cisco

IT Essentials Course Booklet

PC Hardware and Software

Version 4.0

Cisco | Networking Academy
Mind Wide Open

ciscopress.com

IT Essentials Course Booklet

Cisco Networking Academy

Published by:
Cisco Press
800 East 96th Street
Indianapolis, IN 46240 USA

Printed in the United States of America

First Printing August 2010

Library of Congress Cataloging-in-Publication Data is available upon request.

ISBN-13: 978-1-58713-252-0

ISBN-10: 1-58713-252-4

Warning and Disclaimer

This book is designed to provide information about PC Hardware and Software. Every effort has been made to make this book as complete and as accurate as possible, but no warranty or fitness is implied.

The information is provided on an "as is" basis. The authors, Cisco Press, and Cisco Systems, Inc. shall have neither liability nor responsibility to any person or entity with respect to any loss or damages arising from the information contained in this book or from the use of the discs or programs that may accompany it.

The opinions expressed in this book belong to the author and are not necessarily those of Cisco Systems, Inc.

Publisher
Paul Boger

Associate Publisher
Dave Dusthimer

Cisco Representative
Erik Ullanderson

Cisco Press Program Manager
Anand Sundaram

Executive Editor
Mary Beth Ray

Managing Editor
Patrick Kanouse

Project Editor
Bethany Wall

Editorial Assistant
Vanessa Evans

Designer
Louisa Adair

Composition
Mark Shirar

This book is part of the Cisco Networking Academy® series from Cisco Press. The products in this series support and complement the Cisco Networking Academy curriculum. If you are using this book outside the Networking Academy, then you are not preparing with a Cisco trained and authorized Networking Academy provider.

For more information on the Cisco Networking Academy or to locate a Networking Academy, Please visit www.cisco.com/edu.

cisco.

Trademark Acknowledgments

All terms mentioned in this book that are known to be trademarks or service marks have been appropriately capitalized. Cisco Press or Cisco Systems, Inc., cannot attest to the accuracy of this information. Use of a term in this book should not be regarded as affecting the validity of any trademark or service mark.

Feedback Information

At Cisco Press, our goal is to create in-depth technical books of the highest quality and value. Each book is crafted with care and precision, undergoing rigorous development that involves the unique expertise of members from the professional technical community.

Readers' feedback is a natural continuation of this process. If you have any comments regarding how we could improve the quality of this book, or otherwise alter it to better suit your needs, you can contact us through email at feedback@ciscopress.com. Please make sure to include the book title and ISBN in your message.

We greatly appreciate your assistance.

Americas Headquarters
Cisco Systems, Inc.
San Jose, CA

Asia Pacific Headquarters
Cisco Systems (USA) Pte. Ltd.
Singapore

Europe Headquarters
Cisco Systems International BV
Amsterdam, The Netherlands

Cisco has more than 200 offices worldwide. Addresses, phone numbers, and fax numbers are listed on the Cisco Website at **www.cisco.com/go/offices.**

Contents at a Glance

Chapter 1 Introduction to the Personal Computer 1

Chapter 2 Safe Lab Procedures and Tool Use 23

Chapter 3 Computer Assembly - Step by Step 39

Chapter 4 Basics of Preventive Maintenance and Troubleshooting 51

Chapter 5 Fundamental Operating Systems 59

Chapter 6 Fundamental Laptops and Portable Devices 85

Chapter 7 Fundamental Printers and Scanners 109

Chapter 8 Fundamental Networks 129

Chapter 9 Fundamental Security 161

Chapter 10 Communication Skills 175

Chapter 11 Advanced Personal Computers 187

Chapter 12 Advanced Operating Systems 205

Chapter 13 Advanced Laptops and Portable Devices 221

Chapter 14 Advanced Printers and Scanners 235

Chapter 15 Advanced Networks 251

Chapter 16 Advanced Security 271

Glossary 285

Contents

Chapter 1 Introduction to the Personal Computer 1

Introduction 1

1.2 Explain IT industry certifications 1

1.1.1 Identify education and certifications 2

1.1.2 Describe the A+ certification 2

1.1.3 Describe the EUCIP certification 3

1.2 Describe a computer system 4

1.3 Identify the names, purposes, and characteristics of cases and power supplies 4

1.3.1 Describe cases 5

1.3.2 Describe power supplies 5

1.4 Identify the names, purposes, and characteristics of internal components 7

1.4.1 Identify the names, purposes, and characteristics of motherboards 8

1.4.2 Explain the names, purposes, and characteristics of CPUs 8

1.4.3 Identify the names, purposes, and characteristics of cooling systems 9

1.4.4 Identify the names, purposes, and characteristics of ROM and RAM 10

1.4.5 Identify the names, purposes, and characteristics of adapter 11

1.4.6 Identify the names, purposes, and characteristics of storage drives 11

1.4.7 Identify the names, purposes, and characteristics of internal cables 13

1.5 Identify the names, purposes, and characteristics of ports and cables 15

1.5.1 Serial Ports and Cables 14

1.5.2 USB Ports and Cables 14

1.5.3 FireWire Ports and Cables 14

1.5.4 Parallel Ports and Cables 15

1.5.5 SCSI Ports and Cables 15

1.5.6 Network Ports and Cables 15

1.5.7 PS/2 Ports 15

1.5.8 Audio Ports 15

1.5.9 Video Ports and Connectors 16

1.6 Identify the names, purposes, and characteristics of input devices 16

1.7 Identify the names, purposes, and characteristics of output devices 17

1.7.1 Monitors and Projectors 17

1.7.2 Printers, Scanners, and Fax Machines 18

1.7.3 Speakers and Headphones 18

1.8 Explain system resources and their purposes 18

1.8.1 Interrupt Requests 19

1.8.2 Input/Output (I/O) Port Addresses 19

1.8.3 Direct Memory Access 19

Summary 20

Chapter 2 Safe Lab Procedures and Tool Use 23

Introduction 23

2.1 Explain the purpose of safe working conditions and procedures 23

2.1.1 Identify safety procedures and potential hazards for users and technicians 23

2.1.2 Identify safety procedures to protect equipment from damage and data from loss 25

2.1.3 Identify safety procedures to protect the environment from contamination 26

2.2 Identify tools and software used with personal computer components and their purposes 28

2.2.1 Identify hardware tools and their purpose 29

2.2.2 Identify software tools and their purpose 29

2.3 Implement proper tool use 31

2.3.1 Demonstrate proper use of an antistatic wrist strap 32

2.3.2 Demonstrate proper use of an antistatic mat 32

2.3.3 Demonstrate proper use of various hand tools 33

2.3.4 Demonstrate proper use of cleaning materials 34

Summary 36

Chapter 3 Computer Assembly - Step by Step 39

Introduction 39

3.1 Open the case 39

3.2 Install the power supply 39

3.3.1 Install a CPU and a heat sink/fan assembly 40

3.3.2 Install the RAM 41

3.3.3 Install the motherboard 41

3.4 Install internal drives 42

3.5 Install drives in external bays 42

3.5.1 Install the optical drive 42

3.5.2 Install the floppy drive 42

3.6 Install adapter cards 43

3.6.1 Install the NIC 43

3.6.2 Install the wireless NIC 43

3.6.3 Install the video adapter card 43

3.7 Connect all internal cables 44

3.7.1 Connect the power cables 44

3.7.2 Connect the data cables 45

3.8 Re-attach the side panels and connect external cables to the computer 46

3.8.1 Re-attach the side panels to the case 46

3.8.2 Connect external cables to the computer 47

3.9 Boot the computer for the first time 47

3.9.1 Identify beep codes 47

3.9.2 Describe BIOS setup 48

Summary 49

Chapter 4 **Basics of Preventive Maintenance and Troubleshooting 51**

Introduction 51

4.1 Explain the purpose of preventive maintenance 51

4.1.1 Hardware 51

4.1.2 Software 51

4.1.3 Benefits 52

4.2 Identify the steps of the troubleshooting process 52

4.2.1 Explain the purpose of data protection 53

4.2.2 Gather data from the customer 53

4.2.3 Verify the obvious issues 54

4.2.4 Try quick solutions first 54

4.2.5 Gather data from the computer 54

4.2.6 Evaluate the problem and implement the solution 56

4.2.7 Close with the customer 56

Summary 57

Chapter 5 **Fundamental Operating Systems 59**

Introduction 59

5.1 Explain the purpose of an operating system 59

5.1.1 Describe characteristics of modern operating systems 59

5.1.2 Explain operating system concepts 60

5.2 Describe and compare operating systems to include purpose, limitations, and compatibilities 62

5.2.1 Describe desktop operating systems 62

5.2.2 Describe network operating systems 63

5.3 Determine operating system based on customer needs 63

5.3.1 Identify applications and environments that are compatible with an operating system 63

5.3.2 Determine minimum hardware requirements and compatibility with the OS platform 64

5.4 Install an operating system 65

5.4.1 Identify hard drive setup procedures 65

5.4.2 Prepare hard drive 66

5.4.3 Install the operating system using default settings 66

5.4.4 Create accounts 67

5.4.5 Complete the installation 67

5.4.6 Describe custom installation options 68

5.4.7 Identify the boot sequence files and registry files 68

5.4.8 Describe how to manipulate operating system files 69

5.4.9 Describe directory structures 70

5.5 Navigate a GUI (Windows) 72

5.5.1 Manipulate items on the desktop 72

5.5.2 Explore Control Panel applets 73

5.5.3 Explore administrative tools 74

5.5.4 Install, navigate, and uninstall an application 75

5.5.5 Describe upgrading an operating system 76

5.6 Identify and apply common preventive maintenance techniques for operating systems 77

5.6.1 Create a preventive maintenance plan 77

5.6.2 Schedule a task 78

5.6.3 Backup the hard drive 79

5.7 Troubleshoot operating systems 81

5.7.1 Review the troubleshooting process 81

5.7.2 Identify common problems and solutions 81

Summary 82

Chapter 6 Fundamental Laptops and Portable Devices 85

Introduction 85

6.1 Describe laptops and other portable devices 85

Laptops 85

PDAs and Smartphones 86

6.1.1 Identify some common uses of laptops 86

6.1.2 Identify some common uses of PDAs and Smartphones 86

6.2 Identify and describe the components of a laptop 87

6.2.1 Describe the components found on the outside of the laptop 87

6.2.2 Describe the components found on the inside of the laptop 89

6.2.3 Describe the components found on the laptop docking station 90

6.3 Compare and contrast desktop and laptop components 92

6.3.1 Compare and contrast desktop and laptop motherboards 92

6.3.2 Compare and contrast desktop and laptop processors 92

6.3.3 Compare and contrast desktop and laptop power management 92

6.3.4 Compare and contrast desktop and laptop expansion capabilities 93

6.4 Explain how to configure laptops 94

6.4.1 Describe how to configure power settings 95

6.4.2 Describe the safe installation and removal of laptop components 97

6.5 Compare the different mobile phone standards 99

6.6 Identify common preventive maintenance techniques for laptops and portable devices 100

6.6.1 Identify appropriate cleaning procedures 100

6.6.2 Identify optimal operating environments 102

6.7 Describe how to troubleshoot laptops and portable devices 103

6.7.1 Review the troubleshooting process 103

6.7.2 Identify common problems and solutions 104

Summary 105

Chapter 7 Fundamental Printers and Scanners 109

Introduction 109

7.1 Describe the types of printers currently available 109
7.1.1 Describe characteristics and capabilities of printers 110
7.1.2 Describe printer to computer interfaces 111
7.1.3 Describe laser printers 112
7.1.4 Describe impact printers 113
7.1.5 Describe inkjet printers 114
7.1.6 Describe solid-ink printers 115
7.1.7 Describe other printer types 115
7.2 Describe the installation and configuration process 116
7.2.1 Describe how to set up a printer 116
7.2.2 Explain how to power and connect the device using a local or network port 116
7.2.3 Describe how to install and update the device driver, firmware, and RAM 117
7.2.4 Identify configuration options and default settings 118
7.2.5 Describe how to optimize printer performance 118
7.2.6 Describe how to print a test page 119
7.2.7 Describe how to share a printer 119
7.3 Describe the types of scanners currently available 120
7.3.1 Describe scanner types, resolution, and interfaces 120
7.3.2 Describe all-in-one devices 121
7.3.3 Describe flatbed scanners 121
7.3.4 Describe handheld scanners 121
7.3.5 Describe drum scanners 122
7.4 Describe the installation and configuration process for scanners 122
7.4.1 Explain how to power and connect a scanner 122
7.4.2 Describe how to install and update the device driver 122
7.4.3 Identify configuration options and default settings 123
7.5 Identify and apply common preventive maintenance techniques for printers and scanners 123
7.5.1 Describe printer maintenance 123
7.5.2 Describe scanner maintenance 124
7.6 Troubleshoot printers and scanners 124
7.6.1 Review the troubleshooting process 124
7.6.2 Identify common problems and solutions 125
Summary 126
Chapter 8 Fundamental Networks 129
Introduction 129
8.1Explain the principles of networking 129
8.1.1 Define computer networks 130
8.1.2 Explain the benefits of networking 131
8.2 Describe types of networks 132
8.2.1 Describe a LAN 132
8.2.2 Describe a WAN 132

8.2.3 Describe a WLAN 133
8.2.4 Explain peer-to-peer networks 133
8.2.5 Explain client/server networks 133

8.3 Describe basic networking concepts and technologies 134
8.3.1 Explain bandwidth and data transmission 134
8.3.2 Describe IP addressing 135
8.3.3 Define DHCP 137
8.3.4 Describe Internet protocols and applications 138
8.3.5 Define ICMP 138

8.4 Describe the physical components of a network 139
8.4.1 Identify names, purposes, and characteristics of network devices 139
8.4.2 Identify names, purposes, and characteristics of common network cables 141

8.5 Describe LAN topologies and architectures 142
8.5.1 Describe LAN topologies 143
8.5.2 Describe LAN architectures 144

8.6 Identify standards organizations 145

8.7 Identify Ethernet standards 145
8.7.1 Explain cabled Ethernet standards 145
8.7.2 Explain wireless Ethernet standards 147

8.8 Explain OSI and TCP/IP data models 148
8.8.1 Define the TCP/IP model 148
8.8.2 Define the OSI model 149
8.8.3 Compare OSI and TCP/IP 149

8.9 Describe how to configure a NIC and modem 150
8.9.1 Install or update a NIC driver 150
8.9.2 Attach computer to existing network 151
8.9.3 Describe the installation of a modem 151

8.10 Identify names, purposes, and characteristics of other technologies used to establish connectivity 152
8.10.1 Describe telephone technologies 153
8.10.2 Define power line communication 154
8.10.3 Define broadband 154
8.10.4 Define VoIP 155

8.11 Identify and apply common preventive maintenance techniques us 155

8.12 Troubleshoot a network 156
8.12.1 Review the troubleshooting process 156
8.12.2 Identify common network problems and solutions 156

Summary 157

Chapter 9 Fundamental Security 161

Introduction 161

9.1 Explain why security is important 161

9.2 Describe security threats 162

9.2.1 Define viruses, worms, and Trojans 162

9.2.2 Explain web security 163

9.2.3 Define adware, spyware, and grayware 163

9.2.4 Explain Denial of Service 164

9.2.5 Describe spam and popup windows 164

9.2.6 Explain social engineering 165

9.2.7 Explain TCP/IP attacks 165

9.2.8 Explain hardware deconstruction and recycling 166

9.3 Identify security procedures 166

9.3.1 Explain what is required in a basic local security policy 166

9.3.2 Explain the tasks required to protect physical equipment 167

9.3.3 Describe ways to protect data 167

9.3.4 Describe wireless security techniques 169

9.4 Identify common preventive maintenance techniques for security 169

9.4.1 Explain how to update signature files for anti-virus and anti-spyware software 170

9.4.2 Explain how to install operating systems service packs and security patches 170

9.5 Troubleshoot Security 171

9.5.1 Review the troubleshooting process 171

9.5.2 Identify common problems and solutions 172

Summary 173

Chapter 10 Communication Skills 175

Introduction 175

10.1 Explain the relationship between communication and troubleshooting 175

10.2 Describe good communication skills and professional behavior 176

10.2.1 Determine the computer problem of the customer 176

10.2.2 Display professional behavior with the customer 177

10.2.3 Focus the customer on the problem during the call 178

10.2.4 Use proper netiquette 178

10.2.5 Implement time and stress management techniques 179

10.2.6 Observe Service Level Agreements (SLAs) 180

10.2.7 Follow business policies 180

10.3 Explain ethics and legal aspects of working with computer technology 181

Ethical Customs 182

Legal Rules 182

10.4 Describe call center environment and technician responsibilities 182

10.4.1 Describe the call center environment 183

10.4.2 Describe level-one technician responsibilities 183

10.4.3 Describe level-two technician responsibilities 183

Summary 185

Chapter 11 Advanced Personal Computers 187

Introduction 187

11.1 Give an overview of field, remote, and bench technician jobs 188

11.2 Explain safe lab procedures and tool use 188

11.2.1 Review safe working environments and procedures 188

11.2.2 Review names, purposes, characteristics, and safe and appropriate use of tools 189

11.2.3 Identify potential safety hazards and implement proper safety procedures for computer components 190

11.2.4 Describe environmental issues 190

11.3 Describe situations requiring replacement of computer components 191

11.3.1 Select a case and power supply 191

11.3.2 Select a motherboard 192

11.3.3 Select the CPU and heat sink/fan assembly 192

11.3.4 Select RAM 192

11.3.5 Select adapter cards 193

11.3.6 Select storage devices and hard drives 193

11.3.7 Select input and output devices 194

11.4 Upgrade and configure personal computer components and peripherals 195

11.4.1 Upgrade and configure a motherboard 195

11.4.2 Upgrade and configure a CPU and a heat sink/fan assembly 196

11.4.3 Upgrade and configure RAM 197

11.4.4 Upgrade and configure BIOS 198

11.4.5 Upgrade and configure storage devices and hard drives 198

11.4.6 Upgrade and configure input and output devices 199

11.5 Identify and apply common preventive maintenance techniques for personal computer components 199

11.5.1 Clean internal components 200

11.5.2 Clean the case 200

11.5.3 Inspect computer components 200

11.6 Troubleshoot computer components 201

11.6.1 Review the troubleshooting process 202

11.6.2 Identify common problems and solutions 202

11.6.3 Apply troubleshooting skills 202

Summary 203

Chapter 12 Advanced Operating Systems 205

Introduction 205

12.1 Select the appropriate operating system based on customer needs 205

12.1.1 Describe operating systems 206

12.1.2 Describe network operating systems 206

12.2 Install, configure, and optimize an operating system 207

12.2.1 Compare and contrast a default installation and a custom installation 207

12.2.2 Install Windows XP Professional using a custom installation 208

12.2.3 Create, view, and manage disks, directories, and files 209

12.2.4 Identify procedures and utilities used to optimize the performance of operating systems 210

12.2.5 Identify procedures and utilities used to optimize the performance of browsers 211

12.2.6 Describe installation, use, and configuration of e-mail software 212

12.2.7 Set screen resolution and update video driver 213

12.2.8 Describe installation of a second operating system 214

12.3 Describe how to upgrade operating systems 214

12.4 Describe preventive maintenance procedures for operating systems 215

12.4.1 Schedule automatic tasks and updates 215

12.4.2 Set restore points 216

12.5 Troubleshoot operating systems 217

12.5.1 Review the troubleshooting process 217

12.5.2 Identify common problems and solutions 217

12.5.3 Apply troubleshooting skills 217

Summary 219

Chapter 13 Advanced Laptops and Portable Devices 221

Introduction 221

13.1 Describe wireless communication methods for laptops and portable devices 221

13.1.1 Describe Bluetooth Technology 222

13.1.2 Describe Infrared Technology 222

13.1.3 Describe Cellular WAN Technology 223

13.1.4 Describe Wi-Fi Technology 224

13.1.5 Describe Satellite Technology 224

13.2 Describe repairs for laptops and portable devices 225

13.3 Select laptop components 226

13.3.1 Select batteries 226

13.3.2 Select a docking station or port replicator 227

13.3.3 Select storage devices 228

13.3.4 Select additional RAM 228

13.4 Describe preventive maintenance procedures for laptops 229

13.4.1 Describe how to schedule and perform maintenance for laptops 229

13.4.2 Explain how to manage data version control between desktops and laptops 231

13.5 Describe how to troubleshoot a laptop 231

13.5.1 Review the troubleshooting process 232

13.5.2 Identify common problems and solutions 232

13.5.3 Apply troubleshooting skills 232

Summary 233

Chapter 14 Advanced Printers and Scanners 235

Introduction 235

14.1 Describe potential safety hazards and safety procedures associated with printers and scanners 235

14.2 Install and configure a local printer and scanner 236

14.2.1 Connect the device to a local port 236

14.2.2 Install and configure the driver and software 236

14.2.3 Configure options and default settings 237

14.2.4 Verify functionality 239

14.3.1 Describe types of print servers 240

14.3.2 Describe how to install network printer software and driver 241

14.4.1 Describe printer upgrades 242

14.4.2 Describe scanner optimization 243

14.5 Describe printer and scanner preventive maintenance techniques 244

14.5.1 Determine scheduled maintenance according to vendor guidelines 244

14.5.2 Describe a suitable environment for printers and scanners 245

14.5.3 Describe cleaning methods 245

14.5.4 Describe checking capacity of ink cartridges and toners 246

14.6 Troubleshoot printers and scanners 247

14.6.1 Review the troubleshooting process 247

14.6.2 Identify common problems and solutions 247

14.6.3 Apply troubleshooting skills 247

Summary 249

Chapter 15 Advanced Networks 251

Introduction 251

15.1 Identify potential safety hazards and implement proper safety procedures related to networks 251

15.1.1 Explain fiber-optic safety 252

15.1.2 Explain cable, cable cutters, and cable cutting safety hazards 253

15.2 Design a network based on the customer's needs 253

15.2.1 Determine a topology 254

15.2.2 Determine protocols and network applications 254

15.3 Determine the components for your customer's network 255

15.3.1 Select cable types 255

15.3.2 Select ISP connection type 256

15.3.3 Select network cards 257

15.3.4 Select the network device 258

15.4 Implement the customer's network 259

15.4.1 Install and test the customer's network 259

15.4.2 Configure the customer's Internet and network resources 260

15.5 Upgrade the customer's network 261

15.5.1 Install and configure wireless NIC 262

15.5.2 Install and configure wireless routers 262

15.5.3 Test connection 263

15.6 Describe installation, configuration and management of a simple mail server 264

15.6.1 SMTP 264

15.6.2 POP 264

15.6.3 IMAP 265

15.6.4 E-mail Server 265

15.6.5 E-mail Server Installation 265

15.7 Describe preventive maintenance procedures for networks 266

15.8 Troubleshoot the network 267

15.8.1 Review the troubleshooting process 267

15.8.2 Identify common problems and solutions 267

15.8.3 Apply troubleshooting skills 267

Summary 269

Chapter 16 Advanced Security 271

Introduction 271

16.1 Outline security requirements based on customer needs 271

16.1.1 Outline a local security policy 272

16.1.2 Explain when and how to use security hardware 272

16.1.3 Explain when and how to use security application software 273

16.2 Select security components based on customer needs 274

16.2.1 Describe and compare security techniques 274

16.2.2 Describe and compare access control devices 275

16.2.3 Describe and compare firewall types 276

16.3 Implement customer's security policy 277

16.3.1 Configure security settings 277

16.3.2 Describe configuring firewall types 278

16.3.3 Describe protection against malicious software 278

16.4 Perform preventive maintenance on security 279

16.4.1 Describe the configuration of operating system updates 279

16.4.2 Maintain accounts 280

16.4.3 Explain data backup procedures, access to backups, and secure physical backup media 280

16.5 Troubleshoot security 281

16.5.1 Review the troubleshooting process 281

16.5.2 Identify common problems and solutions 281

16.5.3 Apply troubleshooting skills 282

Summary 283

Glossary 285

Command Syntax Conventions

The conventions used to present command syntax in this book are the same conventions used in the IOS Command Reference. The Command Reference describes these conventions as follows:

- **Boldface** indicates commands and keywords that are entered literally as shown. In actual configuration examples and output (not general command syntax), boldface indicates commands that are manually input by the user (such as a **show** command).
- *Italic* indicates arguments for which you supply actual values.
- Vertical bars (|) separate alternative, mutually exclusive elements.
- Square brackets ([ ]) indicate an optional element.
- Braces ({ }) indicate a required choice.
- Braces within brackets ([{ }]) indicate a required choice within an optional element.

About This Course Booklet

Your Cisco Networking Academy Course Booklet is designed as a study resource you can easily read, highlight, and review on the go, wherever the Internet is not available or practical:

- The text is extracted directly, word-for-word, from the online course so you can highlight important points and take notes in the "Your Chapter Notes" section.
- Headings with the exact page correlations provide a quick reference to the online course for your classroom discussions and exam preparation.
- An icon system directs you to the online curriculum to take full advantage of the images imbedded within the Networking Academy online course interface and reminds you to perform the labs, worksheets, interactive activities, and chapter quizzes.

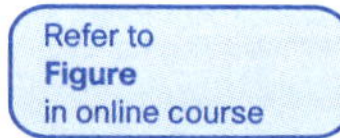

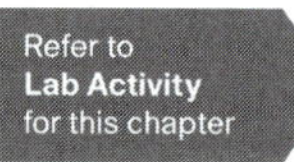

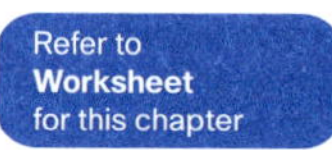

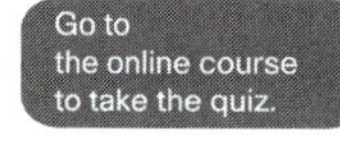

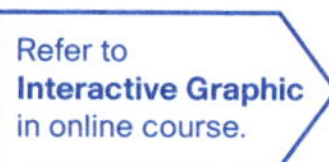

The *Course Booklet* is a basic, economical paper-based resource to help you succeed with the Cisco Networking Academy online course.

CHAPTER 1

Introduction to the Personal Computer

Introduction

Information technology (IT) is the design, development, implementation, support, and management of computer hardware and software applications. An IT professional is knowledgeable about computer systems and operating systems. This chapter will review IT certifications and the components of a basic personal computer system.

After completing this chapter, you will meet these objectives:

- Explain IT industry certifications.
- Describe a computer system.
- Identify the names, purposes, and characteristics of cases and power supplies.
- Identify the names, purposes, and characteristics of internal components.
- Identify the names, purposes, and characteristics of ports and cables.
- Identify the names, purposes, and characteristics of input devices.
- Identify the names, purposes, and characteristics of output devices.
- Explain system resources and their purposes.

Refer to **Figure** in online course

1.1 Explain IT industry certifications

This course will focus on desktop and laptop computers. It will also discuss electronic devices, such as personal digital assistants and cell phones.

Training and experience will qualify a technician to service these computers and personal electronic devices. You will gain the specialized technical skills needed to install, maintain, and repair computers. Earning an industry standard certification will give you confidence and increase your opportunities in IT.

This course is focused on the following two industry standard certifications:

- The CompTIA A+
- The European Certification of Informatics Professional (EUCIP) IT Administrator Certification (Modules 1- 3)

After completing this section, you will meet these objectives:

- Identify education and certifications.
- Describe the A+ Certification.
- Describe the EUCIP Certification.

Refer to **Figure** in online course

1.1.1 Identify education and certifications

Information Technology (IT) is a term that encompasses the relationship between hardware, software, networks, and technical assistance provided to users. **IT Essentials: PC Hardware and Software** covers the information that a technician needs to be successful in IT. This course covers the following topics:

- Personal computers
- Safe lab procedures
- Troubleshooting
- Operating systems
- Laptop computers
- Printers and scanners
- Networks
- Security
- Communication skills

The IT Essentials course focuses on two hardware and software skills-based industry certifications: CompTIA A+ and EUCIP. This course is only an introduction into the world of IT. A technician may continue to study and earn the following certifications:

- CCNA – Cisco Certified Networking Associate
- CCNP – Cisco Certified Networking Professional
- CCIE – Cisco Certified Internetworking Expert
- CISSP – Certified Information Systems Security Professional
- MCP – Microsoft Certified Professional
- MCSA – Microsoft Certified Systems Administrator
- MCSE – Microsoft Certified Systems Engineer
- Network+ – CompTIA Network Certification
- Linux+ – CompTIA Linux Certification

IT certifications can be used as credits for university and college degrees in areas such as computer science and telecommunications.

Refer to **Figure** in online course

1.1.2 Describe the A+ certification

Computing Technology Industry Association (CompTIA) developed the A+ Certification program. A CompTIA A+ certification, as shown in Figure 1, signifies that a candidate is a qualified PC hardware and software technician. CompTIA certifications are known throughout the IT community as one of the best ways to enter the information technology field and build a solid career.

An A+ Certification candidate must pass two exams. The first exam is CompTIA A+ Essentials. The second advanced exam depends on the type of certification desired. Each advanced exam assesses specialized skills in one of the following areas:

- IT Technician
- Remote Support Technician
- Depot Technician

CompTIA A+ Exam – Essentials

All certification candidates must pass the A+ Essentials Exam (220-601). The exam covers the basic skills needed to install, build, upgrade, repair, configure, troubleshoot, optimize, diagnose, and maintain basic personal computer hardware and operating systems.

CompTIA A+ Exam – IT Technician

The CompTIA A+ (220-602) exam assesses the field-service technician. Field technicians work in both mobile and corporate technical environments.

CompTIA A+ Exam – Remote Support Technician

The CompTIA A+ (220-603) exam assesses remote support technicians who are responsible for assisting a customer without physically touching the customer's computer. A remote technician will often work in a call center environment where technicians resolve operating system and connectivity issues over the telephone or Internet.

A remote support technician is also called a help-desk technician, a call-center technician, a technical specialist, or a technical representative.

CompTIA A+ Exam – Depot Technician

The CompTIA A+ (220-604) examination assesses the depot technician. The depot technician has limited interaction with the customer and works primarily in a workshop or lab. A depot technician is also called a bench technician.

Refer to **Worksheet** for this chapter

IT Jobs

Research IT Jobs

Refer to **Figure** in online course

1.1.3 Describe the EUCIP certification

The EUCIP IT Administrator program offers a recognized certification of competence in IT. The certification covers the standards prescribed by the Council of European Professional Informatics Societies (CEPIS). The EUCIP IT Administrator Certification consists of five modules, with a corresponding exam for each module. This course will prepare you for Modules 1–3.

Module 1: Computer Hardware

The Computer Hardware module requires that the candidate understand the basic makeup of a personal computer and the functions of the components. The candidate should be able to effectively diagnose and repair hardware problems. The candidate should be able to advise customers of appropriate hardware to buy.

Module 2: Operating Systems

The Operating Systems module requires that the candidate be familiar with the procedures for installing and updating most common operating systems and applications. The candidate should know how to use system tools for troubleshooting and repairing operating systems.

Module 3: Local Area Network and Network Services

The Local Area Network and Network Services module requires that the candidate be familiar with the procedure of installing, using, and managing local area networks. The candidate should be able to add and remove users and shared resources. The candidate should know how to use system tools for troubleshooting and repairing networks.

Module 4: Expert Network Use

This module is beyond the scope of the IT Essentials course, although some of the topics are covered. The Expert Network Use module requires that the candidate understand LAN communication.

Module 5: IT Security

This module is beyond the scope of the IT Essentials course, although some of the topics are covered. The IT Security module requires that the candidate be familiar with security methods and features that are available for a standalone or networked computer.

Refer to **Figure** in online course

1.2 Describe a computer system

A computer system consists of hardware and software components. Hardware is the physical equipment such as the case, storage drives, keyboards, monitors, cables, speakers, and printers. The term software includes the operating system and programs. The operating system instructs the computer how to operate. These operations may include identifying, accessing, and processing information. Programs or applications perform different functions. Programs vary widely depending on the type of information that will be accessed or generated. For example, instructions for balancing a checkbook are very different from instructions for simulating a virtual reality world on the Internet.

The following sections in this chapter discuss the hardware components found in a computer system.

Refer to **Figure** in online course

1.3 Identify the names, purposes, and characteristics of cases and power supplies

The computer case provides protection and support for the internal components of the computer. All computers need a power supply to convert alternating-current (AC) power from the wall socket into direct-current (DC) power. The size and shape of the computer case is usually determined by the motherboard and other internal components.

You can select a large computer case to accommodate additional components that may be required in the future. Other users may select a smaller case that requires minimal space. In general, the computer case should be durable, easy to service, and have enough room for expansion.

The power supply must provide enough power for the components that are currently installed and allow for additional components that may be added at a later time. If you choose a power supply that powers only the current components, it may be necessary to replace the power supply when other components are upgraded.

After completing this section, you will meet these objectives:

- Describe cases.
- Describe power supplies.

Refer to **Figure** in online course

1.3.1 Describe cases

A computer case contains the framework to support the internal components of a computer while providing an enclosure for added protection. Computer cases are typically made of plastic, steel, and aluminum and are available in a variety of styles.

The size and layout of a case is called a form factor. There are many types of cases, but the basic form factors for computer cases include desktop and tower. Desktop cases may be slimline or full-sized, and tower cases may be mini or full-sized, as shown in Figure 1.

Computer cases are referred to in a number of ways:

- Computer chassis
- Cabinet
- Tower
- Box
- Housing

In addition to providing protection and support, cases also provide an environment designed to keep the internal components cool. Case fans are used to move air through the computer case. As the air passes warm components, it absorbs heat and then exits the case. This process keeps the components of the computer from overheating.

There are many factors that must be considered when choosing a case:

- The size of the motherboard
- The number of external or internal drive locations called bays
- Available space

See Figure 2 for a list of features.

In addition to providing protection from the environment, cases help to prevent damage from static electricity. Internal components of the computer are grounded by attachment to the case.

Note

You should select a case that matches the physical dimensions of the power supply and motherboard.

Refer to **Figure** in online course

1.3.2 Describe power supplies

The power supply, shown in Figure 1, converts alternating-current (AC) power coming from a wall outlet into direct-current (DC) power, which is a lower voltage. DC power is required for all of the components inside the computer.

Connectors

Most connectors today are keyed connectors. Keyed connectors are designed to be inserted in only one direction. Each part of the connector has a colored wire with a different voltage running through it, as seen in Figure 2. Different connectors are used to connect specific components and various locations on the motherboard:

- A Molex connector is a keyed connector used to connect to an optical drive or a hard drive.

- A Berg connector is a keyed connector used to connect to a floppy drive. A Berg connector is smaller than a Molex connector.
- A 20-pin or 24-pin slotted connector is used to connect to the motherboard. The 24-pin slotted connector has two rows of 12-pins each, and the 20-pin slotted connector has two rows of 10-pins each.
- A 4-pin to 8-pin auxiliary power connector has two rows of two to four pins and supplies power to all areas of the motherboard. The 4-pin to 8-pin auxiliary power connector is the same shape as the main power connector, but smaller.
- Older standard power supplies used two connectors called P8 and P9 to connect to the motherboard. P8 and P9 were unkeyed connectors. They could be installed backwards, potentially damaging the motherboard or power supply. The installation required that the connectors were lined up with the black wires together in the middle.

Note

If you have a difficult time inserting a connector, try a different way, or check to make sure that there are no bent pins or foreign objects in the way. Remember, if it seems difficult to plug in any cable or other part, there is something wrong. Cables, connectors, and components are designed to fit together snugly. Never force any connector or component. The connectors that are plugged in incorrectly will damage the plug and the connector. Take your time and make sure that you are handling the hardware correctly.

Electricity and Ohm's Law

These are the four basic units of electricity:

- Voltage **(V)**
- Current **(I)**
- Power **(P)**
- Resistance **(R)**

Voltage, current, power, and resistance are electronic terms that a computer technician must know:

- Voltage is a measure of the force required to push electrons through a circuit.
- Voltage is measured in volts (V). A computer power supply usually produces several different voltages.
- Current is a measure of the amount of electrons going through a circuit.
- Current is measured in amperes, or amps (A). Computer power supplies deliver different amperages for each output voltage.
- Power is a measure of the pressure required to push electrons through a circuit, called voltage, multiplied by the number of electrons going through that circuit, called current. The measurement is called watts (W). Computer power supplies are rated in watts.
- Resistance is the opposition to the flow of current in a circuit. Resistance is measured in ohms. Lower resistance allows more current, and therefore more power, to flow through a circuit. A good fuse will have low resistance or a measurement of almost 0 ohms.

There is a basic equation that expresses how three of the terms relate to each other. It states that voltage is equal to the current multiplied by the resistance. This is known as Ohm's Law.

V = IR

In an electrical system, power (P) is equal to the voltage multiplied by the current.

P = VI

In an electrical circuit, increasing the current or the voltage will result in higher power.

As an example of how this works, imagine a simple circuit that has a 9 V light bulb hooked up to a 9-V battery. The power output of the light bulb is 100-W. Using the equation above, we can calculate how much current in amps would be required to get 100-W out of this 9-V bulb.

To solve this equation, we know the following information:

- **P = 100 W**
- **V = 9 V**
- **I = 100 W/9 V = 11.11 A**

What happens if a 12-V battery and a 12-V light bulb are used to get 100 W of power?

100 W / 12 V = 8.33 amps

This system produces the same power, but with less current.

Computers normally use power supplies ranging from 200-W to 500-W. However, some computers may need 500-W to 800-W power supplies. When building a computer, select a power supply with sufficient wattage to power all of the components. Obtain the wattage information for the components from the manufacturer's documentation. When deciding on a power supply, make sure to choose a power supply that has more than enough power for the current components.

Caution

Do not open a power supply. Electronic capacitors located inside of a power supply, shown in Figure 3, can hold a charge for extended periods of time.

Refer to **Figure** in online course

1.4 Identify the names, purposes, and characteristics of internal components

This section discusses the names, purposes, and characteristics of the internal components of a computer.

After completing this section, you will meet these objectives:

- Identify the names, purposes, and characteristics of motherboards.
- Explain the names, purposes, and characteristics of CPUs.
- Identify the names, purposes, and characteristics of cooling systems.
- Identify the names, purposes, and characteristics of ROM and RAM.
- Identify the names, purposes, and characteristics of adapter cards.
- Identify the names, purposes, and characteristics of storage drives.
- Identify the names, purposes, and characteristics of internal cables.

Refer to **Figure** in online course

1.4.1 Identify the names, purposes, and characteristics of motherboards

The motherboard is the main printed circuit board and contains the buses, or electrical pathways, found in a computer. These buses allow data to travel between the various components that comprise a computer. Figure 1 shows a variety of motherboards. A motherboard is also known as the system board, the backplane, or the main board.

The motherboard accommodates the central processing unit (CPU), RAM, expansion slots, heat sink/fan assembly, BIOS chip, chip set, and the embedded wires that interconnect the motherboard components. Sockets, internal and external connectors, and various ports are also placed on the motherboard.

The form factor of motherboards pertains to the size and shape of the board. It also describes the physical layout of the different components and devices on the motherboard. Various form factors exist for motherboards, as shown in Figure 2.

An important set of components on the motherboard is the chip set. The chip set is composed of various integrated circuits attached to the motherboard that control how system hardware interacts with the CPU and motherboard. The CPU is installed into a slot or socket on the motherboard. The socket on the motherboard determines the type of CPU that can be installed.

The chip set of a motherboard allows the CPU to communicate and interact with the other components of the computer, and to exchange data with system memory, or RAM, hard disk drives, video cards, and other output devices. The chip set establishes how much memory can be added to a motherboard. The chip set also determines the type of connectors on the motherboard.

Most chip sets are divided into two distinct components, Northbridge and Southbridge. What each component does varies from manufacturer to manufacturer, but in general the Northbridge controls access to the RAM, video card, and the speeds at which the CPU can communicate with them. The video card is sometimes integrated into the Northbridge. The Southbridge, in most cases, allows the CPU to communicate with the hard drives, sound card, USB ports, and other I/O ports.

Refer to **Figure** in online course

1.4.2 Explain the names, purposes, and characteristics of CPUs

The central processing unit (CPU) is considered the brain of the computer. It is sometimes referred to as the processor. Most calculations take place in the CPU. In terms of computing power, the CPU is the most important element of a computer system. CPUs come in different form factors, each style requiring a particular slot or socket on the motherboard. Common CPU manufacturers include Intel and AMD.

The CPU socket or slot is the connector that interfaces between the motherboard and the processor itself. Most CPU sockets and processors in use today are built around the pin grid array (PGA) architecture, in which the pins on the underside of the processor are inserted into the socket, usually with zero insertion force (ZIF). ZIF refers to the amount of force needed to install a CPU into the motherboard socket or slot. Slot-based processors are cartridge-shaped and fit into a slot that looks similar to an expansion slot. Figure 1 lists common CPU socket specifications.

The CPU executes a program, which is a sequence of stored instructions. Each model of processor has an instruction set, which it executes. The CPU executes the program by processing each piece of data as directed by the program and the instruction set. While the CPU is executing one step of the program, the remaining instructions and the data are stored nearby in a special memory called cache. There are two major CPU architectures related to instruction sets:

- ***Reduced Instruction Set Computer (RISC)* –** Architectures use a relatively small set of instructions, and RISC chips are designed to execute these instructions very rapidly.
- ***Complex Instruction Set Computer (CISC)* –** Architectures use a broad set of instructions, resulting in fewer steps per operation.

Some CPUs incorporate hyperthreading to enhance the performance of the CPU. With hyperthreading, the CPU has multiple pieces of code being executed simultaneously on each pipeline. To an operating system, a single CPU with hyperthreading appears to be two CPUs.

The power of a CPU is measured by the speed and the amount of data that it can process. The speed of a CPU is rated in cycles per second. The speed of current CPUs is measured in millions of cycles per second, called megahertz (MHz), or billions of cycles per second, called gigahertz (GHz). The amount of data that a CPU can process at the one time depends on the size of the processor data bus. This is also called the CPU bus or the front side bus (FSB). The wider the processor data bus width, the more powerful the processor is. Current processors have a 32-bit or a 64-bit processor data bus.

Overclocking is a technique used to make a processor work at a faster speed than its original specification. Overclocking is not a reliable way to improve computer performance and can result in damaging the CPU.

MMX is a set of multimedia instructions built into Intel processors. MMX enabled microprocessors can handle many common multimedia operations that are normally handled by a separate sound or video card. However, only software especially written to call MMX instructions can take advantage of the MMX instruction set.

The latest processor technology has resulted in CPU manufacturers finding ways to incorporate more than one CPU core onto a single chip. Many CPUs are capable of processing multiple instructions concurrently:

- ***Single Core CPU* –** One core inside a single CPU chip that handles all of the processing capability. A motherboard manufacturer may provide sockets for more than one single processor, providing the ability to build a powerful, multi-processor computer.
- ***Dual Core CPU* –** Two cores inside a single CPU chip in which both cores can process information at the same time.

Refer to **Figure** in online course

1.4.3 Identify the names, purposes, and characteristics of cooling systems

Electronic components generate heat. Heat is caused by the flow of current within the components. Computer components perform better when kept cool. If the heat is not removed, the computer may run slower. If too much heat builds up, computer components can be damaged.

Increasing the air flow in the computer case allows more heat to be removed. A case fan, shown in Figure 1, is installed in the computer case to make the cooling process more efficient.

In addition to case fans, a heat sink draws heat away from the core of the CPU. A fan on top of the heat sink, shown in Figure 2, moves the heat away from the CPU.

Other components are also susceptible to heat damage and are sometimes equipped with fans. Video adapter cards also produce a great deal of heat. Fans are dedicated to cool the graphics-processing unit (GPU), as seen in Figure 3.

Computers with extremely fast CPUs and GPUs may use a water-cooling system. A metal plate is placed over the processor and water is pumped over the top to collect the heat that the CPU creates. The water is pumped to a radiator to be cooled by the air, and then re-circulated.

Refer to **Figure** in online course

1.4.4 Identify the names, purposes, and characteristics of ROM and RAM

ROM

Read-only memory (ROM) chips are located on the motherboard. ROM chips contain instructions that can be directly accessed by the CPU. Basic instructions for booting the computer and loading the operating system are stored in ROM. ROM chips retain their contents even when the computer is powered down. The contents cannot be erased or changed by normal means. The different types of ROM are shown in Figure 1.

Note

ROM is sometimes called firmware. This is misleading because firmware is actually the software that is stored in a ROM chip.

RAM

Random access memory (RAM) is the temporary storage for data and programs that are being accessed by the CPU. RAM is volatile memory, which means that the contents are erased when the computer is powered off. The more RAM in a computer, the more capacity the computer has to hold and process large programs and files, as well as enhance system performance. The different types of RAM are shown in Figure 2.

Memory Modules

Early computers had RAM installed on the motherboard as individual chips. The individual memory chips, called dual inline package (DIP) chips, were difficult to install and often became loose on the motherboard. To solve this problem, designers soldered the memory chips on a special circuit board called a memory module. The different types of memory modules are shown in Figure 3.

Note

Memory modules can be single-sided or double-sided. Single-sided memory modules only contain RAM on one side of the module. Double-sided memory modules contain RAM on both sides of the module.

Cache

SRAM is used as cache memory to store the most frequently used data. SRAM provides the processor with faster access to the data than retrieving it from the slower DRAM, or main memory. The three types of cache memory are shown in Figure 4.

Error Checking

Memory errors occur when the data is not stored correctly in the RAM chips. The computer uses different methods to detect and correct data errors in memory. Figure 5 shows three different methods of memory error checking.

Refer to **Figure** in online course

1.4.5 Identify the names, purposes, and characteristics of adapter cards

Adapter cards increase the functionality of a computer by adding controllers for specific devices or by replacing malfunctioning ports. Figure 1 shows several types of adapter cards. Adapter cards are used to expand and customize the capability of the computer:

- ***NIC –*** Connects a computer to a network using a network cable
- ***Wireless NIC –*** Connects a computer to a network using radio frequencies
- ***Sound adapter –*** Provides audio capability
- ***Video adapter –*** Provides graphic capability
- ***Modem adapter –*** Connects a computer to the Internet using a phone line
- ***SCSI adapter –*** Connects SCSI devices, such as hard drives or tape drives, to a computer
- ***RAID adapter –*** Connects multiple hard drives to a computer to provide redundancy and to improve performance
- ***USB port –*** Connects a computer to peripheral devices
- ***Parallel port –*** Connects a computer to peripheral devices
- ***Serial port –*** Connects a computer to peripheral devices

Computers have expansion slots on the motherboard to install adapter cards. The type of adapter card connector must match the expansion slot. A riser card was used in computer systems with the LPX form factor to allow adapter cards to be installed horizontally. The riser card was mainly used in slim line desktop computers. The different types of expansion slots are shown in Figure 2.

Refer to **Figure** in online course

1.4.6 Identify the names, purposes, and characteristics of storage drives

A storage drive reads or writes information to magnetic or optical storage media. The drive can be used to store data permanently or to retrieve information from a media disk. Storage drives can be installed inside the computer case, such as a hard drive. For portability, some storage drives can connect to the computer using a USB port, a FireWire port, or an SCSI port. These portable storage drives are sometimes referred to as removable drives and can be used on multiple computers. Here are some common types of storage drives:

- Floppy drive
- Hard drive
- Optical drive
- Flash drive
- Network drive

Floppy Drive

A floppy drive, or floppy disk drive, is a storage device that uses removable 3.5-inch floppy disks. These magnetic floppy disks can store 720 KB or 1.44 MB of data. In a computer, the floppy drive is usually configured as the A: drive. The floppy drive can be used to boot the computer if it contains a bootable floppy disk. A 5.25-inch floppy drive is older technology and is seldom used.

Hard Drive

A hard drive, or hard disk drive, is a magnetic storage device that is installed inside the computer. The hard drive is used as permanent storage for data. In a computer, the hard drive is usually configured as the C: drive and contains the operating system and applications. The hard drive is usually configured as the first drive in the boot sequence. The storage capacity of a hard drive is measured in billions of bytes, or gigabytes (GB). The speed of a hard drive is measured in revolutions per minute (RPM). Multiple hard drives can be added to increase storage capacity.

Optical Drive

An optical drive is a storage device that uses lasers to read data on the optical media. There are two types of optical drives:

- Compact disc (CD)
- Digital versatile disc (DVD)

CD and DVD media can be pre-recorded (read-only), recordable (write once), or re-recordable (read and write multiple times). CDs have a data storage capacity of approximately 700 MB. DVDs have a data storage capacity of approximately 8.5 GB on one side of the disc.

There are several types of optical media:

- CD-ROM – CD read-only memory media that is pre-recorded.
- CD-R –CD-recordable media that can be recorded once.
- CD-RW – CD-rewritable media that can be recorded, erased, and re-recorded.
- DVD-ROM – DVD read-only memory media that is pre-recorded.
- DVD-RAM – DVD-random access memory media that can be recorded, erased, and re-recorded.
- DVD+/-R – DVD-recordable media that can be recorded once.
- DVD+/-RW – DVD-rewritable media that can be recorded, erased, and re-recorded.

Flash Drive

A flash drive, also known as a thumb drive, is a removable storage device that connects to a USB port. A flash drive uses a special type of memory that requires no power to maintain the data. These drives can be accessed by the operating system in the same way other types of drives are accessed.

Types of Drive Interfaces

Hard drives and optical drives are manufactured with different interfaces that are used to connect the drive to the computer. To install a storage drive in a computer, the connection interface on the drive must be the same as the controller on the motherboard. Here are some common drive interfaces:

- ***IDE –*** Integrated Drive Electronics, also called Advanced Technology Attachment (ATA) is an early drive controller interface that connects computers and hard disk drives. An IDE interface uses a 40-pin connector.

- ***EIDE –*** Enhanced Integrated Drive Electronics, also called ATA-2, is an updated version of the IDE drive controller interface. EIDE supports hard drives larger than 512 MB, enables Direct Memory Access (DMA) for speed, and uses the AT Attachment Packet Interface (ATAPI) to accommodate optical drives and tape drives on the EIDE bus. An EIDE interface uses a 40-pin connector.
- ***PATA –*** Parallel ATA refers to the parallel version of the ATA drive controller interface.
- ***SATA –*** Serial ATA refers to the serial version of the ATA drive controller interface. A SATA interface uses a 7-pin connector.
- ***SCSI –*** Small Computer System Interface is a drive controller interface that can connect up to 15 drives. SCSI can connect both internal and external drives. An SCSI interface uses a 50-pin, 68-pin, or 80-pin connector.

Refer to **Figure** in online course

1.4.7 Identify the names, purposes, and characteristics of internal cables

Drives require both a power cable and a data cable. A power supply will have a SATA power connector for SATA drives, a Molex power connector for PATA drives, and a Berg 4-pin connector for floppy drives. The buttons and the LED lights on the front of the case connect to the motherboard with the front panel cables.

Data cables connect drives to the drive controller, which is located on an adapter card or on the motherboard. Here are some common types of data cables:

- ***Floppy disk drive (FDD) data cable –*** Data cable has up to two 34-pin drive connectors and one 34-pin connector for the drive controller.
- ***PATA(IDE/EIDE) 40-conductor data cable -*** Originally, the IDE interface supported two devices on a single controller. With the introduction of Extended IDE, two controllers capable of supporting two devices each were introduced. 40-pin connectors are used on 40-conductor ribbon cable. The cable has two connectors for the drives and a third for the controller.
- ***PATA (EIDE) 80-conductor cable -*** As the data rates available over the EIDE interface increased, the chances of corruption of the data being transmitted increased. the use of 80-conductor cable was introduced for devices transmitting at 33.3MBps and over, allowing for a more reliable balanced data transmission. The connectors are still of the 40-pin variety.
- ***SATA data cable –*** Serial ATA data cable has seven conductors, one keyed connector for the drive, and one keyed connector the drive controller.
- ***SCSI data cable –*** There are three types of SCSI data cables. A narrow SCSI data cable has 50-conductors, up to seven 50-pin connectors for drives, and one 50-pin connector for the drive controller, also called the host adapter. A wide SCSI data cable has 68-conductors, up to fifteen 68-pin connectors for drives, and one 68-pin connector for the host adapter. An Alt-4 SCSI data cable has 80-conductors, up to "15" 80-pin connectors for drives, and one 80-pin connector for the host adapter.

Note

A colored stripe on a cable identifies Pin 1 on the cable. When installing a data cable, always ensure that Pin 1 on the cable aligns with Pin 1 on the drive or drive controller. Some cables may be keyed and therefore they can only be connected one way to the drive and drive controller.

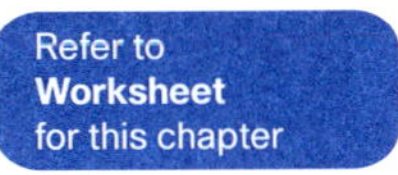

Computer Components

Research computer components

1.5 Identify the names, purposes, and characteristics of ports and cables

Refer to **Figure** in online course

Input/output (I/O) ports on a computer connect peripheral devices, such as printers, scanners, and portable drives. The following ports and cables are commonly used:

- Serial
- USB
- FireWire
- Parallel
- SCSI
- Network
- PS/2
- Audio
- Video

1.5.1 Serial Ports and Cables

A serial port can be either a DB-9, as shown in Figure 1, or a DB-25 male connector. Serial ports transmit one bit of data at a time. To connect a serial device, such as a modem or printer, a serial cable must be used. A serial cable has a maximum length of 50 feet (15.2 m).

1.5.2 USB Ports and Cables

The Universal Serial Bus (USB) is a standard interface that connects peripheral devices to a computer. It was originally designed to replace serial and parallel connections. USB devices are hot-swappable, which means that users can connect and disconnect the devices while the computer is powered on. USB connections can be found on computers, cameras, printers, scanners, storage devices, and many other electronic devices. A USB hub is used to connect multiple USB devices. A single USB port in a computer can support up to 127 separate devices with the use of multiple USB hubs. Some devices can also be powered through the USB port, eliminating the need for an external power source. Figure 2 shows USB cables with connectors.

USB 1.1 allowed transmission rates of up to 12 Mbps in full-speed mode and 1.5 Mbps in low speed mode. USB 2.0 allows transmission speeds up to 480 Mbps. USB devices can only transfer data up to the maximum speed allowed by the specific port.

1.5.3 FireWire Ports and Cables

FireWire is a high-speed, hot-swappable interface that connects peripheral devices to a computer. A single FireWire port in a computer can support up to 63 devices. Some devices can also be powered through the FireWire port, eliminating the need for an external power source. FireWire uses the IEEE 1394 standard and is also known as i.Link.

The IEEE 1394a standard supports data rates up to 400 Mbps and cable lengths up to 15 feet (4.5 m). This standard uses a 6-pin connector or a 4-pin connector. The IEEE 1394b standard allows for a greater range of connections, including CAT5 UTP and optical fiber. Depending on the media used, data rates are supported up to 3.2 Gbps over a 100m distance. Figure 3 shows FireWire cables with connectors.

1.5.4 Parallel Ports and Cables

A parallel port on a computer is a standard Type A DB-25 female connector. The parallel connector on a printer is a standard Type B 36-pin Centronics connector. Some newer printers may use a Type C high-density 36-pin connector. Parallel ports can transmit 8 bits of data at one time and use the IEEE 1284 standard. To connect a parallel device, such as a printer, a parallel cable must be used. A parallel cable, as shown in Figure 4, has a maximum length of 15 feet (4.5 m).

1.5.5 SCSI Ports and Cables

A SCSI port can transmit parallel data at rates in excess of 320 Mbps and can support up to 15 devices. If a single SCSI device is connected to an SCSI port, the cable can be up to 80 feet (24.4 m) in length. If multiple SCSI devices are connected to an SCSI port, the cable can be up to 40 (12.2 m) feet in length. An SCSI port on a computer can be one of three different types, as shown in Figure 5:

- 50-pin connector
- 68-pin connector
- 80-pin connector

Note

SCSI devices must be terminated at the endpoints of the SCSI chain. Check the device manual for termination procedures.

Caution

Some SCSI connectors resemble parallel connectors. Be careful not to connect the cable to the wrong port. The voltage used in the SCSI format may damage the parallel interface. SCSI connectors should be clearly labeled.

1.5.6 Network Ports and Cables

A network port, also known as an RJ-45 port, connects a computer to a network. The connection speed depends on the type of network port. Standard Ethernet can transmit up to 10 Mbps, Fast Ethernet can transmit up to 100 Mbps, and Gigabit Ethernet can transmit up to 1000 Mbps. The maximum length of network cable is 328 feet (100 m). A network connector is shown in Figure 6.

1.5.7 PS/2 Ports

A PS/2 port connects a keyboard or a mouse to a computer. The PS/2 port is a 6-pin mini-DIN female connector. The connectors for the keyboard and mouse are often colored differently, as shown in Figure 7. If the ports are not color-coded, look for a small figure of a mouse or keyboard next to each port.

1.5.8 Audio Ports

An audio port connects audio devices to the computer. The following audio ports are commonly used, as shown in Figure 8:

- Line In – Connects to an external source, such as a stereo system

- Microphone – Connects to a microphone
- Line Out – Connects to speakers or headphones
- Gameport/MIDI – Connects to a joystick or MIDI-interfaced device

1.5.9 Video Ports and Connectors

A video port connects a monitor cable to a computer. Figure 9 shows two of the most common video ports. There are several video port and connector types:

- *Video Graphics Array (VGA) –* VGA has a 3-row 15-pin female connector and provides analog output to a monitor.
- *Digital Visual Interface (DVI) –* DVI has a 24-pin female connector or a 29-pin female connector and provides a compressed digital output to a monitor. DVI-I provides both analog and digital signals. DVI-D provides digital signals only.
- *High-Definition Multimedia Interface (HDMi) –* HDMi has a 19-pin connector and provides digital video and digital audio signals.
- *S-Video –* S-Video has a 4-pin connector and provides analog video signals.
- *Component/RGB –* RGB has three shielded cables (red, green, blue) with RCA jacks and provides analog video signals.

Refer to **Figure** in online course

1.6 Identify the names, purposes, and characteristics of input devices

An input device is used to enter data or instructions into a computer. Here are some examples of input devices:

- Mouse and keyboard
- Digital camera and digital video camera
- Biometric authentication device
- Touch screen
- Scanner

The mouse and keyboard are the two most commonly used input devices. The mouse is used to navigate the graphical user interface (GUI). The keyboard is used to enter text commands that control the computer.

Digital cameras and digital video cameras, shown in Figure 1, create images that can be stored on magnetic media. The image is stored as a file that can be displayed, printed, or altered.

Biometric identification makes use of features that are unique to an individual user, such as fingerprints, voice recognition, or a retinal scan. When combined with ordinary usernames, biometrics guarantees that the authorized person is accessing the data. Figure 2 shows a laptop that has a built-in fingerprint scanner.

A touch screen has a pressure-sensitive transparent panel. The computer receives instructions specific to the place on the screen that the user touches.

A scanner digitizes an image or document. The digitization of the image is stored as a file that can be displayed, printed, or altered. A bar code reader is a type of scanner that reads universal product code (UPC) bar codes. It is widely used for pricing and inventory information.

Refer to **Figure** in online course

1.7 Identify the names, purposes, and characteristics of output devices

An output device is used to present information to the user from a computer. Here are some examples of output devices:

- Monitors and projectors
- Printers, scanners, and fax machines
- Speakers and headphones

1.7.1 Monitors and Projectors

Monitors and projectors are primary output devices for a computer. There are different types of monitors, as shown in Figure 1. The most important difference between these monitor types is the technology used to create an image:

- ***CRT*** **–** Cathode-ray tube monitor is the most common monitor type. There are three electron beams. Each focused to hit colored phosphor on the screen which will glow either red, blue or green. Areas not struck by the electron beam do not glow. The combination of glowing and non-glowing areas is what creates the image on the screen. Most televisions also use this technology.
- ***LCD*** **–** Liquid crystal display is commonly used in laptops and some projectors. It consists of two polarizing filters with a liquid crystal solution between them. An electronic current aligns the crystals so that light can either pass through or not pass through. The effect of light passing through in certain areas and not in others is what creates the image. LCD comes in two forms, active matrix and passive matrix. Active matrix is sometimes called thin film transistor (TFT). TFT allows each pixel to be controlled, which creates very sharp color images. Passive matrix is less expensive than active matrix but does not provide the same level of image control.
- ***DLP*** **–** Digital light processing is another technology used in projectors. DLP projectors use a spinning color wheel with a microprocessor-controlled array of mirrors called a digital micromirror device (DMD). Each mirror corresponds to a specific pixel. Each mirror reflects light toward or away from the projector optics. This creates a monochromatic image of up to 1024 shades of gray in between white and black. The color wheel then adds the color data to complete the projected, color image.

Monitor resolution refers to the level of image detail that can be reproduced. Figure 2 is a chart of common monitor resolutions. Higher resolution settings produce better image quality. There are several factors involved in monitor resolution:

- ***Pixels*** **–** The term pixel is an abbreviation for picture element. Pixels are the tiny dots that comprise a screen. Each pixel consists of red, green, and blue.
- ***Dot Pitch*** **–** Dot pitch is the distance between pixels on the screen. A lower dot pitch number produces a better image.
- ***Refresh Rate*** **–** The refresh rate is how often per second the image is rebuilt. A higher refresh rate produces a better image and reduces the level of flicker.
- ***Interlace/Non-Interlace*** **–** Interlaced monitors create the image by scanning the screen two times. The first scan covers the odd lines, top to bottom, and the second scan covers the even

lines. Non-interlaced monitors create the image by scanning the screen, one line at a time from top to bottom. Most CRT monitors today are non-interlaced.

- ***Horizontal Vertical Colors (HVC) –*** The number of pixels in a line is the horizontal resolution. The number of lines in a screen is the vertical resolution. The number of colors that can be reproduced is the color resolution.
- ***Aspect Ratio –*** Aspect ratio is the horizontal to vertical measurement of the viewing area of a monitor. For example, a 4:3 aspect ratio would apply to a viewing area that is 16 inches wide by 12 inches high. A 4:3 aspect radio would also apply to a viewing area that is 24 inches wide by 18 inches high. A viewing area that is 22 inches wide by 12 inches high has an aspect ratio of 11:6.

Monitors have controls for adjusting the quality of the image. Here are some common monitor settings:

- Brightness – Intensity of the image
- Contrast – Ratio of light to dark
- Position – Vertical and horizontal location of image on the screen
- Reset – Returns the monitor settings to factory settings

1.7.2 Printers, Scanners, and Fax Machines

Printers are output devices that create hard copies of computer files. Some printers specialize in particular applications, such as printing color photographs. Other all-in-one type printers, like the one shown in Figure 3, are designed to provide multiple services such as printing, fax, and copier functions.

1.7.3 Speakers and Headphones

Speakers and headphones are output devices for audio signals. Most computers have audio support either integrated into the motherboard or on an adapter card. Audio support includes ports that allow input and output of audio signals. The audio card has an amplifier to power headphones and external speakers, which are shown in Figure 4.

Refer to **Figure** in online course

1.8 Explain system resources and their purposes

System resources are used for communication purposes between the CPU and other components in a computer. There are three common system resources:

- Interrupt Requests (IRQ)
- Input/Output (I/O) Port Addresses
- Direct Memory Access (DMA)

1.8.1 Interrupt Requests

IRQs are used by computer components to request information from the CPU. The IRQ travels along a wire on the motherboard to the CPU. When the CPU receives an interrupt request, the CPU determines how to fulfill this request. The priority of the request is determined by the IRQ number assigned to that computer component. Older computers only had eight IRQs to assign to devices. Newer computers have 16 IRQs, which are numbered 0 to 15, as shown in Figure 1. As a general rule, each component in the computer must be assigned a unique IRQ. IRQ conflicts can cause components to stop functioning and even cause the computer to crash. With the numerous components that can be installed in a computer, it is difficult to assign a unique IRQ to every component. Today, most IRQ numbers are assigned automatically with plug and play (PnP) operating systems and the implementation of PCI slots, USB ports, and FireWire ports.

1.8.2 Input/Output (I/O) Port Addresses

Input/output (I/O) port addresses are used to communicate between devices and software. The I/O port address is used to send and receive data for a component. As with IRQs, each component will have a unique I/O port assigned. There are 65,535 I/O ports in a computer, and they are referenced by a hexadecimal address in the range of 0000h to FFFFh. Figure 2 shows a chart of common I/O ports.

1.8.3 Direct Memory Access

Refer to **Figure** in online course

DMA channels are used by high-speed devices to communicate directly with main memory. These channels allow the device to bypass interaction with the CPU and directly store and retrieve information from memory. Only certain devices can be assigned a DMA channel, such as SCSI host adapters and sound cards. Older computers only had four DMA channels to assign to components. Newer computers have eight DMA channels that are numbered 0 to 7, as shown in Figure 3.

Summary

This chapter introduced the IT industry, options for training and employment, and some of the industry-standard certifications. This chapter also covered the components that comprise a personal computer system. Much of the content in this chapter will help you throughout this course:

- Information Technology encompasses the use of computers, network hardware, and software to process, store, transmit, and retrieve information.
- A personal computer system consists of hardware components and software applications.
- The computer case and power supply must be chosen carefully to support the hardware inside the case and allow for the addition of components.
- The internal components of a computer are selected for specific features and functions. All internal components must be compatible with the motherboard.
- You should use the correct type of ports and cables when connecting devices.
- Typical input devices include the keyboard, mouse, touch screen, and digital cameras.
- Typical output devices include monitors, printers, and speakers.
- System resources must be assigned to computer components. System resources include IRQs, I/O port addresses, and DMAs.

Chapter 1 Quiz

Take the chapter quiz to test your knowledge.

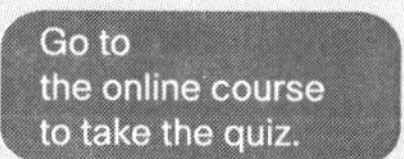

Your Chapter Notes

CHAPTER 2

Safe Lab Procedures and Tool Use

Introduction

This chapter covers basic safety practices for the workplace, hardware and software tools, and the disposal of hazardous materials. Safety guidelines help protect individuals from accidents and injury and protect equipment from damage. Some of these guidelines are designed to protect the environment from contamination by discarded materials. Stay alert to situations that could result in injury or damage to equipment. Warning signs are designed to alert you to danger. Always watch for these signs and take the appropriate action according to the warning given.

After completing this chapter, you will meet these objectives:

- Explain the purpose of safe working conditions and procedures.
- Identify tools and software used with personal computer components and their purposes.
- Implement proper tool use.

Refer to **Figure** in online course

2.1 Explain the purpose of safe working conditions and procedures

Safe working conditions help to prevent injury to people and damage to computer equipment. A safe workspace is clean, organized, and properly lighted. Everyone must understand and follow safety procedures.

Follow proper procedures for handling computer equipment to reduce the risk of personal injury, damage to property, and loss of data. Any damage or loss may result in claims for damage from the owner of the property and data.

The proper disposal or recycling of hazardous computer components is a global issue. Make sure to follow regulations that govern how to dispose of specific items. Organizations that violate these regulations can be fined or face expensive legal battles.

After completing this section, you will meet these objectives:

- Identify safety procedures and potential hazards for users and technicians.
- Identify safety procedures to protect equipment from damage and data from loss.
- Identify safety procedures to protect the environment from contamination.

Refer to **Figure** in online course

2.1.1 Identify safety procedures and potential hazards for users and technicians

General Safety Guidelines

Follow the basic safety guidelines to prevent cuts, burns, electrical shock, and damage to eyesight. As is best practice, make sure that a fire extinguisher and first-aid kit are available in case of fire or injury. Figure 1 shows a list of general safety guidelines.

Caution

Power supplies and monitors contain very high voltage. Do not wear the antistatic wrist strap when repairing power supplies or monitors.

Caution

Some printer parts may become very hot when in use and other parts may contain very high voltages. Make sure that the printer has had time to cool before making the repair. Check the printer manual for locations of various components that may contain high voltages. Some components may retain high voltages even after the printer is turned off.

Fire Safety Guidelines

Follow fire safety guidelines to protect lives, structures, and equipment. To avoid an electrical shock, and to prevent damage to the computer, turn off and unplug the computer before beginning a repair.

Fire can spread rapidly and be very costly. Proper use of a fire extinguisher can prevent a small fire from getting out of control. When working with computer components, always consider the possibility of an accidental fire and know how to react. If there is a fire, you should follow these safety procedures:

- Never fight a fire that is out of control or not contained.
- Always have a planned fire escape route before beginning any work.
- Get out of the building quickly.
- Contact emergency services for help.

Be sure to locate and read the instructions on the fire extinguishers in your workplace before you have to use them. Safety training may be available in your organization.

In the United States, there are four classifications for fire extinguishers. A different letter, color, and shape identifies each fire extinguisher classification, as shown in Figure 2. Each type of fire extinguisher has specific chemicals to fight different types of fires:

- Class A – Paper, wood, plastics, cardboard
- Class B – Gasoline, kerosene, organic solvents
- Class C – Electrical equipment
- Class D – Combustible metals

What types of fire extinguisher classifications are there in your country?

It is important to know how to use a fire extinguisher. Use the memory aid P-A-S-S to help you remember the basic rules of fire extinguisher operation:

P - Pull the pin.

A - Aim at the base of the fire, not at the flames.

S - Squeeze the lever.

S - Sweep the nozzle from side to side.

Refer to **Figure** in online course

2.1.2 Identify safety procedures to protect equipment from damage and data from loss

Electrostatic discharge (ESD), harsh climates, and poor-quality sources of electricity can cause damage to computer equipment. Follow proper handling guidelines, be aware of environmental issues, and use equipment that stabilizes power to prevent equipment damage and data loss.

ESD

Static electricity is the buildup of an electric charge resting on a surface. This buildup may zap a component and cause damage. This is known as electrostatic discharge (ESD). ESD can be destructive to the electronics in a computer system.

At least 3,000 volts of static electricity must build up before a person can feel ESD. For example, static electricity can build up on you as they walk across a carpeted floor. When you touch another person, you both receive a shock. If the discharge causes pain or makes a noise, the charge was probably above 10,000 volts. By comparison, less than 30 volts of static electricity can damage a computer component.

ESD Protection Recommendations

ESD can cause permanent damage to electrical components. Follow these recommendations to help prevent ESD damage:

- Keep all components in antistatic bags until you are ready to install them.
- Use grounded mats on workbenches.
- Use grounded floor mats in work areas.
- Use antistatic wrist straps when working on computers.

Climate

Climate affects computer equipment in a variety of ways:

- If the environment temperature is too high, equipment can overheat.
- If the humidity level is too low, the chance of ESD increases.
- If the humidity level is too high, equipment can suffer from moisture damage.

Figure 1 shows how environmental conditions increase or decrease the risk of ESD.

Power Fluctuation Types

Voltage is the force that moves electrons through a circuit. The movement of electrons is called current. Computer circuits need voltage and current to operate electronic components. When the voltage in a computer is not accurate or steady, computer components may not operate correctly. Unsteady voltages are called power fluctuations.

The following types of AC power fluctuations can cause data loss or hardware failure:

- ***Blackout*** – complete loss of AC power. A blown fuse, damaged transformer, or downed power line can cause a blackout.
- ***Brownout*** – reduced voltage level of AC power that lasts for a period of time. Brownouts occur when the power line voltage drops below 80% of the normal voltage level. Overloading electrical circuits can cause a brownout.

- ***Noise –*** interference from generators and lightning. Noise results in unclean power, which can cause errors in a computer system.
- ***Spike –*** sudden increase in voltage that lasts for a very short period and exceeds 100% of the normal voltage on a line. Spikes can be caused by lightning strikes, but can also occur when the electrical system comes back on after a blackout.
- ***Power surge –*** dramatic increase in voltage above the normal flow of electrical current. A power surge lasts for a few nanoseconds, or one-billionth of a second.

Power Protection Devices

To help shield against power fluctuation issues, use protection devices to protect the data and computer equipment:

- ***Surge Suppressor –*** helps protect against damage from surges and spikes. A surge suppressor diverts extra electrical voltage on the line to the ground.
- ***Uninterruptible Power Supply (UPS) –*** helps protect against potential electrical power problems by supplying electrical power to a computer or other device. The battery is constantly recharging while the UPS is in use. The UPS is able to supply a consistent quality of power when brownouts and blackouts occur. Many UPS devices are able to communicate directly with the operating system on a computer. This communication allows the UPS to safely shut down the computer and save data prior to the UPS losing all electrical power.
- ***Standby Power Supply (SPS) –*** helps protect against potential electrical power problems by providing a backup battery to supply power when the incoming voltage drops below the normal level. The battery is on standby during the normal operation. When the voltage decreases, the battery provides DC power to a power inverter, which converts it to AC power for the computer. This device is not as reliable as a UPS because of the time it takes to switch over to the battery. If the switching device fails, the battery will not be able to supply power to the computer. Figure 2 shows some examples of surge suppressors, UPS, and SPS devices.

Caution

Never plug a printer into a UPS device. UPS manufacturers suggest not plugging a printer into a UPS for fear of overloading the UPS.

Refer to **Figure** in online course

2.1.3 Identify safety procedures to protect the environment from contamination

Computers and peripherals, as shown in Figure 1, contain materials that can be harmful to the environment. Hazardous materials are sometimes called toxic waste. These materials can contain high concentrations of heavy metals such as cadmium, lead, or mercury. The regulations for the disposal of hazardous materials vary according to state or country. Contact the local recycling or waste removal authorities in your community for information about disposal procedures and services.

Material Safety and Data Sheet

A Material Safety and Data Sheet (MSDS) is a fact sheet that summarizes information about material identification, including hazardous ingredients that can affect personal health, fire hazards, and first aid requirements. In Figure 2, the MSDS sheet contains chemical reactivity and incompatibility information that includes spill, leak, and disposal procedures. It also includes protective measures for the safe handling and storage of materials.

To determine if a material is classified as hazardous, consult the manufacturer's MSDS. In the U.S., the Occupational Safety and Health Administration (OSHA) requires that all hazardous materials must be accompanied by an MSDS when transferred to a new owner. The MSDS information included with products purchased for computer repairs or maintenance can be relevant to computer technicians. OSHA also requires that employees be informed about the materials that they are working with and be provided with material safety information. In the United Kingdom, Chemicals Hazard Information and Packaging for Supply Regulations 2002 (CHIP3) oversees the handling of hazardous materials. CHIP3 requires chemical suppliers to safely package and transport dangerous chemicals and to include a data sheet with the product.

Note

The MSDS is valuable in determining how to dispose of any potentially hazardous materials in the safest manner. Always check local regulations concerning acceptable disposal methods before disposing of any electronic equipment.

What organization governs the use of hazardous chemicals in your country? Are MSDS sheets mandatory?

The MSDS contains valuable information:

- The name of the material
- The physical properties of the material
- Any hazardous ingredients contained in the material
- Reactivity data, such as fire and explosion data
- Procedures for spills or leaks
- Special precautions
- Health hazards
- Special protection requirements

Computers and other computing devices are eventually discarded because of one of the following reasons:

- Parts or components begin to fail more frequently as the device ages.
- The computer becomes obsolete for the application for which it was originally intended.
- Newer models have improved features.

Before discarding a computer or any of its components, it is crucial to consider safe disposal of each separate component.

Proper Disposal of Batteries

Batteries often contain rare earth metals that can be harmful to the environment. Batteries from portable computer systems may contain lead, cadmium, lithium, alkaline manganese, and mercury. These metals do not decay and will remain in the environment for many years. Mercury is commonly used in the manufacturing of batteries and is extremely toxic and harmful to humans.

Recycling batteries should be a standard practice for a technician. All batteries, including lithium-ion, nickel-cadmium, nickel-metal hydride, and lead-acid are subject to disposal procedures that comply with local environmental regulations.

Proper Disposal of Monitors or CRTs

Handle monitors and CRTs with care. Extremely high voltage can be stored in monitors and CRTs, even after being disconnected from a power source. CRTs contain glass, metal, plastics, lead, barium, and rare earth metals. According to the U.S. Environmental Protection Agency (EPA), CRTs may contain approximately 4 lbs (1.8 kg) of lead. Monitors must be disposed of in compliance with environmental regulations.

Proper Disposal of Toner Kits, Cartridges, and Developers

Used printer toner kits and printer cartridges must be disposed of properly or recycled. Some toner cartridge suppliers and manufacturers will take empty cartridges for refilling. There are also companies that specialize in refilling empty cartridges. Kits to refill inkjet printer cartridges are available but are not recommended, because the ink may leak into the printer, causing irreversible damage. This can be especially costly because using refilled inkjet cartridges may also void the inkjet printer warranty.

Proper Disposal of Chemical Solvents and Aerosol Cans

Contact the local sanitation company to learn how and where to dispose of the chemicals and solvents used to clean computers. Never dump chemicals or solvents down a sink or dispose of them in any drain that connects to public sewers.

The cans or bottles that contain solvents and other cleaning supplies must be handled carefully. Make sure that they are identified and treated as special hazardous waste. For example, some aerosol cans may explode when exposed to heat if the contents are not completely used.

Refer to **Figure** in online course

2.2 Identify tools and software used with personal computer components and their purposes

For every job there is the right tool. Make sure that you are familiar with the correct use of each tool and that the right tool is used for the current task. Skilled use of tools and software makes the job less difficult and ensures that tasks are performed properly and safely.

Software tools are available that help diagnose problems. Use these tools to determine which computer device is not functioning correctly.

A technician must document all repairs and computer problems. The documentation can then be used as a reference for future problems or for other technicians who may not have encountered the problem before. The documents may be paper based, but electronic forms are preferred because they can be easily searched for specific problems.

After completing this section, you will meet these objectives:

- Identify hardware tools and their purpose.
- Identify software tools and their purpose.
- Identify organizational tools and their purpose.

Refer to **Figure** in online course

2.2.1 Identify hardware tools and their purpose

A toolkit should contain all of the tools necessary to complete hardware repairs. As you gain experience, you will learn which tools to have available for different types of jobs. Hardware tools are grouped into these four categories:

- ESD tools
- Hand tools
- Cleaning tools
- Diagnostic tools

ESD Tools

There are two ESD tools: the antistatic wrist strap and the antistatic mat. The antistatic wrist strap protects computer equipment when grounded to a computer chassis. The antistatic mat protects computer equipment by preventing static electricity from accumulating on the hardware or on the technician. Click each of the items in Figure 1 for more information on ESD tools.

Hand Tools

Most tools used in the computer assembly process are small hand tools. They are available individually or as part of a computer repair toolkit. Toolkits range widely in size, quality, and price. Click each of the items in Figure 2 for more information on hand tools.

Cleaning Tools

Having the appropriate cleaning tools is essential when maintaining or repairing computers. Using these tools ensures that computer components are not damaged during cleaning. Click each of the items in Figure 3 for more information on cleaning tools.

Diagnostic Tools

A digital multimeter and a loopback adapter are used to test hardware. Click each of the items in Figure 4 for more information on diagnostic tools.

Refer to **Figure** in online course

2.2.2 Identify software tools and their purpose

A technician must be able to use a range of software tools to help diagnose problems, maintain hardware, and protect the data stored on a computer.

Disk Management Tools

You must be able to identify which software to use in different situations. Disk management tools help detect and correct disk errors, prepare a disk for data storage, and remove unwanted files.

Click each of the buttons in Figure 1 to see screen shots of the following disk management tools:

- ***Fdisk or Disk Management –*** used to create and delete partitions on a hard drive
- ***Format –*** used to prepare a hard drive to store information

- ***Scandisk or Chkdsk –*** used to check the integrity of files and folders on a hard drive by scanning the file system. They may also check the disk surface for physical errors
- ***Defrag –*** used to optimize space on a hard drive to allow faster access to programs and data
- ***Disk Cleanup –*** used to clear space on a hard drive by searching for files that can be safely deleted
- ***Disk Management –*** a system utility used to manage hard drives and partitions, which peforms tasks such as initializing disks, creating partitions, and formatting partitions
- ***System File Checker (SFC) –*** a command-line utility that scans the operating system critical files and replaces any files that are corrupted

Use the Windows XP boot disk for troubleshooting and repairing corrupted files. The Windows XP boot disk is designed to repair Windows system files, restore damaged or lost files, and reinstall the operating system. Third-party software tools are available to assist in troubleshooting problems.

Protection Software Tools

Each year, viruses, spyware, and other types of malicious attacks infect millions of computers. These attacks can damage an operating system, application, and data. Computers that have been infected may even have problems with hardware performance or component failure.

To protect data and the integrity of the operating system and hardware, use software designed to guard against attacks and to remove malicious programs.

Various types of software are used to protect hardware and data. Click each of the buttons in Figure 2 to see screen shots of these protection software tools:

- ***Windows XP Security Center –*** allows you to check the status of essential security settings on the computer. The Security Center continuously checks to make sure that the software firewall and antivirus programs are running. It also ensures that automatic updates are set to download and install automatically.
- ***Antivirus Program –*** protects a computer against virus attacks.
- ***Spyware Remover –*** protects against software that sends information about web surfing habits to an attacker. Spyware can be installed without the knowledge or consent of the user.
- ***Firewall –*** a program that runs continuously to protect against unauthorized communications to and from your computer.

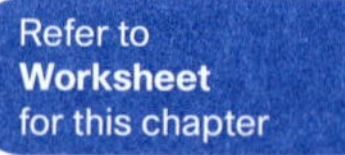

Diagnostic Software

Research hard drive diagnostic software

Refer to **Figure** in online course

2.2.3 Identify organizational tools and their purpose

It is important that a technician document all services and repairs. These documents need to be stored centrally and made available to all other technicians. The documentation can then be used as reference material for similar problems that are encountered in the future. Good customer service includes providing the customer with a detailed description of the problem and the solution.

Personal Reference Tools

Personal Reference tools include troubleshooting guides, manufacturer manuals, quick reference guides, and a repair journal. In addition to an invoice, a technician keeps a journal of upgrades and repairs. The documentation in the journal should include descriptions of the problem, possible solutions that have been tried in order to correct the problem, and the steps taken to repair the problem. Be sure to note any configuration changes made to the equipment and any replacement parts used in the repair. This documentation will be valuable when you encounter similar situations in the future.

- ***Notes* –** Make notes as you go through the investigation and repair process. Refer to these notes to avoid repeating previous steps and to determine what steps to take next.
- ***Journal* –** Document the upgrades and repairs that you perform. The documentation should include descriptions of the problem, possible solutions that have been tried in order to correct the problem, and the steps taken to repair the problem. Be sure to note any configuration changes made to the equipment and any replacement parts used in the repair. Your journal, along with your notes, can be valuable when you encounter similar situations in the future.
- ***History of repairs* –** Make a detailed list of problems and repairs, including the date, replacement parts, and customer information. The history allows a technician to determine what work has been performed on a computer in the past.

Internet Reference Tools

The Internet is an excellent source of information about specific hardware problems and possible solutions:

- Internet search engines
- News groups
- Manufacturer FAQs
- Online computer manuals
- Online forums and chat
- Technical websites

Figure 1 shows an example of a technical website.

Miscellaneous Tools

With experience, you will discover many additional items to add to the toolkit. Figure 2 shows how a roll of masking tape can be used to label parts that have been removed from a computer when a parts organizer is not available.

A working computer is also a valuable resource to take with you on computer repairs in the field. A working computer can be used to research information, download tools or drivers, or communicate with other technicians.

Figure 3 shows the types of computer replacement parts to include in a toolkit. Make sure that the parts are in good working order before you use them. Using known good working components to replace possible bad ones in computers will help you quickly determine which component may not be working properly.

Refer to **Figure** in online course

2.3 Implement proper tool use

Safety in the workplace is everyone's responsibility. You are much less likely to injure yourself or damage components when using the proper tool for the job.

Before cleaning or repairing equipment, check to make sure that your tools are in good condition. Clean, repair, or replace any items that are not functioning adequately.

After completing this section, you will meet these objectives:

- Demonstrate proper use of an antistatic wrist strap.
- Demonstrate proper use of an antistatic mat.
- Demonstrate proper use of various hand tools.
- Demonstrate proper use of cleaning materials.

Refer to **Figure** in online course

2.3.1 Demonstrate proper use of an antistatic wrist strap

As discussed previously, an example of ESD is the small shock that someone receives when you walk across a room with carpet and touch a doorknob. Although the small shock is harmless to you, the same electrical charge passing from you to a computer can damage its components. Wearing an antistatic wrist strap can prevent ESD damage to computer components.

The purpose of an antistatic wrist strap is to equalize the electrical charge between you and the equipment. The antistatic wrist strap is a conductor that connects your body to the equipment that you are working on. When static electricity builds up in your body, the connection made by the wrist strap to the equipment, or ground, channels the electricity through the wire that connects the strap.

As shown in Figure 1, the wrist strap has two parts and is easy to wear:

Step 1. Wrap the strap around your wrist and secure it using the snap or Velcro. The metal on the back of the wrist strap must remain in contact with the skin at all times.

Step 2. Snap the connector on the end of the wire to the wrist strap and connect the other end either to the equipment or to the same grounding point that the antistatic mat is connected to. The metal skeleton of the case is a good place to connect the wire. When connecting the wire to equipment you are working on, choose an unpainted metal surface. A painted surface does not conduct the electricity as well as unpainted metal.

Note

Attach the wire on the same side of the equipment as the arm wearing the antistatic wrist strap. This will help to keep the wire out of the way while you are working.

Although wearing a wrist strap will help to prevent ESD, you can further reduce the risks by not wearing clothing made of silk, polyester, or wool. These fabrics are more likely to generate a static charge.

Note

Technicians should roll up their sleeves, remove scarfs or ties, and tuck in their shirts to prevent interference from clothing. Ensure that earrings, necklaces, and other loose jewelry are properly secured.

Caution

Never wear an antistatic wrist strap if you are repairing a monitor or CRT.

Refer to **Figure** in online course

2.3.2 Demonstrate proper use of an antistatic mat

You may not always have the option to work on a computer in a properly equipped workspace. If you can control the environment, try to set up your workspace away from carpeted areas. Carpets can cause the buildup of electrostatic charges. If you cannot avoid the carpeting, ground yourself to the unpainted portion of the case of the computer on which you are working before touching any components.

Antistatic Mat

An antistatic mat is slightly conductive. It works by drawing static electricity away from a component and transferring it safely from equipment to a grounding point, as shown in Figure 1:

Step 1. Lay the mat on the workspace next to or under the computer case.

Step 2. Clip the mat to the case to provide a grounded surface on which you can place parts as you remove them from the system.

Reducing the potential for ESD reduces the likelihood of damage to delicate circuits or components.

Note
Always handle components by the edges.

Workbench

When you are working at a workbench, ground the workbench and the antistatic floor mat. By standing on the mat and wearing the wrist strap, your body has the same charge as the equipment and reduces the probability of ESD.

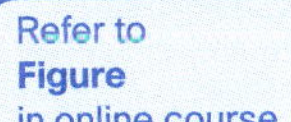

2.3.3 Demonstrate proper use of various hand tools

A technician needs to be able to properly use each tool in the toolkit. This topic covers many of the various hand tools used when repairing computers.

Screws

Match each screw with the proper screwdriver. Place the tip of the screwdriver on the head of the screw. Turn the screwdriver clockwise to tighten the screw and counterclockwise to loosen the screw, as shown in Figure 1.

Screws can become stripped if you over-tighten them with a screwdriver. A stripped screw, shown in Figure 2, may get stuck in the screw hole, or it may not tighten firmly. Discard stripped screws.

Flat Head Screwdriver

As shown in Figure 3, use a flat head screwdriver when you are working with a slotted screw. Do not use a flat head screwdriver to remove a Phillips head screw. Never use a screwdriver as a pry bar. If you can not remove a component, check to see if there is a clip or latch that is securing the component in place.

Caution
If excessive force is needed to remove or add a component, something is probably wrong. Take a second look to make sure that you have not missed a screw or a locking clip that is holding the component in place. Refer to the device manual or diagram for additional information.

Phillips Head Screwdriver

As shown in Figure 4, use a Phillips head screwdriver with crosshead screws. Do not use this type of screwdriver to puncture anything. This will damage the head of the screwdriver.

Hex Driver

As shown in Figure 5, use a hex driver to loosen and tighten bolts that have a hexagonal (six-sided) head. Hex bolts should not be over-tightened because the threads of the bolts can be stripped. Do not use a hex driver that is too large for the bolt that you are using.

Caution

Some tools are magnetized. When working around electronic devices, be sure that the tools you are using have not been magnetized. Magnetic fields can be harmful to data stored on magnetic media. Test your tool by touching the tool with a screw. If the screw is attracted to the tool, do not use the tool.

Part Retriever, Needle-Nose Pliers, or Tweezers

As shown in Figure 6, the part retriever, needle-nose pliers, and tweezers can be used to place and retrieve parts that may be hard to reach with your fingers. Do not scratch or hit any components when using these tools.

Caution

Pencils should not be used inside the computer to change the setting of switches or to pry off jumpers. The pencil lead can act as a conductor and may damage the computer components.

2.3.4 Demonstrate proper use of cleaning materials

Refer to **Figure** in online course

Keeping computers clean inside and out is a vital part of a maintenance program. Dirt can cause problems with the physical operation of fans, buttons, and other mechanical components. Figure 1 shows severe dust buildup on computer components. On electrical components, an excessive buildup of dust will act like an insulator and trap the heat. This insulation will impair the ability of heat sinks and cooling fans to keep components cool, causing chips and circuits to overheat and fail.

Caution

Before cleaning any device, turn it off and unplug the device from the power source.

Computer Cases and Monitors

Clean computer cases and the outside of monitors with a mild cleaning solution on a damp, lint-free cloth. Mix one drop of dishwashing liquid with four ounces of water to create the cleaning solution. If any water drips inside the case, allow enough time for the liquid to dry before powering on the computer.

LCD Screens

Do not use ammoniated glass cleaners or any other solution on an LCD screen unless the cleaner is specifically designed for the purpose. Harsh chemicals will damage the coating on the screen.

There is no glass protecting these screens, so be gentle when cleaning them and do not press firmly on the screen.

CRT Screens

To clean the screens of CRT monitors, dampen a soft, clean, lint-free cloth with distilled water and wipe the screen from top to bottom. Then use a soft, dry cloth to wipe the screen and remove any streaking after you have cleaned the monitor.

Clean dusty components with a can of compressed air. Compressed air does not cause electrostatic buildup on components. Make sure that you are in a well-ventilated area before blowing the dust out of the computer. A best practice is to wear a dust mask to make sure that you do not breathe in the dust particles.

Blow out the dust using short bursts from the can. Never tip the can or use the compressed air can upside down. Do not allow the fan blades to spin from the force of the compressed air. Hold the fan in place. Fan motors can be ruined from spinning when the motor is not turned on.

Component Contacts

Clean the contacts on components with isopropyl alcohol. Do not use rubbing alcohol. Rubbing alcohol contains impurities that can damage contacts. Make sure that the contacts do not collect any lint from the cloth or cotton swab. Blow any lint off the contacts with compressed air before reinstallation.

Keyboard

Clean a desktop keyboard with compressed air or a small, hand-held vacuum cleaner with a brush attachment.

Caution

Never use a standard vacuum cleaner inside a computer case. The plastic parts of the vacuum cleaner can build up static electricity and discharge to the components. Use only a vacuum approved for electronic components.

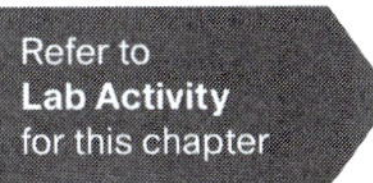

Computer Dissasembly

Disassemble a computer

Mouse

Refer to **Figure** in online course

Use glass cleaner and a soft cloth to clean the outside of the mouse. Do not spray glass cleaner directly on the mouse. If cleaning a ball mouse, you can remove the ball and clean it with glass cleaner and a soft cloth. Wipe the rollers clean inside the mouse with the same cloth. You may need to use a nail file to clean the rollers on the mouse. Do not spray any liquids inside the mouse.

The chart in Figure 2 indicates the computer items that you should clean and the cleaning materials you should use in each case.

Summary

This chapter discussed safe lab procedures, correct tool usage, and the proper disposal of computer components and supplies. You have familiarized yourself in the lab with many of the tools used to build, service, and clean computer and electronic components. You have also learned the importance of organizational tools and how these tools help you work more efficiently.

The following are some of the important concepts to remember from this chapter:

- Work in a safe manner to protect both users and equipment.
- Follow all safety guidelines to prevent injuries to yourself and to others.
- Know how to protect equipment from ESD damage.
- Know about and be able to prevent power issues that can cause equipment damage or data loss.
- Know which products and supplies require special disposal procedures.
- Familiarize yourself with MSDS sheets for both safety issues and disposal restrictions to help protect the environment.
- Be able to use the correct tools for the task.
- Know how to clean components safely.
- Use organizational tools during computer repairs.

Chapter 2 Quiz

Take the chapter quiz to test your knowledge.

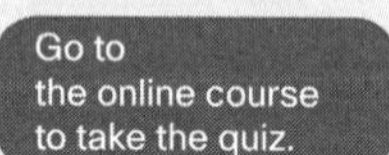

Your Chapter Notes

CHAPTER 3

Computer Assembly - Step by Step

Introduction

Assembling computers is a large part of a technician's job. As a technician, you will need to work in a logical, methodical manner when working with computer components. As with any learned trade, computer assembly skills will improve dramatically with practice.

After completing this chapter, you will meet these objectives:

- Open the case.
- Install the power supply.
- Attach the components to the motherboard and install the motherboard.
- Install internal drives.
- Install drives in external bays.
- Install adapter cards.
- Connect all internal cables.
- Re-attach the side panels and connect external cables to the computer.
- Boot the computer for the first time.

Refer to **Figure** in online course

3.1 Open the case

Computer cases are produced in a variety of form factors. Form factors refer to the size and shape of the case.

Prepare the workspace before opening the computer case. There should be adequate lighting, good ventilation, and a comfortable room temperature. The workbench or table should be accessible from all sides. Avoid cluttering the surface of the workbench or table with tools and computer components. An antistatic mat on the table will help prevent physical and ESD damage to equipment. Small containers can be used to hold small screws and other parts as they are being removed.

There are different methods for opening cases. To learn how to open a particular computer case, consult the user manual or manufacturer's website. Most computer cases are opened in one of the following ways:

- The computer case cover can be removed as one piece.
- The top and side panels of the case can be removed.
- The top of the case may need to be removed before the side panels can be removed.

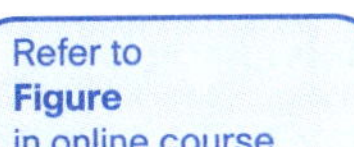

3.2 Install the power supply

Refer to **Figure** in online course

A technician may be required to replace or install a power supply. Most power supplies can only fit one way in the computer case. There are usually three or four screws that attach the power supply to the case. Power supplies have fans that can vibrate and loosen screws that are not secured. When installing a power supply, make sure that all of the screws are used and that they are properly tightened.

These are the power supply installation steps:

Step 1. Insert the power supply into the case.

Step 2. Align the holes in the power supply with the holes in the case.

Step 3. Secure the power supply to the case using the proper screws.

Refer to **Lab Activity** for this chapter

Power Supply Installation

Install the power supply in the computer

Refer to **Figure** in online course

3.3 Attach the components to the motherboard and install the motherboard

This section details the steps to install components on the motherboard and then install the motherboard into the computer case.

After completing this section, you will meet these objectives:

- Install a CPU and a heat sink/fan assembly.
- Install the RAM.
- Install the motherboard.

Refer to **Figure** in online course

3.3.1 Install a CPU and a heat sink/fan assembly

The CPU and the heat sink/fan assembly may be installed on the motherboard before the motherboard is placed in the computer case.

CPU

Figure 1 shows a close-up view of the CPU and the motherboard. The CPU and motherboard are sensitive to electrostatic discharge. When handling a CPU and motherboard, make sure that you place them on a grounded antistatic mat. You should wear an antistatic wrist strap while working with these components.

Caution

When handling a CPU, do not touch the CPU contacts at any time.

The CPU is secured to the socket on the motherboard with a locking assembly. The CPU sockets today are ZIF sockets. You should be familiar with the locking assembly before attempting to install a CPU into the socket on the motherboard.

Thermal compound helps to keep the CPU cool. Figure 2 shows thermal compound being applied to the CPU.

When you are installing a used CPU, clean the CPU and the base of the heat sink with isopropyl alcohol. Doing this removes all traces of old thermal compound. The surfaces are now ready for a new layer of thermal compound. Follow all manufacturer recommendations about applying the thermal compound.

Heat Sink/Fan Assembly

Figure 3 shows the heat sink/fan assembly. It is a two-part cooling device. The heat sink draws heat away from the CPU. The fan moves the heat away from the heat sink. The heat sink/fan assembly usually has a 3-pin power connector.

Figure 4 shows the connector and the motherboard header for the heat sink/fan assembly.

Follow these instructions for CPU and heat sink/fan assembly installation:

Step 1. Align the CPU so that the Connection 1 indicator is lined up with Pin 1 on the CPU socket. Doing this ensures that the orientation notches on the CPU are aligned with the orientation keys on the CPU socket.

Step 2. Place the CPU gently into the socket.

Step 3. Close the CPU load plate and secure it in place by closing the load lever and moving it under the load lever retention tab.

Step 4. Apply a small amount of thermal compound to the CPU and spread it evenly. Follow the application instructions provided by the manufacturer.

Step 5. Align the heat sink/fan assembly retainers with the holes on the motherboard.

Step 6. Place the heat sink/fan assembly onto the CPU socket, being careful not to pinch the CPU fan wires.

Step 7. Tighten the heat sink/fan assembly retainers to secure the assembly in place.

Step 8. Connect the heat sink/fan assembly power cable to the header on the motherboard.

Refer to **Figure** in online course

3.3.2 Install the RAM

Like the CPU and the heat sink/fan assembly, RAM is installed in the motherboard before the motherboard is secured in the computer case. Before you install a memory module, consult the motherboard documentation or website of the manufacturer to ensure that the RAM is compatible with the motherboard.

RAM provides temporary data storage for the CPU while the computer is operating. RAM is volatile memory, which means that its contents are lost when the computer is shut down. Typically, more RAM will enhance the performance of your computer.

Follow these steps for RAM installation:

- Align the notches on the RAM module to the keys in the slot and press down until the side tabs click into place.
- Make sure that the side tabs have locked the RAM module. Visually check for exposed contacts.

Repeat these steps for additional RAM modules.

Refer to **Figure** in online course

3.3.3 Install the motherboard

The motherboard is now ready to install in the computer case. Plastic and metal standoffs are used to mount the motherboard and to prevent it from touching the metal portions of the case. You should install only the standoffs that align with the holes in the motherboard. Installing any additional standoffs may prevent the motherboard from being seated properly in the computer case.

Follow these steps for motherboard installation:

- Install standoffs in the computer case.
- Align the I/O connectors on the back of the motherboard with the openings in the back of the case.
- Align the screw holes of the motherboard with the standoffs.
- Insert all all of the motherboard screws.
- Tighten all of the motherboard screws.

Refer to **Lab Activity** for this chapter

Motherboard Installation
Install the CPU, heat sink/fan assembly, RAM, and motherboard

Refer to **Figure** in online course

3.4 Install internal drives

Drives that are installed in internal bays are called internal drives. A hard disk drive (HDD) is an example of an internal drive.

Follow these steps for HDD installation:

- Position the HDD so that it aligns with the 3.5-inch drive bay.
- Insert the HDD into the drive bay so that the screw holes in the drive line up with the screw holes in the case.
- Secure the HDD to the case using the proper screws.

Refer to **Figure** in online course

3.5 Install drives in external bays

Drives, such as optical drives and floppy drives, are installed in drive bays that are accessed from the front of the case. Optical drives and floppy drives store data on removable media. Drives in external bays allow access to the media without opening the case.

After completing this section, you will meet these objectives:

- Install the optical drive.
- Install the floppy drive.

Refer to **Figure** in online course

3.5.1 Install the optical drive

An optical drive is a storage device that reads and writes information to CDs and DVDs. A Molex power connector provides the optical drive with power from the power supply. A PATA cable connects the optical drive to the motherboard.

Follow these steps for optical drive installation:

- Position the optical drive so that it aligns with the 5.25-inch drive bay.
- Insert the optical drive into the drive bay so that the optical drive screw holes align with the screw holes in the case.
- Secure the optical drive to the case using the proper screws.

Refer to **Figure** in online course

3.5.2 Install the floppy drive

A floppy disk drive (FDD) is a storage device that reads and writes information to a floppy disk. A Berg power connector provides the FDD with power from the power supply. A floppy data cable connects the FDD to the motherboard.

A floppy disk drive fits into the 3.5-inch bay on the front of the computer case.

Follow these steps for FDD installation:

- Position the FDD so that it aligns with the 3.5-inch drive bay.
- Insert the FDD into the drive bay so that the FDD screw holes align with the screw holes in the case.
- Secure the FDD to the case using the proper screws.

Refer to **Lab Activity** for this chapter

Drive Installation
Install the hard drive, optical drive, and floppy drive

3.6 Install adapter cards

Refer to **Figure** in online course

Adapter cards are installed to add functionality to a computer. Adapter cards must be compatible with the expansion slot. This section focuses on the installation of three types of adapter cards:

- PCIe x1 NIC
- PCI Wireless NIC
- PCIe x16 video adapter card

After completing this section, you will meet these objectives:

- Install the NIC.
- Install the wireless NIC.
- Install the video adapter card.

3.6.1 Install the NIC

Refer to **Figure** in online course

A NIC enables a computer to connect to a network. NICs use PCI and PCIe expansion slots on the motherboard.

Follow these steps for NIC installation:

- Align the NIC to the appropriate expansion slot on the motherboard.
- Press down gently on the NIC until the card is fully seated.
- Secure the NIC PC mounting bracket to the case with the appropriate screw.

3.6.2 Install the wireless NIC

Refer to **Figure** in online course

A wireless NIC enables a computer to connect to a wireless network. Wireless NICs use PCI and PCIe expansion slots on the motherboard. Some wireless NICs are installed externally with a USB connector.

Follow these steps for wireless NIC installation:

- Align the wireless NIC to the appropriate expansion slot on the motherboard.
- Press down gently on the wireless NIC until the card is fully seated.
- Secure the wireless NIC PC mounting bracket to the case with the appropriate screw.

3.6.3 Install the video adapter card

Refer to **Figure** in online course

A video adapter card is the interface between a computer and a display monitor. An upgraded video adapter card can provide better graphic capabilities for games and graphic programs. Video adapter cards use PCI, AGP, and PCIe expansion slots on the motherboard.

Follow these steps for video adapter card installation:

- Align the video adapter card to the appropriate expansion slot on the motherboard.
- Press down gently on the video adapter card until the card is fully seated.
- Secure the video adapter card PC mounting bracket to the case with the appropriate screw.

Refer to **Lab Activity** for this chapter

Adapter Card Installation
Install the NIC, wireless NIC, and video adapter card

Refer to **Figure** in online course

3.7 Connect all internal cables

Power cables are used to distribute electricity from the power supply to the motherboard and other components. Data cables transmit data between the motherboard and storage devices, such as hard drives. Additional cables connect the buttons and link lights on the front of the computer case to the motherboard.

After completing this section, you will meet these objectives:

- Connect the power cables.
- Connect the data cables.

Refer to **Figure** in online course

3.7.1 Connect the power cables

Motherboard Power Connections

Just like other components, motherboards require power to operate. The Advanced Technology Extended (ATX) main power connector will have either 20 or 24 pins. The power supply may also have a 4-pin or 6-pin Auxiliary (AUX) power connector that connects to the motherboard. A 20-pin connector will work in a motherboard with a 24-pin socket.

Follow these steps for motherboard power cable installation:

- Align the 20-pin ATX power connector to the socket on the motherboard. [Figure 1]
- Gently press down on the connector until the clip clicks into place.
- Align the 4-pin AUX power connector to the socket on the motherboard. [Figure 2]
- Gently press down on the connector until the clip clicks into place.

SATA Power Connectors

SATA power connectors use a 15-pin connector. SATA power connectors are used to connect to hard disk drives, optical drives, or any devices that have a SATA power socket.

Molex Power Connectors

Hard disk drives and optical drives that do not have SATA power sockets use a Molex power connector.

Caution

Do not use a Molex connector and a SATA power connector on the same drive at the same time.

Berg Power Connectors

The 4-pin Berg power connector supplies power to a floppy drive.

Follow these steps for power connector installation:

- Plug the SATA power connector into the HDD. [Figure 3]
- Plug the Molex power connector into the optical drive. [Figure 4]
- Plug the 4-pin Berg power connector into the FDD. [Figure 5]
- Connect the 3-pin fan power connector into the appropriate fan header on the motherboard, according to the motherboard manual. [Figure 6]
- Plug the additional cables from the case into the appropriate connectors according to the motherboard manual.

Refer to **Figure** in online course

3.7.2 Connect the data cables

Drives connect to the motherboard using data cables. The drive being connected determines the type of data cable used. The types of data cables are PATA, SATA, and floppy disk.

PATA Data Cables

The PATA cable is sometimes called a ribbon cable because it is wide and flat. The PATA cable can have either 40 or 80 conductors. A PATA cable usually has three 40-pin connectors. One connector at the end of the cable connects to the motherboard. The other two connectors connect to drives. If multiple hard drives are installed, the master drive will connect to the end connector. The slave drive will connect to the middle connector.

A stripe on the data cable denotes pin 1. Plug the PATA cable into the drive with the pin 1 indicator on the cable aligned to the pin 1 indicator on the drive connector. The pin 1 indicator on the drive connector is usually closest to the power connector on the drive. Many motherboards have two PATA drive controllers, which provides support for a maximum of four PATA drives.

SATA Data Cables

The SATA data cable has a 7-pin connector. One end of the cable is connected to the motherboard. The other end is connected to any drive that has a SATA data connector.

Floppy Data Cables

The floppy drive data cable has a 34-pin connector. Like the PATA data cable, the floppy drive data cable has a stripe to denote the location of pin 1. A floppy drive cable usually has three 34-pin connectors. One connector at the end of the cable connects to the motherboard. The other two connectors connect to drives. If multiple floppy drives are installed, the A: drive will connect to the end connector. The B: drive will connect to the middle connector.

Plug the floppy drive data cable into the drive with the pin 1 indicator on the cable aligned to the pin 1 indicator on the drive connector. Motherboards have one floppy drive controller, which provides support for a maximum of two floppy drives.

Note

If pin 1 on the floppy drive data cable is not aligned with pin 1 on the drive connector, the floppy drive will not function. This misalignment will not damage the drive, but the drive activity light will display continuously. To fix this problem, turn off the computer and re-connect the data cable so that the pin 1 on the cable and the pin 1 on the connector are aligned. Reboot the computer.

Follow these steps for data cable installation:

- Plug the motherboard end of the PATA cable into the motherboard socket. [Figure 1]
- Plug the connector at the far end of the PATA cable into the optical drive. [Figure 2]
- Plug one end of the SATA cable into the motherboard socket. [Figure 3]
- Plug the other end of the SATA cable into the HDD. [Figure 4]
- Plug the motherboard end of the FDD cable into the motherboard socket. [Figure 5]
- Plug the connector at the far end of the FDD cable into the floppy drive. [Figure 6]

Refer to **Lab Activity** for this chapter

Internal Cables

Install internal power and data cables in the computer

Refer to **Figure** in online course

3.8 Re-attach the side panels and connect external cables to the computer

Now that all the internal components have been installed and connected to the motherboard and power supply, the side panels are re-attached to the computer case. The next step is to connect the cables for all computer peripherials and the power cable.

After completing this section, you will meet these objectives:

- Re-attach the side panels to the case.
- Connect external cables to the computer.

Refer to **Figure** in online course

3.8.1 Re-attach the side panels to the case

Most computer cases have two panels, one on each side. Some computer cases have one three-sided cover that slides down over the case frame.

Once the cover is in place, make sure that it is secured at all screw locations. Some computer cases use screws that are inserted with a screwdriver. Other cases have knob-type screws that can be tightened by hand.

If you are unsure about how to remove or replace the computer case, refer to the documentation or website of the manufacturer for more information.

Caution

Handle case parts with care. Some computer case covers have sharp or jagged edges.

Refer to **Figure** in online course

3.8.2 Connect external cables to the computer

After the case panels have been re-attached, connect the cables to the back of the computer. Here are some common external cable connections:

- Monitor

- Keyboard
- Mouse
- USB
- Ethernet
- Power

When attaching cables, ensure that they are connected to the correct locations on the computer. For example, some mouse and keyboard cables use the same type of PS/2 connector.

Caution

When attaching cables, never force a connection.

Note

Plug in the power cable after you have connected all other cables.

Follow these steps for external cable installation:

. Attach the monitor cable to the video port. [Figure 1]

. Secure the cable by tightening the screws on the connector.

. Plug the keyboard cable into the PS/2 keyboard port. [Figure 2]

. Plug the mouse cable into the PS/2 mouse port. [Figure 3]

. Plug the USB cable into a USB port. [Figure 4]

. Plug the network cable into the network port. [Figure 5]

. Connect the wireless antenna to the antenna connector. [Figure 6]

. Plug the power cable into the power supply. [Figure 7]

Figure 8 shows all of the external cables plugged into the back of the computer.

Refer to **Lab Activity** for this chapter

Complete the Computer Assembly

Reattach the case and connect the external cables to complete the computer assembly

3.9 Boot the computer for the first time

Refer to **Figure** in online course

When the computer is booted, the basic input/output system (BIOS) performs a check on all of the internal components. This check is called a power-on self test (POST).

After completing this section, you will meet these objectives:

- Identify beep codes.
- Describe BIOS setup.

3.9.1 Identify beep codes

Refer to **Figure** in online course

POST checks to see that all of the hardware in the computer is operating correctly. If a device is malfunctioning, an error or a beep code alerts the technician that there is a problem. Typically, a single beep denotes that the computer is functioning properly. If there is a hardware problem, the computer may emit a series of beeps. Each BIOS manufacturer uses different codes to indicate hardware problems. Figure 1 shows a sample chart of beep codes. The beep codes for your computer may be different. Consult the motherboard documentation to view beep codes for your computer.

Refer to **Figure** in online course

3.9.2 Describe BIOS setup

The BIOS contains a setup program used to configure settings for hardware devices. The configuration data is saved to a special memory chip called a complementary metal-oxide semiconductor (CMOS), as shown in Figure 1. CMOS is maintained by the battery in the computer. If this battery dies, all BIOS setup configuration data will be lost. If this occurs, replace the battery and reconfigure the BIOS settings.

To enter the BIOS setup program, you must press the proper key or key sequence during POST. Most computers use the DEL key. Your computer may use another key or combination of keys.

Figure 2 shows an example of a BIOS setup program. Here are some common BIOS setup menu options:

- Main – System time, date, HDD type, etc.
- Advanced – Infrared port settings, parallel port settings, etc.
- Security – Password settings to setup utility
- Others – Low battery alarm, system beep, etc.
- Boot – Boot order of the computer
- Exit – Setup utility exit

Refer to **Lab Activity** for this chapter

Boot the Computer

Boot the computer and verify BIOS settings

Summary

This chapter detailed the steps used to assemble a computer and to boot the system for the first time. These are some important points to remember:

- Computer cases come in a variety of sizes and configurations. Many of the components of the computer must match the form factor of the case.
- The CPU is installed on the motherboard with a heat sink/fan assembly.
- RAM is installed in RAM slots found on the motherboard.
- Adapter cards are installed in PCI and PCIe expansion slots found on the motherboard.
- Hard disk drives are installed in 3.5-inch drive bays located inside the case.
- Optical drives are installed in 5.25-inch drive bays that can be accessed from outside the case.
- Floppy drives are installed in 3.5-inch drive bays that can be accessed from outside the case.
- Power supply cables are connected to all drives and the motherboard.
- Internal data cables transfer data to all drives.
- External cables connect peripheral devices to the computer.
- Beep codes signify when hardware malfunctions.
- The BIOS setup program is used to display information about the computer components and allows the user to change system settings.

Chapter 3 Quiz

Take the chapter quiz to test your knowledge.

Your Chapter Notes

CHAPTER 4

Basics of Preventive Maintenance and Troubleshooting

Introduction

This chapter introduces preventive maintenance and the troubleshooting process. Preventive maintenance is a regular and systematic inspection, cleaning, and replacement of worn parts, materials, and systems. Preventive maintenance helps to prevent failure of parts, materials, and systems by ensuring that they are in good working order. Troubleshooting is a systematic approach to locating the cause of a fault in a computer system. A good preventive maintenance program helps minimize failures. With fewer failures, there is less troubleshooting to do, thus saving an organization time and money.

Troubleshooting is a learned skill. Not all troubleshooting processes are the same, and technicians tend to refine their own troubleshooting skills based on knowledge and personal experience. Use the guidelines in this chapter as a starting point to help develop your troubleshooting skills. Although each situation is different, the process described in this chapter will help you to determine your course of action when you are trying to solve a technical problem for a customer.

After completing this chapter, you will meet these objectives:

- Explain the purpose of preventive maintenance.
- Identify the steps of the troubleshooting process.

Refer to **Figure** in online course

4.1 Explain the purpose of preventive maintenance

Preventive maintenance is used to reduce the probability of hardware or software problems by systematically and periodically checking hardware and software to ensure proper operation.

4.1.1 Hardware

Check the condition of cables, components, and peripherals. Clean components in order to reduce the likelihood of overheating. Repair or replace any components that show signs of abuse or excess wear. Use the tasks listed in Figure 1 as a guide to create a hardware maintenance program.

What additional hardware maintenance tasks can you add to the list?

4.1.2 Software

Verify that installed software is current. Follow the policies of the organization when installing security updates, operating system updates, and program updates. Many organizations do not allow updates until extensive testing has been completed. This testing is done to confirm that the update will not cause problems with the operating system and software. Use the tasks listed in Figure 2 as a guide to create a software maintenance schedule that fits the needs of your computer equipment.

Refer to **Figure** in online course

What other software maintenance tasks can you add to the list?

4.1.3 Benefits

Be proactive in computer equipment maintenance and data protection. By performing regular maintenance routines, you can reduce potential hardware and software problems. Doing this will reduce computer down time and repair costs.

A preventive maintenance plan is developed based on the needs of the equipment. A computer exposed to a dusty environment, such as a construction site, will need more attention than equipment in an office environment. High-traffic networks, such as a school network, may require additional scanning and removal of malicious software or unwanted files. Document the routine maintenance tasks that must be performed on the computer equipment and the frequency of each task. This list of tasks can then be used to create a maintenance program.

Some benefits of preventive maintenance are listed in Figure 3. Can you think of any other benefits that preventive maintenance provides?

Refer to **Figure** in online course

4.2 Identify the steps of the troubleshooting process

Troubleshooting requires an organized and logical approach to problems with computers and other components. A logical approach to troubleshooting allows you to eliminate variables in a systematic order. Asking the right questions, testing the right hardware, and examining the right data helps you understand the problem. This helps you form a proposed solution to try.

Troubleshooting is a skill that you will refine over time. Each time you solve another problem, you will increase your troubleshooting skills by gaining more experience. You will learn how and when to combine, as well as skip, steps to reach a solution quickly. The troubleshooting process is a guideline that can be modified to fit your needs.

In this section, you will learn an approach to problem solving that can be applied to both hardware and software. Many of the steps can also be applied to problem solving in other work-related areas.

Note

The term customer, as used in this course, is any user that requires technical computer assistance.

After completing this section, you will meet these objectives:

- Explain the purpose of data protection.
- Gather data from the customer.
- Verify the obvious issues.
- Try quick solutions first.
- Gather data from the computer.
- Evaluate the problem and implement the solution.
- Close with the customer.

Refer to **Figure** in online course

4.2.1 Explain the purpose of data protection

Before you begin troubleshooting problems, always follow the necessary precautions to protect data on a computer. Some repairs, such as replacing a hard drive or reinstalling an operating system, may put the data on the computer at risk. Make sure that you do everything possible to prevent data loss while attempting repairs.

Caution

Although data protection is not one of the six troubleshooting steps, you must protect data before beginning any work on a customer's computer. If your work results in data loss for the customer, you or your company could be held liable.

Backup Data

A backup is a copy of the data on a computer hard drive that is saved to media such as a CD, DVD, or tape drive. In an organization, backups are routinely done on a daily, weekly, and monthly basis.

If you are unsure that a backup has been done, do not attempt any troubleshooting activities until you check with the customer. Here is a list of items to verify with the customer about data backups:

- Date of the last backup
- Contents of the backup
- Data integrity of the backup
- Availability of all backup media for a data restore

If the customer does not have a current backup and you are not able to create one, you should ask the customer to sign a liability release form. A liability release form should contain at least the following information:

- Permission to work on the computer without a current backup available
- Release from liability if data is lost or corrupted
- Description of the work to be performed

Refer to **Figure** in online course

4.2.2 Gather data from the customer

During the troubleshooting process, gather as much information from the customer as possible. The customer will provide you with the basic facts about the problem. Figure 1 lists some of the important information to gather from the customer.

Conversation Etiquette

When you are talking to the customer, you should follow these guidelines:

- Ask direct questions to gather information.
- Do not use industry jargon when talking to customers.
- Do not talk down to the customer.

- Do not insult the customer.
- Do not accuse the customer of causing the problem.

By communicating effectively, you will be able to elicit the most relevant information about the problem from the customer.

Open-Ended Questions

Open-ended questions are used to obtain general information. Open-ended questions allow customers to explain the details of the problem in their own words. Figure 2 shows some examples of open-ended questions.

Closed-Ended Questions

Based on the information from the customer, you can proceed with closed-ended questions. Closed-ended questions generally require a "yes" or "no" answer. These questions are intended to get the most relevant information in the shortest time possible. Figure 3 shows some examples of closed-ended questions.

The information obtained from the customer should be documented in the work order and in the repair journal. Write down anything that you think may be important for you or another technician. Often, the small details can lead to the solution of a difficult or complicated problem.

Refer to **Figure** in online course

4.2.3 Verify the obvious issues

The second step in the troubleshooting process is to verify the obvious issues. Even though the customer may think that there is a major problem, start with the obvious issues before moving to more complex diagnoses.

If the problem is not resolved when you verify the obvious issues, you will need to continue with the troubleshooting process. If you find an obvious issue that fixes the problem, you can go to the last step and close with the customer. These steps are simply a guideline to help you solve problems in an efficient manner.

Refer to **Figure** in online course

4.2.4 Try quick solutions first

The next step in the troubleshooting process is to try quick solutions first. Obvious issues and quick solutions sometimes overlap each other and can be used together to repair the problem. Document each solution that you try. Information about the solutions that you have tried is vital if the problem needs to be escalated to another technician.

Figure 1 identifies some common quick solutions. If a quick solution does not resolve the problem, document your results and try the next most likely solution. Continue this process until you have solved the problem or have tried all of the quick solutions. Document the resolution for future reference, as shown in Figure 2.

Refer to **Figure** in online course

4.2.5 Gather data from the computer

The next step in the troubleshooting process is to gather data from the computer, as shown in Figure 1. You have tried all of the quick solutions, but the problem is still not resolved. It is now time to verify the customer's description of the problem by gathering data from the computer.

Event Viewer

When system, user, or software errors occur on a computer, the Event Viewer is updated with information about the errors. The Event Viewer application shown in Figure 2 records the following information about the problem:

- What problem occurred
- The date and time of the problem
- The severity of the problem
- The source of the problem
- Event ID number
- Which user was logged in when the problem occurred

Although this utility lists details about the error, you may still need to research the solution.

Device Manager

The Device Manager shown in Figure 3 displays all of the devices that are configured on a computer. Any device that the operating system determines to be acting incorrectly will be flagged with an error icon. This type of error is denoted as a yellow circle with an exclamation point ("!"). If a device is disabled, it will be flagged with a red circle and an "X". A yellow question mark "?" indicates that the hardware is not functioning properly because the system does not know what driver to install for the hardware.

Beep Codes

Each BIOS manufacturer has a unique beep sequence for hardware failures. When troubleshooting, power on the computer and listen. As the system proceeds through the POST, most computers will emit one beep to indicate that the system is booting properly. If there is an error, you may hear multiple beeps. Document the beep code sequence and research the code to determine the specific hardware failure.

BIOS Information

If the computer boots and stops after the POST, you should investigate the BIOS settings to determine where to find the problem. A device may not be detected or configured properly. Refer to the motherboard manual to make sure that the BIOS settings are accurate.

Diagnostic Tools

Conduct research to determine what software is available to help diagnose and solve problems. There are many programs available that can help you troubleshoot hardware. Often, manufacturers of system hardware provide diagnostic tools of their own. A hard drive manufacturer, for instance, may provide a tool that can be used to boot the computer and diagnose problems with the hard drive when it will not boot Windows.

Do you know of any third-party tools that you can use to troubleshoot computers?

Refer to **Figure** in online course

4.2.6 Evaluate the problem and implement the solution

The next step in the troubleshooting process is to evaluate the problem and implement the solution. Evaluate the problem and research possible solutions. Figure 1 lists possible research locations. Divide larger problems into smaller problems that can be analyzed and solved individually. Solutions should be prioritized, starting with the the easiest and fastest to implement.

Create a list of possible solutions and implement them one at a time. If you implement a possible solution and it does not work, reverse the solution and try another.

Refer to **Figure** in online course

4.2.7 Close with the customer

After the repairs to the computer have been completed, finish the troubleshooting process by closing with the customer. Communicate the problem and the solution to the customer verbally and in all documentation. Figure 1 shows the steps to be taken when you have finished a repair and are closing with the customer.

Verify the solution with the customer. If the customer is available, demonstrate how the solution has corrected the computer problem. Have the customer test the solution and try to reproduce the problem. When the customer can verify that the problem has been resolved, you can complete the documentation for the repair in the work order and in your journal. The documentation should include the following information:

Refer to **Interactive Graphic** in online course.

- The description of the problem
- The steps to resolve the problem
- The components used in the repair

Summary

This chapter discussed the concepts of preventive maintenance and the troubleshooting process.

- Regular preventive maintenance reduces hardware and software problems.
- Before beginning any repair, back up the data on a computer.
- The troubleshooting process is a guideline to help you solve computer problems in an efficient manner.
- Document everything that you try, even if it fails. The documentation that you create will become a useful resource for you and other technicians.

Chapter 4 Quiz

Take the chapter quiz to test your knowledge.

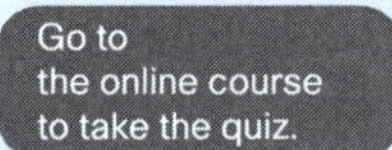

Your Chapter Notes

CHAPTER 5

Fundamental Operating Systems

Introduction

The operating system (OS) controls almost all functions on a computer. In this chapter, you will learn about the components, functions, and terminology related to the Windows 2000 and Windows XP operating systems.

After completing this chapter, you will meet these objectives:

- Explain the purpose of an operating system.
- Describe and compare operating systems to include purpose, limitations, and compatibilities.
- Determine the operating system based on customer needs.
- Install an operating system.
- Navigate a GUI.
- Identify and apply common preventive maintenance techniques for operating systems.
- Troubleshoot operating systems.

5.1 Explain the purpose of an operating system

All computers rely on an operating system (OS) to provide the interface for interaction between users, applications, and hardware. The operating system boots the computer and manages the file system. Almost all modern operating systems can support more than one user, task, or CPU.

After completing this section, you will meet these objectives:

- Describe characteristics of modern operating systems.
- Explain operating system concepts.

Refer to **Figure** in online course

5.1.1 Describe characteristics of modern operating systems

Regardless of the size and complexity of the computer and the operating system, all operating systems perform the same four basic functions. Operating systems control hardware access, manage files and folders, provide a user interface, and manage applications.

Control Hardware Access

The operating system manages the interaction between applications and the hardware. To access and communicate with the hardware, the operating system installs a device driver for each hardware component. A device driver is a small program written by the hardware manufacturer and supplied with the hardware component. When the hardware device is installed, the device driver is also installed, allowing the OS to communicate with the hardware component.

The process of assigning system resources and installing drivers can be performed with Plug and Play (PnP). The PnP process was introduced in Windows 95 to simplify the installation of new hardware. All modern operating systems are PnP-compatible. With PnP, the operating system automatically detects the PnP-compatible hardware and installs the driver for that component. The operating system then configures the device and updates the registry, which is a database that contains all the information about the computer.

Note

The registry contains information about applications, users, hardware, network settings, and file types.

File and Folder Management

The operating system creates a file structure on the hard disk drive to allow data to be stored. A file is a block of related data that is given a single name and treated as a single unit. Program and data files are grouped together in a directory. The files and directories are organized for easy retrieval and use. Directories can be kept inside other directories. These nested directories are referred to as subdirectories. Directories are called folders in Windows operating systems, and subdirectories are called subfolders.

User Interface

The operating system enables the user to interact with software and hardware. There are two types of user interfaces:

- Command Line Interface (CLI) – The user types commands at a prompt, as shown in Figure 1.
- Graphical User Interface (GUI) – The user interacts with menus and icons, as shown in Figure 2.

Most operating systems, such as Windows 2000 and Windows XP, include both a GUI and a CLI.

Application Management

The operating system locates an application and loads it into the RAM of the computer. Applications are software programs, such as word processors, databases, spreadsheets, games, and many other applications. The operating system ensures that each application has adequate system resources.

Application programming interface (API) is a set of guidelines used by programmers to ensure that the application they are developing is compatible with an operating system. Here are two examples of APIs:

- Open Graphics Library (OpenGL) – Cross-platform standard specification for multimedia graphics
- DirectX – Collection of APIs related to multimedia tasks for Microsoft Windows

Refer to **Figure** in online course

5.1.2 Explain operating system concepts

To understand the capabilities of an operating system, it is important to understand some basic terms. The following terms are often used when comparing operating systems:

- ***Multi-user –*** Two or more users can work with programs and share peripheral devices, such as printers, at the same time.

- ***Multi-tasking –*** The computer is capable of operating multiple applications at the same time.
- ***Multi-processing –*** The computer can have two or more central processing units (CPUs) that programs share.
- ***Multi-threading –*** A program can be broken into smaller parts that can be loaded as needed by the operating system. Multi-threading allows individual programs to be multi-tasked.

Almost all modern operating systems are multi-user and multi-tasking, and they support multi-processing and multi-threading.

Modes of Operation

All modern CPUs can run in different modes of operation. The mode of operation refers to the capability of the CPU and the operating environment. The mode of operation determines how the CPU will manage applications and memory. Figure 1 shows an example of the logical memory allocation. The four common modes of operation are real mode, protected mode, virtual real mode, and compatible mode.

Real Mode

A CPU that operates in real mode can only execute one program at a time, and it can only address 1 MB of system memory at a time. Although all modern processors have real mode available, it is only used by DOS and DOS applications or by 16-bit operating systems, such as Windows 3.x. In real mode, when an application creates an error, the entire computer can be affected because the program has direct access to memory. This can cause the computer to stop responding, restart, or shut down due to corruption of the memory space. Figure 2 is a chart of some common DOS commands that can still be used in modern operating systems, such as Windows XP.

Protected Mode

A CPU that operates in protected mode has access to all of the memory in the computer, including virtual memory. Virtual memory is hard disk space that is used to emulate RAM. Operating systems that use protected mode can manage multiple programs simultaneously. Protected mode provides 32-bit access to memory, drivers, and transfers between input and output (I/O) devices. Protected mode is used by 32-bit operating systems, such as Windows 2000 or Windows XP. In protected mode, applications are protected from using the memory reserved for another application that is currently running.

Virtual Real Mode

A CPU that operates in virtual real mode allows a real-mode application to run within a protected-mode operating system. This can be demonstrated when a DOS application runs in a 32-bit operating system, such as Windows XP.

Compatibility Mode

Compatibility mode creates the environment of an earlier operating system for applications that are not compatible with the current operating system. As an example, an application that checks the version of the operating system may be written for Windows NT and require a particular service pack. Compatibility mode can create the proper environment or version of the operating system to allow the application to run as if it is in the intended environment.

Refer to **Figure** in online course

5.2 Describe and compare operating systems to include purpose, limitations, and compatibilities

A technician may be asked to choose and install an operating system for a customer. The type of OS selected depends on the customer's requirements for the computer. There are two distinct types of operating systems: desktop operating systems and network operating systems. A desktop operating system is intended for use in a small office/home office (SOHO) with a limited number of users. A network operating system (NOS) is designed for a corporate environment serving multiple users with a wide range of needs.

After completing this section, you will meet these objectives:

- Describe desktop operating systems.
- Describe network operating systems.

Refer to **Figure** in online course

5.2.1 Describe desktop operating systems

A desktop OS has the following characteristics:

- Supports a single user
- Runs single-user applications
- Shares files and folders on a small network with limited security

In the current software market, the most commonly used desktop operating systems fall into three groups: Microsoft Windows, Apple Mac OS, and UNIX/Linux.

Microsoft Windows

Windows is one of the most popular operating systems today. The following products are desktop versions of the Microsoft Windows operating systems:

- Windows XP Professional – Used on most computers that will connect to a Windows Server on a network
- Windows XP Home Edition – Used on home computers and has very limited security
- Windows XP Media Center – Used on entertainment computers for viewing movies and listening to music
- Windows XP Tablet PC Edition – Used for tablet PCs
- Windows XP 64-bit Edition – Used for computers with 64-bit processors
- Windows 2000 Professional – Older Windows operating system that has been replaced by Windows XP Professional
- Windows Vista – Newest version of Windows

Apple Mac OS

Apple computers are proprietary and use an operating system called Mac OS. Mac OS is designed to be a user-friendly GUI operating system. Current versions of Mac OS are now based on a customized version of UNIX.

UNIX/Linux

UNIX, which was introduced in the late 1960s, is one of the oldest operating systems. There are many different versions of UNIX today. One of the most recent is the extremely popular Linux.

Linux was developed by Linus Torvalds in 1991, and it is designed as an open-source operating system. Open-source programs allow the source code to be distributed and changed by anyone as a free download or from developers at a much lower cost than other operating systems.

Refer to **Figure** in online course

5.2.2 Describe network operating systems

A network OS has the following characteristics:

- Supports multiple users
- Runs multi-user applications
- Is robust and redundant
- Provides increased security compared to desktop operating systems

These are the most common network operating systems:

- ***Microsoft Windows* –** Network operating systems offered by Microsoft are Windows 2000 Server and Windows Server 2003. Windows Server operating systems use a central database called Active Directory to manage network resources.
- ***Novell Netware* –** Novell NetWare was the first OS to meet network OS requirements and enjoy widespread deployment in PC-based LANs back in the 1980s.
- ***Linux* –** Linux operating systems include Red Hat, Caldera, SuSE, Debian, and Slackware.
- ***UNIX* –** Various corporations offered proprietary operating systems, based on UNIX.

Refer to **Worksheet** for this chapter

NOS Jobs
Research NOS jobs

Refer to **Figure** in online course

5.3 Determine operating system based on customer needs

To select the proper operating system to meet the requirements of your customer, you need to understand how the customer wants to use the computer. The operating system that you recommend should be compatible with any applications that will be used and should support all hardware that is installed in the computer. If the computer will be attached to a network, the new operating system should also be compatible with other operating systems on the network.

After completing this section, you will meet these objectives:

- Identify applications and environments that are compatible with an operating system.
- Determine minimum hardware requirements and compatibility with the OS platform.

Refer to **Figure** in online course

5.3.1 Identify applications and environments that are compatible with an operating system

An operating system should be compatible with all applications that are installed on a computer. Before recommending an OS to your customer, investigate the types of applications that your customer will be using. If the computer will be part of a network, the operating system must also be compatible with the operating systems of the other computers in the network. The network type determines what operating systems are compatible. Microsoft Windows networks can have multiple computers using different versions of Microsoft operating systems. These are some guidelines that will help you determine the best operating system for your customer:

- Does the computer have "off-the-shelf" applications or customized applications that were programmed specifically for this customer? If the customer will be using a customized application, the programmer of that application will specify which operating system is compatible with it. Most off-the-shelf applications specify a list of compatible operating systems on the outside of the application package.

- Are the applications programmed for a single user or multiple users? This information will help you decide whether to recommend a desktop OS or a network OS. If the computer will be connected to a network, make sure to recommend the same OS platform that the other computers on the network use.
- Are any data files shared with other computers, such as a laptop or home computer? To ensure compatibility of file formats, recommend the same OS platform that the other data file-sharing computers use.

As an example, your customer may have a Windows network installed and wants to add more computers to the network. In this case, you should recommend a Windows OS for the new computers. If the customer does not have any existing computer equipment, the choice of available OS platforms increases. To make an OS recommendation, you will need to review budget constraints, learn how the computer will be used, and determine what types of applications will be installed.

Refer to **Figure** in online course

5.3.2 Determine minimum hardware requirements and compatibility with the OS platform

Operating systems have minimum hardware requirements that must be met for the OS to install and function correctly. Figure 1 is a chart of the minimum hardware requirements for Windows 2000, Windows XP Pro, and Windows XP Home operating systems.

Identify the equipment that your customer has in place. If hardware upgrades are necessary to meet the minimum requirements for an OS, conduct a cost analysis to determine the best course of action. In some cases, it may be less expensive for the customer to purchase a new computer than to upgrade the current system. In other cases, it may be cost-effective to upgrade one or more of the following components:

- RAM
- Hard disk drive
- CPU
- Video adapter card

Note

In some cases, the application requirements may exceed the hardware requirements of the operating system. For the application to function properly, it will be necessary to satisfy the additional requirements.

Once you have determined the minimum hardware requirements for an OS, you should ensure that all of the hardware in the computer is compatible with the operating system that you have selected for your customer.

Hardware Compatibility List

Most operating systems have a hardware compatibility list (HCL) that can be found on the manufacturer's website, as shown in Figure 2. These lists provide a detailed inventory of hardware that has been tested and is known to work with the operating system. If any of your customer's existing hardware is not on the list, those components may need to be upgraded to match components on the HCL.

Note

An HCL may not be continuously maintained and therefore may not be a comprehensive reference.

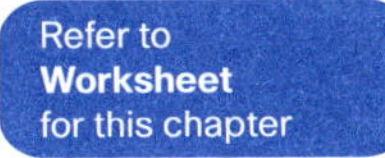

Upgrade Components

Research additional hardware components to upgrade a computer

Refer to **Figure** in online course

5.4 Install an operating system

As a technician, you may have to perform a clean installation of an operating system. Perform a clean install in the following situations:

- When a computer is passed from one employee to another
- When the operating system is corrupted
- When a new replacement hard drive is installed in a computer

After completing this section, you will meet these objectives:

- Identify hard drive setup procedures.
- Prepare the hard drive.
- Install the operating system using default settings.
- Create user accounts.
- Complete the installation.
- Describe custom installation options.
- Identify the boot sequence files and Registry files.
- Describe how to manipulate operating system files.
- Describe directory structures.

Refer to **Figure** in online course

5.4.1 Identify hard drive setup procedures

The installation and initial booting of the operating system is called the operating system setup. Although it is possible to install an operating system over a network from a server or from a local hard drive, the most common installation method is with CDs and DVDs. To install an OS from a CD or DVD, first configure the BIOS setup to boot the system from the CD or DVD.

Partitioning and Formatting

Before installing an operating system on a hard drive, the hard drive must be partitioned and formatted. When a hard drive is partitioned, it is logically divided into one or more areas. When a hard drive is formatted, the partitions are prepared to hold files and applications. During the installation phase, most operating systems automatically partition and format the hard drive. A technician should understand the process relating to hard drive setup. The following terms are used when referring to hard drive setup:

- ***Primary partition –*** This partition is usually the first partition. A primary partition cannot be subdivided into smaller sections. There can be up to four partitions per hard drive.
- ***Active partition –*** This partition is the partition used by the operating system to boot the computer. Only one primary partition can be marked active.

- ***Extended partition –*** This partition normally uses the remaining free space on a hard drive or takes the place of a primary partition. There can be only one extended partition per hard drive, and it can be subdivided into smaller sections called logical drives.
- ***Logical drive –*** This drive is a section of an extended partition that can be used to separate information for administrative purposes.
- ***Formatting –*** This process prepares a file system in a partition for files to be stored.
- ***Sector –*** A sector contains a fixed number of bytes, generally at least 512.
- ***Cluster –*** A cluster is also called a file allocation unit. It is the smallest unit of space used for storing data. It is made up of one or more sectors.
- ***Track –*** A track is one complete circle of data on one side of a hard drive platter. A track is broken into groups of sectors.
- ***Cylinder –*** A cylinder is a stack of tracks lined up one on top of another to form a cylinder shape.
- ***Drive mapping –*** Drive mapping is a letter assigned to a physical or logical drive.

Refer to **Figure** in online course

5.4.2 Prepare hard drive

A clean installation of an operating system proceeds as if the disk were brand new; there is no attempt to preserve any information that is currently on the hard drive. The first phase of the installation process entails partitioning and formatting the hard drive. This process prepares the disk to accept the file system. The file system provides the directory structure that organizes the user's operating system, application, configuration, and data files.

The Windows XP operating system can use one of two file systems:

- ***File Allocation Table, 32-bit (FAT32) –*** A file system that can support partition sizes up to 2 TB or 2,048 GB. The FAT32 file system is supported by Windows 9.x, Windows Me, Windows 2000, and Windows XP.
- ***New Technology File System (NTFS) –*** A file system that can support partition sizes up to 16 exabytes, in theory. NTFS incorporates more file system security features and extended attributes than the FAT file system.

Figure 1 shows the steps required to partition and format a drive in Windows XP. Click the **Start** button in the lower right corner to see the hard drive setup steps.

Refer to **Lab Activity** for this chapter

Install Windows XP

Install Windows XP using FAT32 on a 5GB partition

5.4.3 Install the operating system using default settings

When installing Windows XP, the installation wizard gives the option to install using typical (default) settings or custom settings. Using the typical settings increases the likelihood of a successful installation. However, the user must still provide the following information during the setup:

- Standards and formats that define currency and numerals
- Text input language
- Name of the user and company
- Product key
- Computer name

- Administrator password
- Date and time settings
- Network settings
- Domain or workgroup information

When a computer boots up with the Windows installation CD, the Windows XP installation starts with three options:

- Setup XP – To run the setup and install the XP operating system, press ENTER.
- Repair XP – To repair an installation, press R to open the Recovery Console.
- Quit – To quit Setup without installing Windows XP, press F3.

For this section, select the Setup XP option.

Refer to **Figure** in online course

5.4.4 Create accounts

An administrator account is automatically created when Windows XP is installed. The default administrator account is named “administrator”. For security purposes, change this name as soon as possible. This privileged account should only be used to manage the computer—it should not be used as a daily account. People have accidentally made drastic changes while using the administrator account instead of a regular user account. Attackers seek out the administrative account because it is so powerful.

Create a user account when prompted during the installation process. Unlike the administrator account, user accounts can be created at any time. A user account has fewer permissions than the computer administrator. For example, users may have the right to read, but not modify, a file.

Refer to **Figure** in online course

5.4.5 Complete the installation

After the Windows installation copies all of the necessary operating system files to the hard drive, the computer will reboot and prompt you to log in for the first time.

You must register Windows XP. As shown in Figure 1, you must also complete the verification that ensures that you are using a legal copy of the OS. Doing so will enable you to download patches and service packs. Performing this step requires a connection to the Internet.

Depending on the age of the media at the time of your installation, there may be updates to install. As shown in Figure 2, you can use the Microsoft Update Manager from the Start menu to scan for new software and to do the following:

- Install all service packs
- Install all patches

Start > All Programs > Accessories > System Tools > Windows Update

You should also verify that all hardware is installed correctly. As shown in Figure 3, you can use Device Manager to locate problems and to install the correct or updated drivers using the following path:

Start > Control Panel > System > Hardware > Device Manager

In Device Manager, warning icons are represented by a yellow exclamation point or a red “X”. A yellow exclamation point represents a problem with the device. To view the problem description, right-click the device and select **Properties**. A red "X" represents a device that has been disabled. To enable the device, right-click the disabled device and select **Enable**. To open a category that is not yet expanded, click the plus (+) sign.

Note

When Windows detects a system error, Windows reporting displays a dialog box. If you choose to send the report, then Microsoft Windows error reporting (WER) collects information about the application and the module involved in the error and sends the information to Microsoft.

Refer to **Lab Activity** for this chapter

Windows XP User Accounts and Updates

Create user accounts and checks for Windows updates

Refer to **Figure** in online course

5.4.6 Describe custom installation options

Installing an operating system on a single computer takes time. Imagine the time it would take to install operating systems on multiple computers, one at a time, in a large organization. To simplify this activity, you can use the Microsoft System Preparation (Sysprep) tool to install and configure the same operating system on multiple computers. Sysprep prepares an operating system that will be used on computers with different hardware configurations. With Sysprep and a disk cloning application, technicians are able to quickly install an operating system, complete the last configuration steps for the OS setup, and install applications.

Disk Cloning

Disk cloning creates an image of a hard drive in a computer. Follow these steps for disk cloning:

- Create a master installation on one computer. This master installation includes the operating system, software applications, and configuration settings that will be used by the other computers in the organization.
- Run Sysprep.
- Create a disk image of the configured computer using a third-party disk-cloning program.
- Copy the disk image onto a server. When the destination computer is booted, a shortened version of the Windows setup program runs. The setup will create a new system security identifier (SID), install drivers for hardware, create user accounts, and configure network settings to finish the OS install.

Refer to **Figure** in online course

5.4.7 Identify the boot sequence files and Registry files

You should know the process that Windows XP uses when booting. Understanding these steps can help you to troubleshoot boot problems. Figure 1 shows the boot sequence for Windows XP.

The Windows XP Boot Process

To begin the boot process, you first turn on the computer, which is called a cold boot. The computer performs the power-on self test (POST). Because the video adapter has not yet been initialized, any errors that occur at this point in the boot process will be reported by a series of audible tones, called beep codes.

After POST, the BIOS locates and reads the configuration settings that are stored in the CMOS. This configuration setting is the order in which devices will be tried to see if an operating system is located there. The BIOS boots the computer using the first drive that contains an operating system.

Once the drive with the operating system is located, the BIOS locates the Master Boot Record (MBR). The MBR locates the operating system boot loader. For Windows XP, the boot loader is called NT Loader (NTLDR).

NTLDR and the Windows Boot Menu

At this point NTLDR controls several installation steps. For instance, if more than one OS is present on the disk, BOOT.INI gives the user a chance to select which one to use. If there are no other operating systems, or if the user does not make a selection before the timer expires, then the following steps occur:

- NTLDR runs NTDETECT.COM to get information about installed hardware.
- NTLDR then uses the path specified in the BOOT.INI to find the boot partition.
- NTLDR loads two files that make up the core of XP: NTOSKRNL.EXE and HAL.DLL.
- NTLDR reads the Registry files, chooses a hardware profile, and loads device drivers.

The Windows Registry

The Windows Registry files are an important part of the Windows XP boot process. These files are recognized by their distinctive names, which begin with HKEY_, as shown in Figure 2, followed by the name of the portion of the operating system under their control. Every setting in Windows—from the background of the desktop and the color of the screen buttons to the licensing of applications—is stored in the Registry. When a user makes changes to the Control Panel settings, File Associations, System Policies, or installed software, the changes are stored in the Registry.

Each user has a unique section of the Registry. The Windows login process pulls system settings from the Registry to reconfigure the system to the state that it was in the last time that the user turned it on.

The NT Kernel

At this point, the NT kernel, the heart of the Windows operating system, takes over. The name of this file is NTOSKRNL.EXE. It starts the login file called WINLOGON.EXE and displays the XP welcome screen.

Refer to **Figure** in online course

Note

If a SCSI drive will boot the computer, Windows will copy the NTBOOTDD.SYS file during installation. This file will not be copied if SCSI drives are not being used.

5.4.8 Describe how to manipulate operating system files

After you have installed Windows XP, you may want to make changes to the configuration. The following applications are used extensively for post-installation modifications:

- ***Msconfig* –** This boot configuration utility allows you to set the programs that will run at startup and to edit configuration files. It also offers simplified control over Windows Services, as shown in Figure 1.
- ***Regedit* –** This application allows you to edit the registry, as shown in Figure 2.

Note

REGEDT32 was used with Windows NT. In Windows XP, and Windows Server 2003, the REGEDT32 file is nothing more than a shortcut to the REGEDIT.EXE command. In Windows XP, you can enter **REGEDT32.EXE** or **REGEDIT.EXE**; both commands run the same program.

Caution

Using REGEDT32.EXE or **REGEDIT.EXE** incorrectly may cause configuration problems that could require you to reinstall the operating system.

Startup Modes

You can boot Windows in one of many different modes. Pressing the F8 key during the boot process opens the Windows Advanced Startup Options menu, which allows you to select how to boot Windows. The following startup options are commonly used:

- ***Safe Mode* –** Starts Windows but only loads drivers for basic components, such as the keyboard and display.
- ***Safe Mode with Networking Support* –** Starts Windows identically to Safe Mode and also loads the drivers for network components.
- ***Safe Mode with Command Prompt* –** Starts Windows and loads the command prompt instead of the GUI interface.
- ***Last Known Good Configuration* –** Enables a user to load the configurations settings of Windows that was used the last time that Windows successfully started. It does this by accessing a copy of the registry that is created for this purpose.

Refer to **Figure** in online course

Note

Last Known Good Configuration is not useful unless it is applied immediately after a failure occurs. If the machine is restarted and, despite its difficulties, manages to open Windows, the registry key for Last Known Good Configuration will probably be updated with the faulty information.

5.4.9 Describe directory structures

File Extensions and Attributes

In Windows, files are organized in a directory structure. The root level of the Windows partition is usually labeled drive C:\. Next, there is an initial set of standardized directories, called folders, for the operating system, applications, configuration information, and data files. Following the initial installation, users can install most applications and data in whatever directory they choose.

Files in the directory structure adhere to a Windows naming convention:

- Maximum of 255 characters may be used.
- Characters such as a period (.) or a slash (\ /) are not allowed.
- An extension of three or four letters is added to the filename to identify the file type.
- Filenames are not case sensitive.

The following filename extensions are commonly used:

- .doc – Microsoft Word

- .txt – ASCII text only
- .jpg – Graphics format
- .ppt – Microsoft PowerPoint
- .zip – Compression format

The directory structure maintains a set of attributes for each file that controls how the file may be viewed or altered. These are the most common file attributes:

- R – The file is read-only.
- A – The file will be archived the next time that the disk is backed up.
- S – The file is marked as a system file and a warning is given if an attempt is made to delete or modify the file.
- H – The file is hidden in the directory display.

The filenames, extensions, and attributes can be viewed by entering a DOS window and using the ATTRIB command, as shown in Figure 1. Use the following path:

Start > Run > cmd

Navigate to the folder that contains the file that you are interested in. Type ATTRIB followed by the file name. Use a wildcard such as *.* to view many files at once. The attributes of each file will appear in the left column of the screen. Information about the ATTRIB command can be found at the command prompt by typing:

ATTRIB/?

The Windows equivalent of the ATTRIB command can be accessed by right-clicking a file in Windows Explorer and choosing **Properties**.

Note

To see the properties of a file in Windows Explorer, you must first set Windows Explorer to "Show Hidden Files". Use this path:

Right-click **Start > Explore > Tools > Folder Options > View**

NTFS and FAT32

Windows XP and Windows 2000 use FAT32 and NTFS file systems. Security is one of the most important differences between these file systems. NTFS can support more and larger files than FAT32 and provides more flexible security features for files and folders. Figures 2 and 3 shows the file permission properties for FAT32 and NTFS.

Partitions can be converted from FAT32 to NTFS using the CONVERT.EXE utility. Doing this will provide the extra security advantages of NTFS. To restore an NTFS partition back to a FAT32 partition, reformat the partition and restore the data from a backup.

Refer to **Figure** in online course

Caution

Before converting a file system, remember to back up the data.

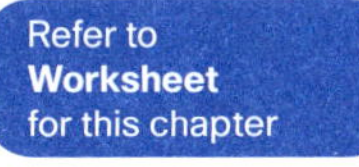

FAT32 and NTFS

Answer NTFS and FAT32 questions

5.5 Navigate a GUI (Windows)

The operating system provides a user interface that allows you to interact with the computer. There are two methods that you can use to navigate the file system and run applications within an operating system:

- A Graphical User Interface (GUI) provides graphical representations (icons) of all of the files, folders, and programs on a computer. You manipulate these icons using a pointer that is controlled with a mouse or similar device. The pointer allows you to move icons by dragging and dropping, and execute programs by clicking.
- A Command Line Interface (CLI) is text-based. You must type commands to manipulate files and execute programs.

After completing this section, you will meet these objectives:

- Manipulate items on the desktop.
- Explore Control Panel applets.
- Explore administrative tools.
- Install, navigate, and uninstall an application.
- Describe upgrading operating systems.

5.5.1 Manipulate items on the desktop

Refer to **Figure** in online course

Once the operating system has been installed, the desktop can be customized to suit individual needs. A desktop on a computer is a graphical representation of a workspace. The desktop has icons, toolbars, and menus to manipulate files. The desktop can be customized with images, sounds, and colors to provide a more personalized look and feel.

Desktop Properties

To customize the GUI interface of your desktop, right-click the desktop and choose **Properties**, as shown in Figure 1. The **Display Properties** menu has five tabs: Themes, Desktop, Screen Saver, Appearance, and Settings. Click any of these tabs to customize your display settings.

Desktop Items

There are several items on the desktop that can be customized, such as the Taskbar and Recycle Bin. To customize any item, right-click the item and then choose **Properties**.

Start Menu

On the desktop, the Start menu is accessed by clicking the **Start** button. The **Start** menu, shown in Figure 2, displays all of the applications installed in the computer, a list of recently opened documents, and a listing of other elements, such as a search feature, help center, and system settings. The **Start** menu can also be customized. There are two styles of Start menu: XP and Classic. The XP-style **Start** menu will be used throughout this course for demonstrating command sequences.

My Computer

To access the various drives installed in the computer, double-click the **My Computer** icon that appears on the desktop. To customize certain settings, right-click **My Computer** and choose **Properties**. Settings that can be customized include the following:

- Computer name
- Hardware settings
- Virtual memory
- Automatic updates
- Remote access

Launching Applications

Applications can be launched in several ways:

- Click the application on the **Start** menu.
- Double-click the application shortcut icon on the desktop.
- Double-click the application executable file in **My Computer**.
- Launch the application from the **Run** window or command line.

My Network Places

To view and configure network connections, right-click the **My Network Places** icon on the desktop. In My Network Places, you can connect to or disconnect from a network drive. Click **Properties** to configure existing network connections, such as a wired or wireless LAN connection

Refer to **Lab Activity** for this chapter

Run Commands

Explore CLI commands

Refer to **Figure** in online course

5.5.2 Explore Control Panel applets

Windows centralizes the settings for many features that control the behavior and appearance of the computer. These settings are categorized in applets, or small programs, found in the Control Panel, as shown in Figure 1. Adding or removing programs, changing network settings, and changing the security settings are some of the configuration options available in the Control Panel.

Control Panel Applets

The names of various applets in the Control Panel differ slightly depending on the version of Windows installed. In Windows XP, the icons are grouped into categories:

- ***Appearance and Themes –*** applets that control the look of windows:
  - Display
  - Taskbar and Start menu
  - Folder options
- ***Network and Internet Connections –*** applets that configure all of the connection types:
  - Internet options
  - Network connections
- ***Add or Remove Programs –*** an applet to add or remove programs and windows components safely

- ***Sounds, Speech, and Audio Devices –*** applets that control all of the settings for sound:
  - Sounds and audio devices
  - Speech
  - Portable Media Devices
- ***Performance and Maintenance –*** applets to find information about your computer or perform maintenance:
  - Administrative tools
  - Power options
  - Scheduled tasks
  - System
- ***Printers and Other Hardware –*** applets to configure devices connected to your computer:
  - Game controllers
  - Keyboard
  - Mouse
  - Phone and modem options
  - Printers and faxes
  - Scanners and cameras
- ***User Accounts –*** applets to configure options for users and their e-mail:
  - E-mail
  - User accounts
- ***Date, Time, Language, and Regional Options –*** applets to change settings based on your location and language:
  - Date and time
  - Regional and language options
- ***Accessibility Options –*** a wizard used to configure windows for vision, hearing, and mobility needs
- ***Security Center –*** applet used to configure security settings for:
  - Internet options
  - Automatic updates
  - Windows firewall

Display Settings

You can change the display settings by using the Display Settings applet. Change the appearance of the desktop by modifying the resolution and color quality, as shown in Figure 2. You can change more advanced display settings, such as wallpaper, screen saver, power settings, and other options, with the following path:

Start > Control Panel > Display > Settings tab > Advanced

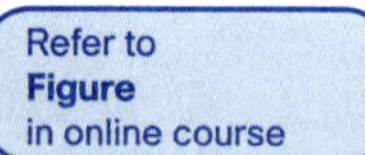

5.5.3 Explore administrative tools

Device Manager

The Device Manager, shown in Figure 1, allows you to view all of the settings for devices in the computer. A common task for technicians is to view the values assigned for the IRQ, I/O address, and the DMA setting for all of the devices in the computer. To view the system resources in the Device Manager, use the following path:

Start > Control Panel > System > Hardware > Device Manager > View > Resources

Task Manager

The Task Manager, shown in Figure 2, allows you to view all applications that are currently running and to close any applications that have stopped responding. The Task Manager allows you to monitor the performance of the CPU and virtual memory, view all processes that are currently running, and view information about the network connections. To view information in the Task Manager, use the following path:

CTRL-ALT-DEL > Task Manager

Event Viewer

The Event Viewer, shown in Figure 3, logs a history of events regarding applications, security, and the system. These log files are a valuable troubleshooting tool. To access the Event Viewer, use the following path:

Start > Control Panel > Administrative Tools > Event Viewer

Remote Desktop

The Remote Desktop allows one computer to remotely take control of another computer. This troubleshooting feature is only available with Windows XP Professional. To access the Remote Desktop, use the following path:

Start > All Programs > Accessories > Communications > Remote Desktop Connection

Performance Settings

To enhance the performance of the operating system, you can change some of the settings that your computer uses, such as virtual memory configuration settings, which are shown in Figure 4. To change the virtual memory setting, use the following path:

Start > Control Panel > System > Advanced > Performance area > Settings button

Refer to **Figure** in online course

5.5.4 Install, navigate, and uninstall an application

As a technician, you will be responsible for adding and removing software from your customers' computers. Most applications use an automatic installation process when an application CD is inserted in the optical drive. The installation process updates the Add or Remove Programs utility. The user is required to click through the installation wizard and provide information when requested.

Add or Remove Programs Applet

Microsoft recommends that users always use the Add or Remove Programs utility, as shown in Figure 1, when installing or removing applications. When you use the Add or Remove Programs utility to install an application, the utility tracks installation files so that the application can be uninstalled completely, if desired. To open the Add or Remove Programs applet, use the following path:

Start > Control Panel > Add or Remove Programs

Add an Application

If a program or application is not automatically installed when the CD is inserted, you can use the Add or Remove Programs applet to install the application, as shown in Figure 2. Click the **Add New Programs** button and select the location where the application is located. Windows will install the application for you.

Once the application is installed, the application can be started from the Start menu or a shortcut icon that the application installs on the desktop. Check the application to ensure that it is functioning properly. If there are problems with the application, make the repair or uninstall the application. Some applications, such as Microsoft Office, provide a repair option in the install process. You can use this function to try to correct a program that is not working properly.

Uninstall an Application

If an application is not uninstalled properly, you may be leaving files on the hard drive and unnecessary settings in the registry. Although this may not cause any problems, it depletes available hard drive space, system resources, and the speed at which the registry is read. Figure 3 shows the Add or Remove Programs applet to use to uninstall programs that you no longer need. The wizard will guide you through the software removal process and remove every file that was installed.

Refer to **Lab Activity** for this chapter

Install Third-Party Software

Install and remove an application

Refer to **Figure** in online course

5.5.5 Describe upgrading an operating system

Sometimes it may be necessary to upgrade an operating system. Before upgrading the operating system, check the minimum requirements of the new operating system to ensure that the computer meets the minimum specifications required. Check the HCL to ensure that the hardware is compatible with the new operating system. Back up all data before upgrading the operating system in case there is a problem with the installation.

The process of upgrading a computer system from Windows 2000 to Windows XP is quicker than performing a new installation of Windows XP. The Windows XP setup utility replaces the existing Windows 2000 files with Windows XP files during the upgrade process. However, the existing applications and settings will be saved.

Upgrading the Operating System

- Insert the Windows XP CD into the CD-ROM drive to start the upgrade process. Select **Start > Run**.
- In the Run box, where D is the drive letter for the CD-ROM, type **D:\i386\winnt32** and press **Enter**. The Welcome to the Windows XP Setup Wizard displays.
- Choose **Upgrade to Windows XP** and click **Next**. The License Agreement page displays.
- Read the license agreement and click the button to accept this agreement.
- Click **Next**. The Upgrading to the Windows XP NTFS File System page displays.
- Follow the prompts and complete the upgrade. When the install is complete, the computer will restart.

Refer to **Figure** in online course

Note

The Windows XP Setup Wizard may automatically start when the CD is inserted into the optical drive.

5.6 Identify and apply common preventive maintenance techniques for operating systems

Preventive maintenance for an operating system includes organizing the system, defragmenting the hard drive, keeping applications current, removing unused applications, and checking the system for errors.

After completing this section, you will meet these objectives:

- Create a preventive maintenance plan.
- Schedule a task.
- Backup the hard drive.

Refer to **Figure** in online course

5.6.1 Create a preventive maintenance plan

The goal of an operating system preventive maintenance plan is to avoid problems in the future. You should perform preventive maintenance regularly, and you should also record all actions taken and observations made. Some preventative maintenance should take place when it will cause the least amount of disruption to the people who use the computers. This often means scheduling tasks at night, early in the morning, or over the weekend. There are also tools and techniques that can automate many preventive maintenance tasks.

Preventive Maintenance Planning

Preventive maintenance plans should include detailed information about the maintenance of all computers and network equipment, with emphasis on equipment that could impact the organization the most. Preventive maintenance includes the following Important tasks:

- Updates to the operating system and applications
- Updates to anti-virus and other protective software
- Hard drive error checking
- Hard drive backup
- Hard drive defragmentation

A preventive maintenance program that is designed to fix things before they break, and to solve small problems before they affect productivity, can provide the following benefits to users and organizations:

- Decreased downtime
- Improved performance
- Improved reliability
- Decreased repair costs

An additional part of preventive maintenance is documentation. A repair log will help you to figure out which equipment is the most or least reliable. It will also provide a history of when a computer was last fixed, how it was fixed, and what the problem was.

Refer to **Figure** in online course

5.6.2 Schedule a task

Some preventive maintenance consists of cleaning, inspecting, and doing minor repairs. Some preventive maintenance uses application tools that are either already in the operating system or can be loaded onto the user's hard drive. Most preventive maintenance applications can be set to run automatically according to a schedule.

Windows has the following utilities that will launch tasks when you schedule them:

- The DOS AT command launches tasks at a specified time using the command line interface.
- The Windows Task Scheduler launches tasks at a specified time using a graphical user interface.

Information about the AT command is available at this path:

Start > Run > cmd

Then type **AT /?** at the command line.

Access the Windows Task Scheduler by following this path:

Start > All Programs > Accessories > System Tools > Scheduled Tasks

Both of these tools allow users to set commands to run at a certain time just once, or to repeat at selected days or times. The Windows Task Scheduler, shown in Figure 1, is easier to learn and use than the AT command, especially when it comes to recurring tasks and deleting tasks already scheduled.

System Utilities

There are several utilities included with DOS and Windows that help maintain system integrity. Two utilities that are useful tools for preventive maintenance are:

- ***ScanDisk or CHKDSK –*** ScanDisk (Windows 2000) and CHKDSK (Windows XP) check the integrity of files and folders and scan the hard disk surface for physical errors. Consider using them at least once a month and also whenever a sudden loss of power causes the system to shut down.
- ***Defrag –*** As files increase in size, some data is written to the next available space on the disk. In time, data becomes fragmented, or spread all over the hard drive. It takes time to seek each section of the data. Defrag gathers the noncontiguous data into one place, making files run faster.

You can access both of these utilities by using this path:

Start > All Programs > Accessories > System Tools > Disk Defragmenter

Automatic Updates

If every maintenance task had to be scheduled every time it was run, repairing computers would be much harder than it is today. Fortunately, tools such as the Scheduled Task Wizard allow many functions to be automated. But how can you automate the update of software that has not been written?

Operating systems and applications are constantly being updated for security purposes and for added functionality. It is important that Microsoft and others provide an update service, as shown in Figure 2. The update service can scan the system for needed updates and then recommend what should be downloaded and installed. The update service can download and install updates as soon as they are available, or it can download updates as required, and install them when the computer is next rebooted. The Microsoft Update Wizard is available at this path:

Start > Control Panel > System > Automatic Updates

Most anti-virus software contains its own update facility. It can update both its application software and its database files automatically. This feature allows it to provide immediate protection as new threats develop.

Restore Point

An update can sometimes cause serious problems. Perhaps an older program is in the system that is not compatible with the current operating system. An automatic update may install code that will work for most users but does not work with your system.

Windows Restore Point, shown in Figure 3, is the solution for this problem. Windows XP can create an image of current computer settings, called a restore point. Then, if the computer crashes, or an update causes system problems, the computer can roll back to a previous configuration.

A technician should always create a restore point before updating or replacing the operating system. Restore points should also be created at the following times:

- When an application is installed
- When a driver is installed

Note

A restore point backs up drivers, system files, and registry settings but not application data.

To restore or create a restore point, use the following path:

Start > All Programs > Accessories > System Tools > System Restore

ERD and ASR

Windows 2000 offers the ability to create an emergency repair disk (ERD) that saves critical boot files and configuration information necessary to troubleshoot problems in Windows. Windows XP offers the same features with the Automated System Recovery (ASR) wizard. Although both ERD and ASR are powerful troubleshooting tools, they should never replace a good backup.

A recovery CD contains the essential files used to repair the system after a serious issue, such as a hard drive crash. The recovery CD can contain the original version of Windows, hardware drivers, and application software. When the recovery CD is used, the computer will be restored to the original default configuration.

Refer to **Lab Activity** for this chapter

Restore Point

Create and execute a restore point

5.6.3 Backup the hard drive

Refer to **Figure** in online course

Just as the system restore points allow the restoration of OS configuration files, backup tools allow the recovery of data. You can use the Microsoft Backup Tool, shown in Figure 1, to perform backups as required. It is important to establish a backup strategy that includes data recovery. The organization's requirements will determine how often the data must be backed up and the type of backup to perform.

It can take a long time to run a backup. If the back up strategy is followed carefully, it will not be necessary to backup every file at every backup. It is only necessary to make copies of the files that have changed since the last backup. For this reason, there are several different types of backup.

Normal Backup

A normal backup is also called a full backup. During a normal backup, all selected files on the disk are archived to the backup medium. These files are marked as having been archived by clearing the archive bit.

Copy Backup

A copy backup will copy all selected files. It does not mark the files as having been archived.

Differential Backup

A differential backup backs up all the files and folders that have been created or modified since either the last normal backup or the last incremental backup (see below). The differential backup does not mark the files as having been archived. Copies will be made from the same starting point until the next incremental or full backup is performed. Making differential backups is important because only the last full and differential backups are needed to restore all the data.

Incremental Backup

An incremental backup procedure backs up all the files and folders that have been created or modified since either the last normal or incremental backup. It marks the files as having been archived by clearing the archive bit. This has the effect of advancing the starting point of differential backups without having to re-archive the entire contents of the drive. If you have to perform a system restore, you would have to first restore the last full backup, then restore every incremental backup in order, and then restore any differential backups made since the last incremental backup.

Daily Backup

Daily backups only back up the files that are modified on the day of the backup. Daily backups do not modify the archive bit.

To access the daily backup utility on a Windows XP Professional system, use the following path:

Start > All Programs > Accessories > System Tools > Backup

Backup Media

There are many types of backup media available for computers:

- Tape drives are devices that are used for data backup on a network server drive. Tapes drives are an inexpensive way to store a lot of data.
- The Digital Audio Tape (DAT) tape standard uses 4 mm digital audiotapes to store data in the Digital Data Storage (DSS) format.
- Digital Linear Tape (DLT) technology offers high-capacity and relatively high-speed tape backup capabilities.
- USB flash memory can hold hundreds of times the data that a floppy disk can hold. USB flash memory devices are available in many capacities and offer better transfer rates than tape devices.

Refer to **Lab Activity** for this chapter

Windows Backup and Recovery

Backup and Restore a computer registry in Windows XP

Refer to **Figure** in online course

5.7 Troubleshoot operating systems

Most operating systems contain utilities to assist in the troubleshooting process. These utilities help technicians determine why the computer crashes or does not boot properly. The utilities also help identify the problem and how to resolve it.

Follow the steps outlined in this section to accurately identify, repair, and document the problem. The troubleshooting process is shown in Figure 1.

After completing this section, you will meet these objectives:

- Review the troubleshooting process.
- Identify common problems and solutions.

Refer to **Figure** in online course

5.7.1 Review the troubleshooting process

Operating system problems can result from a combination of hardware, application, and configuration issues. Computer technicians must be able to analyze the problem and determine the cause of the error in order to repair the operating system. This process is called troubleshooting.

The first step in the troubleshooting process is to gather data from the customer. Figures 1 and 2 list open-ended and closed-ended questions to ask the customer.

Once you have talked to the customer, you should verify the obvious issues. Figure 3 lists some issues for operating systems.

After the obvious issues have been verified, try some quick solutions. Figure 4 lists quick solutions for operating systems.

If quick solutions did not correct the problem, use Step 4 in the troubleshooting process to gather data from the computer. Figure 5 shows different ways to gather information about the problem from the computer.

At this point, you will have enough information to evaluate the problem and to research and implement possible solutions. Figure 6 shows resources for possible solutions.

After you have solved the operating system problem, you will close with the customer. Figure 7 is a list of the tasks required to complete this step.

Refer to **Figure** in online course

5.7.2 Identify common problems and solutions

Operating system problems can be attributed to hardware, application, or configuration issues, or to some combination of the three. You will resolve some types of operating system problems more often than others. Figure 1 is a chart of common operating system problems and solutions.

Summary

This chapter introduced computer operating systems. As a technician, you should be skilled at installing, configuring, and troubleshooting an operating system. The following concepts from this chapter are important to remember:

- There are several different operating systems available, and you must consider the customer's needs and environment when choosing an operating system.
- The main steps in setting up a customer's computer include preparing the hard drive, installing an operating system, creating user accounts, and configuring installation options.
- A GUI shows icons of all files, folders, and applications on the computer. A pointing device, such as a mouse, is used to navigate in a GUI desktop.
- You should establish a backup strategy that allows for the recovery of data. Normal, copy, differential, incremental, and daily backups are all optional backup tools available in Windows operating systems.
- Preventive maintenance techniques help to ensure optimal operation of the operating system.
- Some of the tools available for troubleshooting an operating system problem include Windows Advanced Options menu, event logs, device manager, and system files.

Chapter 5 Quiz

Take the chapter quiz to test your knowledge.

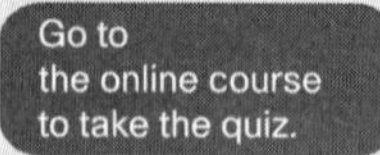

Your Chapter Notes

CHAPTER 6

Fundamental Laptops and Portable Devices

Introduction

Do you know when the first laptops were developed? Who do you think used the early laptops?

One of the original laptops was the GRiD Compass 1101. It was used by astronauts on space missions in the early 1980s. It weighed 11 lb (5 kg) and cost US $8,000 - $10,000! Laptops today often weigh less than one-half the weight and cost less than one-third the price of the GRiD. The compact design, convenience, and evolving technology of laptops have made them as popular as desktops.

Laptops, Personal Digital Assistants (PDAs), and Smartphones are becoming more popular as their prices decrease and technology continues to progress. As a computer technician, you need to have knowledge of portable devices of all kinds. This chapter focuses on the differences between laptops and desktops and describes the features of PDAs and Smartphones.

After completing this chapter, you will meet these objectives:

- Describe laptops and other portable devices.
- Identify and describe the components of a laptop.
- Compare and contrast desktop and laptop components.
- Explain how to configure laptops.
- Compare the different mobile phone standards.
- Identify common preventive maintenance techniques for laptops and portable devices.
- Describe how to troubleshoot laptops and portable devices.

6.1 Describe laptops and other portable devices

Note

Notebooks, laptops, and tablets are types of portable computers. For clarity and consistency in this course, all portable computers will be called laptops.

Laptops

Early laptops were heavy and expensive. Today, laptops are very popular because advances in technology have resulted in laptops that cost less, weigh less, and have improved capabilities. Many laptops can be configured with an additional video port, a FireWire port, an infrared port, or an integrated camera.

Refer to **Figure** in online course

PDAs and Smartphones

PDAs and Smartphones are examples of portable, hand-held devices that are becoming more popular. PDAs offer features such as games, web surfing, e-mail, instant messaging, and many other features offered by PCs. Smartphones are cell phones with many built-in PDA capabilities. PDAs and Smartphones can run some of the same software as laptops.

After completing this section, you will meet these objectives:

- Identify some common uses of laptops.
- Identify some common uses of PDAs and Smartphones.

Refer to **Figure** in online course

6.1.1 Identify some common uses of laptops

The most significant feature of a laptop is its compact size. The design of the laptop places the keyboard, screen, and internal components into a small, portable case.

Another popular feature of the laptop is its portability. A rechargeable battery allows the laptop to function when it is disconnected from an AC power source.

The first laptops were used primarily by business people who needed to access and enter data when they were away from the office. The use of laptops was limited due to expense, weight, and limited capabilities compared to less expensive desktops.

Today, laptops have lower prices and increased capabilities. A laptop is now a real alternative to a desktop computer.

Here are some common uses for the laptop:

- Taking notes in school or researching papers
- Presenting information in business meetings
- Accessing data away from home or the office
- Playing games while traveling
- Watching movies while traveling
- Accessing the Internet in a public place
- Sending and receiving e-mail in a public place

Can you think of other uses for laptops?

Refer to **Figure** in online course

6.1.2 Identify some common uses of PDAs and Smartphones

The concept of the PDA has existed since the 1970s. The earliest models were computerized personal organizers designed to have a touch screen or a keyboard. Today, some models have both a touch screen and a keyboard and use an operating system that is similar to operating systems used on desktop computers.

The PDA is an electronic personal organizer with tools to help organize information:

- Address book
- Calculator
- Alarm clock

- Internet access
- E-mail
- Global positioning

The Smartphone is a mobile phone with PDA capabilities. Smartphones combine cell phone and computer functions in a single, handheld device. The technology of the PDA and the technology of the Smartphone continue to merge.

Smartphones may include these additional options:

- Built-in camera
- Document access
- E-mail
- Abbreviated note-taking
- Television

Smartphone connectivity and PDA connectivity include Bluetooth and regular USB cable connections.

Can you think of other uses for the PDA and the Smartphone?

Refer to **Worksheet** for this chapter

Laptop, Smartphone, and PDA

Research laptop, Smartphone, and PDA specifications

Refer to **Figure** in online course

6.2 Identify and describe the components of a laptop

What are some common laptop features?

- They are small and portable.
- They have an integrated display screen in the lid.
- They have an integrated keyboard in the base.
- They run on AC power or a rechargeable battery.
- They support hot-swappable drives and peripherals.
- Most laptops can use docking stations and port replicators to connect peripherals.

In this section, you will look closely at the components of a laptop. You will also examine a docking station. Remember, laptops and docking stations come in many models. Components may be located in different places on different models.

After completing this section, you will meet these objectives:

- Describe the components found on the outside of the laptop.
- Describe the components found on the inside of the laptop.
- Describe the components found on the laptop docking station.

Refer to **Figure** in online course

6.2.1 Describe the components found on the outside of the laptop

Laptop and desktop computers use the same types of ports so that peripherals can be interchangeable. These ports are specifically designed for connecting peripherals, providing network connectivity, and providing audio access.

Ports, connections, and drives are located on the front, back, and sides of the laptop due to the compact design. Laptops contain PC Card or ExpressCard slots to add functionality such as more memory, a modem, or a network connection.

Laptops require a port for external power. Laptops can operate using either a battery or an AC power adapter. This port can be used to power the computer or to charge the battery.

There are status indicators, ports, slots, connectors, bays, jacks, vents, and a keyhole on the exterior of the laptop. Click the highlighted areas in Figures 1 to 7 to discover additional information about each of these components.

Figure 1 shows three LEDs on the top of the laptop. Click the three highlighted areas for more information about what the LEDs indicate:

Step 1. Bluetooth

Step 2. Battery

Step 3. Standby

Note

LED displays vary among laptops. Technicians should consult the laptop manual for a list of specific status displays.

Figure 2 shows three components on the back of the laptop. Click the three highlighted areas for more information about the components:

Step 1. Parallel port

Step 2. AC power connector

Step 3. Battery bay

A laptop operates using either a battery or an AC power adapter. Laptop batteries are manufactured in various shapes and sizes. They use different types of chemicals and metals to store power. Refer to Figure 3 to compare rechargeable batteries.

The left side of the laptop shown in Figure 4 has ten components. Click the ten highlighted areas for more information about the components:

Step 1. Security keyhole

Step 2. USB

Step 3. S-video connector

Step 4. Modem

Step 5. Ethernet

Step 6. Network LEDs

Step 7. Stereo headphone jack

Step 8. Microphone jack

Step 9. Ventilation

Step 10. PC combo expansion slot

The front of the laptop shown in Figure 5 has the components listed here. Click the four highlighted areas for more information about the components:

Step 1. Ventilation

Step 2. Speakers

Step 3. Infrared port

Step 4. Laptop latch

The right side of the laptop shown in Figure 6 contains four components. Click the four highlighted areas for more information about the components:

Step 1. VGA port

Step 2. Drive bay status indicator

Step 3. Optical drive activity indicator

Step 4. Optical drive

The bottom of the laptop shown in Figure 7 has the components listed here. Click the four highlighted areas for more information about the components:

Step 1. Docking station connector

Step 2. Battery latches

Step 3. RAM access panel

Step 4. Hard drive access panel

Refer to **Figure** in online course

6.2.2 Describe the components found on the inside of the laptop

Laptops have a "clamshell" design. Typically, the laptop is closed when not in use. By opening the lid of the laptop, you can access a variety of input devices, LEDs, and a display screen.

There are several input devices available when the laptop lid is open. Click the five highlighted areas in Figure 1 for more information about the input devices:

Step 1. Keyboard

Step 2. Input devices

Step 3. Fingerprint reader

Step 4. Volume controls

Step 5. Power button

Refer to Figure 1. Do you know which of those devices perform the following functions?

- Move the pointer
- Turn up the volume
- Log on to the laptop
- Type a document

- Turn on the laptop
- Switch to external monitor

Can you think of other information you may input?

At the bottom of the screen is a row of LEDs that shows the status of specific functions. Click the eight highlighted areas in Figure 2 for more information on these LEDs:

Step 1. Wireless.

Step 2. Bluetooth

Step 3. Num Lock

Step 4. Caps Lock

Step 5. Hard drive activity

Step 6. Power on

Step 7. Battery status

Step 8. Hibernate/Standby

Note

Indicators may vary by laptop.

A laptop monitor is a built-in LCD. It is similar to a desktop LCD monitor, except that the resolution, brightness, and contrast settings can be adjusted using software or button controls. The laptop monitor cannot be adjusted for height and distance because it is integrated into the lid of the case. A desktop monitor can be added to a laptop. A function key on the laptop keyboard toggles between the laptop display and the desktop monitor, as shown in Figure 3.

On many laptops, a small pin on the laptop cover contacts a switch when the case is closed, called an LCD cutoff switch. The LCD cutoff switch tells the CPU to conserve power by extinguishing the backlight and turning off the LCD. If this switch breaks or is dirty, the LCD will remain dark while the laptop is open. Carefully clean this switch to restore normal operation.

Refer to **Figure** in online course

6.2.3 Describe the components found on the laptop docking station

A base station is a device that attaches to AC power and to desktop peripherals. When you plug the laptop into the base station, you have convenient access to power and the attached peripherals.

There are two types of base stations: docking stations and port replicators. Docking stations and port replicators are used for the same purpose. Port replicators are usually smaller than docking stations and do not have speakers or PCI slots. Figures 1 to 3 illustrate a docking station.

Click the three highlighted areas in Figure 1 for more information about components on the top of the docking station:

Step 1. Power button

Step 2. Eject button

Step 3. Docking connector

Some docking stations include the following drive bays and ports to provide additional functionality:

- Parallel

- USB
- Ethernet
- Video
- Audio

The back of the docking station contains ports and connectors used to attach to desktop peripherals such as a mouse, a monitor, or a printer. A vent is also necessary to expel hot air from the docking station. Click the 15 highlighted areas in Figure 2 for more information about the components located on the back of the docking station:

Step 1. Exhaust vent

Step 2. AC power connector

Step 3. PC Card/ExpressCard slot

Step 4. VGA port

Step 5. DVI port

Step 6. Line In connector

Step 7. Headphone connector

Step 8. USB port

Step 9. Mouse port

Step 10. Keyboard port

Step 11. External-diskette-drive connector

Step 12. Parallel port.

Step 13. Serial port

Step 14. Modem port

Step 15. Ethernet port

Secure the laptop to the docking station with a key lock. Click the highlighted areas in Figure 3 for more information about the key lock located on the right side of the docking station.

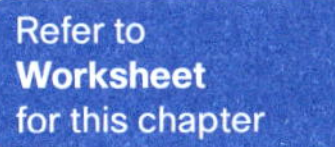

Laptop Docking Stations

True/False statements about docking stations

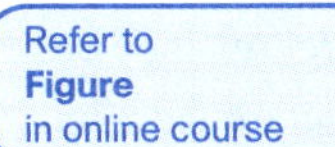

6.3 Compare and contrast desktop and laptop components

Most of the functions that a desktop can perform can also be performed by a laptop. However, these two kinds of computers are built very differently and the parts are not interchangeable. As an example, a plane and a helicopter can each travel to the same destination, but they cannot be repaired with the same spare parts. This is also true for laptops and desktops. Few components can be shared between desktops and laptops.

Desktop components tend to be standardized. They usually meet universal form factors. Desktops made by different manufacturers can often use the same components. A DVD/CD-RW drive is an example of a desktop component that has a standard form factor.

Laptop components are much more specialized than desktop components. This difference is because laptop manufacturers focus on refining laptop components to make them more efficient and compact. As a result, manufacturers design laptop components to follow their own specific form factors. Laptop components are proprietary. As a result, you may not be able to use components made by one laptop manufacturer to repair a laptop made by another manufacturer.

Note

Technicians may have to obtain certification for each laptop manufacturer that they support.

After completing this section, you will meet these objectives:

- Compare and contrast desktop and laptop motherboards.
- Compare and contrast desktop and laptop processors.
- Compare and contrast desktop and laptop power management.
- Compare and contrast desktop and laptop expansion capabilities.

Refer to **Figure** in online course

6.3.1 Compare and contrast desktop and laptop motherboards

Desktop motherboards have standard form factors. The standard size and shape allow motherboards from different manufacturers to be interchangeable.

Laptop motherboards vary by manufacturer and are proprietary. When you repair a laptop, it is strongly recommended that you obtain a replacement motherboard from the manufacturer of the laptop. Figure 1 shows a desktop motherboard and a laptop motherboard.

Laptop motherboards and desktop motherboards are designed differently. Components designed for a laptop generally cannot be used in a desktop. Figure 2 shows a few examples of the design differences.

Refer to **Figure** in online course

6.3.2 Compare and contrast desktop and laptop processors

The central processing unit (CPU), or processor, is the brain of the computer. The CPU interprets and processes instructions that are used to manipulate data.

Laptop processors are designed to use less power and create less heat than desktop processors. As a result, laptop processors do not require cooling devices that are as large as those found in desktops. Laptop processors also use CPU throttling to modify the clock speed as needed to reduce power consumption and heat. This results in a slight decrease in performance. It also increases the lifespan of some components. These specially designed processors allow laptops to operate for a longer period of time when using a battery power source. Figure 1 shows laptop processor specifications.

Note

Technicians should refer to the laptop manual for processors that can be used as replacement processors and for processor replacement instructions.

Refer to **Figure** in online course

6.3.3 Compare and contrast desktop and laptop power management

Power management controls the flow of electricity to the components of a computer.

Desktops are usually set up in a location where they remain plugged into a power source. Desktop power management distributes electricity from the source to the components of the desktop. There is also a small battery in the desktop that provides electricity to maintain the internal clock and BIOS settings when the desktop is powered off.

Laptops are small and portable. This portability feature is achieved by combining the small size and weight of a laptop with the ability to operate from a battery. When the laptop is plugged in, laptop power management sends electricity from the AC power source to the laptop components. The laptop power management also recharges the battery. When the laptop is unplugged, laptop power management takes electricity from the battery and sends it to the laptop components.

There are two methods of power management:

- Advanced Power Management (APM)
- Advanced Configuration and Power Interface (ACPI)

APM is an earlier version of power management. With APM, the BIOS was used to control the settings for power management.

ACPI has replaced APM. ACPI offers additional power management features. With ACPI, the operating system controls power management.

Refer to **Figure** in online course

6.3.4 Compare and contrast desktop and laptop expansion capabilities

Expansion capabilities add functionality to a computer. Many expansion devices can be used with both laptops and desktops:

- External drives
- Modems
- Network cards
- Wireless adapters
- Printers
- Other peripherals

Expansion devices are attached to laptops and desktops differently. A desktop attaches these devices with serial, parallel, USB, and FireWire ports. A laptop attaches these devices with the same ports and PC Cards.

The standardized use of USB and FireWire ports makes it possible to connect many types of external components to laptops, docking stations, port replicators, and desktops. The USB and FireWire standards make it possible to connect and remove external components without the need to power off the system. USB and FireWire ports are used to connect a range of external components:

- Printers
- Scanners
- Floppy disk drives
- Mice

- Cameras
- Keyboards
- Hard drives
- Flash drives
- Optical drives
- MP3 players

Laptops and desktops have similar expansion capabilities. It is the difference in form factor between the computers that determines which type of expansion device is used. Desktops have internal bays that support 5.25″ and 3.5″ drives. Additionally, there is space to install other permanent expansion drives. Laptops have limited space; therefore, the expansion bays on laptops are designed to allow different types of drives to fit into the same bay. Drives are hot-swappable and are inserted or removed as needed. Figure 1 shows a comparison of desktop and laptop expansion components.

Laptops use the PC Card slot to add functionality. The PC Card slot uses an open standard interface to connect to peripheral devices using the CardBus standard. Here are some examples of devices that connect using PC Cards:

- Memory
- Modems
- Hard drives
- Network cards

PC Cards follow the PCMCIA standard. They come in three types: Type I, Type II, and Type III. Each type of PC Card is different in size and can attach to different devices. A newer type of PC Card is called the PC ExpressCard. Figure 2 shows a comparison of PC Cards and PC ExpressCards. The PC ExpressCard comes in 34mm and 54mm widths. Figure 3 shows an example of a PC Card and PC ExpressCards.

Suppose that you need to purchase a wireless NIC for a laptop. Which type of PC Card would you select?

Refer to **Worksheet** for this chapter

Laptop Expansion

Fill in the blank for laptop specifications

Refer to **Figure** in online course

6.4 Explain how to configure laptops

To allow applications and processes to run smoothly, it may be necessary to configure and allocate system resources, install additional components and plug-ins, or change environmental settings to match software requirements. Adding external components is usually accomplished through the use of Plug and Play, but occasionally driver installation and additional configuration may be required. Proper configuration of the power settings will help you get the maximum performance from a laptop, such as increasing the length of time the laptop can be used on battery power.

With laptops, it may be necessary to exchange components as needed to accomplish different tasks and respond to changing situations and needs. A laptop can be customized for specific purposes by adding external components. For example, a second hard drive can be installed in a laptop to provide additional storage capacity. Components need to be carefully inserted or connected to bays, connectors, and proprietary expansion areas to avoid damage to the equipment. It is important to follow safe removal procedures when disconnecting hot-swappable and non-hot-swappable devices.

After completing this section, you will meet these objectives:

- Describe how to configure power settings.
- Describe the safe installation and removal of laptop components.

Refer to **Figure** in online course

6.4.1 Describe how to configure power settings

One of the most popular features of a laptop is the ability to operate using batteries. This feature allows laptops to operate in locations where AC power is not available or is inconvenient. Advances in power management and battery technology are increasing the time that laptop users can remain disconnected from AC power. Current batteries can last anywhere between 2 to 10 hours without recharging. Managing the power by configuring the power settings on a laptop is important to ensure that the battery charge is used efficiently.

The Advanced Configuration and Power Interface (ACPI) standards create a bridge between the hardware and OS and allow technicians to create power management schemes to get the best performance from the computer. The ACPI standards can be applicable to most computers, but they are particularly important when managing power in laptops. Click the power states in Figure 1 to view more information about each power state.

Technicians frequently are required to configure power settings by changing the settings found in BIOS. Configuring power settings in BIOS affects the following conditions:

- System states
- Battery and AC modes
- Thermal management
- CPU PCI bus power management

Figure 2 shows an example of power settings in BIOS.

Note

When working in Windows XP, the ACPI power management mode must be enabled in BIOS to allow the OS to configure all of the power management states.

Note

There is no standard name for each power management state. Manufacturers may use different names for the same state.

Here are the steps to check the ACPI settings in the BIOS:

- Enter BIOS setup by pressing the appropriate key or key combination while the computer is booting. Typically this is the **Delete** key or the **F2** key, but there are several other options.
- Locate and enter the Power Management settings menu item.
- Use the appropriate keys to enable ACPI mode.
- Save and exit BIOS setup.

Note

These steps are common to most laptops and should be used only as a guideline. Be sure to check your laptop manual for specific configuration settings.

The Power Options feature in Windows XP allows you to reduce the power consumption of a number of devices or of the entire system. Use Power Options to control the power management features of the following:

- Hard Drive
- Display
- Shut Down, Hibernate, and Standby modes
- Low-battery warnings

Configuring Power Settings in Windows XP

You can adjust power management by using Power Options in the Control Panel. The **Power Options** displays only the options that can be controlled.

Note

Power Options will automatically detect devices that may be unique to your computer. Therefore, the Power Options windows may vary by the hardware that is detected.

To configure your power settings, click:

Start > Control Panel > Power Options

Power Schemes

Power Schemes are a collection of settings that manage the power usage of the computer. Both the hard drive and the display consume large amounts of power. They can be configured under the Power Schemes tab.

When you open Power Options, you will notice that Windows XP has preset power schemes. These are the default settings and were created when Windows XP was installed. You can use the default Power Schemes or create customized schemes that are based on specific work requirements. Figure 3 shows the Power Scheme set for a laptop.

Customize the Display and Hard Drive Power Setting

In this scenario, the student needs access to the display, but rarely accesses the hard drive. For example; a student that uses a laptop for research on the Internet, but does not create or save files often.

Power Management for the Hard Drive

One of the biggest power consumers on a laptop is the hard drive. In our example, the hard drive is not accessed often. The "Turn off hard disks" time is set for 1 hour when the laptop is plugged in, and 3 minutes when the laptop is "Running on batteries".

You decide that the default settings for the Standby and Hibernate modes are acceptable and no changes are made. Power Schemes can be saved with a customized name. Saving the Power Scheme with a custom name allows the user to easily switch back to the default settings. In this example, save the Power Scheme settings as "Research" as shown in Figure 4.

Setting the Laptop to the Standby or Hibernate Sleep State

If you do not want to completely shut down the laptop, you have two options: Standby and Hibernate.

- ***Standby*** – Documents and applications are saved in RAM, allowing the computer to power on quickly.

- ***Hibernate –*** Documents and applications are saved to a temporary file on the hard drive, and will take a little longer than Standby to power on.

Figure 5 shows Hibernate enabled in the Power Options properties.

Adjusting Low Battery Warnings

In Windows XP, you can set the low battery warnings. There are two levels: Low Battery Alarm and Critical Battery Alarm. The Low Battery Alarm will warn you that the battery is low. The Critical Battery Alarm will initiate a forced standby, hibernate, or shut down, as shown in Figure 6.

Refer to **Worksheet** for this chapter

ACPI Standards

Select the ACPI standard for each characteristic

Refer to **Figure** in online course

6.4.2 Describe the safe installation and removal of laptop components

There are a number of components on a laptop that may need to be replaced. Remember always to make sure that you have the correct replacement component and tools as recommended by the manufacturer. Some components are hot-swappable, which means that they can be removed and replaced while the computer is on. These are some components that may need to be replaced:

- Battery
- Optical drive
- Hard drive
- Memory
- PC cards

Figure 1 shows an example of a laptop.

Note

Each laptop manufacturer uses unique hardware installation and removal procedures. Check the laptop manual for specific installation information and follow safety installation and ESD precautions.

Caution

Always disconnect power and remove the battery before installing or removing laptop components that are not hot-swappable.

Battery Replacement Steps [Figure 2]

Remove the battery from the battery bay:

- Move the battery lock to the unlocked position.
- Hold the release lever in the unlock position and remove the battery.

Install the battery into the battery bay:

- Insert the battery.
- Make sure that both battery levers are locked.

Optical Drive Replacement Steps

[Figure 3]

Remove the DVD/CD-RW drive:

- Press the button to open the drive and remove any media in the drive. Close the tray.
- Slide the latch to release the lever that secures the drive.
- Pull on the lever to expose the drive. Remove the drive.

Install the DVD/CD-RW drive:

- Insert the drive securely.
- Push the lever inward.

Hard Drive Replacement Steps

[Figure 4]

Remove the hard drive:

- On the bottom of the laptop, remove the screw that holds the hard drive in place.
- Slide the assembly outward. Remove the hard drive assembly.
- Remove the hard drive faceplate from the hard drive.

Install the hard drive:

- Attach the hard drive faceplate to the hard drive.
- Slide the hard drive into the hard drive bay.
- On the bottom of the laptop, install the screw that holds the hard drive in place.

Expansion Memory Replacement Steps

[Figure 5]

Laptop expansion memory is also called SODIMM. Remove the existing SODIMM if there are no available slots for the new SODIMM:

- Remove screw to expose the SODIMM.
- Press outward on the clips that hold the sides of the SODIMM.
- Lift up to loosen the SODIMM from the slot and remove the SODIMM.

Install the SODIMM:

- Align the notch at a 45-degree angle.
- Gently press down until clips lock.
- Replace cover and install screw.

PC Expansion Card Replacement Steps

[Figure 6]

Remove the PC expansion card:

- Press the top eject button to release the PC expansion card.

Note

There are two buttons. The bottom blue button ejects the Type II PC card.

Install the PC expansion card:

- Press the blue button inward.
- Insert the PC expansion card into the express slot.

Caution

On some laptops, the PC Card, Optical Drive, and USB devices are hot-swappable. However, the internal hard drive, RAM and battery are NOT hot-swappable.

Hot-Swappable Device Removal Steps

- Left-click the Safely Remove Hardware icon in the Windows system tray to ensure that the device is not in use.
- Left-click the device that you want to remove. A message pops up to tell you that it is safe to remove the device.
- Remove the hot-swappable device from the laptop.

Refer to **Figure** in online course

6.5 Compare the different mobile phone standards

When people began to use cell phones, there were few industry-wide standards applying to cell phone technology. Without standards, it was difficult and expensive to make calls to people that were on another network. Today, cell phone providers use industry standards, which make it easier to use cell phones to make calls.

When the industry started, most cell phone standards were analog. Today, cell phone standards are mostly digital.

Note

Cell phone standards have not been adopted uniformly around the world. Some cell phones are capable of using multiple standards, whereas others can use only one standard. As a result, some cell phones can operate in many countries and other cell phones can only be used locally.

The first generation (1G) of cell phones began service in the 1980s. First-generation phones primarily used analog standards, including Advanced Mobile Phone System (AMPS) and Nordic Mobile Telephone (NMT). In an analog system, the voice information is sent by varying the radio signals used by the phone in the same pattern as the speakers' voices. Unfortunately, this means that interference and noise, which also vary the signal, cannot easily be separated from the voice in the signal. This factor limits the usefulness of analog systems.

Digital signals convert the speakers' voices into a series of ones and zeros. This technology degrades the signal a little, because ones and zeros are not a faithful representation of your voice. However, the digital signal is robust. It can be fixed using error correction routines if there is interference. Also, digital signals can be compressed, making the systems much more efficient than analog.

In the 1990s, the second generation (2G) of cell phones was marked by a switch from analog to digital standards. Second-generation cell standards included Global System for Mobile (GSM), Integrated Digital Enhanced Network (iDEN), and Code Division Multiple Access (CDMA).

Third-generation standards enable cell phones to go beyond simple voice and data communications. It is now common for cell phones to send and receive text, photos, and video. It is also common for 3G cell phones to access the Internet and to use the Global Positioning System (GPS).

Note

As 3G cell phone standards were being developed, extensions to the existing 2G standards were added. These transitional standards are known as 2.5G standards.

Fourth-generation (4G) standards have been championed by many users, in response to the availability of increased data rates. Higher data rates will allow users to download files, such as video and music, faster than what was available with standards of previous generations.

Click the five generation tabs in Figure 1 to view more information about the different cell phone standards.

New technologies that add multimedia and networking functionality can be bundled with cell phone standards. Figure 2 lists common technologies that may be added to the cell phone bundle of services. Most cell phone providers will charge extra for adding these features.

Refer to **Figure** in online course

6.6 Identify common preventive maintenance techniques for laptops and portable devices

Because laptops are mobile, they are used in different types of environments. Some environments can be hazardous to a laptop. Even eating or drinking around a laptop creates a potentially hazardous condition.

Consider what would happen if a drink were spilled onto the keyboard of a laptop. Many components are placed in a very small area directly beneath the keyboard. Spilling liquid or dropping debris onto the keyboard can result in severe internal damage.

It is important to keep a laptop clean and to ensure that it is being used in the most optimal environment possible. This section covers preventive maintenance techniques for the laptop.

After completing this section, you will meet these objectives:

- Identify appropriate cleaning procedures.
- Identify optimal operating environments.

Refer to **Figure** in online course

6.6.1 Identify appropriate cleaning procedures

Proper routine cleaning is the easiest, least expensive way to protect and to extend the life of a laptop. It is very important to use the right products and procedures when cleaning a laptop. Always read all warning labels on the cleaning products. The components are very sensitive and should be handled with care. Consult the laptop manual for additional information and cleaning suggestions.

Laptop Keyboard Cleaning Procedures

. Turn off the laptop.

. Disconnect all attached devices.

- Disconnect laptop from the electrical outlet.
- Remove all installed batteries.
- Wipe laptop and keyboard with a soft, lint-free cloth that is lightly moistened with water or computer-screen cleaner.

Ventilation Cleaning Procedures

- Turn off the laptop.
- Disconnect all attached devices.
- Disconnect laptop from the electrical outlet.
- Remove all installed batteries.
- Use compressed air or a non-electrostatic vacuum to clean out the dust from the vents and the fan behind the vent.
- Use tweezers to remove any debris.

LCD Cleaning Procedures

- Turn off the laptop.
- Disconnect all attached devices.
- Disconnect laptop from the electrical outlet.
- Remove all installed batteries.
- Wipe display with a soft, lint-free cloth that is lightly moistened with a mild cleaning solution.

Caution

Do not spray cleaning solution directly onto the LCD display. Use products specifically designed for cleaning LCD displays.

Touch Pad Cleaning Procedures

- Turn off the laptop.
- Disconnect all attached devices.
- Disconnect laptop from the electrical outlet.
- Remove all installed batteries.
- Wipe surface of touch pad gently with a soft, lint-free cloth that is moistened with an approved cleaner. Never use a wet cloth.

The small screen of a PDA or Smartphone requires special care. The user operates these devices by touching the screen with a stylus. If dirt is present, the PDA may not accurately detect the stylus position or movement. The dirt can also scratch the screen. Clean the screen with a small amount of non-abrasive cleaning solution on a soft cloth. To protect the screen surface from a stylus, use self-adhesive screen covers.

Caution

Use a soft, lint-free cloth with an approved cleaning solution to avoid damaging laptop surfaces. Apply the cleaning solution to the lint-free cloth, not directly to the laptop.

Floppy Drive Cleaning Procedures

Use a commercially-available cleaning kit to clean a floppy drive. Floppy drive cleaning kits include pre-treated floppy discs that remove contaminants from the floppy drive heads that have accumulated through normal operation.

- Remove all media from the floppy drive.
- Insert the cleaning disc and let it spin for the suggested amount of time.

Optical Drive Cleaning Procedures

Dirt, dust, and other contaminants can collect in the optical drives. Contaminated drives can cause malfunctions, missing data, error messages, and lost productivity.

- Use a commercially-available CD or DVD drive cleaning disc. Many floppy disc cleaning kits include an optical disc cleaner. Like the floppy disc cleaner, optical disc cleaner kits contain a cleaning solution and a non-abrasive disc that is inserted into the optical drive.
- Remove all media from the optical drive.
- Insert the cleaning disc and let it spin for the suggested amount of time to clean all contact areas.

Cleaning a CD or DVD Disc

Inspect the disc for scratches. Replace discs that contain deep scratches; they may cause data errors. If you notice problems such as skipping or degraded playback quality with your CDs or DVDs, clean the discs. Commercial products are available that clean discs and provide protection from dust, fingerprints, and scratches. Cleaning products for CDs are safe to use on DVDs.

- Hold the disc by the outer edge or by the inside edge.
- Gently wipe the disc with a lint-free cotton cloth. Never use paper or any material that may scratch the disc or leave streaks.
- Wipe from the center of the disc outward. Never use a circular motion.
- Apply a commercial CD or DVD cleaning solution to the lint-free cotton cloth, and wipe again if any contaminates remain on the disc.
- Allow the disc to dry before it is inserted into the drive.

6.6.2 Identify optimal operating environments

Refer to **Figure** in online course

An optimal operating environment for a laptop is clean, free of potential contaminants, and within the temperature and humidity range specified by the manufacturer. Figure 1 shows examples of operating environments. With most desktop computers, the operating environment can be controlled. However, due to the portable nature of laptops, it is not always possible to control the temperature, humidity, and working conditions. Laptops are built to resist adverse environments, but technicians should always take precautions to protect the equipment from damage and loss of data.

It is important to transport or ship laptops carefully. Use a padded laptop case to store your laptop. When you carry it, use an approved computer bag. If the laptop is shipped, use sufficient packing material. Figure 2 shows examples of laptop carrying cases and packing boxes.

Caution

Be sure to pack laptops and all accessories securely to prevent damage during transport.

Laptops are transported to many types of environments. Dust particles, temperature, and humidity can affect the performance of a laptop.

Follow these guidelines to help ensure optimal operating performance from your laptop:

- Clean the laptop frequently to remove dust and potential contaminants.
- Do not obstruct vents or airflow to internal components. A laptop can overheat if air circulation is obstructed.
- Keep the room temperature between 45 to 90 degrees Fahrenheit (7 to 32 degrees Celsius).
- Keep the humidity level between 10 to 80 percent.

Caution

Use a soft, lint-free cloth with an approved cleaning solution to avoid damaging laptop surfaces. Apply the cleaning solution to the lint-free cloth, not directly to the laptop.

Temperature and humidity recommendations will vary by laptop manufacturer. You should research these recommended values, especially if you plan to use the laptop in extreme conditions. Refer to Figure 3 for humidity and temperature examples.

Refer to **Figure** in online course

6.7 Describe how to troubleshoot laptops and portable devices

When troubleshooting problems with laptops or portable devices, you should determine if a repair is cost-effective. To determine the best course of action, compare the cost of the repair with the replacement cost of the laptop or portable device less the salvage value.

Because many portable devices change rapidly in design and functionality, portable devices are often more expensive to repair than to replace. For this reason, portable devices are usually replaced, whereas laptops can be replaced or repaired.

Follow the steps outlined in this section to accurately identify, repair, and document the problem. The troubleshooting process is shown in Figure 1.

After completing this section, you will meet these objectives:

- Review the troubleshooting process.
- Identify common problems and solutions.

Refer to **Figure** in online course

6.7.1 Review the troubleshooting process

Computer problems can result from a combination of hardware, software, and network issues. Computer technicians must be able to analyze the problem and determine the cause of the error in order to repair the computer. This process is called troubleshooting.

The first step in the troubleshooting process is to gather data from the customer. Figures 1 and 2 list open-ended and closed-ended questions to ask the customer.

Once you have talked to the customer, you should verify the obvious issues. Figure 3 lists some issues for laptops.

After the obvious issues have been verified, try some quick solutions. Figure 4 lists quick solutions for laptops.

If quick solutions did not correct the problem, use Step 4 in the troubleshooting process to gather data from the computer. Figure 5 shows different ways to gather information about the problem from the computer.

At this point, you will have enough information to evaluate the problem, research, and implement possible solutions. Figure 6 shows resources for possible solutions.

After you have solved the laptop problem, you will close with the customer. Figure 7 is a list of the tasks required to complete this step.

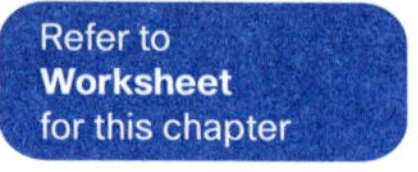

6.7.2 Identify common problems and solutions

Computer problems can be attributed to hardware, software, networks, or some combination of the three. You will resolve some types of computer problems more often than others. Figure 1 is a chart of common laptop problems and solutions.

Refer to **Worksheet** for this chapter

Research Laptop Problems

Research laptop issues

Summary

This chapter discussed the features of laptops, portable devices (PDAs) and Smartphones. The following concepts from this chapter are important to remember:

- Laptops and PDAs are becoming increasingly popular due to reduced costs, lighter weights, increased capabilities, and battery power for portability.
- PDAs and Smartphones are small, handheld devices with many of the capabilities of a computer, such as an address book, calendar, e-mail, and Internet access.
- Laptops and desktops have ports that are virtually the same; therefore, the peripherals are interchangeable. Laptops can use docking stations or port replicators to quickly connect to desktop peripherals and AC power.
- Desktop and laptop components, such as motherboards, are not interchangeable. Additionally, laptop components tend to be proprietary to each manufacturer and designed with unique form factors.
- The laptop CPU is designed to use less power and create less heat than the desktop computer. It uses CPU throttling to reduce power consumption and heat.
- Functionality of the laptop can be expanded by adding components via PC Card or ExpressCard slots and USB, FireWire, or parallel ports.
- An important component of laptop portability is the ability to run on battery power. The current method of managing power is through the operating system with the Advanced Configuration and Power Interface (ACPI). The ACPI standard defines six power management states.
- There are several components of a laptop that may need to be replaced. Steps are defined to replace the battery, optical drive, hard drive, memory, and PC Cards.
- Cell phone standards were developed in the 1980s. The current third-generation standards enable cell phones to share some laptop functions, such as e-mail, Internet access, address, and calendar functions. Standards have not been adopted worldwide.
- Preventive maintenance will ensure optimal operation of the laptop. It is important to keep the laptop clean and in safe environments. It is critical to use the correct materials and techniques when cleaning the various components of a laptop. Procedures for cleaning the components are presented.
- Dust, temperature, and humidity can affect laptop performance. Basic guidelines are to keep the laptop clean, with good ventilation, and room temperature between 45 and 90 degrees F (7 to 32 degrees C) and humidity levels in the range of 10 to 80 percent.
- Always verify that repair of a laptop is cost-effective.
- Troubleshooting laptop problems requires the technician to identify, repair, and document the problem. Troubleshooting steps include: Gather data from customer, verify the obvious issues, try quick solutions first, gather data from the computer, evaluate the problem, implement the solution, and close with the customer.
- When troubleshooting wireless-capable devices, check all status LEDs and signal strength indicators. Remove all unnecessary peripherals to isolate the problem.
- Check for external problems, such as connection errors, power errors, and function key errors. Connection errors can often be solved by removing and reinserting components. Check in Device Manager for errors. Power errors can be caused by the use of incorrect adaptors,

damaged batteries, damaged AC adaptors, or dead wall outlets. Check components controlled by Function keys.

- Try quick solutions first to solve laptop problems. Reboot and verify the BIOS settings, start the laptop in safe mode, and use the Last Known Good Configuration Option.
- For problem resolution, gather information from the computer from the Device Manager, Network Settings, Power Options, Event Viewer, and System Configuration.
- Resources for troubleshooting should include other technicians, Internet resources, manufacturers' FAQs, and online forums.
- The final steps in the troubleshooting process are to test the laptop in all scenarios, discuss the solution with the customer, fill out all necessary paperwork and billing documents, and document the solution.

The Advanced Laptops and Portable Devices chapter will focus on troubleshooting more difficult problems.

Chapter 6 Quiz

Take the chapter quiz to test your knowledge.

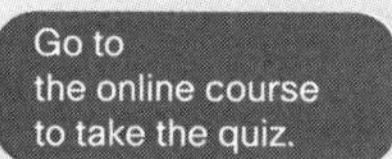

Your Chapter Notes

CHAPTER 7

Fundamental Printers and Scanners

Introduction

This chapter will provide essential information about printers and scanners. You will learn how printers operate, what to consider when purchasing a printer, and how to connect printers to an individual computer or to a network.

Printers produce paper copies of electronic files. Scanners allow users to convert paper documents into electronic files. Many government regulations require physical records; therefore, hard copies of computer documents are often as important today as they were when the paperless revolution began several years ago.

You must understand the operation of various types of printers and scanners to be able to install and maintain them, as well as troubleshoot any problems that may arise.

After completing this chapter, you will meet these objectives:

- Describe the types of printers currently available.
- Describe the installation and configuration process for printers.
- Describe the types of scanners currently available.
- Describe the installation and configuration process for scanners.
- Identify and apply common preventive maintenance techniques for printers and scanners.
- Troubleshoot printers and scanners.

Refer to **Figure** in online course

7.1 Describe the types of printers currently available

As a computer technician, you may be required to purchase, repair, or maintain a printer. The customer may request you to perform the following tasks:

- Select a printer.
- Install and configure a printer.
- Troubleshoot a printer.

After completing this section, you will meet these objectives:

- Describe characteristics and capabilities of printers.
- Describe printer-to-computer interfaces.
- Describe laser printers.
- Describe impact printers.
- Describe inkjet printers.

- Describe solid-ink printers.
- Describe other printer types.

Refer to **Figure** in online course

7.1.1 Describe characteristics and capabilities of printers

Printers available today are usually either laser printers using electrophotographic technology or inkjet printers using electrostatic spray technology. Dot matrix printers using impact technology are used in applications that require carbon copies. Figure 1 shows a list of printer selection criteria.

Capacity and Speed

Printer capacity and speed are factors to consider when selecting a printer. Inkjet printers are usually slower, but they may be adequate for a home or small office. The speed of a printer is measured in pages per minute (ppm). The speed of an inkjet printer is 2 – 6 ppm. The speed of an laser printer is 8 – 200 ppm.

Color or Black and White

A computer monitor produces colors through the additive mixing of dots that are displayed on the screen. The eye picks up the colors directly. The dots produce the color range using red, green, and blue (RGB) dots.

A printer produces colors using subtractive mixing. The eye sees a color that reflects from the combination of colors on the paper. Figure 2 shows a CMYK color wheel.

The choice between a black-and-white printer and a color printer depends on the needs of your customer. If your customer is primarily printing letters and does not need color capability, a black-and-white printer will be sufficient. However, an elementary school teacher might need a color printer to add excitement to lessons.

Quality

The quality of printing is measured in dots per inch (dpi). The more dpi, the higher the resolution. When the resolution is higher, text and images are usually clearer. To produce the best high-resolution images, you should use both high-quality ink or toner and high-quality paper.

Reliability

A printer should be reliable. Because there are so many types of printers on the market, you should research the specifications of several printers before selecting one. Here are some of the options available from the manufacturer:

- ***Warranty*** – Identify what is covered within the warranty.
- ***Scheduled servicing*** – Servicing is based on expected usage. Information is found in the manual or on the manufacturer's website.
- ***Mean time between failures (MTBF)*** – There is an average length of time that the printer will work without failing. Information is found in the manual or on the manufacturer's website.

Total Cost of Ownership

Consider the cost when selecting hardware. When buying a printer, there is more than just the initial cost of the printer to consider. The total cost of ownership (TCO) includes a number of factors:

- Initial purchase price

- Cost of supplies, such as paper and ink
- Price per page
- Maintenance costs
- Warranty costs

When calculating the TCO, you should also consider the amount of material printed and the expected lifetime of the printer.

Refer to **Figure** in online course

7.1.2 Describe printer to computer interfaces

A computer must have a compatible interface with the printer to be able to print documents. Typically, printers connect to home computers using a parallel, USB, or wireless interface. Corporate printers may connect to a network using a network cable.

Serial

Serial data transfer is the movement of single bits of information in a single cycle. A serial connection can be used for dot matrix printers because the printers do not require high-speed data transfer.

Parallel

Parallel data transfer is faster than serial data transfer. Parallel data transfer is the movement of multiple bits of information in a single cycle. The path is wider for information to move to or from the printer.

IEEE 1284 is the current standard for parallel printer ports. Enhanced Parallel Port (EPP) and Enhanced Capabilities Port (ECP) are two modes of operation within the IEEE 1284 standard that allow bi-directional communication.

SCSI

Small Computer System Interface (SCSI) is a type of interface that uses parallel communication technology to achieve high data-transfer rates.

USB

USB is a common interface for printers and other devices. The speed and simple setup has made USB very practical. Newer operating systems offer PnP USB support. When a USB device is added to a computer system supporting PnP, the device is automatically detected and starts the driver installation process.

FireWire

FireWire, also known as i.LINK or IEEE 1394, is a high-speed communication bus that is platform independent. FireWire connects digital devices such as digital printers, scanners, digital cameras, and hard drives.

FireWire allows a peripheral device, such as a printer, to seamlessly plug into a computer. It also allows a device such as printer to be hot-swappable. FireWire provides a single plug-and-socket connection that can attach up to 63 devices. FireWire has a data transfer rate of up to 400 Mbps.

Ethernet

Printers can be shared over a network. Connecting a printer to the network requires cabling that is compatible with both the existing network and the network port installed in the printer. Most network printers use an RJ-45 interface to connect to a network.

Wireless

Wireless printing technology is available in infrared, Bluetooth, and wireless fidelity (Wi-Fi) technology.

For infrared communication to take place between a printer and a computer, transmitters and receivers are required on both devices. There must be a clear line of sight between the transmitter and receiver on both devices, with a maximum distance of 12 feet (3.7 m). Infrared uses a type of light that is invisible to the human eye.

Bluetooth technology uses an unlicensed radio frequency for short-range communication and is popular for wireless headsets and synching PDAs to laptops and desktop computers. A Bluetooth adapter will allow a Bluetooth device to connect to a printer, usually by using a USB port.

Wi-Fi is the popular name for a relatively new technology that allows the connection of computers to a network without using cables. There are two common standards for Wi-Fi technology, both of which begin with the number of the IEEE standard 802.11:

- 802.11b transfers data at a rate of 11 Mbps.
- 802.11g transfers data at a rate of 54 Mbps. 802.11g products are backwards-compatible with 802.11b.

Refer to **Figure** in online course

7.1.3 Describe laser printers

A laser printer is a high-quality, fast printer that uses a laser beam to create an image. The central part of the laser printer is its electrophotographic drum. The drum is a metal cylinder that is coated with a light-sensitive insulating material. When a beam of laser light strikes the drum, it becomes a conductor at the point where the light hits it. As the drum rotates, the laser beam draws an electrostatic image upon the drum, called the image. The undeveloped or latent image is passed by a supply of dry ink or toner that is attracted to it. The drum turns and brings this image in contact with the paper, which attracts the toner from the drum. The paper is passed through a fuser that is made up of hot rollers, which melts the toner into the paper.

Printing Process

The laser printer process involves six steps to print information onto a single sheet of paper.

Step 1: Cleaning

When an image has been deposited on the paper and the drum has separated from the paper, any remaining toner must be removed from the drum. A printer may have a blade that scrapes all excess toner from the drum. Some printers use an AC voltage on a wire that removes the charge from the drum surface and allows the excess toner to fall away from the drum. The excess toner is stored in a used toner container that may be emptied or discarded.

Step 2: Conditioning

This step involves removing the old latent image from the drum and conditioning the drum for a new latent image. Conditioning is done by placing a special wire, grid, or roller that receives a negative charge of approximately – 600 volts DC uniformly across the surface of the drum. The charged wire or grid is called the primary corona. The roller is called a conditioning roller.

Step 3: Writing

The writing process involves scanning the photosensitive drum with the laser beam. Every portion of the drum that is exposed to the light has the surface charge reduced to about – 100 volts DC. This electrical charge has a lower negative charge than the remainder of the drum. As the drum turns, an invisible latent image is created on the drum.

Step 4: Developing

In the developing phase, the toner is applied to the latent image on the drum. The toner is a negatively-charged combination of plastic and metal particles. A control blade holds the toner at a microscopic distance from the drum. The toner then moves from the control blade to the more positively-charged latent image on the drum.

Step 5: Transferring

In this step, the toner attached to the latent image is transferred to the paper. The transfer, or secondary corona, places a positive charge on the paper. Because the drum was charged negatively, the toner on the drum is attracted to the paper. The image is now on the paper and is held in place by the positive charge.

Step 6: Fusing

In this step, the toner is permanently fused to the paper. The printing paper is rolled between a heated roller and a pressure roller. As the paper moves through the heated roller and the pressure roller, the loose toner is melted and fused with the fibers in the paper. The paper is then moved to the output tray as a printed page.

The following mnemonic will help you to memorize the order of the steps of the laser printing process: Continuous Care Will Delay Trouble Forever (Cleaning, Conditioning, Writing, Developing, Transferring, Fusing).

Warning

The primary corona wire or grid, or the conditioning roller, can be very dangerous. The voltage runs as high as – 6000 volts. Only certified technicians should work on the unit. Before working inside a laser printer, you should make sure that voltage is properly discharged.

7.1.4 Describe impact printers

Refer to **Figure** in online course

Impact printers are very basic printers. Impact printers have print heads that strike the inked ribbon, causing characters to be imprinted on the paper. Dot-matrix and daisy-wheel are examples of impact printers.

The following are some advantages of an impact printer:

- Uses inexpensive consumables
- Uses continuous feed paper
- Has carbon copy printing ability

The following are some disadvantages of an impact printer:

- Noisy
- Low resolution graphics
- Limited color capability
- Slow printing, normally in the range of 32 to 76 characters per second (cps)

Types of Impact Printers

In the daisy-wheel printer, the wheel contains the letters, numbers, and special characters. The wheel is rotated until the required character is in place, and an electromechanical hammer pushes the character into the ink ribbon. The character then strikes the paper, imprinting the character on the paper.

The dot-matrix printer is similar to the daisy-wheel printer, except that instead of a wheel containing the characters, a print head contains pins that are surrounded by electromagnets. When energized, the pins push forward onto the ink ribbon, creating a character on the paper.

The number of pins on a print head, 9 or 24, indicates the quality of the print. The highest quality of print that is produced by the dot matrix printer is referred to as near letter quality (NLQ).

Most dot-matrix printers use continuous feed paper. The paper has perforations between each sheet and perforated strips on the side used to feed the paper and to prevent skewing or shifting. Sheet feeders that print one page at a time are available in some of the higher-quality office printers. A large roller, called the platen, applies pressure to keep the paper from slipping. If a multiple-copy paper is used, the platen gap can be adjusted to the thickness of the paper.

Refer to **Figure** in online course

7.1.5 Describe inkjet printers

Inkjet printers produce high-quality prints. Inkjet printers are easy to use and inexpensive compared to laser printers. The print quality of an inkjet printer is measured in dots per inch (dpi). Higher dpi numbers provide greater image details. Figure 1 shows an all-in-one device that contains an inkjet printer. Figure 2 shows ink jet printer components.

Inkjet printers use ink-filled cartridges that spray ink onto a page through tiny holes. The tiny holes are called nozzles. The ink is sprayed in a pattern on the page.

There are two types of inkjet nozzles:

- ***Thermal*** **–** A pulse of electrical current is applied to heating chambers around the nozzles. The heat creates a bubble of steam in the chamber. The steam forces ink out through the nozzle and onto the paper.
- ***Piezoelectric*** **–** Piezoelectric crystals are located in the ink reservoir at the back of each nozzle. A charge is applied to the crystal, causing it to vibrate. This vibration of the crystal controls the flow of ink onto the paper.

Inkjet printers use plain paper to make economical prints. Special-purpose paper may be used to create high-quality prints of photographs. When the inkjet print is complete and the paper leaves the printer, the ink is often wet. You should avoid touching printouts for 10 to 15 seconds in order to prevent the images from smearing.

These are some advantages of an inkjet printer:

- Low cost

- High resolution
- Quick to warm up

These are some disadvantages of an inkjet printer:

- Nozzles are prone to clogging.
- Ink cartridges are expensive.
- Ink is wet after printing.

Refer to **Figure** in online course

7.1.6 Describe solid-ink printers

Solid-ink printers use solid sticks of ink rather than toner or ink cartridges. Solid-ink printers produce high-quality images. The ink sticks are nontoxic and can be handled safely.

Solid-ink printers melt ink sticks and spray the ink through nozzles. The ink is sprayed onto a drum. The drum transfers the ink to paper.

These are some advantages of solid-ink printers:

- Produces vibrant color prints
- Easy to use
- Can use many different paper types

These are some disadvantages of solid-ink printers:

- Printers are expensive
- Ink is expensive
- They are slow to warm up

Refer to **Figure** in online course

7.1.7 Describe other printer types

Two other printing technologies that you may work with are thermal and dye-sublimation.

Thermal Printers

Some retail cash registers or older fax machines may contain thermal printers, as shown in Figure 1. The thermal paper used in thermal printers is chemically treated and has a waxy quality. Thermal paper becomes black when heated. Most thermal printer print heads are the width of the paper. Areas of the print head are heated as required to make the pattern on the paper. The paper is supplied in the form of a roll.

A thermal printer has the following advantage:

- Longer life because there are few moving parts

A thermal printer has the following disadvantages:

- Paper is expensive.
- Paper has a short shelf life.
- Images are poor quality.
- Paper must be stored at room temperature.

Dye-Sublimation Printers

Dye-sublimation printers produce photo-quality images for graphic printing. See Figure 2 for an example of a dye-sublimation printer. This type of printer uses solid sheets of ink that change directly from solid to gas, in a process called sublimating. The print head passes over a sheet of cyan, magenta, yellow, and a clear overcoat (CMYO). There is a pass for each color.

Dye-sublimation printers have the following advantages:

- Printers produce high-quality images.
- Overcoat layer reduces smearing and increases moisture resistance.

Dye-sublimation printers have the following disadvantages:

- Media can be expensive.
- Printers are better for color than for grayscale (black and white).

In photography, both dye-sublimation printers and small color ink-jet printers provide quality prints.

Refer to **Figure** in online course

7.2 Describe the installation and configuration process for printers

When you purchase a printer, the installation and configuration information is usually supplied by the manufacturer. An installation CD that includes drivers, manuals, and diagnostic software will be included with the printer. The same tools may also be available as downloads from the manufacturer's website.

After completing this section, you will meet these objectives:

- Describe how to set up a printer.
- Explain how to power and connect the device using a local or network port.
- Describe how to install and update the device driver, firmware, and RAM.
- Identify configuration options and default settings.
- Describe how to optimize printer performance.
- Describe how to print a test page.
- Describe how to share a printer.

Refer to **Figure** in online course

7.2.1 Describe how to set up a printer

Although all types of printers are somewhat different to connect and configure, there are procedures that should be applied to all printers. After the printer has been unpacked and placed in position, connect it to the computer, network, or print server and plug it into an electrical outlet.

Refer to **Figure** in online course

7.2.2 Explain how to power and connect the device using a local or network port

Now that the printer has been unpacked and placed in position, you must connect it to the computer, network, or print server and plug it into an electrical outlet.

First, connect the appropriate data cable to the communication port on the back of the printer. If the printer has a USB, FireWire, or parallel port, connect the corresponding cable to the printer port. Connect the other end of the data cable to the corresponding port on the back of the computer. If you are installing a network printer, connect the network cable to the network port.

After the data cable has been properly connected, attach the power cable to the printer. Connect the other end of the power cable to an available electrical outlet.

Warning

Never plug a printer into a UPS. The power surge that occurs when the printer is turned on will damage the UPS unit.

Refer to **Figure** in online course

7.2.3 Describe how to install and update the device driver, firmware, and RAM

After you have connected the power and data cables to the printer, the operating system may discover the printer and attempt to install a driver. If you have a driver disc from the manufacturer, use this driver. The driver that is included with the printer is usually more current than the drivers used by the operating system. Figure 1 shows the Add Printer wizard, which can also be used to install the new printer.

Printer Driver

Printer drivers are software programs that enable the computer and the printer to communicate with each other. Drivers also provide an interface for the user to configure printer options. Every printer model has a unique driver. Printer manufacturers frequently update drivers to increase the performance of the printer, to add options, or to fix problems. You can download new printer drivers from the manufacturer's website.

Step 1: Find Out If a Newer Driver Is Available

Go to the printer manufacturer's website. Most manufacturers' websites have a link from the main page to a page that offers drivers and support. Make sure the driver is compatible with the computer that you are updating.

Step 2: Download the Driver

Download the printer driver files to your computer. Most driver files will come in a compressed or "zipped" format. Download the file to a folder and uncompress or "unzip" the contents. Save instructions or documentation to a separate folder on your computer.

Step 3: Install the Downloaded Driver

Install the downloaded driver automatically or manually. Most printer drivers have a setup file that will automatically search the system for older drivers and replace them with the new one. If there is no setup file available, follow the directions that are supplied by the manufacturer.

Step 4: Test the New Printer Driver

Run multiple tests to make sure the printer works properly. Use a variety of applications to print different types of documents. Change and test each printer option.

Firmware

Firmware is a set of instructions stored on the printer. The firmware controls how the printer operates. Figure 2 shows a firmware upgrade utility. The procedure to upgrade firmware is very similar to the procedure for installing printer drivers.

Printer Memory

Adding printer memory to a printer can improve printing speed and allow the printer to handle more complex print jobs. All printers have at least some amount of memory inside. Generally, the more memory a printer has, the more efficiently it will operate. Figure 3 is a generic list of steps to follow to upgrade printer memory.

Consult the printer documentation for memory requirements:

- ***Memory specifications –*** Some printer manufacturers use standard types of memory and other manufacturers use proprietary memory. Check the documentation for the type of memory, the speed of the memory, and the capacity of memory.
- ***Memory population and availability –*** Some printers have multiple memory slots. To find out how many memory slots are used and how many are available, you may need to open a compartment on the printer to check memory population.

Refer to **Figure** in online course

7.2.4 Identify configuration options and default settings

Each printer may have different configurations and default options. Check the printer documentation for information about configurations and default settings.

Here are some common configurations that are available for printers:

- Paper type – standard, draft, gloss, or photo
- Print quality – draft, normal, photo, or automatic
- Color printing – multiple colors used
- Black-and-white printing – only black ink used
- Grayscale printing – color image printed using only black ink in different shades
- Paper size – standard paper sizes or envelopes and business cards
- Paper orientation – landscape or portrait
- Print layout – normal, banner, booklet, or poster
- Duplex – normal or two-sided printing

Refer to **Figure** in online course

7.2.5 Describe how to optimize printer performance

With printers, most optimization is completed through the software supplied with the drivers.

In the software, there are tools available to optimize performance:

- Print spool settings – Ability to cancel or pause current print jobs in the printer queue
- Color calibration – Ability to adjust settings to match the colors on the screen to the colors on the printed sheet
- Paper orientation – Ability to select landscape or portrait image layout

Refer to **Figure** in online course

7.2.6 Describe how to print a test page

After installing a printer, you should print a test page to verify that the printer is operating properly. The test page confirms that the driver software is installed and working correctly, and that the printer and computer are communicating.

Print a Test Page

To print a test page manually, use the following path:

Start > Printers and Faxes to display the Printers and Faxes menu.

Right-click the desired printer and follow this path:

Properties > General Tab > Print Test Page

A dialog box will open, asking if the page printed correctly. If the page did not print, built-in help files will assist you in troubleshooting the problem.

Print from an Application

You can also test a printer by printing a test page from an application such as Notepad or WordPad. To access Notepad, use the following path:

Start > Programs > Accessories > Notepad

A blank document will open. Enter some text in the document. Print it using the following path:

File > Print

Test a Printer

You can also print from the command line to test the printer. Printing from the command line is limited to ASCII files only, such as .txt and .bat files. To send a file to the printer from the command line, use this path:

Start > Run

The Run box should pop up. Type cmd in the Run box, and then click **OK**.

At the command line prompt, enter the following command:

Print thefile.txt

Test the Printer from the Printer Panel

Most printers have a front panel with controls to allow you to generate test pages. This method of printing enables you to verify the printer operation separately from the network or computer. Consult the printer manufacturer's website or documentation to learn how to print a test page from the front panel of the printer.

Refer to **Figure** in online course

7.2.7 Describe how to share a printer

Printer sharing enables multiple users or clients to access a printer that they are not directly connected to. Figure 1 shows several computers with different operating systems, all connected to the same shared printer. This arrangement reduces the expense on a network, because fewer printers are required.

Setting up printer sharing is simple with Windows XP. The following steps enable a computer to share a printer:

- Click **Start > Printers and Faxes**.
- Right-click the printer and choose **Properties**.
- Select the **Share** tab.
- Click the **Share this printer** radio button, as shown in Figure 2.
- Keep or change the share name.
- Click **Apply**.

All of the computers that use the shared printer must have the correct drivers installed. Drivers for other operating systems can be installed on the print server.

To connect to the printer from another computer on the network, choose **Start > Printers and Faxes > Add Printer**. The Add Printer Wizard will appear. Follow the steps using the wizard.

Refer to **Figure** in online course

7.3 Describe the types of scanners currently available

As a computer technician, you may be required to purchase, repair, or maintain a scanner. The customer may request you to perform the following tasks:

- Select a scanner.
- Install and configure a scanner.
- Troubleshoot a scanner.

Figure 1 shows some of the different types of scanners.

After completing this section, you will meet the following objectives:

- Describe scanner types, resolution, and interfaces.
- Describe all-in-one devices.
- Describe flatbed scanners.
- Describe handheld scanners.
- Describe drum scanners.
- Compare costs of different types of scanners.

Refer to **Figure** in online course

7.3.1 Describe scanner types, resolution, and interfaces

Scanners are used to convert printed data or images into an electronic data format that a computer can store or process as required. After an image has been scanned, it can be saved, modified, and even e-mailed as you would with any other file. Although most scanners perform the same operation, there are different types of scanners available, as shown in Figure 1. Click on each type of scanner to learn more information.

As with printers, the features, quality, and speed of the different types of scanners vary. Scanners typically create an RGB image that can be converted into common image formats such as JPEG, TIFF, Bitmap, and PNG. An RGB image has three channels: red, green, and blue. RGB channels generally follow the color receptors of the human eye, and are used in computer displays and image scanners.

Some scanners have the ability to create text documents using optical character recognition (OCR) software. OCR software is used to convert a scanned printed page into text that can be edited with a word processor. The resolution of a scanner is measured in dots per inch (dpi). Like printers, the higher the dpi, the better the quality of the image.

To allow communication of data, the scanner and computer must have compatible interfaces. The interfaces and cables used for printers are typically the same as the interfaces and cables used for scanners, as shown in Figure 2.

Refer to **Figure** in online course

7.3.2 Describe all-in-one devices

An all-in-one device combines the functionality of multiple devices into one physical piece of hardware. The devices may include media card readers and hard drives for storage. All-in-one devices generally include these functions:

- Scanner
- Printer
- Copier
- Fax

All-in-one devices are typically used in home-office environments or where space is limited. These devices are often used with a computer but can operate alone to copy and fax documents.

Refer to **Figure** in online course

7.3.3 Describe flatbed scanners

Flatbed scanners are often used to scan books and photographs for archiving. An electronic image is acquired by placing the book or photograph face down on the glass. The scanner head, consisting of an array of image sensors, lies beneath the glass and moves along the item, capturing the image.

Sheet feeders can be used with flatbed scanners to scan multiple images. A sheet feeder is a device that can be attached to some flatbed scanners to hold multiple sheets and feed them into the scanner, one at a time. This feature allows for faster scanning; however, the image quality is usually not as good as a flatbed scanner that does not use a sheet feeder.

Refer to **Figure** in online course

7.3.4 Describe handheld scanners

A handheld scanner is small and portable. It is difficult to smoothly scan an image using a handheld scanner. To scan an item, carefully pass the scanner head across the item that you want to scan. As with a flatbed scanner, digital images are made from the images collected by the handheld scanner.

When you want to scan an item larger than the head of the handheld scanner, you must make more than one pass to capture the full image. It may be difficult to recreate the original image digitally when it is scanned in more than one pass. The images must be put back together to form a single image of the item that was scanned.

Refer to **Figure** in online course

7.3.5 Describe drum scanners

Drum scanners produce a high-quality transfer of an image. Drum scanners are usually used commercially but are being replaced by lower-priced, high-quality flatbed scanners. Many drum scanners are still in use for high-end reproductions, such as archiving photographs in museums.

To scan an image using a drum scanner, you attach the image to a revolving drum or load it into a supporting canister. The drum is rotated at high speed across optical scanners. The optical scanners move slowly across the drum surface until the entire image is captured. The captured image is then reproduced by the computer as a digital image file.

Refer to **Figure** in online course

7.4 Describe the installation and configuration process for scanners

When you purchase a scanner, the installation and configuration information is usually supplied by the manufacturer. An installation CD that includes drivers, manuals, and diagnostic software will be included with the scanner. The same tools may also be available as downloads from the manufacturer's website.

After completing this section, you will meet the following objectives:

- Explain how to power and connect a scanner.
- Describe how to install and update the device driver.
- Identify configuration options and default settings.

Refer to **Figure** in online course

7.4.1 Explain how to power and connect a scanner

Like printers, scanners can connect to a computer using the USB, FireWire, network, or parallel port interface. Some scanners may connect using a SCSI interface.

Scanners that are built into an all-in-one device should be plugged directly into an AC wall outlet. This will provide the AC current necessary to operate all-in-one device. Other types of scanners may acquire power through the USB or FireWire connector.

After unpacking the scanner, connect the appropriate power and data cables. Use the scanner documentation as your guide, or check the manufacturer's website for instructions.

Refer to **Figure** in online course

7.4.2 Describe how to install and update the device driver

Once you have connected and started the scanner, the computer operating system may be able to discover the scanner through the PnP process. If the scanner is discovered, a driver may be installed automatically by the operating system.

After you set up a scanner, install the driver software that the manufacturer includes with the scanner. This driver is usually more current than the drivers on your computer. It may also provide more functionality than the basic driver from Windows.

As with a printer, you may want to install drivers from the manufacturer's website to gain additional functionality, diagnostic tools, and troubleshooting utilities. Download software from the manufacturer's website and follow any directions provided to install the software and utilities for your scanner. Some scanning software will automatically download and install updated software, drivers, or firmware. Follow directions provided by the update utility to install these files.

Refer to **Lab Activity** for this chapter

All-in-One Device

Install and configure an all-in-one device

Refer to **Figure** in online course

7.4.3 Identify configuration options and default settings

Scanners have configuration options and default settings that differ between model types and manufacturers.

A scanner may come with a basic graphic editing software package for editing photographs and other images. Editing software packages may include OCR software that allows text in a scanned image to be manipulated as text.

These are some of the configurations that may be available on a scanner:

- Color, grayscale, or black-and-white scanning
- One-touch scanning into your choice of software
- Quality and resolution choices
- Sheet feeders

Color calibration between devices is important so that you see true representations of color. To calibrate a scanner, scan a graphic that contains specific colors. A calibration application installed on the computer compares the output of the scanner against the known colors of the sample graphic on the display. The software will adjust the color of the scanner accordingly. When your scanner, monitor, and printer treat the same colors in the same way, the image you print will match the image you scan.

Refer to **Figure** in online course

7.5 Identify and apply common preventive maintenance techniques for printers and scanners

Printers and scanners have many moving parts that can wear out over time or through extended use. They must be maintained regularly to operate correctly.

Moving parts can be affected by dust and other air particles. Clean printers and scanners regularly to avoid downtime, loss of productivity, and high repair costs.

After completing this section, you will meet the following objectives:

- Describe printer maintenance.
- Describe scanner maintenance.

Refer to **Figure** in online course

7.5.1 Describe printer maintenance

Printers have many moving parts and require a higher level of maintenance than most other electronic devices. Impurities are produced by the printer and collect on the internal components. Over time, if the impurities are not removed, the printer may malfunction. The maintenance schedule for a printer can be found in the manual or on the manufacturer's website.

Caution

Be sure to unplug the printer from the electrical source before beginning any type of maintenance.

Most printers come with printer monitoring and diagnostic software from the manufacturer that can help you maintain the printer. Observe the guidelines from the manufacturer for cleaning the following printer and scanner components:

- Printer roller surfaces
- Printer and scanner paper-handling mechanisms

The type and quality of paper and ink used can affect the life of the printer:

- ***Paper selection –*** High-quality paper can help to ensure that the printer operates efficiently and for a long time. Many types of printer paper are available, including inkjet and laser. The printer manufacturer may recommend the type of paper that should be used for best results. Some papers, especially photo paper and transparencies, have a right and wrong side. Load the paper according to the manufacturer's instructions.
- ***Ink selection –*** The manufacturer will recommend the brand and type of ink that you should use. If the wrong type of ink is installed, the printer may not work or the print quality may be reduced. You should avoid refilling the ink cartridges because the ink may leak.

Refer to **Figure** in online course

7.5.2 Describe scanner maintenance

The scanner surface should be kept clean. If the glass becomes dirty, consult the manufacturer's user manual for cleaning recommendations. To prevent liquid from leaking into the scanner case, do not spray glass cleaner directly on the device. Dampen a cloth with the cleaner, and then apply the cleaner gently to the glass.

If the inside of the glass becomes dirty, check the manual for instructions on how to open the unit or remove the glass from the scanner. If possible, thoroughly clean both sides of the glass, and replace the glass as it was originally set in the scanner. When the scanner is not in use, keep the lid closed. In the case of the handheld scanner, put it in a safe place. Also, never lay anything heavy on a scanner because you may damage the casing or internal parts.

Refer to **Figure** in online course

7.6 Troubleshoot printers and scanners

With printer and scanner problems, a technician must be able to determine if the problem exists with the device, cable connection, or the computer that it is attached to. Follow the steps outlined in this section to accurately identify, repair, and document the problem.

After completing this section, you will meet these objectives:

- Review the troubleshooting process.
- Identify common problems and solutions.

Refer to **Figure** in online course

7.6.1 Review the troubleshooting process

Printer problems can result from a combination of hardware, software, and network issues. Computer technicians must be able to analyze the problem and determine the cause of the error in order to repair the printer. This process is called troubleshooting.

The first step in the troubleshooting process is to gather data from the customer. Figures 1 and 2 list open-ended and closed-ended questions to ask the customer.

Once you have talked to the customer, you should verify the obvious issues. Figure 3 lists some issues for printers and scanners.

After the obvious issues have been verified, try some quick solutions. Figure 4 lists quick solutions for printers and scanners.

If quick solutions did not correct the problem, use Step 4 in the troubleshooting process to gather data from the computer. Figure 5 shows different ways to gather information about the problem from the computer.

At this point, you will have enough information to evaluate the problem, research, and implement possible solutions. Figure 6 shows resources for possible solutions.

After you have solved the printer or scanner problem, you will close with the customer. Figure 7 is a list of the tasks required to complete this step.

Refer to **Figure** in online course

7.6.2 Identify common problems and solutions

Printer or scanner problems can be attributed to hardware, software, networks, or some combination of the three. You will resolve some types of printer and scanner problems more often than others. Figure 1 is a chart of common printer and scanner problems and solutions.

Summary

In this chapter, various types of printers and scanners were discussed. You learned that there are many different types and sizes of printers and scanners, each with different capabilities, speeds, and uses. You also learned that both printers and scanners can be connected directly to computers, as well as shared across a network. The chapter also introduced the different types of cables and interfaces available to connect a printer or scanner. The customer may request you to perform the following tasks:

- Some printers and scanners have low output and are adequate for home use, whereas other printers and scanners have high output and are designed for commercial use.
- Printers may have different speeds and quality of print.
- Older printers and scanners use parallel cables and ports. Newer printers and scanners typically use USB or FireWire cables and connectors.
- Larger printers and scanners may also have an NIC port to connect to a network.
- Newer printers and scanners are PnP. The computer will automatically install the necessary drivers.
- If the device drivers are not automatically installed by the computer, you will have to supply the drivers on a CD or download them from the manufacturer's website.
- Most optimization is done through software drivers and utilities.
- After you have set up the printer or scanner, you can share the device with other users on the network. This arrangement is cost-efficient because there is no need for every user to have a printer or scanner.
- A good preventative maintenance program will extend the life of the printer and scanner and keep them performing well.
- Troubleshooting printer and scanner problems requires the technician to identify, repair, and document the problem. Troubleshooting steps include: Gather data from customer, verify the obvious issues, try quick solutions first, gather data from the computer, evaluate the problem, implement the solution, and close with the customer.

Chapter 7 Quiz

Take the chapter quiz to test your knowledge.

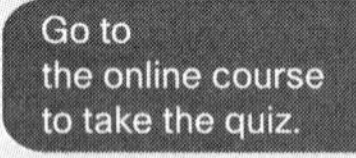

Your Chapter Notes

CHAPTER 8

Fundamental Networks

Introduction

This chapter will provide an overview of network principles, standards, and purposes. The following types of networks will be discussed in this chapter:

- Local Area Network (LAN)
- Wide Area Network (WAN)
- Wireless LAN (WLAN)

The different types of network topologies, protocols, and logical models as well as the hardware needed to create a network will also be discussed in this chapter. Configuration, troubleshooting, and preventive maintenance will be covered. You will also learn about network software, communication methods, and hardware relationships.

After completing this chapter, you will meet these objectives:

- Explain the principles of networking.
- Describe types of networks.
- Describe basic networking concepts and technologies.
- Describe the physical components of a network.
- Describe LAN topologies and architectures.
- Identify standards organizations.
- Identify Ethernet standards.
- Explain OSI and TCP/IP data models.
- Describe how to configure a NIC and a modem.
- Identify names, purposes, and characteristics of other technologies used to establish connectivity.
- Identify and apply common preventive maintenance techniques used for networks.
- Troubleshoot a network.

8.1 Explain the principles of networking

Refer to **Figure** in online course

Networks are systems that are formed by links. Websites that allow individuals to link to each other's pages are called social networking sites. A set of related ideas can be called a conceptual network. The connections you have with all your friends can be called your personal network.

People use the following networks every day:

- Mail delivery system

- Telephone system
- Public transportation system
- Corporate computer network
- The Internet

Computers can be linked by networks to share data and resources. A network can be as simple as two computers connected by a single cable or as complex as hundreds of computers connected to devices that control the flow of information. Converged data networks can include general purpose computers, such as PCs and servers, as well as devices with more specific functions, including printers, phones, televisions, and game consoles.

All data, voice, video, and converged networks share information and use various methods to direct how this information flows. The information on the network goes from one place to another, sometimes via different paths, to arrive at the appropriate destination.

The public transportation system is similar to a data network. The cars, trucks, and other vehicles are like the messages that travel within the network. Each driver defines a starting point (source) and an ending point (destination). Within this system, there are rules such as stop signs and traffic lights that control the flow from the source to the destination.

After completing this section, you will meet these objectives:

- Define computer networks.
- Explain the benefits of networking.

Refer to **Figure** in online course

8.1.1 Define computer networks

A computer data network is a collection of hosts connected by networking devices. A host is any device that sends and receives information on the network. Peripherals are devices that are connected to hosts. Some devices can serve either as hosts or peripherals. For example, a printer connected to your laptop which is on a network is acting as a peripheral. If the printer is connected directly to a networking device, such as a hub, switch, or router, it is acting as a host.

Computer networks are used globally in businesses, homes, schools, and government agencies. Many of the networks are connected to each other through the Internet.

Many different types of devices can connect to a network:

- Desktop computers
- Laptop computers
- Printers
- Scanners
- PDAs
- Smartphones
- File/print servers

A network can share many different types of resources:

- Services, such as printing or scanning
- Storage space on removable devices, such as hard drives or optical drives

- Applications, such as databases

You can use networks to access information stored on other computers, print documents using shared printers, and synchronize the calendar between your computer and your Smartphone.

Network devices link together using a variety of connections:

- Copper cabling – Uses electrical signals to transmit data between devices
- Fiber-optic cabling – Uses glass or plastic wire, also called fiber, to carry information as light pulses
- Wireless connection – Uses radio signals, infrared technology (laser), or satellite transmissions

Refer to **Figure** in online course

8.1.2 Explain the benefits of networking

The benefits of networking computers and other devices include lower costs and increased productivity. With networks, resources can be shared, which results in less duplication and corruption of data.

Fewer Peripherals Needed

Figure 1 shows that many devices can be connected on a network. Each computer on the network does not need to have its own printer, scanner, or backup device. Multiple printers can be set up in a central location and shared among the network users. All network users send print jobs to a central print server that manages the print requests. The print server can distribute print jobs over multiple printers, or queue jobs that require a specific printer.

Increased Communication Capabilities

Networks provide several different collaboration tools that can be used to communicate between network users. Online collaboration tools include e-mail, forums and chats, voice and video, and instant messaging. With these tools, users can communicate with friends, family, and colleagues.

Avoid File Duplication and Corruption

A server manages network resources. Servers store data and share it with users on a network. Confidential or sensitive data can be protected and shared with the users who have permission to access that data. Document tracking software can be used to prevent users from overwriting files, or changing files that others are accessing at the same time.

Lower Cost Licensing

Application licensing can be expensive for individual computers. Many software vendors offer site licenses for networks, which can dramatically reduce the cost of software. The site license allows a group of people or an entire organization to use the application for a single fee.

Centralized Administration

Centralized administration reduces the number of people needed to manage the devices and data on the network, reducing time and cost to the company. Individual network users do not need to manage their own data and devices. One administrator can control the data, devices, and permissions of users on the network. Backing up data is easier because the data is stored in a central location.

Conserve Resources

Data processing can be distributed across many computers to prevent one computer from becoming overloaded with processing tasks.

Refer to **Interactive Graphic** in online course.

Refer to **Figure** in online course

8.2 Describe types of networks

Data networks continue to evolve in complexity, use, and design. To communicate about networks, different types of networks are given different descriptive names. A computer network is identified by the following specific characteristics:

- The area it serves
- How the data is stored
- How the resources are managed
- How the network is organized
- The type of networking devices used
- The type of media used to connect the devices

After completing this section, you will meet these objectives:

- Describe a LAN.
- Describe a WAN.
- Describe a WLAN.
- Explain peer-to-peer networks.
- Explain client/server networks.

Refer to **Figure** in online course

8.2.1 Describe a LAN

Local Area Network (LAN) refers to a group of interconnected devices that is under the same administrative control. In the past, LANs were considered to be small networks that existed in a single physical location. Àlthough LANs can be as small as a single local network installed in a home or small office, over time, the definition of LANs has evolved to include interconnected local networks consisting of many hundreds of devices, installed in multiple buildings and locations.

The important thing to remember is that all of the local networks within a LAN are under one administrative control group that governs the security and access control policies that are in force on the network. In this context, the word "Local" in Local Area Network refers to local consistent control rather than being physically close to each other. Devices in a LAN may be physically close, but it is not a requirement.

Refer to **Figure** in online course

8.2.2 Describe a WAN

Wide Area Networks (WANs) are networks that connect LANs in geographically separated locations. The most common example of a WAN is the Internet. The Internet is a large WAN that is composed of millions of interconnected LANs. Telecommunications service providers (TSP) are used to interconnect these LANs at different locations.

Refer to **Figure** in online course

8.2.3 Describe a WLAN

In a traditional LAN, devices are connected together using copper cabling. In some environments, installing copper cabling may not be practical, desirable, or even possible. In these situations, wireless devices are used to transmit and receive data using radio waves. These networks are called wireless LANs, or WLANs. As with LANs, on a WLAN you can share resources, such as files and printers, and access the Internet.

In a WLAN, wireless devices connect to access points within a specified area. Access points are typically connected to the network using copper cabling. Instead of providing copper cabling to every network host, only the wireless access point is connected to the network with copper cabling. The range (radius of coverage) for typical WLAN systems varies from under 30m indoors to much greater distances outdoors, depending on the technology used.

Refer to **Interactive Graphic** in online course.

Refer to **Figure** in online course

8.2.4 Explain peer-to-peer networks

In a peer-to-peer network there are no dedicated servers or hierarchy among the computers. In this type of network, each device has equivalent capabilities and responsibilities. Individual users are responsible for their own resources and can decide which data and devices to share. Because individual users are responsible for the resources on their own computers, there is no central point of control or administration in the network.

Peer-to-peer networks work best in environments with ten or fewer computers. Because individual users are in control of their own computers, there is no need to hire a dedicated network administrator.

Peer-to-peer networks have several disadvantages:

- There is no centralized network administration which makes it difficult to determine who controls resources on the network.
- There is no centralized security. Each computer must use separate security measures for data protection.
- The network becomes more complex and difficult to manage as the number of computers on the network increases.
- There may be no centralized data storage. Separate data backups must be maintained. This responsibility falls on the individual users.

Peer-to-peer networks still exist inside larger networks today. Even on a large client network, users can still share resources directly with other users without using a network server. In your home, if you have more than one computer, you can set up a peer-to-peer network. You can share files with other computers, send messages between computers, and print documents to a shared printer.

Refer to **Figure** in online course

8.2.5 Explain client/server networks

In a client/server network, the client requests information or services from the server. The server provides the requested information or service to the client. Servers on a client/server network commonly perform some of the processing work for client machines; for example, sorting through a database before delivering only the records requested by the client.

One example of a client/server network is a corporate environment in which employees use a company e-mail server to send, receive, and store e-mail. The e-mail client on an employee computer issues a request to the e-mail server for any unread e-mail. The server responds by sending the requested e-mail to the client.

In a client/server model, the servers are maintained by network administrators. Data backups and security measures are implemented by the network administrator. The network administrator also controls user access to the network resources. All of the data on the network is stored on a centralized file server. Shared printers on the network are managed by a centralized print server. Network users with the proper permissions can access both the data and shared printers. Each user must provide an authorized username and password to gain access to network resources that they are permitted to use.

For data protection, an administrator performs a routine backup of all the files on the servers. If a computer crashes, or data is lost, the administrator can easily recover the data from a recent backup.

Refer to **Figure** in online course

8.3 Describe basic networking concepts and technologies

As a computer technician, you will be required to configure and troubleshoot computers on a network. To effectively configure a computer on the network, you should understand IP addressing, protocols, and other network concepts.

After completing this section, you will meet these objectives:

- Explain bandwidth and data transmission.
- Describe IP addressing.
- Define DHCP.
- Describe Internet protocols and applications.
- Define ICMP.

Refer to **Figure** in online course

8.3.1 Explain bandwidth and data transmission

Bandwidth is the amount of data that can be transmitted within a fixed time period. When data is sent over a computer network, it is broken up into small chunks called packets. Each packet contains headers. A header is information added to each packet that contains the source and destination of the packet. A header also contains information that describes how to put all of the packets back together again at the destination. The size of the bandwidth determines the amount of information that can be transmitted.

Bandwidth is measured in bits per second and is usually denoted by any of the following units of measure:

- bps – bits per second
- kbps – kilobits per second
- Mbps – megabits per second

Note

One byte is equal to 8 bits, and is abbreviated with a capital B. One MBps is approximately 8 Mbps.

Figure 1 shows how bandwidth on a network can be compared to a highway. In the highway example, the cars and trucks represent the data. The number of lanes on the highway represents the amount of cars that could travel on the highway at the same time. An eight-lane highway can handle four times the number of cars that a two-lane highway can hold.

The data that is transmitted over the network can flow using one of three modes: simplex, half-duplex, or full-duplex.

Simplex

Simplex, also called unidirectional, is a single, one-way transmission. An example of simplex transmission is the signal that is sent from a TV station to your home TV.

Half-Duplex

When data flows in one direction at a time, it is known as half-duplex. With half-duplex, the channel of communications allows alternating transmission in two directions, but not in both directions simultaneously. Two-way radios, such as police or emergency communications mobile radios, work with half-duplex transmissions. When you press the button on the microphone to transmit, you cannot hear the person on the other end. If people at both ends try to talk at the same time, neither transmission gets through.

Full-Duplex

When data flows in both directions at the same time, it is known as full-duplex. Although the data flows in both directions, the bandwidth is measured in only one direction. A network cable with 100 Mbps in full-duplex mode has a bandwidth of 100 Mbps.

A telephone conversation is an example of full-duplex communication. Both people can talk and be heard at the same time.

Full-duplex networking technology increases network performance because data can be sent and received at the same time. Broadband technology allows multiple signals to travel on the same wire simultaneously. Broadband technologies, such as digital subscriber line (DSL) and cable, operate in full-duplex mode. With a DSL connection, for example, users can download data to the computer and talk on the telephone at the same time.

Refer to **Figure** in online course

8.3.2 Describe IP addressing

An IP address is a number that is used to identify a device on the network. Each device on a network must have a unique IP address to communicate with other network devices. As noted earlier, a host is a device which sends or receives information on the network. Network devices are devices that move data across the network including hubs, switches, and routers. On a LAN, each host and network device must have an IP address within the same network to be able to communicate with each other.

A person's name and fingerprints usually do not change. They provide a label or address for the physical aspect of the person – the body. A person's mailing address, on the other hand, relates to where the person lives or picks up mail. This address can change. On a host, the Media Access Control (MAC) address (explained below) is assigned to the host NIC and is known as the physical address. The physical address remains the same regardless of where the host is placed on the network in the same way that fingerprints remain with the person regardless of where the person goes.

The IP address is similar to the mailing address of a person. It is known as a logical address because it is logically assigned based on the host location. The IP address, or network address, is based on the local network and is assigned to each host by a network administrator. This process is similar to the local government assigning a street address based on the logical description of the city or village and neighborhood.

An IP address consists of a series of 32 binary bits (ones and zeros). It is very difficult for humans to read a binary IP address. For this reason, the 32 bits are grouped into four 8-bit bytes called octets. An IP address, even in this grouped format, is hard for humans to read, write and remember; therefore, each octet is presented as its decimal value, separated by a decimal point or period. This format is referred to as dotted-decimal notation. When a host is configured with an IP address, it is entered as a dotted decimal number, such as 192.168.1.5. Imagine if you had to enter the 32-bit binary equivalent of this: 11000000101010000000000100000101. If just one bit were mistyped, the address would be different and the host may not be able to communicate on the network.

The logical 32-bit IP address is hierarchical and is composed of two parts. The first part identifies the network and the second part identifies a host on that network. Both parts are required in an IP address. As an example, if a host has IP address 192.168.18.57, the first three octets, 192.168.18, identify the network portion of the address, and the last octet, 57 identifies the host. This is known as hierarchical addressing, because the network portion indicates the network on which each unique host address is located. Routers only need to know how to reach each network and not the location of each individual host.

IP addresses are divided into the following five classes:

- Class A – Large networks, implemented by large companies and some countries
- Class B – Medium-sized networks, implemented by universities
- Class C – Small networks, implemented by ISP for customer subscriptions
- Class D – Special use for multicasting
- Class E – Used for experimental testing

Subnet Mask

The subnet mask is used to indicate the network portion of an IP address. Like the IP address, the subnet mask is a dotted decimal number. Usually all hosts within a LAN use the same subnet mask. Figure 1 shows default subnet masks for usable IP addresses that are mapped to the first three classes of IP addresses:

- 255.0.0.0 – Class A, which indicates that the first octet of the IP address is the network portion
- 255.255.0.0 – Class B, which indicates that the first two octets of the IP address is the network portion
- 255.255.255.0 – Class C, which indicates that the first three octets of the IP address is the network portion

If an organization owns one Class B network but needs to provide IP addresses for four LANs, the organization would have to subdivide the Class B address into four smaller parts. Subnetting is a logical division of a network. It provides the means to divide a network, and the subnet mask specifies how it is subdivided. An experienced network administrator typically performs subnetting. After the subnetting scheme has been created, the proper IP addresses and subnet masks can be configured on the hosts in the four LANs. These skills are taught in the Cisco Networking Academy courses related to CCNA level networking skills.

Manual Configuration

In a network with a small number of hosts, it is easy to manually configure each device with the proper IP address. A network administrator who understands IP addressing should assign the addresses and should know how to choose a valid address for a particular network. The IP address that is entered is unique for each host within the same network or subnet.

To manually enter an IP address on a host, go to the TCP/IP settings in the Properties window for the Network Interface Card (NIC). The NIC is the hardware that enables a computer to connect to a network. It has an address called the Media Access Control (MAC) address. Whereas the IP address is a logical address that is defined by the network administrator, a MAC address is "burned-in" or permanently programmed into the NIC when it is manufactured. The IP address of a NIC can be changed, but the MAC address never changes.

The main difference between an IP address and a MAC address is that the MAC address is used to deliver frames on the LAN, while an IP address is used to transport frames outside the LAN. A frame is a data packet, along with address information added to the beginning and end of the packet before transmission over the network. Once a frame is delivered to the destination LAN, the MAC address is used to deliver the frame to the end host on that LAN.

If more than a few computers comprise the LAN, manually configuring IP addresses for every host on the network can be time-consuming and prone to errors. In this case, the use of a Dynamic Host Configuration Protocol (DHCP) server would automatically assign IP addresses and greatly simplify the addressing process.

Refer to **Worksheet** for this chapter

IP Address Class

Identify the IP address class for an IP address

8.3.3 Define DHCP

Refer to **Figure** in online course

Dynamic Host Configuration Protocol (DHCP) is a software utility used to dynamically assign IP addresses to network devices. This dynamic process eliminates the need for manually assigning IP addresses. A DHCP server can be set up and the hosts can be configured to automatically obtain an IP address. When a computer is set to obtain an IP address automatically, all of the other IP addressing configuration boxes are dimmed, as shown in Figure 1. The server maintains a list of IP addresses to assign, and manages the process so that every device on the network receives a unique IP address. Each address is held for a predetermined amount of time. When the time expires, the DHCP server can use this address for any computer that joins the network.

This is the IP address information that a DHCP server can assign to hosts:

- IP address
- Subnet mask
- Default gateway
- Optional values, such as a Domain Name System (DNS) server address

The DHCP server receives a request from a host. The server then selects IP address information from a set of predefined addresses that are stored in a database. Once the IP address information is selected, the DHCP server offers these values to the requesting host on the network. If the host accepts the offer, the DHCP server leases the IP address for a specific period of time.

Using a DHCP server simplifies the administration of a network because the software keeps track of IP addresses. Automatically configuring TCP/IP also reduces the possibility of assigning duplicate or invalid IP addresses. Before a computer on the network can take advantage of the DHCP server services, the computer must be able to identify the server on the local network. A computer can be configured to accept an IP address from a DHCP server by clicking the "Obtain an IP address automatically" option in the NIC configuration window, as shown in Figure 2.

If your computer cannot communicate with the DHCP server to obtain an IP address, the Windows operating system will automatically assign a private IP address. If your computer is assigned an IP address in the range of 169.254.0.0 to 169.254.255.255, your computer will only be able to communicate with other computers in the same range. An example of when these private addresses would be useful is in a classroom lab where you want to prevent access outside of your network. This operating system feature is called Automatic Private IP Addressing (APIPA). APIPA will continually request an IP address from a DHCP server for your computer.

Refer to **Figure** in online course

8.3.4 Describe Internet protocols and applications

A protocol is a set of rules. Internet protocols are sets of rules governing communication within and between computers on a network. Protocol specifications define the format of the messages that are exchanged. A letter sent through the postal system also uses protocols. Part of the protocol specifies the position on the envelope that the delivery address needs to be written. If the delivery address is written in the wrong place, the letter cannot be delivered.

Timing is crucial to network operation. Protocols require messages to arrive within certain time intervals so that computers will not wait indefinitely for messages that may have been lost. Therefore, systems maintain one or more timers during transmission of data. Protocols also initiate alternative actions if the network does not meet the timing rules. Many protocols consist of a suite of other protocols that are stacked in layers. These layers depend on the operation of the other layers in the suite to function properly.

These are the main functions of protocols:

- Identifying errors
- Compressing the data
- Deciding how data is to be sent
- Addressing data
- Deciding how to announce sent and received data

Although there are many other protocols, Figure 1 summarizes some of the more common protocols used on networks and the Internet.

To understand how networks and the Internet work, you must be familiar with the commonly used protocols. These protocols are used to browse the web, send and receive e-mail, and transfer data files. You will encounter other protocols as your experience in IT grows, but they are not used as often as the common protocols described here.

In Figure 2, click the protocol names to learn more about each one.

The more you understand about each of these protocols, the more you will understand how networks and the Internet work.

Refer to **Interactive Graphic** in online course.

Refer to **Figure** in online course

8.3.5 Define ICMP

Internet Control Message Protocol (ICMP) is used by devices on a network to send control and error messages to computers and servers. There are several different uses for ICMP, such as announcing network errors, announcing network congestion, and troubleshooting.

Packet internet groper (ping) is commonly used to test connections between computers. Ping is a simple but highly useful command line utility used to determine whether a specific IP address is accessible. You can ping the IP address to test IP connectivity. Ping works by sending an ICMP echo request to a destination computer or other network device. The receiving device then sends back an ICMP echo reply message to confirm connectivity.

Ping is a troubleshooting tool used to determine basic connectivity. The command line switches that can be used with the ping command are shown in Figure 1. Four ICMP echo requests (pings) are sent to the destination computer. If it is reachable, the destination computer responds with four ICMP echo replies. The percentage of successful replies can help you to determine the reliability and accessibility of the destination computer.

You can also use ping to find the IP address of a host when the name is known. If you ping the name of a website, for example, cisco.com, as shown in Figure 2, the IP address of the server displays.

Other ICMP messages are used to report undelivered packets, data on an IP network that includes source and destination IP addresses, and whether a device is too busy to handle the packet. Data, in the form of a packet, arrives at a router, which is a networking device that forwards data packets across networks toward their destinations. If the router does not know where to send the packet, the router deletes it. The router then sends an ICMP message back to the sending computer informing it that the data was deleted. When a router becomes very busy, it may send a different ICMP message to the sending computer indicating that it should slow down because there is congestion on the network.

Refer to **Figure** in online course

8.4 Describe the physical components of a network

There are many devices that can be used in a network to provide connectivity. The device you use will depend on how many devices you are connecting, the type of connections that they use, and the speed at which the devices operate. These are the most common devices on a network:

- Computers
- Hubs
- Switches
- Routers
- Wireless access points

The physical components of a network are needed to move data between these devices. The characteristics of the media determine where and how the components are used. These are the most common media used on networks:

- Twisted-pair
- Fiber-optic cabling
- Radio waves

After completing this section, you will meet these objectives:

- Identify names, purposes, and characteristics of network devices.
- Identify names, purposes, and characteristics of common network cables.

Refer to **Figure** in online course

8.4.1 Identify names, purposes, and characteristics of network devices

To make data transmission more extensible and efficient than a simple peer-to-peer network, network designers use specialized network devices, such as hubs, switches, routers, and wireless access points, to send data between devices.

Hubs

Hubs, shown in Figure 1, are devices that extend the range of a network by receiving data on one port, and then regenerating the data and sending it out to all other ports. This process means that all traffic from a device connected to the hub is sent to all the other devices connected to the hub every time the hub transmits data. This causes a great amount of network traffic. Hubs are also called concentrators, because they serve as a central connection point for a LAN.

Bridges and Switches

Files are broken up into small pieces of data, called packets, before they are transmitted over a network. This process allows for error checking and easier retransmission if the packet is lost or corrupted. Address information is added to the beginning and to the end of packets before they are transmitted. The packet, along with the address information, is called a frame.

LANs are often divided into sections called segments, similar to the way a company is divided into departments. The boundaries of segments can be defined using a bridge. A bridge is a device used to filter network traffic between LAN segments. Bridges keep a record of all the devices on each segment to which the bridge is connected. When the bridge receives a frame, the destination address is examined by the bridge to determine if the frame is to be sent to a different segment, or dropped. The bridge also helps to improve the flow of data by keeping frames confined to only the segment to which the frame belongs.

Switches, shown in Figure 2, are sometimes called multiport bridges. A typical bridge may have just two ports, linking two segments of the same network. A switch has several ports, depending on how many network segments are to be linked. A switch is a more sophisticated device than a bridge. A switch maintains a table of the MAC addresses for computers that are connected to each port. When a frame arrives at a port, the switch compares the address information in the frame to its MAC address table. The switch then determines which port to use to forward the frame.

Routers

Whereas a switch connects segments of a network, routers, shown in Figure 3, are devices that connect entire networks to each other. Switches use MAC addresses to forward a frame within a single network. Routers use IP addresses to forward frames to other networks. A router can be a computer with special network software installed, or a router can be a device built by network equipment manufacturers. Routers contain tables of IP addresses along with optimal destination routes to other networks.

Wireless Access Points

Wireless access points, shown in Figure 4, provide network access to wireless devices such as laptops and PDAs. The wireless access point uses radio waves to communicate with radios in computers, PDAs, and other wireless access points. An access point has limited range of coverage. Large networks require several access points to provide adequate wireless coverage.

Multipurpose Devices

There are network devices that perform more than one function. It is more convenient to purchase and configure one device that serves all of your needs than to purchase a separate device for each function. This is especially true for the home user. In your home, you would purchase a multipurpose device instead of a switch, a router, and a wireless access point. The Linksys 300N, shown in Figure 5, is an example of a multipurpose device.

Refer to **Figure** in online course

8.4.2 Identify names, purposes, and characteristics of common network cables

Until recently, cables were the only medium used to connect devices on networks. A wide variety of networking cables are available. Coaxial and twisted-pair cables use copper to transmit data. Fiber-optic cables use glass or plastic to transmit data. These cables differ in bandwidth, size, and cost. You need to know what type of cable to use in different situations so that you are able to install the correct cables for the job. You will also need to be able to troubleshoot and repair problems that you encounter.

Twisted-Pair

Twisted-pair is a type of copper cabling that is used for telephone communications and most Ethernet networks. A pair of wires forms a circuit that can transmit data. The pair is twisted to provide protection against crosstalk, which is the noise generated by adjacent pairs of wires in the cable. Pairs of copper wires are encased in color-coded plastic insulation and twisted together. An outer jacket protects the bundles of twisted pairs.

When electricity flows through a copper wire, a magnetic field is created around the wire. A circuit has two wires, and in a circuit, the two wires have oppositely-charged magnetic fields. When the two wires of the circuit are next to each other, the magnetic fields cancel each other out. This is called the cancellation effect. Without the cancellation effect, your network communications become slow due to the interference caused by the magnetic fields.

There are two basic types of twisted-pair cables:

- ***Unshielded twisted-pair (UTP)*** – Cable that has two or four pairs of wires. This type of cable relies solely on the cancellation effect produced by the twisted-wire pairs that limits signal degradation caused by electromagnetic interface (EMI) and radio frequency interference (RFI). UTP is the most commonly used cabling in networks. UTP cables have a range of 328 feet (100 m).
- ***Shielded twisted-pair (STP)*** – Each pair of wires is wrapped in metallic foil to better shield the wires from noise. Four pairs of wires are then wrapped in an overall metallic braid or foil. STP reduces electrical noise from within the cable. It also reduces EMI and RFI from outside the cable.

Although STP prevents interference better than UTP, STP is more expensive because of extra shielding, and more difficult to install because of the thickness. In addition, the metallic shielding must be grounded at both ends. If improperly grounded, the shield acts like an antenna picking up unwanted signals. STP is primarily used outside North America.

Category Rating

UTP comes in several categories that are based on two factors:

- The number of wires in the cable
- The number of twists in those wires

Category 3 is the wiring used for telephone systems and for Ethernet LAN at 10 Mbps. Category 3 has four pairs of wires.

Category 5 and Category 5e have four pairs of wires with a transmission rate of 100 Mbps. Category 5 and 5e are the most common network cables used. Category 5e has more twists per foot than Category 5 wiring. These extra twists further prevent interference from outside sources and the other wires within the cable.

Some Category 6 cables use a plastic divider to separate the pairs of wires, which prevents interference. The pairs also have more twists than Category 5e cable. A twisted pair cable is shown in Figure 1.

Coaxial Cable

Coaxial cable is a copper-cored cable surrounded by a heavy shielding. Coaxial cable is used to connect computers in a network. There are several types of coaxial cable:

- ***Thicknet or 10BASE5 –*** Coax cable that was used in networks and operated at 10 megabits per second with a maximum length of 500 meters
- ***Thinnet 10BASE2 –*** Coax cable that was used in networks and operated at 10 megabits per second with a maximum length of 185 meters
- ***RG-59 –*** Most commonly used for cable television in the U.S.
- ***RG-6 –*** Higher quality cable than RG-59, with more bandwidth and less susceptibility to interference

A coaxial cable is shown in Figure 2.

Fiber-Optic Cable

An optical fiber is a glass or plastic conductor that transmits information using light. Fiber-optic cable, shown in Figure 3, has one or more optical fibers enclosed in a sheath or jacket. Because it is made of glass, fiber-optic cable is not affected by electromagnetic interference or radio frequency interference. All signals are converted to light pulses to enter the cable, and converted back into electrical signals when they leave it. This means that fiber-optic cable can deliver signals that are clearer, can go farther, and have greater bandwidth than cable made of copper or other metals.

Fiber-optic cable can reach distances of several miles or kilometers before the signal needs to be regenerated. Fiber-optic cable is usually more expensive to use than copper cable and the connectors are more costly and harder to assemble. Common connectors for fiber-optic networks are SC, ST, and LC. These three types of fiber-optic connectors are half-duplex, which allows data to flow in only one direction. Therefore, two cables are needed.

These are the two types of glass fiber-optic cable:

- ***Multimode –*** Cable that has a thicker core than single-mode cable. It is easier to make, can use simpler light sources (LEDs), and works well over distances of a few kilometers or less.
- ***Single-mode –*** Cable that has a very thin core. It is harder to make, uses lasers as a light source, and can transmit signals dozens of kilometers with ease.

Refer to **Figure** in online course

8.5 Describe LAN topologies and architectures

Most of the computers that you work on will be part of a network. Topologies and architectures are building blocks for designing a computer network. While you may not build a computer network, you need to understand how they are designed in order to work on computers that are part of a network.

There are two types of LAN topologies: physical and logical. A physical topology, shown in Figure 1, is the physical layout of the components on the network. A logical topology, shown in Figure 2, determines how the hosts communicate across a medium, such as a cable or the airwaves. Topologies are commonly represented as network diagrams.

A LAN architecture is built around a topology. LAN architecture comprises all the components that make up the structure of a communications system. These components include the hardware, software, protocols, and sequence of operations.

After completing this section, you will meet these objectives:

- Describe LAN topologies.
- Describe LAN architectures.

Refer to **Figure** in online course

8.5.1 Describe LAN topologies

A physical topology defines the way in which computers, printers, and other devices are connected to a network. A logical topology describes how the hosts accesses the medium and communicates on the network. The type of topology determines the capabilities of the network, such as ease of setup, speed, and cable lengths.

Physical Topologies

Figure 1 shows the common LAN physical topologies:

- Bus
- Ring
- Star
- Hierarchical or Extended Star
- Mesh

Bus Topology

In the bus topology, each computer connects to a common cable. The cable connects one computer to the next, like a bus line going through a city. The cable has a small cap installed at the end, called a terminator. The terminator prevents signals from bouncing back and causing network errors.

Ring Topology

In a ring topology, hosts are connected in a physical ring or circle. Because the ring topology has no beginning or end, the cable does not need to be terminated. A specially-formatted frame, called a token, travels around the ring, stopping at each host. If a host wants to transmit data, the host adds the data and the destination address to the frame. The frame then continues around the ring until the frame stops at the host with the destination address. The destination host takes the data out of the frame.

Star Topology

The star topology has a central connection point, which is normally a device such as a hub, switch, or router. Each host on a network has a cable segment that attaches the host directly to the central connection point. The advantage of a star topology is that it is easy to troubleshoot. Each host is connected to the central device with its own wire. If there is a problem with that cable, only that host is affected. The rest of the network remains operational.

Hierarchical or Extended Star Topology

A hierarchical or extended star topology is a star network with an additional networking device connected to the main networking device. Typically, a network cable connects to one hub, and then several other hubs connect to the first hub. Larger networks, such as those of corporations or universities, use the hierarchical star topology.

Mesh Topology

The mesh topology connects all devices to each other. When every device is connected to every other device, a failure of any cable will not affect the network. The mesh topology is used in WANs that interconnect LANs.

Logical Topologies

The two most common types of logical topologies are broadcast and token passing.

In a broadcast topology, each host addresses either data to a particular host or to all hosts connected on a network. There is no order that the hosts must follow to use the network – it is first come, first served for transmitting data on the network.

Token passing controls network access by passing an electronic token sequentially to each host. When a host receives the token, it can send data on the network. If the host has no data to send, it passes the token to the next host and the process repeats itself.

Refer to **Figure** in online course

8.5.2 Describe LAN architectures

LAN architecture describes both the physical and logical topologies used in a network. Figure 1 shows the three most common LAN architectures.

Ethernet

The Ethernet architecture is based on the IEEE 802.3 standard. The IEEE 802.3 standard specifies that a network use the Carrier Sense Multiple Access with Collision Detection (CSMA/CD) access control method. In CSMA/CD, hosts access the network using the first come, first served broadcast topology method to transmit data.

Ethernet uses a logical bus or broadcast topology and either a bus or star physical topology. As networks expand, most Ethernet networks are implemented using an extended star or hierarchical star topology. Standard transfer rates are 10 Mbps and 100 Mbps, but new standards outline Gigabit Ethernet, which is capable of attaining speeds up to 1000 Mbps (1 Gbps).

Token Ring

IBM originally developed Token Ring as a reliable network architecture based on the token-passing access control method. Token Ring is often integrated with IBM mainframe systems. Token Ring is used with computers and mainframes.

Token Ring is an example of an architecture in which the physical topology is different from its logical topology. The Token Ring topology is referred to as a star-wired ring because the outer appearance of the network design is a star. The computers connect to a central hub, called a multistation access unit (MSAU). Inside the device, however, the wiring forms a circular data path, creating a logical ring. The logical ring is created by the token traveling out of an MSAU port to a computer. If the computer does not have any data to send, the token is sent back to the MSAU port and then out the next port to the next computer. This process continues for all computers and therefore resembles a physical ring.

FDDI

Fiber distributed data interface (FDDI) is a type of Token Ring network. The implementation and topology of FDDI differs from the IBM Token Ring LAN architecture. FDDI is often used to connect several buildings in an office complex or on a university campus.

FDDI runs on fiber-optic cable. FDDI combines high-speed performance with the advantages of the token-passing ring topology. FDDI runs at 100 Mbps on a dual-ring topology. The outer ring is called the primary ring and the inner ring is called the secondary ring.

Normally, traffic flows only on the primary ring. If the primary ring fails, the data automatically flows onto the secondary ring in the opposite direction.

An FDDI dual ring supports a maximum of 500 computers per ring. The total distance of each length of the cable ring is 62 miles (100 km). A repeater, which is a device that regenerates signals, is required every 1.2 miles (2 km). In recent years, many token ring networks have been replaced by faster Ethernet networks.

Refer to **Figure** in online course

8.6 Identify standards organizations

Several worldwide standards organizations are responsible for setting networking standards. Standards are used by manufacturers as a basis for developing technology, especially communications and networking technologies. Standardizing technology ensures that the devices you use will be compatible with other devices using the same technology. The standards groups create, examine, and update standards. These standards are applied to the development of technology to meet the demands for higher bandwidth, efficient communication, and reliable service.

Click each of the standards in Figure 1 to learn more information.

Refer to **Figure** in online course

8.7 Identify Ethernet standards

Ethernet protocols describe the rules that control how communication occurs on an Ethernet network. To ensure that all Ethernet devices are compatible with each other, the IEEE developed standards for manufacturers and programmers to follow when developing Ethernet devices.

After completing this section, you will meet these objectives:

- Explain cabled Ethernet standards.
- Explain wireless Ethernet standards.

Refer to **Figure** in online course

8.7.1 Explain cabled Ethernet standards

IEEE 802.3

The Ethernet architecture is based on the IEEE 802.3 standard. The IEEE 802.3 standard specifies that a network implement the CSMA/CD access control method.

In CSMA/CD, all end stations "listen" to the network wire for clearance to send data. This process is similar to waiting to hear a dial tone on a phone before dialing a number. When the end station detects that no other host is transmitting, the end station will attempt to send data. If no other station sends any data at the same time, this transmission will arrive at the destination computer with no problems. If another end station observed the same clear signal and transmitted at the same time, a collision will occur on the network media.

The first station that detects the collision, or the doubling of voltage, sends out a jam signal that tells all stations to stop transmitting and to run a backoff algorithm. A backoff algorithm calculates random times in which the end station will start to try network transmission again. This random time is typically in one or two milliseconds (ms), or thousandths of a second. This sequence occurs every time there is a collision on the network and can reduce Ethernet transmission by up to 40%.

Ethernet Technologies

The IEEE 802.3 standard defines several physical implementations that support Ethernet. Some of the common implementations are described here.

Ethernet

10BASE-T is an Ethernet technology that uses a star topology. 10BASE-T is a popular Ethernet architecture whose features are indicated in its name:

- The ten (10) represents a speed of 10 Mbps.
- BASE represents baseband transmission. In baseband transmission, the entire bandwidth of a cable is used for one type of signal.
- The T represents twisted-pair copper cabling.

Advantages of 10BASE-T:

- Installation of cable is inexpensive compared to fiber-optic installation.
- Cables are thin, flexible, and easier to install than coaxial cabling.
- Equipment and cables are easy to upgrade.

Disadvantages of 10BASE-T:

- The maximum length for a 10BASE-T segment is only 328 feet (100 m).
- Cables are susceptible to electromagnetic interference (EMI).

Fast Ethernet

The high bandwidth demands of many modern applications, such as live video conferencing and streaming audio, have created a need for higher data-transfer speeds. Many networks require more bandwidth than 10 Mbps Ethernet.

100BASE-TX is much faster than 10BASE-T and has a theoretical bandwidth of 100 Mbps.

Advantages of 100BASE-TX:

- At 100 Mbps, transfer rates of 100BASE-TX are ten times that of 10BASE-T.
- 100BASE-X uses twisted-pair cabling, which is inexpensive and easy to install.

Disadvantages of 100BASE-TX:

- The maximum length for a 100BASE-TX segment is only 328 feet (100 m).
- Cables are susceptible to electromagnetic interference (EMI).

1000BASE -T is commonly known as Gigabit Ethernet. Gigabit Ethernet is a LAN architecture.

Advantages of 1000BASE-T:

- The 1000BASE-T architecture supports data transfer rates of 1 Gbps. At 1 Gbps, it is ten times faster than Fast Ethernet, and 100 times faster than Ethernet. This increased speed makes it possible to implement bandwidth-intensive applications, such as live video.
- The 1000BASE-T architecture has interoperability with 10BASE-T and 100BASE-TX.

Disadvantages of 1000BASE-T:

- The maximum length for a 1000BASE-T segment is only 328 feet (100 m).
- It is susceptible to interference.
- Gigabit NICs and switches are expensive.
- Additional equipment is required.

10BASE-FL, 100BASE-FX, 1000BASE-SX and LX are fiber-optic Ethernet Technologies.

Refer to **Figure** in online course

8.7.2 Explain wireless Ethernet standards

IEEE 802.11 is the standard that specifies connectivity for wireless networks. IEEE 802.11, or Wi-Fi, refers to the collective group of standards – 802.11a, 802.11b, 802.11g, and 802.11n. These protocols specify the frequencies, speeds, and other capabilities of the different Wi-Fi standards.

802.11a

Devices conforming to the 802.11a standard allow WLANs to achieve data rates as high as 54 Mbps. IEEE 802.11a devices operate in the 5 GHz radio frequency range and within a maximum range of 150 feet (45.7 m).

802.11b

802.11b operates in the 2.4 GHz frequency range with a maximum theoretical data rate of 11 Mbps. These devices operate within a maximum range of 300 feet (91 m).

802.11g

IEEE 802.11g provides the same theoretical maximum speed as 802.11a, which is 54 Mbps, but operates in the same 2.4 GHz spectrum as 802.11b. Unlike 802.11a, 802.11g is backward-compatible with 802.11b. 802.11g also has a maximum range of 300 feet (91 m).

802.11n

802.11n is a newer wireless standard that has a theoretical bandwidth of 540 Mbps and operates in either the 2.4 GHz or 5 GHz frequency range with a maximum range of 984 feet (250 m).

Refer to **Figure** in online course

8.8 Explain OSI and TCP/IP data models

An architectural model is a common frame of reference for explaining Internet communications and developing communication protocols. It separates the functions of protocols into manageable layers. Each layer performs a specific function in the process of communicating over a network.

The TCP/IP model was created by researchers in the U.S. Department of Defense (DoD). The TCP/IP model is a tool used to help explain the TCP/IP suite of protocols, which is the dominant standard for transporting data across networks. This model has four layers, as shown in Figure 1.

In the early 1980s, the International Standards Organization (ISO) developed the Open Systems Interconnect (OSI) model, which was defined in ISO standard 7498-1, to standardize the way devices communicate on a network. This model has seven layers, as shown in Figure 1. This model was a major step forward toward ensuring that there would be interoperability between network devices.

After completing this section, you will meet these objectives:

- Define the TCP/IP model.
- Define the OSI model.
- Compare OSI and TCP/IP.

Refer to **Figure** in online course

8.8.1 Define the TCP/IP model

The TCP/IP reference model provides a common frame of reference for the development of the protocols used on the Internet. It consists of layers that perform functions necessary to prepare data for transmission over a network. The chart in Figure 1 shows the four layers of the TCP/IP model.

A message begins at the top layer, the Application layer and moves down the TCP/IP layers to the bottom layer, the Network Access layer. Header information is added to the message as it moves down through each layer and is then transmitted. After reaching the destination, the message travels back up through each layer of the TCP/IP model. The header information that was added to the message is stripped away as the message moves up through the layers toward its destination.

Application Protocols

Application layer protocols provide network services to user applications such as web browsers and e-mail programs. Explore some of the more common Internet protocols in Figure 2, the Application layer, to learn more about the protocols that operate in this layer.

Transport Protocols

Transport layer protocols provide end-to-end management of the data. One of the functions of these protocols is to divide the data into manageable segments for easier transport across the network. Explore each of the protocols in Figure 3, the Transport layer, to learn more about the protocols that operate in this layer.

Internet Protocols

Internet layer protocols operate in the third layer from the top in the TCP/IP model. These protocols are used to provide connectivity between hosts in the network. Explore each of the protocols in Figure 4, the Internet layer, to learn more about the protocols that operate in this layer.

Refer to **Figure** in online course

Network Access Protocols

Network Access layer protocols describe the standards that hosts use to access the physical media. The IEEE 802.3 Ethernet standards and technologies, such as CSMA/CD and 10BASE-T are defined in this layer.

8.8.2 Define the OSI model

The OSI model is an industry standard framework that is used to divide network communications into seven distinct layers. Although other models exist, most network vendors today build their products using this framework.

A system that implements protocol behavior consisting of a series of these layers is known as a protocol stack. Protocol stacks can be implemented either in hardware or software, or a combination of both. Typically, only the lower layers are implemented in hardware, and the higher layers are implemented in software.

Each layer is responsible for part of the processing to prepare data for transmission on the network. The chart in Figure 1 shows what each layer of the OSI model does.

In the OSI model, when data is transferred, it is said to virtually travel down the OSI model layers of the sending computer, and up the OSI model layers of the receiving computer.

When a user wants to send data, such as an e-mail, the encapsulation process starts at the Application layer. The Application layer is responsible for providing network access to applications. Information flows through the top three layers and is considered to be data when it gets down to the Transport layer.

At the Transport layer, the data is broken down into more manageable segments, or Transport layer protocol data units (PDUs), for orderly transport across the network. A PDU describes data as it moves from one layer of the OSI model to another. The Transport layer PDU also contains information such as port numbers, sequence numbers, and acknowledgement numbers, which is used for reliable data transport.

At the Network layer, each segment from the Transport layer becomes a packet. The packet contains logical addressing and other layer-3 control information.

At the Data Link layer, each packet from the Network layer becomes a frame. The frame contains physical address and error correction information.

At the Physical layer, the frame becomes bits. These bits are transmitted one at a time across the network medium.

At the receiving computer, the de-encapsulation process reverses the process of encapsulation. The bits arrive at the Physical layer of the OSI model of the receiving computer. The process of virtually traveling up the OSI model of the receiving computer will bring the data to the Application layer, where an e-mail program will display the e-mail.

Note

Mnemonics can help you remember the seven layers of the OSI. Some examples include: "All People Seem To Need Data Processing" and "Please Do Not Throw Sausage Pizza Away".

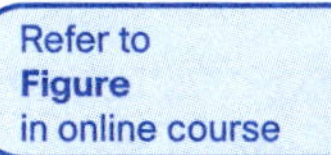

8.8.3 Compare OSI and TCP/IP

The OSI model and the TCP/IP model are both reference models used to describe the data communication process. The TCP/IP model is used specifically for the TCP/IP suite of protocols and the OSI model is used for development of standard communication for equipment and applications from different vendors.

The TCP/IP model performs the same process as the OSI model, but uses four layers instead of seven. The chart in Figure 1 shows how the layers of the two models compare.

Refer to **Interactive Graphic** in online course.

8.9 Describe how to configure a NIC and a modem

Refer to **Figure** in online course

A network interface card (NIC) is required to connect to the Internet. The NIC may come preinstalled or you may have to purchase one on your own. In rare cases, you may need to update the driver. You can use the driver disc that comes with the motherboard or adapter card, or you can supply a driver that you downloaded from the manufacturer.

After the NIC and the driver have been installed, you can connect the computer to the network.

In addition to installing a NIC, you may also need to install a modem to connect to the Internet.

After completing this section, you will meet these objectives:

- Install or update a NIC driver.
- Attach the computer to an existing network.
- Describe the installation of a modem.

Refer to **Figure** in online course

8.9.1 Install or update a NIC driver

Sometimes, a manufacturer will publish new driver software for a NIC. A new driver may enhance the functionality of the NIC, or it may be needed for operating system compatibility.

When installing a new driver, be sure to disable virus protection software so that none of the files is incorrectly installed. Some virus scanners detect a driver update as a possible virus attack. Also, only one driver should be installed at a time; otherwise, some updating processes may conflict updating processes may conflict.

A best practice is to close all applications that are running so that they are not using any files associated with the driver update. Before updating a driver, you should visit the manufacturer's website. In many cases, you can download a self-extracting executable driver file that will automatically install or update the driver. Alternatively, you can click the **Update Driver** button in the toolbar of the Device Manager.

The "+" next to the Network adapters category allows you to expand the category and show the network adapters installed in your system. To view and change the properties of the adapter, or update the driver, double-click the adapter. In the adapter properties window select the **Driver** tab.

After the update has been completed, it is a good idea to reboot the computer even if you do not receive a message telling you to reboot. Rebooting the computer will ensure that the installation has gone as planned and that the new driver is working properly. When installing multiple drivers, reboot the computer between each update to make sure that there are no conflicts. This step takes extra time but will ensure a clean installation of the driver.

Uninstall a NIC Driver

If a new NIC driver does not perform as expected after it has been installed, the driver can be uninstalled, or rolled back, to the previous driver. Double-click the adapter in the Device Manager. In the Adapter Properties window, select the **Driver** tab and click **Roll Back Driver**. If there was no driver installed before the update, this option will not be available. In that case, you will need to find a driver for the device and install it manually if the operating system could not find a suitable driver for the NIC.

Refer to **Worksheet** for this chapter

Internet Search for NIC Drivers

Research NIC drivers

Refer to **Figure** in online course

8.9.2 Attach computer to existing network

Now that the NIC drivers are installed, you are ready to connect to the network. Plug a network cable, also called an Ethernet patch or straight-through cable, into the network port on the computer. Plug the other end into the network device or wall jack.

After connecting the network cable, look at the LEDs, or link lights, next to the Ethernet port on the NIC to see if there is any activity. Figure 1 shows network activity on a NIC. If there is no activity, this may indicate a faulty cable, a faulty hub port, or even a faulty NIC. You may have to replace one or more of these devices to correct the problem.

After you have confirmed that the computer is connected to the network and the link lights on the NIC indicate a working connection, the computer will need an IP address. Most networks are set up so that the computer will receive an IP address automatically from a local DHCP server. If the computer does not have an IP address, you will need to enter a unique IP address in the TCP/IP properties of the NIC.

Every NIC must be configured with the following information:

- ***Protocols*** **–** The same protocol must be implemented between any two computers that communicate on the same network.
- ***IP address*** **–** This address is configurable and must be unique to each device. The IP address can be manually configured or automatically assigned by DHCP.
- ***MAC address*** **–** Each device has a unique MAC address. The MAC address is assigned by the manufacturer and cannot be changed.

After the computer is connected to the network, you should test connectivity with the **ping** command. Use the **ipconfig** command, shown in Figure 2, to find out what your IP address is. Ping your own IP address to make sure that your NIC is working properly. After you have determined that your NIC is working, ping your default gateway or another computer on your network, as shown in Figure 3. A default gateway allows a host to communicate outside of your network. If you have an Internet connection, ping a popular website, such as www.cisco.com. If you can ping an Internet site or another computer on your network successfully, everything is working properly with your connection. If you cannot ping one of these, you will need to begin troubleshooting the connection.

Refer to **Lab Activity** for this chapter

DHCP Configuration for Ethernet NIC

Configure NIC to use DHCP from 300N

Refer to **Figure** in online course

8.9.3 Describe the installation of a modem

A modem is an electronic device that transfers data between one computer and another using analog signals over a telephone line. Examples of modems are shown in Figure 1. The modem converts digital data to analog signals for transmission. The modem at the receiving end reconverts the analog signals back to digital data to be interpreted by the computer. The process of converting analog signals to digital and back again is called modulation/demodulation. Modem-based transmission is very accurate, despite the fact that telephone lines can be noisy due to clicks, static, and other problems.

An internal modem plugs into an expansion slot on the motherboard. To configure a modem, jumpers may have to be set to select the IRQ and I/O addresses. No configuration is needed for a plug-and-play modem, which can only be installed on a motherboard that supports plug-and-play. A modem using a serial port that is not yet in use must be configured. Additionally, the software drivers that come with the modem must be installed for the modem to work properly. Drivers for modems are installed the same way drivers are installed for NICs.

External modems connect to a computer through the serial and USB ports.

When computers use the public telephone system to communicate, it is called dial-up networking (DUN). Modems communicate with each other using audio tone signals. This means that modems are able to duplicate the dialing characteristics of a telephone. DUN creates a Point-to-Point Protocol (PPP) connection between two computers over a phone line.

After the line connection has been established, a "handshaking sequence" takes place between the two modems and the computers. The handshaking sequence is a series of short communications that occur between the two systems. This is done to establish the readiness of the two modems and computers to engage in data exchange. Dial-up modems send data over the serial telephone line in the form of an analog signal. Because the analog signals change gradually and continuously, they can be drawn as waves. In this system, the digital signals are represented by 1s and 0s. The digital signals must be converted to a waveform to travel across telephone lines. They are converted back to the digital form, 1s and 0s, by the receiving modem so that the receiving computer can process the data.

AT Commands

All modems require software to control the communication session. Most modem software uses the Hayes-compatible command set. The Hayes command set is based on a group of instructions that always begins with a set of attention characters (AT), followed by the command characters. These are known as AT commands. The AT command set is shown in Figure 2.

The AT commands are modem control commands. The AT command set is used to issue dial, hang up, reset, and other instructions to the modem. Most user manuals that come with a modem contain a complete listing of the AT command set.

The standard Hayes-compatible code to dial is ATDxxxxxxx. There are usually no spaces in an AT string. If a space is inserted, most modems will ignore it. The "x" signifies the number dialed. There will be seven digits for a local call and 11 digits for a long-distance call. A W indicates that the modem will wait for an outside line, if necessary, to establish a tone before proceeding. Sometimes, a T is added to signify tone dialing or a P is added to signify pulse dialing.

Refer to **Figure** in online course

8.10 Identify names, purposes, and characteristics of other technologies used to establish connectivity

There are many ways to connect to the Internet. Phone, cable, satellite, and private telecommunications companies offer Internet connections for businesses and home use.

In the 1990s, the Internet was typically used for data transfer. Transmission speeds were slow compared to the high-speed connections that are available today. Most Internet connections were analog modems that used the "plain old telephone system" (POTS) to send and receive data. In recent years, many businesses and home users have switched to high-speed Internet connections. The additional bandwidth allows for transmission of voice and video as well as data.

You should understand how users connect to the Internet and the advantages and disadvantages of different connection types.

After completing this section, you will meet these objectives:

- Describe telephone technologies.
- Define power line communication.
- Define broadband.
- Define VOIP.

Refer to **Figure** in online course

8.10.1 Describe telephone technologies

There are several WAN solutions available for connecting between sites or to the Internet. WAN connection services provide different speeds and levels of service. Before committing to any type of Internet connection, research all available services to determine the best solution to match the needs of your customer.

Analog Telephone

This technology uses standard voice telephone lines. This type of service uses a modem to place a telephone call to another modem at a remote site, such as an Internet Service provider. There are two major disadvantages of using the phone line with an analog modem. The first is that the telephone line cannot be used for voice calls while the modem is in use. The second is the limited bandwidth provided by analog phone service. The maximum bandwidth using an analog modem is 56 Kbps, but in reality, it is usually much lower than that. An analog modem is not a good solution for the demands of busy networks.

Integrated Services Digital Network (ISDN)

The next advancement in WAN service is ISDN. ISDN is a standard for sending voice, video, and data over normal telephone wires. ISDN technology uses the telephone wires as an analog telephone service. However, ISDN uses digital technology to carry the data. Because it uses digital technology, ISDN provides higher-quality voice and higher-speed data transfer than traditional analog telephone service.

There are three services offered by ISDN digital connections: Basic Rate Interface (BRI), Primary Rate Interface (PRI), and Broadband ISDN (BISDN). ISDN uses two different types of communications channels. The "B" channel is used to carry the information – data, voice, or video and the "D" channel is usually used for controlling and signaling, but can be used for data.

Click the names of the types of ISDN in Figure 1 to learn more.

Digital Subscriber Line (DSL)

DSL is an "always-on" technology. "Always on" means that there is no need to dial up each time to connect to the Internet. DSL uses the existing copper telephone lines to provide high-speed digital data communication between end users and telephone companies. Unlike ISDN, where the digital data communications replaces the analog voice communications, DSL shares the telephone wire with analog signals.

The telephone company limits the bandwidth of the analog voice on the lines. This limit allows the DSL to place digital data on the phone wire in the unused portion of the bandwidth. This sharing of the phone wire allows voice calls to be placed while DSL is connecting to the Internet.

There are two major considerations when selecting DSL. DSL has distance limitations. The phone lines used with DSL were designed to carry analog information. Therefore, the length that the digital signal can be sent is limited and cannot pass through any form of multiplexer used with analog phone lines. The other consideration is that the voice information and the data carried by DSL must be separated at the customer site. A device called a splitter separates the connection to the phones and the connection to the local network devices.

Asymmetric Digital Subscriber Line (ADSL)

ADSL is currently the most commonly used DSL technology. ADSL has different bandwidth capabilities in each direction. ADSL has a fast downstream speed – typically 1.5 Mbps. Downstream is the process of transferring data from the server to the end user. This is beneficial to users who are downloading large amounts of data. The high speed upload rate of ADSL is slower. ADSL does not perform well when hosting a web server or FTP server, both of which involve upload-intensive Internet activities.

Click the types of DSL in Figure 2 to learn more.

Refer to **Figure** in online course

8.10.2 Define power line communication

Power line communication (PLC) is a communication method that uses power distribution wires (local electric grid) to send and receive data.

PLC is known by other names:

- Power Line Networking (PLN)
- Mains Communication
- Power Line Telecoms (PLT)

With PLC, an electric company can superimpose an analog signal over the standard 50 or 60 Hz AC that travels in power lines. The analog signal can carry voice and data signals.

PLC may be available in areas where other high-speed connections are not. PLC is faster than an analog modem, and may cost much less than other high-speed connection types. As this technology matures, it will become more common to find and may increase in speed.

You can use PLC to network computers within your home instead of installing network cabling or wireless technology. PLC connections can be used anywhere there is an electrical outlet. You can control lighting and appliances using PLC without installing control wiring.

Refer to **Figure** in online course

8.10.3 Define broadband

Broadband is a technique used to transmit and receive multiple signals using multiple frequencies over one cable. For example, the cable used to bring cable television to your home can carry computer network transmissions at the same time. Because the two transmission types use different frequencies, they do not interfere with each other.

Broadband is a signaling method that uses a wide range of frequencies that can further be divided into channels. In networking, the term broadband describes communication methods that transmit two or more signals at the same time. Sending two or more signals simultaneously increases the rate of transmission. Some common broadband network connections include cable, DSL, ISDN, and satellite.

Cable

A cable modem connects your computer to the cable company using the same coaxial cable that connects to your cable television. A cable modem is shown in the figure. You can plug your computer directly into the cable modem, or you can connect a router, switch, hub, or multipurpose network device so that multiple computers can share the connection to the Internet.

DSL

With DSL, the voice and data signals are carried on different frequencies on the copper telephone wires. A filter is used to prevent DSL signals from interfering with phone signals. A DSL filter is shown in the figure. Plug the filter into a phone jack and plug the phone into the filter.

The DSL modem does not require a filter. The DSL modem is not affected by the frequencies of the telephone. Like a cable modem, a DSL modem can connect directly to your computer, or it can be connected to a networking device to share the Internet connection with multiple computers.

ISDN

ISDN is another example of broadband. ISDN uses multiple channels and can carry different types of services; therefore, it is considered a type of broadband. ISDN can carry voice, video, and data.

Satellite

Broadband satellite is an alternative for customers who cannot get cable or DSL connections. A satellite connection does not require a phone line or cable, but uses a satellite dish for two-way communication. Download speeds are typically up to 500 Kbps; uploads are closer to 56 Kbps. It takes time for the signal from the satellite dish to relay to your Internet Service Provider (ISP) through the satellite orbitting the Earth.

People who live in rural areas often use satellite broadband because they need a faster connection than dial-up and no other broadband connection is available.

Refer to **Worksheet** for this chapter

Broadband

Identify the different types of broadband

Refer to **Figure** in online course

8.10.4 Define VoIP

Voice over IP (VoIP) is a method to carry telephone calls over the data networks and Internet. VoIP converts the analog signals of our voices into digital information that is transported in IP packets. VoIP can also use an existing IP network to provide access to the public switched telephone network (PSTN).

When using VoIP, you are dependent on an Internet connection. This can be a disadvantage if the Internet connection experiences an interruption in service. When a service interruption occurs, the user cannot make phone calls.

Refer to **Figure** in online course

8.11 Identify and apply common preventive maintenance techniques used for networks

There are common preventive maintenance techniques that should continually be performed for a network to operate properly. In an organization, if there is one malfunctioning computer, generally only one user is affected. But if the network is malfunctioning, many or all users will be unable to work.

One of the biggest problems with network devices, especially in the server room, is heat. Network devices, such as computers, hubs, and switches, do not perform well when over heated. Often, excess heat is generated by accumulated dust and dirty air filters. When dust gathers in and on network devices, it impedes the proper flow of cool air and sometimes even clogs fans. It is important to keep network rooms clean and change air filters often. It is also a good idea to have replacement filters available for prompt maintenance.

Preventive maintenance involves checking the various components of a network for wear. Check the condition of network cables because they are often moved, unplugged, and kicked. Many network problems can be traced to a faulty cable. You should replace any cables that have exposed wires, are badly twisted, or are bent.

Label your cables. This practice will save troubleshooting time later. Refer to wiring diagrams and always follow your company's cable labeling guidelines.

Refer to **Figure** in online course

8.12 Troubleshoot a network

Network issues can be simple or complex. To assess how complicated the problem is, you should determine how many computers on the network are experiencing the problem.

If there is a problem with one computer on the network, start the troubleshooting process at that computer. If there is a problem with all computers on the network, start the troubleshooting process in the network room where all computers are connected. As a technician, you should develop a logical and consistent method for diagnosing network problems by eliminating one problem at a time.

Follow the steps outlined in this section to accurately identify, repair, and document the problem. The troubleshooting process is shown in Figure 1.

After completing this section, you will meet these objectives:

- Review the troubleshooting process.
- Identify common network problems and solutions.

Refer to **Figure** in online course

8.12.1 Review the troubleshooting process

Network problems can result from a combination of hardware, software, and connectivity issues. Computer technicians must be able to analyze the problem and determine the cause of the error in order to repair the network issue. This process is called troubleshooting.

The first step in the troubleshooting process is to gather data from the customer. Figures 1 and 2 list open-ended and closed-ended questions to ask the customer.

Once you have talked to the customer, you should verify the obvious issues. Figure 3 lists some issues for networks.

After the obvious issues have been verified, try some quick solutions. Figure 4 lists some quick solutions for networks.

If quick solutions did not correct the problem, it is time to gather data from the computer. Figure 5 shows different ways to gather information about the problem from the network.

At this point, you will have enough information to evaluate the problem, research, and implement possible solutions. Figure 6 shows resources for possible solutions.

After you have solved the network problem, you will close with the customer. Figure 7 is a list of the tasks required to complete this step.

Refer to **Figure** in online course

8.12.2 Identify common network problems and solutions

Network problems can be attributed to hardware, software, connectivity issues, or some combination of the three. You will resolve some types of network problems more often than others. Figure 1 is a chart of common network problems and solutions.

Refer to **Worksheet** for this chapter

Network Problem

Help desk activity to diagnose a network problem

Summary

This chapter introduced you to the fundamentals of networking, the benefits of having a network, and the ways to connect computers to a network. The different aspects of troubleshooting a network were discussed with examples of how to analyze and implement simple solutions. The following concepts from this chapter are important to remember:

- A computer network is composed of two or more computers that share data and resources.
- A Local Area Network (LAN) refers to a group of interconnected computers that are under the same administrative control.
- A Wide Area Network (WAN) is a network that connects LANs in geographically separated locations.
- In a peer-to-peer network, devices are connected directly to each other. A peer-to-peer network is easy to install, and no additional equipment or dedicated administrator is required. Users control their own resources, and a network works best with a small number of computers. A client/server network uses a dedicated system that functions as the server. The server responds to requests made by users or clients connected to the network.
- A LAN uses a direct connection from one computer to another. It is suitable for a small area, such as in a home, building, or school. A WAN uses point-to-point or point-to-multipoint, serial communications lines to communicate over greater distances. A WLAN uses wireless technology to connect devices together.
- The network topology defines the way in which computers, printers, and other devices are connected. Physical topology describes the layout of the wire and devices, as well as the paths used by data transmissions. Logical topology is the path that signals travel from one point to another. Topologies include bus, star, ring, and mesh.
- Networking devices are used to connect computers and peripheral devices so that they can communicate. These include hubs, bridges, switches, routers, and multipurpose devices. The type of device implemented depends on the type of network.
- Networking media can be defined as the means by which signals, or data, are sent from one computer to another. Signals can be transmitted either by cable or wireless means. The media types discussed were coaxial, twisted-pair, fiber-optic cabling, and radio frequencies.
- Ethernet architecture is now the most popular type of LAN architecture. Architecture refers to the overall structure of a computer or communications system. It determines the capabilities and limitations of the system. The Ethernet architecture is based on the IEEE 802.3 standard. The IEEE 802.3 standard specifies that a network implement the CSMA/CD access control method.
- The OSI reference model is an industry standard framework that is used to divide the functions of networking into seven distinct layers. These layers include Application, Presentation, Session, Transport, Network, Data Link, and Physical. It is important to understand the purpose of each layer.
- The TCP/IP suite of protocols has become the dominant standard for the Internet. TCP/IP represents a set of public standards that specify how packets of information are exchanged between computers over one or more networks.
- A NIC is a device that plugs into a motherboard and provides ports for the network cable connections. It is the computer interface with the LAN.

- A modem is an electronic device that is used for computer communications through telephone lines. It allows data transfer between one computer and another. The modem converts byte-oriented data to serial bit streams. All modems require software to control the communication session. The set of commands that most modem software uses is known as the Hayes-compatible command set.
- The three transmission methods to sending signals over data channels are simplex, half-duplex, and full-duplex. Full-duplex networking technology increases performance because data can be sent and received at the same time. DSL, two-way cable modem, and other broadband technologies operate in full-duplex mode.
- Network devices and media, such as computer components, must be maintained. It is important to clean equipment regularly and use a proactive approach to prevent problems. Repair or replace broken equipment to prevent downtime.
- When troubleshooting network problems, listen to what your customer tells you so that you can formulate open-ended and closed-ended questions that will help you determine where to begin fixing the problem. Verify obvious issues and try quick solutions before escalating the troubleshooting process.

Chapter 8 Quiz

Take the chapter quiz to test your knowledge.

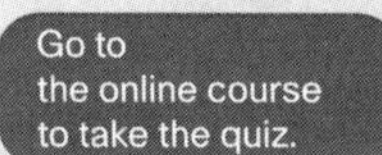

Your Chapter Notes

Fundamental Security

Introduction

Technicians need to understand computer and network security. Failure to implement proper security procedures can have an impact on users, computers, and the general public. Private information, company secrets, financial data, computer equipment, and items of national security are placed at risk if proper security procedures are not followed.

After completing this chapter, you will meet these objectives:

- Explain why security is important.
- Describe security threats.
- Identify security procedures.
- Identify common preventive maintenance techniques for security.
- Troubleshoot security.

Refer to **Figure** in online course

9.1 Explain why security is important

Computer and network security help to keep data and equipment functioning and provide access only to appropriate people. Everyone in an organization should give high priority to security because everyone can be affected by a lapse in security.

Theft, loss, network intrusion, and physical damage are some of the ways a network or computer can be harmed. Damage or loss of equipment can mean a loss of productivity. Repairing and replacing equipment can cost the company time and money. Unauthorized use of a network can expose confidential information and reduce network resources.

An attack that intentionally degrades the performance of a computer or network can also harm the production of an organization. Poorly implemented security measures to wireless network devices demonstrate that physical connectivity is not necessary for unauthorized access by intruders.

The primary responsibilities of a technician include data and network security. A customer or an organization may depend on you to ensure that their data and computer equipment are secure. You will perform tasks that are more sensitive than those assigned to the average employee. You may repair, adjust, and install equipment. You will need to know how to configure settings to keep the network secure but still keep it available to those who need to access it. You will ensure that software patches and updates are applied, anti-virus software is installed, and anti-spyware software is used. You may also be asked to instruct users how to maintain good security practices with computer equipment.

Refer to **Worksheet** for this chapter

Security Attacks

Search for computer crime information

Refer to **Figure** in online course

9.2 Describe security threats

To successfully protect computers and the network, a technician must understand both types of threats to computer security:

- Physical – Events or attacks that steal, damage, or destroy equipment, such as servers, switches, and wiring
- Data – Events or attacks that remove, corrupt, deny access, allow access, or steal information

Threats to security can come from the inside or outside of an organization, and the level of potential damage can vary greatly:

- Internal – Employees have access to data, equipment, and the network
  - Malicious threats are when an employee intends to cause damage.
  - Accidental threats are when the user damages data or equipment unintentionally.
- External – Users outside of an organization that do not have authorized access to the network or resources
  - Unstructured – Attackers use available resources, such as passwords or scripts, to gain access and run programs designed to vandalize
  - Structured – Attackers use code to access operating systems and software

Physical loss or damage to equipment can be expensive, and data loss can be detrimental to your business and reputation. Threats against data are constantly changing as attackers find new ways to gain entry and commit their crimes.

After completing this section, you will meet these objectives:

- Define viruses, worms, and Trojans.
- Explain web security.
- Define adware, spyware, and grayware.
- Explain Denial of Service.
- Describe spam and popup windows.
- Explain social engineering.
- Explain TCP/IP attacks.
- Explain hardware deconstruction and recycling.

Refer to **Figure** in online course

9.2.1 Define viruses, worms, and Trojans

Computer viruses are deliberately created and sent out by attackers. A virus is attached to small pieces of computer code, software, or documents. The virus executes when the software is run on a computer. If the virus is spread to other computers, those computers could continue to spread the virus.

A virus is a program written with malicious intent and sent out by attackers. The virus is transferred to another computer through e-mail, file transfers, and instant messaging. The virus hides by attaching itself to a file on the computer. When the file is accessed, the virus executes and infects the computer. A virus has the potential to corrupt or even delete files on your computer, use your e-mail to spread itself to other computers, or even erase your entire hard drive.

Some viruses can be exceptionally dangerous. The most damaging type of virus is used to record keystrokes. These viruses can be used by attackers to harvest sensitive information, such as passwords and credit card numbers. Viruses may even alter or destroy information on a computer. Stealth viruses can infect a computer and lay dormant until summoned by the attacker.

A worm is a self-replicating program that is harmful to networks. A worm uses the network to duplicate its code to the hosts on a network, often without any user intervention. It is different from a virus because a worm does not need to attach to a program to infect a host. Even if the worm does not damage data or applications on the hosts it infects, it is harmful to networks because it consumes bandwidth.

A Trojan is technically a worm. The Trojan does not need to be attached to other software. Instead, a Trojan threat is hidden in software that appears to do one thing, and yet behind the scenes it does another. Trojans are often disguised as useful software. The Trojan program can reproduce like a virus and spread to other computers. Computer data damage and production loss could be significant. A technician may be needed to perform the repairs, and employees may lose or have to replace data. An infected computer could be sending critical data to competitors, while at the same time infecting other computers on the network.

Virus protection software, known as anti-virus software, is software designed specifically to detect, disable, and remove viruses, worms, and Trojans before they infect a computer. Anti-virus software becomes outdated quickly, however, and it is the responsibility of the technician to apply the most recent updates, patches, and virus definitions as part of a regular maintenance schedule. Many organizations establish a written security policy stating that employees are not permitted to install any software that is not provided by the company. Organizations also make employees aware of the dangers of opening e-mail attachments that may contain a virus or a worm.

Refer to **Worksheet** for this chapter

Third-Party Software

Search for antivirus and anti-spyware software

Refer to **Figure** in online course

9.2.2 Explain web security

Web security is important because so many people visit the World Wide Web every day. Some of the features that make the web useful and entertaining can also make it harmful to a computer.

Tools that are used to make web pages more powerful and versatile, as shown in Figure 1, can also make computers more vulnerable to attacks. These are some examples of web tools:

- ***ActiveX* –** Technology created by Microsoft to control interactivity on web pages. If ActiveX is on a page, an applet or small program has to be downloaded to gain access to the full functionality.
- ***Java* –** Programming language that allows applets to run within a web browser. Examples of applets include a calculator or a counter.
- ***JavaScript* –** Programming language developed to interact with HTML source code to allow interactive websites. Examples include a rotating banner or a popup window.

Attackers may use any of these tools to install a program on a computer. To prevent against these attacks, most browsers have settings that force the computer user to authorize the downloading or use of ActiveX, Java, or JavaScript, as shown in Figure 2.

Refer to **Figure** in online course

9.2.3 Define adware, spyware, and grayware

Adware, spyware, and grayware are usually installed on a computer without the knowledge of the user. These programs collect information stored on the computer, change the computer configuration, or open extra windows on the computer without the user's consent.

Adware is a software program that displays advertising on your computer. Adware is usually distributed with downloaded software. Most often, adware is displayed in a popup window. Adware popup windows are sometimes difficult to control and will open new windows faster than users can close them.

Grayware or malware is a file or program other then a virus that is potentially harmful. Many grayware attacks are phishing attacks that try to persuade the reader to unknowingly provide attackers with access to personal information. As you fill out an online form, the data is sent to the attacker. Grayware can be removed using spyware and adware removal tools.

Spyware, a type of grayware, is similar to adware. It is distributed without any user intervention or knowledge. Once installed, the spyware monitors activity on the computer. The spyware then sends this information to the organization responsible for launching the spyware.

Phishing is a form of social engineering where the attacker pretends to represent a legitimate outside organization, such as a bank. A potential victim is contacted via e-mail. The attacker might ask for verification of information, such as a password or username, to supposedly prevent some terrible consequence from occurring.

Note

There is rarely a need to give out sensitive personal or financial information online. Be suspicious. Use the postal service to share sensitive information.

Refer to **Interactive Graphic** in online course.

Refer to **Figure** in online course

9.2.4 Explain Denial of Service

Denial of service (DoS) is a form of attack that prevents users from accessing normal services, such as e-mail and a web server, because the system is busy responding to abnormally large amounts of requests. DoS works by sending enough requests for a system resource that the requested service is overloaded and ceases to operate.

Common DoS attacks include the following:

- Ping of death – A series of repeated, larger than normal pings that crash the receiving computer
- E-mail bomb – A large quantity of bulk e-mail that overwhelms the e-mail server preventing users from accessing it

Distributed DoS (DDoS) is another form of attack that uses many infected computers, called zombies, to launch an attack. With DDoS, the intent is to obstruct or overwhelm access to the targeted server. Zombie computers located at different geographical locations make it difficult to trace the origin of the attack.

Refer to **Figure** in online course

9.2.5 Describe spam and popup windows

Spam, also known as junk mail, is unsolicited e-mail, as shown in Figure 1. In most cases, spam is used as a method of advertising. However, spam can be used to send harmful links or deceptive content, as shown in Figure 2.

When used as an attack method, spam may include links to an infected website or an attachment that could infect a computer. These links or attachments may result in lots of windows designed to capture your attention and lead you to advertising sites. These windows are called popups. As shown in Figure 2, uncontrolled popup windows can quickly cover the user's screen and prevent any work from getting done.

Many anti-virus and e-mail software programs automatically detect and remove spam from an e-mail inbox. Some spam still may get through, so look for some of the more common indications:

- No subject line
- Incomplete return addresses
- Computer generated e-mails
- Return e-mails not sent by the user

Refer to **Figure** in online course

9.2.6 Explain social engineering

A social engineer is a person who is able to gain access to equipment or a network by tricking people into providing the necessary access information. Often, the social engineer gains the confidence of an employee and convinces the employee to divulge username and password information.

A social engineer may pose as a technician to try to gain entry into a facility, as shown in Figure 1. Once inside, the social engineer may look over shoulders to gather information, seek out papers on desks with passwords and phone extensions, or obtain a company directory with e-mail addresses.

Here are some basic precautions to help protect against social engineering:

- Never give out your password
- Always ask for the ID of unknown persons
- Restrict access of unexpected visitors
- Escort all visitors
- Never post your password in your work area
- Lock your computer when you leave your desk
- Do not let anyone follow you through a door that requires an access card

Refer to **Figure** in online course

9.2.7 Explain TCP/IP attacks

TCP/IP is the protocol suite that is used to control all of the communications on the Internet. Unfortunately, TCP/IP can also make a network vulnerable to attackers.

Some of the most common attacks:

- SYN Flood – Randomly opens TCP ports, tying up the network equipment or computer with a large amount of false requests, causing sessions to be denied to others
- DoS – Sends abnormally large amounts of requests to a system preventing access to the services
- DDoS – Uses "zombies" to make tracing the origin of the DoS attack difficult to locate
- Spoofing – Gains access to resources on devices by pretending to be a trusted computer
- Man-in-the-Middle – Intercepts or inserts false information in traffic between two hosts
- Replay – Uses network sniffers to extract usernames and passwords to be used at a later date to gain access
- DNS Poisoning – Changes the DNS records on a system to point to false servers where the data is recorded

Refer to **Figure** in online course

9.2.8 Explain hardware deconstruction and recycling

Hardware deconstruction is the process of removing sensitive data from hardware and software before recycling or discarding. Hard drives should be fully erased to prevent the possibility of recovery using specialized software. It is not enough to delete files or even format the drive. Use a third party tool to overwrite data multiple times rendering the data unusable. The only way to fully ensure that data cannot be recovered from a hard drive is to carefully shatter the platters with a hammer and safely dispose of the pieces.

Media like CDs and floppy disks must also be destroyed. Use a shredding machine that is designed for the purpose.

Refer to **Figure** in online course

9.3 Identify security procedures

A security plan should be used to determine what will be done in a critical situation. Security plan policies should be constantly updated to reflect the latest threats to a network. A security plan with clear security procedures is the basis for a technician to follow. Security plans should be reviewed on a yearly basis.

Part of the process of ensuring security is to conduct tests to determine areas where security is weak. Testing should be done on a regular basis. New threats are released daily. Regular testing provides details of any possible weaknesses in the current security plan that should be addressed.

There are multiple layers of security in a network, including physical, wireless, and data. Each layer is subject to security attacks. The technician needs to understand how to implement security procedures to protect equipment and data.

After completing this section, you will meet these objectives:

- Explain what is required in a basic local security policy.
- Explain the tasks required to protect physical equipment.
- Describe ways to protect data.
- Describe wireless security techniques.

Refer to **Figure** in online course

9.3.1 Explain what is required in a basic local security policy

Though local security policies may vary between organizations, there are questions all organizations should ask:

- What assets require protection?
- What are the possible threats?
- What to do in the event of a security breach?

Note

The computer itself may be referred to as the central processing unit, or CPU. For this course, the term CPU will only refer to the microprocessor chip.

A security policy should describe how a company addresses security issues:

- Define a process for handling network security incidents

- Define a process to audit existing network security
- Define a general security framework for implementing network security
- Define behaviors that are allowed
- Define behaviors that are prohibited
- Describe what to log and how to store the logs: Event Viewer, system log files, or security log files
- Define network access to resources through account permissions
- Define authentication technologies to access data: usernames, passwords, biometrics, smart cards

Refer to **Figure** in online course

9.3.2 Explain the tasks required to protect physical equipment

Physical security is as important as data security. When a computer is taken, the data is also stolen.

There are several methods of physically protecting computer equipment, as shown in Figures 1 and 2:

- Control access to facilities
- Use cable locks with equipment
- Keep telecommunication rooms locked
- Fit equipment with security screws
- Use security cages around equipment
- Label and install sensors, such as Radio Frequency Identification (RFID) tags, on equipment

For access to facilities, there are several means of protection:

- Card keys that store user data, including level of access
- Biometric sensors that identify physical characteristics of the user, such as fingerprints or retinas
- Posted security guard
- Sensors, such as RFID tags, to monitor equipment

Refer to **Figure** in online course

9.3.3 Describe ways to protect data

The value of physical equipment is often far less than the value of the data it contains. The loss of sensitive data to a company's competitors or to criminals may be costly. Such losses may result in a lack of confidence in the company and the dismissal of computer technicians in charge of computer security. To protect data, there are several methods of security protection that can be implemented.

Password Protection

Password protection can prevent unauthorized access to content, as shown in Figure 1. Attackers are able to gain access to unprotected computer data. All computers should be password protected. Two levels of password protection are recommended:

- BIOS – Prevents BIOS settings from being changed without the appropriate password
- Login – Prevents unauthorized access to the network

Network logins provide a means of logging activity on the network and either preventing or allowing access to resources. This makes it possible to determine what resources are being accessed.

Usually, the system administrator defines a naming convention for the usernames when creating network logins. A common example of a username is the first initial of the person's first name and then the entire last name. You should keep the username naming convention simple so that people do not have a hard time remembering it.

When assigning passwords, the level of password control should match the level of protection required. A good security policy should be strictly enforced and include, but not be limited to, the following rules:

- Passwords should expire after a specific period of time.
- Passwords should contain a mixture of letters and numbers so that they cannot easily be broken.
- Password standards should prevent users from writing down passwords and leaving them unprotected from public view.
- Rules about password expiration and lockout should be defined. Lockout rules apply when an unsuccessful attempt has been made to access the system or when a specific change has been detected in the system configuration.

To simplify the process of administrating security, it is common to assign users to groups, and then to assign groups to resources. This allows the access capability of users on a network to be changed easily by assigning or removing the user from various groups. This is useful when setting up temporary accounts for visiting workers or consultants, giving you the ability to limit access to resources.

Data Encryption

Encrypting data uses codes and ciphers. Traffic between resources and computers on the network can be protected from attackers monitoring or recording transactions by implementing encryption. It may not be possible to decipher captured data in time to make any use of it.

Virtual Private Network (VPN) uses encryption to protect data. A VPN connection allows a remote user to safely access resources as if their computer is physically attached to the local network.

Port Protection

Every communication using TCP/IP is associated with a port number. HTTPS, for instance, uses port 443 by default. A firewall, as shown in Figure 2, is a way of protecting a computer from intrusion through the ports. The user can control the type of data sent to a computer by selecting which ports will be open and which will be secured. Data being transported on a network is called traffic.

Data Backups

Data backup procedures should be included in a security plan. Data can be lost or damaged in circumstances such as theft, equipment failure, or a disaster such as a fire or flood. Backing up data is one of the most effective ways of protecting against data loss. Here are some considerations for data backups:

- ***Frequency of backups –*** Backups can take a long time. Sometimes it is easier to make a full backup monthly or weekly, and then do frequent partial backups of any data that has changed since the last full backup. However, spreading the backups over many recordings increases the amount of time needed to restore the data.
- ***Storage of backups –*** Backups should be transported to an approved offsite storage location for extra security. The current backup media is transported to the offsite location on a daily, weekly, or monthly rotation as required by the local organization.

- ***Security of backups –*** Backups can be protected with passwords. These passwords would have to be entered before the data on the backup media could be restored.

File System Security

All file systems keep track of resources, but only file systems with journals can log access by user, date, and time. The FAT 32 file system, shown in Figure 3, which is used in some versions of Windows, lacks both journaling and encryption capabilities. As a result, situations that require good security are usually deployed using a file system such as NTFS, which is part of Windows 2000 and Windows XP. If increased security is needed, it is possible to run certain utilities, such as CONVERT, to upgrade a FAT 32 file system to NTFS. The conversion process is not reversible. It is important to clearly define your goals before making the transition.

Refer to **Figure** in online course

9.3.4 Describe wireless security techniques

Since traffic flows through radio waves in wireless networks, it is easy for attackers to monitor and attack data without having to physically connect to a network. Attackers gain access to a network by being within range of an unprotected wireless network. A technician needs to know how to configure access points and wireless network interface cards (NICs) to an appropriate level of security.

When installing wireless services, you should apply wireless security techniques immediately to prevent unwanted access to the network as shown in Figure 1. Wireless access points should be configured with basic security settings that are compatible with the existing network security.

An attacker can access data as it travels over the radio signal. A wireless encryption system can be used to prevent unwanted capture and use of data by encoding the information that is sent. Both ends of every link must use the same encryption standard. Figure 2 shows the levels of security described here:

- ***Wired Equivalent Privacy (WEP) –*** the first generation security standard for wireless. Attackers quickly discovered that WEP encryption was easy to break. The encryption keys used to encode the messages could be detected by monitoring programs. Once the keys were obtained, messages could be easily decoded.
- ***Wi-Fi Protected Access (WPA) –*** an improved version of WEP. It was created as a temporary solution until the 802.11i (a security layer for wireless systems) was fully implemented. Now that 802.11i has been ratified, WPA2 has been released. It covers the entire 802.11i standard.
- ***Lightweight Extensible Authentication Protocol (LEAP), also called EAP-Cisco –*** a wireless security protocol created by Cisco to address the weaknesses in WEP and WPA. LEAP is a good choice when using Cisco equipment in conjunction with operating systems like Windows and Linux.

Wireless Transport Layer Security (WTLS) is a security layer used in mobile devices that employ the Wireless Applications Protocol (WAP). Mobile devices do not have a great deal of spare bandwidth to devote to security protocols. WTLS was designed to provide security for WAP devices in a bandwidth-efficient manner.

Refer to **Figure** in online course

9.4 Identify common preventive maintenance techniques for security

Security strategies are constantly changing as are the technologies used to secure equipment and data. New exploits are discovered daily. Attackers are constantly searching for new methods to use in an attack. Software manufacturers have to regularly create and issue new patches to fix flaws and vulnerabilities in products. If a computer is left unprotected by a technician, an attacker can easily gain access. Unprotected computers on the Internet may become infected within a few minutes.

Because of the constantly changing security threats, a technician should understand how to install patches and updates. They should also be able to recognize when new updates and patches are available. Some manufacturers release updates on the same day every month, but also send out critical updates when necessary. Other manufacturers provide automatic update services that patch the software every time the computer is turned on, or e-mail notifications when a new patch or update is released.

After completing this section, you will meet these objectives:

- Explain how to update signature files for anti-virus and anti-spyware software.
- Explain how to install operating systems service packs and security patches.

Refer to **Figure** in online course

9.4.1 Explain how to update signature files for anti-virus and anti-spyware software

Threats to security from viruses and worms are always present. Attackers constantly look for new ways to infiltrate computers and networks. Because new viruses are always being developed, security software must be continually updated. This process can be performed automatically, but a technician should know how to manually update any type of protection software and all customer application programs.

Click on each step in the figure for more information.

Virus, spyware, and adware detection programs look for patterns in the programming code of the software in a computer. These patterns are determined by analyzing viruses that are intercepted on the Internet and on LANs. These code patterns are called signatures. The publishers of protection software compile the signatures into virus definition tables. To update signature files for anti-virus and spyware software, first check to see if the signature files are the most recent files. This can be done by navigating to the "About" option of the protection software, or by launching the update tool for the protection software. If the signature files are out of date, update them manually with the "Update Now" option on most protection software.

You should always retrieve the signature files from the manufacturer's website to make sure the update is authentic and not corrupted by viruses. This can put great demand on the manufacturer's website especially when new viruses are released. To avoid creating too much traffic at a single website, some manufacturers distribute their signature files for download to multiple download sites. These download sites are called mirrors.

Caution

When downloading the signature files from a mirror, ensure that the mirror site is a legitimate site. Always link to the mirror site from the manufacturer's website.

Refer to **Figure** in online course

9.4.2 Explain how to install operating systems service packs and security patches

Viruses and worms can be difficult to remove from a computer. Software tools are required to remove viruses and repair the computer code the virus has modified. These software tools are provided by operating system manufacturers and security software companies. Make sure that you download these tools from a legitimate site.

Manufacturers of operating systems and software applications may provide code updates called patches that prevent a newly discovered virus or worm from making a successful attack. From time to time, manufacturers combine patches and upgrades into a comprehensive update application called a service pack. Many infamous and devastating virus attacks could have been much less severe if more users had downloaded and installed the latest service pack.

The Windows operating system routinely checks the Windows Update website for high-priority updates that can help protect a computer from the latest security threat. These updates can include security updates, critical updates, and service packs. Depending on the setting you choose, Windows automatically downloads and installs any high-priority updates that your computer needs, or notifies you as these updates become available.

Updates must be installed, not just downloaded. If you use the Automatic setting you can schedule the time and day. Otherwise, new updates are installed at 3 A.M. by default. If your computer is turned off during a scheduled update, updates are installed the next time you start your computer. You can also choose to have Windows notify you when a new update is available and install the update yourself.

Follow the steps in Figure 1 to update the operating system with a service pack or security patch.

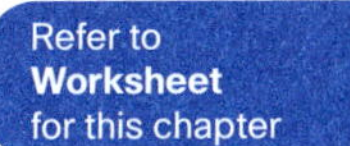

Download Protection Software and Updates

Research the download websites for protection software and updates

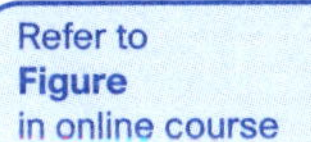

9.5 Troubleshoot security

The troubleshooting process is used to help resolve security issues. These problems range from simple, such as preventing someone from watching over your shoulder, to more complex problems, such as manually removing infected files. Use the troubleshooting steps as a guideline to help you diagnose and repair problems.

After completing this section, you will meet these objectives:

- Review the troubleshooting process.
- Identify common problems and solutions.

Refer to **Figure** in online course

9.5.1 Review the troubleshooting process

Computer technicians must be able to analyze a security threat and determine the appropriate method to protect assets and repair damage. This process is called troubleshooting.

The first step in the troubleshooting process is to gather data from the customer. Figures 1 and 2 list open-ended and closed-ended questions to ask the customer.

Once you have talked to the customer, you should verify the obvious issues. Figure 3 lists issues that apply to laptops.

After the obvious issues have been verified, try some quick solutions. Figure 4 lists some quick solutions to laptop problems.

If quick solutions did not correct the problem, it is time to gather data from the computer. Figure 5 shows different ways to gather information about the problem from the laptop.

At this point, you will have enough information to evaluate the problem, research, and implement possible solutions. Figure 6 shows resources for possible solutions.

After you have solved the problem, you will close with the customer. Figure 7 is a list of the tasks required to complete this step.

Refer to **Figure** in online course

9.5.2 Identify common problems and solutions

Computer problems can be attributed to hardware, software, connectivity issues, or some combination of the three. You will resolve some types of computer problems more often than others. Figure 1 is a chart of common security problems and solutions.

The worksheet is designed to reinforce your communication skills to verify information from the customer.

Refer to **Worksheet** for this chapter

Gather Information from the Customer

Document customer information and problem description in a work order

Summary

This chapter discussed computer security and why it is important to protect computer equipment, networks, and data. Threats, procedures, and preventive maintenance relating to data and physical security were described to help you keep computer equipment and data safe. Security protects computers, network equipment, and data from loss and physical danger. The following are some of the important concepts to remember from this chapter:

- Security threats can come from inside or outside of an organization.
- Viruses and worms are common threats that attack data.
- Develop and maintain a security plan to protect both data and physical equipment from loss.
- Keep operating systems and applications up to date and secure with patches and service packs.

Chapter 9 Quiz

Take the chapter quiz to test your knowledge.

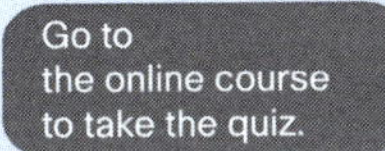

Your Chapter Notes

CHAPTER 10

Communication Skills

Introduction

What is the relationship between communication skills and troubleshooting? As a computer technician, you will not only fix computers but will also interact with people. In fact, troubleshooting is as much about communicating with the customer as it is about knowing how to fix a computer. In this chapter, you will learn to use good communication skills as confidently as you use a screwdriver.

After completing this chapter, you will meet these objectives:

- Explain the relationship between communication and troubleshooting.
- Describe good communication skills and professional behavior.
- Explain ethics and legal aspects of working with computer technology.
- Describe the call center environment and technician responsibilities.

Refer to **Figure** in online course

10.1 Explain the relationship between communication and troubleshooting

Think of a time when you had to call a repair person to get something fixed. Did it feel like an emergency to you? Did you appreciate it when the repair person was sympathetic and responsive? Perhaps you had a bad experience with a repair person. Are you likely to call that same person to fix a problem again?

Good communication skills will enhance a technician's troubleshooting skills. Both of these skill sets take time and experience to develop well. As your hardware, software, and OS knowledge increases, your ability to quickly determine a problem and find a solution will improve. The same principle applies to developing communication skills. The more you practice good communication skills, the more effective you will become when working with customers. A knowledgeable technician who uses good communication skills will always be in demand in the job market.

To troubleshoot a computer, you will need to learn the details of the problem from the customer. Most people who need a computer problem fixed are probably feeling some stress. If you establish a good rapport with the customer, the customer may relax a bit. A relaxed customer is more likely to be able to provide the information that you need to determine the source of the problem and then fix it.

Speaking directly with the customer is usually the first step in resolving the computer problem. As a technician, you will also have access to several communication and research tools. All of these resources can be used to help gather information for the troubleshooting process.

Refer to **Worksheet** for this chapter

Technician Resources

Research online resources for troubleshooting computer problems

Refer to **Figure** in online course

10.2 Describe good communication skills and professional behavior

Whether you are talking with a customer on the phone or in person, it is important to communicate well and to represent yourself professionally. Your professionalism and good communication skills will enhance your creditability with the customer.

Your body language can be seen by your customer. A customer can hear your sighs and sense that you are sneering, even over the phone. Conversely, customers can also sense that you are smiling when you are speaking with them on the phone. Many call-center technicians use a mirror at their desk to monitor their facial expressions.

Successful technicians control their own reactions and emotions from one customer call to the next. A good rule for all technicians to follow is that a new customer call means a fresh start. Never carry your frustration from one call to the next.

After completing this section, you will meet these objectives:

- Determine the computer problem of the customer.
- Display professional behavior with the customer.
- Focus the customer on the problem during the call.
- Use proper Netiquette.
- Implement time and stress management techniques.
- Observe service level agreements (SLAs).
- Follow business policies.

Refer to **Figure** in online course

10.2.1 Determine the computer problem of the customer

One of the first tasks of the technician is to determine the type of computer problem that the customer is experiencing.

Remember these three rules at the beginning of your conversation:

- Know – Call your customer by name
- Relate – Use brief communication to create a one-to-one connection between you and your customer
- Understand – Determine the customer's level of knowledge about the computer to know how to effectively communicate with the customer

To accomplish this, you should practice active listening skills. Allow the customer to tell the whole story. During the time that the customer is explaining the problem, occasionally interject some small word or phrase, such as "I understand", "Yes", "I see", or "Okay." This behavior lets the customer know that you are there and that you are listening. This is not the same as interrupting the customer to ask a question or make a statement.

A technician should not interrupt the customer to ask a question or make a statement. This is rude, disrespectful, and creates tension. Many times in a conversation, you may find yourself thinking of what to say before the other person finishes talking. When you do this, you are not really listening. As practice, try listening carefully when other people speak, and let them finish their thoughts.

After you have listened to the customer explain the whole problem, clarify what the customer has said. This will help convince the customer that you have heard and understand the situation. A good practice for clarification is to paraphrase the customer's explanation by beginning with the words "Let me see if I understand what you have told me...." This is a very effective tool that shows the customer that you have listened and that you are concerned with the issues.

After you have assured the customer that you understand the problem, you will probably have to ask some follow-up questions. Make sure that these questions are pertinent. Do not ask questions that the customer has already answered while describing the problem. Doing this will only irritate the customer and show that you were not listening.

Follow-up questions should be targeted, closed-ended questions based on the information that you have already gathered. Closed-ended questions should focus on obtaining specific information. The customer should be able to answer with a simple "yes" or "no" or with a factual response such as, "Windows XP Pro". Use all of the information that you have gathered from the customer to continue filling out the work order.

Refer to **Figure** in online course

10.2.2 Display professional behavior with the customer

When dealing with customers, it is necessary to be professional in all aspects of your role. You must handle customers with respect and prompt attention. When on a telephone, make sure that you know how to place a customer on hold, as well as how to transfer a customer without losing the call. It is important how you conduct the call, and your job is to help the customer focus on and communicate the problem so that you can solve it.

Be positive when communicating with the customer. Tell the customer what you can do. Do not focus on what you cannot do. Be prepared to explain alternative ways that you can help them, such as e-mailing information, faxing step-by-step instructions, or using remote control software to solve the problem. Customers will quickly sense whether you are interested in helping them.

Figure 1 outlines the process to follow before you put a customer on hold. First, let the customer finish speaking. Then, explain that you have to put the customer on hold, and ask the customer for permission to do so. When the customer agrees to be put on hold, thank the customer. Tell your customer that you will be away only a few minutes and explain what you will be doing during that time.

Figure 2 outlines the process for transferring a call. Follow the same process for a call transfer as you would when placing a customer on hold. Let the customer finish talking and then explain that you have to transfer the call. When the customer agrees to be transferred, tell the customer the phone number that you are transferring the customer to. You should also tell the new technician your name, the name of the customer that you are transferring, and the related ticket number.

When dealing with customers, it is sometimes easier to explain what you should not do. Observe the following list of things that you should not do when communicating with a customer:

- Avoid minimizing customer problems
- Avoid using jargon, abbreviations, and acronyms
- Avoid a negative attitude or tone of voice
- Avoid arguing with customers or becoming defensive
- Avoid being judgmental, insulting, or calling the customer names
- Avoid distractions or interruptions when talking with customers
- Avoid unnecessary holds and abrupt holds
- Avoid transfers without explaining the purpose of the transfer and getting customer consent
- Avoid negative remarks about other technicians to the customer

Refer to **Interactive Graphic** in online course.

Refer to **Figure** in online course

10.2.3 Focus the customer on the problem during the call

Part of your job is to focus the customer during the phone call. When you focus the customer on the problem, it allows you to control the call. This will make the best use of your time and the customer's time on troubleshooting the problem. Do not take any comments personally and do not retaliate with any comments or criticism. If you stay calm with the customer, finding a solution to the problem will remain the focal point of the call.

Just as there are many different computer problems, there are many different types of customers, as shown in Figure 1. The list of problem-customer types below is not comprehensive and often a customer can display a combination of traits. You will need to recognize which traits your customer exhibits. Recognizing these traits will help you to manage the call accordingly.

Talkative Customer

A talkative customer discusses everything except the problem on the call. The customer often uses the call as an opportunity to socialize. It can be difficult to get a talkative customer to focus on the problem.

Rude Customer

A rude customer complains during the call and often makes negative comments about the product, the service, and the technician. This type of customer is sometimes abusive and uncooperative and gets aggravated very easily.

Angry Customer

An angry customer talks loudly during the call and often tries to speak when the technician is talking. Angry customers are usually frustrated that they have a problem and upset that they have to call somebody to fix it.

Knowledgeable Customer

A knowledgeable customer wants to speak with a technician that is equally experienced in computers. This type of customer usually tries to control the call and does not want to speak with a level-one technician.

Inexperienced Customer

An inexperienced customer has difficulty describing the problem. These customers are usually not able to follow directions correctly and not able to communicate the errors that they encounter.

Refer to **Interactive Graphic** in online course.

Refer to **Figure** in online course

10.2.4 Use proper netiquette

Have you read a blog where two or three members have stopped discussing the issue and are simply insulting each other? These are called "flame wars" and they occur in blogs and e-mail threads. Have you ever wondered if they would actually say those things to each other in person? Perhaps you have received an e-mail that had no greeting or was written entirely in capital letters. How did this make you feel while you were reading it?

As a technician, you should be professional in all communications with customers. For e-mail and text communications, there is a set of personal and business etiquette rules called Netiquette.

In addition to the e-mail and text Netiquette, there are general rules that apply to all of your online interactions with customers and coworkers:

- Remember that you are dealing with people.
- Adhere to the same standards of behavior that you follow in real life.
- Know where you are in cyberspace.
- Respect other people's time and bandwidth.
- Share expert knowledge.
- Do not engage in "flame wars" online.
- Respect other people's privacy.
- Be forgiving of other people's mistakes.

The list above is not comprehensive. What other general rules about online communications can you think of?

Refer to **Figure** in online course

10.2.5 Implement time and stress management techniques

As a technician, you are a very busy person. It is important for your own well-being to use proper time and stress management techniques.

Workstation Ergonomics

The ergonomics of your work area can help you do your job or make it more difficult. Because you may spend a major portion of your day at your workstation, make sure that the desk layout works well, as shown in Figure 1. Have your headset and phone in a position that is both easy to reach and easy to use. Your chair should be adjusted to a height that is comfortable. Adjust your computer screen to a comfortable angle so that you do not have to tilt your head up or down to see it. Make sure your keyboard and mouse are also in a position that is comfortable for you. You should not have to bend your wrist in order to type. If possible, try to minimize external distractions such as noise.

Time Management

For time management, it is important to prioritize your activities. Make sure that you carefully follow the business policy of your company. The company policy may state that you must take "down" calls first, even though they may be harder to solve. A "down" call usually means that a server is not working and the entire office or company is waiting for the problem to be resolved in order to resume business.

If you have to call back a customer, make sure that you do it as close to the callback time as possible. Keep a list of callback customers and check them off one at a time as you complete these calls. Doing this will ensure that you do not forget a customer.

When working with many customers, do not give favorite customers faster or better service. When reviewing the call boards, do not take only the easy customer calls. See Figure 2 for a sample customer call board. Do not take the call of another technician unless you have permission to do so.

Stress Management

For stress management, take a moment to compose yourself between customer calls. Every call should be independent of each other, and you should not carry any frustrations from one call to the next.

You may have to do some physical activity to relieve stress. You should stand up and take a short walk. Do a few simple stretch movements or squeeze a tension ball. Take a break if you can, and try to relax. You will then be ready to answer the next customer call effectively.

Figure 3 shows ways to relax. Can you think of any other appropriate activities that might relieve stress at work?

Refer to **Figure** in online course

10.2.6 Observe Service Level Agreements (SLAs)

When dealing with customers, it is important to adhere to that customer's service level agreement (SLA). An SLA is a contract that defines expectations between an organization and the service vendor to provide an agreed upon level of support. As an employee of the service company, your job is to honor the SLA that you have with the customer. Take a closer look at some of the standard sections found in an SLA by moving over the circles in Figure 1.

An SLA is typically a legal agreement that contains the responsibilities and liabilities of all parties involved. Some of the contents of an SLA usually include the following:

- Response time guarantees (often based on type of call and level of service agreement)
- Equipment and/or software that will be supported
- Where service will be provided
- Preventive maintenance
- Diagnostics
- Part availability (equivalent parts)
- Cost and penalties
- Time of service availability (for example, 24X7; Monday to Friday, 8 am to 5 pm EST; and so on)

There may be exceptions to the SLA. Make sure to follow your company business rules in detail. Some of the exceptions may include the ability of the customer to upgrade level of service, or the ability to escalate to management for review. Escalation to management should be reserved for special situations. For example, a long-standing customer or a customer from a very large company may have a problem that falls outside the parameters stated in their SLA with your service company. In these cases, your management may choose to support the customer for customer-relation reasons.

Can you think of any other circumstances in which it might be a good idea to escalate a call to management?

Refer to **Figure** in online course

10.2.7 Follow business policies

As a technician, you should be aware of all business policies related to customer calls. You would not want to make a promise to a customer that you cannot keep. You should also have a good understanding of all rules governing employees.

Customer Call Rules

The following rules are examples of the specific rules a call center may have to handle customer calls:

- Maximum time on call (Example: 15 minutes)
- Maximum call time in queue (Example: three minutes)
- Number of calls per day (Example: Minimum of 30)
- Rules on passing calls on to other technicians (Example: Only when absolutely necessary and not without that technician's permission)
- Rules on what you can and cannot promise to the customer (See that customer's SLA for details)
- When to follow SLA and when to escalate to management

Call Center Employee Rules

There are also other rules to cover general daily activities of employees:

- Arrive at your workstation early enough to become prepared, usually about 15 to 20 minutes before the first call.
- Do not exceed the allowed number and length of breaks.
- Do not take a break or go to lunch if there is a call on the board.
- Do not take a break or go to lunch at the same time as other technicians (stagger breaks among technicians).
- Do not leave an ongoing call to take a break or go to lunch.
- Make sure that another technician is available if you have to leave.
- If no other technician is available, check with the customer to see if you can call back later, possibly in the morning.
- Do not show favoritism to certain customers.
- Do not take another technician's calls without permission.
- Do not talk negatively about the capabilities of another technician.

Can you think of any other rules that might apply in a call center?

Refer to **Figure** in online course

10.3 Explain ethics and legal aspects of working with computer technology

When you are working with customers and their equipment, there are some general ethical customs and legal rules that you should observe. Often, these customs and rules overlap.

Ethical Customs

You should always have respect for your customers, as well as for their property. Property includes any information or data that may be accessible. Such information or data would include any of the following items:

- E-mails
- Phone lists
- Records or data on the computer
- Hard copies of files, information, or data left on desk

Before accessing a computer account, including the administrator account, you should get the permission of the customer. From the troubleshooting process, you may have gathered some private information, such as usernames and passwords. If you document this type of private information, you must keep it confidential. Divulging any customer information to anyone else is not only unethical, but may be illegal. Legal details of customer information are usually covered under the SLA.

Do not send unsolicited messages to a customer. Do not send unsolicited mass mailings or chain letters to customers. Never send forged or anonymous e-mails. All of these activities are considered unethical and in certain circumstances, may be considered illegal.

Legal Rules

There are several computer-related activities that are not only unethical, but are definitely illegal. Be aware that this is not an exhaustive list:

- Do not make any changes to system software or hardware configurations without customer permission.
- Do not access a customer's or co-worker's accounts, private files, or e-mail messages without permission.
- Do not install, copy, or share digital content (including software, music, text, images, and video) in violation of copyright and/or software agreements or applicable federal and state law.
- Do not use a customer's company IT resources for commercial purposes.
- Do not make a customer's IT resources available to unauthorized users.
- Keep sensitive customer information confidential.
- Do not knowingly use a customer's company resources for illegal activities. Criminal or illegal use may include obscenity, child pornography, threats, harassment, copyright infringement, university trademark infringement, defamation, theft, identity theft, and unauthorized access.

Do you know the copyright and trademark laws in your state or country?

Refer to **Interactive Graphic** in online course.

10.4 Describe call center environment and technician responsibilities

Refer to **Figure** in online course

A call center environment is usually very professional and fast-paced. It is a help desk system where customers call in and are placed on a callboard. Available technicians take the customer calls. A technician must supply the level of support that is outlined in the customer's SLA.

After completing this section, you will meet these objectives:

- Describe the call center environment.
- Describe level-one technician responsibilities.
- Describe level-two technician responsibilities.

Refer to **Figure** in online course

10.4.1 Describe the call center environment

A call center may exist within a company and offer service to the employees of that company as well as to the customers of that company's products. Alternatively, a call center may be an independent business that sells computer support as a service to outside customers. In either case, a call center will be a busy, fast-paced work environment, often operating 24 hours a day.

Call centers tend to have a large number of cubicles. As shown in Figure 1, each cubicle has a chair, at least one computer, a phone, and a headset. The technicians working at these cubicles will have varied levels of experience in computers, and some will have specialties in certain types of computers, software, or operating systems.

All of the computers in a call center will have help desk software. The technicians use this software to manage many of their job functions. Although it is not a complete list of most features of help desk software, Figure 2 provides more detail.

Your call center will have its own business policies regarding call priority. Figure 3 provides a sample chart of how calls may be named, defined, and prioritized.

Refer to **Figure** in online course

10.4.2 Describe level-one technician responsibilities

Call centers sometimes have different names for level-one technicians. These technicians may be known as level-one analysts, dispatchers, or incident screeners. Regardless of the title, the level-one technician's responsibilities are fairly similar from one call center to the next.

The primary responsibility of a level-one technician is to gather pertinent information from the customer. The technician has to document all information in the ticket or work order. The information the level-one technician must obtain is shown in Figure 1.

Some problems are very simple to resolve and a level-one technician can usually take care of these without escalating the work order to a level-two technician.

Often, a problem requires the expertise of a level-two technician. In these cases, the level-one technician must be able to translate a customer's problem description into a succinct sentence or two that is entered into the work order. This translation is important so that other technicians can quickly understand the situation without having to ask the customer the same questions again. Figure 2 shows how a customer might describe some of the most common problems and how a technician should document those problems.

Refer to **Figure** in online course

10.4.3 Describe level-two technician responsibilities

As with level-one technicians, call centers sometimes have different names for level-two technicians. These technicians may be known as product specialists or technical-support personnel. The level-two technician's responsibilities are generally the same from one call center to the next.

The level-two technician is usually more knowledgeable than the level-one technician about technology, or has been working for the company for a longer period of time. When a problem cannot be resolved within ten minutes, the level-one technician prepares an escalated work order, as shown in Figure 1. The level-two technician receives the escalated work order with the description of the problem. They then call the customer back to ask any additional questions and resolve the problem.

The following list of guidelines details when to escalate a problem to a more experienced technician. These are generic guidelines; you should follow your company's business policy for problem escalation.

- Escalate problems that require opening the computer case.
- Escalate problems that require installation of applications, operating systems, or drivers.
- Escalate problems that will take a long time to walk a customer through - like CMOS changes.
- Escalate down calls. The entire network is down, and a more experienced tech may be able to resolve the issue faster.

Problems that require opening up the computer will need a level-two technician. Level-two technicians can also use remote diagnostic software to connect to the customer's computer in order to update drivers and software, access the operating system, check BIOS, and gather other diagnostic information to solve the problem.

Summary

In this chapter, you learned about the relationship between communication skills and troubleshooting skills. You have learned that these two skills need to be combined to make you a successful technician. You also learned about the legal aspects and ethics of dealing with computer technology and the property of the customer.

The following concepts from this chapter are important to remember:

- To be a successful technician, you will need to practice good communication skills with customers and co-workers. These skills are as important as technical expertise.
- You should always conduct yourself in a professional manner with your customers and co-workers. Professional behavior increases customer confidence and enhances your credibility. You should also learn to recognize the classic signs of a difficult customer and learn what to do and what not to do when you are on a call with this customer.
- There are a few techniques that you can use to keep a difficult customer focused on the problem during a call. Primarily, you must remain calm and ask pertinent questions in an appropriate fashion. These techniques keep you in control of the call.
- There is a right way and a wrong way to put a customer on hold, or transfer a customer to another technician. Learn and use the right way every time. Doing either of these operations incorrectly can cause serious damage to your company's relationship with its customers.
- Netiquette is a list of rules to use whenever you communicate through e-mail, text messaging, instant messaging, or blogs. This is another area where doing things the wrong way can cause damage to your company's relationship with its customers.
- You must understand and comply with your customer's service level agreement (SLA). If the problem falls outside the parameters of the SLA, you need to find positive ways of telling the customer what you can do to help, and not what you cannot do. In special circumstances, you may decide to escalate the work order to management.
- In addition to the SLA, you must follow the business policies of the company. These policies will include how your company prioritizes calls, how and when to escalate a call to management, and when you are allowed to take breaks and lunch.
- A computer technician's job is stressful. You will rarely get to meet a customer who is having a good day. You can alleviate some of the stress by setting up your workstation in the most ergonomically beneficial way possible. You should practice time and stress management techniques every day.
- There are ethical and legal aspects of working in computer technology. You should be aware of your company's policies and practices. In addition, you may need to familiarize yourself with your state or country's trademark and copyright laws.
- The call center is a fast-paced environment. Level-one technicians and level-two technicians each have specific responsibilities. These responsibilities may vary slightly from one call center to another.

Chapter 10 Quiz

Take the chapter quiz to test your knowledge.

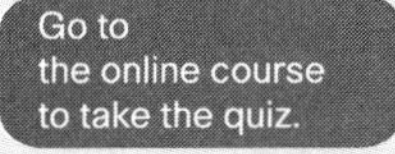

Your Chapter Notes

CHAPTER 11

Advanced Personal Computers

Introduction

In your career as a technician, you may have to determine if a component for a customer's computer should be upgraded or replaced. It is important that you develop advanced skills in installation procedures, troubleshooting techniques, and diagnostic methods for computers. This chapter discusses the importance of component compatibility across hardware and software. It also covers the need for adequate system resources to efficiently run the customer's hardware and software.

After completing this chapter, you will meet these objectives:

- Give an overview of field, remote, and bench technician jobs.
- Explain safe lab procedures and tool use.
- Describe situations requiring replacement of computer components.
- Upgrade and configure personal computer components and peripherals.
- Identify and apply common preventive maintenance techniques for personal computer components.
- Troubleshoot computer components and peripherals.

Refer to **Figure** in online course

11.1 Give an overview of field, remote, and bench technician jobs

Your experience working with computers and earning a technical certification can help you become qualified for employment as any of the following:

- Field technician
- Remote technician
- Bench technician

Technicians in different computer careers work in different environments. The skills required by each career can be very similar. The degree to which different skills are needed vary from one job to the next. When you train to become a computer technician, you are expected to develop the following skills:

- Building and upgrading computers
- Performing installations
- Installing, configuring, and optimizing software
- Performing preventive maintenance
- Troubleshooting and repairing computers

- Communicating clearly with the customer
- Documenting customer feedback and the steps involved in finding the solution to a problem

Field technicians, shown in Figure 1, work in various conditions and businesses. You might work for one company and only repair that company's assets. Alternatively, you may work for a company that provides onsite computer equipment repair for a variety of companies and customers. In either of these situations, you need both excellent troubleshooting skills and customer service skills, because you are in regular contact with customers and work on a wide variety of hardware and software.

If you are a remote technician, you might work at a help desk answering calls or e-mails from customers who have computer problems, as shown in Figure 2. You create work orders and communicate with the customer to try to diagnose and repair the problem.

Good communication skills are valuable because the customer must clearly understand your questions and instructions. Some help desks use software to connect directly to a customer's computer to fix the problem. As a remote technician, you may work on a team of help desk technicians for an organization or from home.

As a bench technician, you typically would not work directly with customers. Bench technicians are often hired to perform computer warranty service in a central depot or work facility, as shown in Figure 3.

Refer to **Worksheet** for this chapter

Job Opportunities

Research computer-related jobs

Refer to **Figure** in online course

11.2 Explain safe lab procedures and tool use

Safety should always be your priority on a job or in the lab. As a computer technician, you should be aware of the many workplace hazards, and you should take the necessary precautions to avoid them.

You should try to practice safety in the lab so that it becomes part of your regular routine. Follow all safety procedures and use the correct tools for the job. This policy will help prevent personal injury and damage to equipment.

To accomplish a safe working environment, it is better to be proactive rather than reactive. Figure 1 gives a list of safety rules to help you maintain a safe working environment.

After completing this section, you will meet these objectives:

- Review safe working environment and procedures.
- Review names, purposes, characteristics, and safe and appropriate use of tools.
- Identify potential safety hazards and implement proper safety procedures for computer components.
- Describe environmental issues.

Refer to **Figure** in online course

11.2.1 Review safe working environments and procedures

Workplace safety is necessary to ensure that you, and everyone near you, stay unharmed. In any situation, you should always follow these basic rules:

- Use antistatic mats and pads to reduce the chance of ESD damaging your equipment.
- Store hazardous or toxic materials in a secured cabinet.

- Keep the floor clear of anything that might trip someone.
- Clean work areas on a regular basis.

You should use caution when you move computer equipment from one place to another. Make sure that customers follow the safety rules in your work area. You may need to explain these rules and assure customers that the rules are there to protect them.

Follow local codes and government rules whenever you dispose of such things as batteries, solvents, computers, and monitors. Failing to do so may result in a fine. Many countries have agencies to enforce safety standards and ensure safe working conditions for employees. What are some of the documents that describe work safety codes and standards in your country?

Refer to **Figure** in online course

11.2.2 Review names, purposes, characteristics, and safe and appropriate use of tools

A computer technician needs proper tools to work safely and prevent damage to the computer equipment. There are many tools that a technician uses to diagnose and repair computer problems:

- Straight-head screwdriver, large and small
- Phillips-head screwdriver, large and small
- Tweezers or part retriever
- Needle-nosed pliers
- Wire cutters
- Chip extractor
- Hex wrench set
- Torx screwdriver
- Nut driver, large and small
- Three-claw component holder
- Digital multimeter
- Wrap plugs
- Small mirror
- Small dust brush
- Soft, lint-free cloth
- Cable ties
- Scissors
- Small flashlight
- Electric tape
- Pencil or pen
- Compressed air

Static electricity is one of the biggest concerns for computer technicians when working in many environments. The tools you use and even your own body can store or conduct thousands of volts of electricity. Walking across carpet or a rug and touching a computer component before grounding yourself can severely damage the component.

Antistatic devices help control static electricity. Use antistatic devices to prevent damage to sensitive components. Before you touch a computer component, be sure to ground yourself by touching a grounded computer chassis or mat. These are some antistatic devices:

- Antistatic wrist strap – Conducts static electricity from your body to ground
- Antistatic mat – Grounds computer frame
- Antistatic bag – Keeps sensitive computer components safe when not installed inside a computer
- Cleaning products – Maintains components without creating a buildup of static electricity

Refer to **Figure** in online course

Caution

Do not wear an antistatic wrist strap when working with high-voltage circuits, such as those found in monitors and printers. Do not open monitors unless you are properly trained.

11.2.3 Identify potential safety hazards and implement proper safety procedures for computer components

Most internal computer components use low-voltage electricity. Some components, however, operate with high voltage and can be dangerous if you do not follow safety precautions. The following dangerous, high-voltage computer components should only be serviced by authorized personnel:

- Power supplies
- Display monitors
- Laser printers

Power Supplies

The cost to repair a power supply can sometimes equal the cost of a new power supply. For this reason, most broken or used power supplies are replaced. Only experienced certified technicians should service power supplies.

Display Monitors

The internal electronic parts of a display monitor cannot be repaired, but they can be replaced. Monitors, especially CRT monitors, operate using high voltages. Only a certified electronic technician should service them.

Laser Printers

Laser printers can be very expensive. It is more cost effective to fix broken printers by repairing or replacing broken parts. Laser printers use high voltages and may have very hot surfaces inside. Use caution when servicing laser printers.

Refer to **Figure** in online course

11.2.4 Describe environmental issues

The Earth's environment is delicately balanced. The hazardous materials found in computer components must be disposed of in specific ways to help maintain this balance. A computer recycling warehouse is a place where discarded computer equipment can be taken apart. Computer parts that are still usable can be recycled for repairing other equipment. Figure 1 shows a computer recycling warehouse.

Recycling warehouses must obey the codes and regulations for the disposal of each type of computer part. Before parts are recycled, they are separated into groups. CRT monitors contain as much as 4 to 5 lbs (1.6 to 2.3 kg) of lead, a dangerous element. Much of the lead is inside cathode ray tubes. Other materials inside computer equipment are also dangerous:

- Mercury
- Cadmium
- Hexavalent chromium

Batteries are used to power laptop computers, digital cameras, camcorders, and remote-control toys. Batteries may contain some of these toxic materials:

- Nickel cadmium (Ni-Cd)
- Nickel metal hydride (Ni-MH)
- Lithium ion (Li-ion)
- Lead (Pb)

Discarding Components

Many organizations have policies that define disposal methods for the hazardous components found in electronic equipment. These methods typically include programs to reuse, recycle, or exchange.

You may need to dispose of computer components because they have become outdated, or you may need additional functionality. In addition to recycling parts, you can donate them to other people or organizations. Some businesses exchange used computer equipment for partial payment of new equipment.

Refer to **Figure** in online course

11.3 Describe situations requiring replacement of computer components

Situations that require the replacement of computer components include the repair of broken parts or an upgrade for functionality.

After completing this section, you will meet these objectives:

- Select a case and power supply.
- Select a motherboard.
- Select a CPU and cooling system.
- Select RAM.
- Select adapter cards.
- Select storage devices and hard drives.
- Select input and output devices.

Refer to **Figure** in online course

11.3.1 Select a case and power supply

You should determine the customer's needs before making any purchases or performing upgrades. Ask your customer what devices will be connected to the computer and what applications will be used.

The computer case holds the power supply, motherboard, memory, and other components. When purchasing a new computer case and power supply separately, you should ensure that all of the components will fit into the new case and that the power supply is powerful enough to operate all of the components. Many times a case comes with a power supply inside. You still need to verify that the power supply provides enough power to operate all the components that will be installed in the case.

Refer to **Figure** in online course

11.3.2 Select a motherboard

New motherboards often have new features or standards that may be incompatible with older components. When you select a replacement motherboard, make sure that it supports the CPU, RAM, video adapter, and other adapter cards. The socket and chip set on the motherboard must be compatible with the CPU. The motherboard must also accommodate the existing heat sink/fan assembly.

The existing power supply must have connections that fit the new motherboard. Pay particular attention to the number and type of expansion slots. Do they match the existing adapter cards? For instance, the new motherboard may lack an AGP connector for an existing video adapter. The motherboard may have PCIe expansion slots that the existing adapter cards cannot use. Finally, the new motherboard must physically fit into the current computer case.

Refer to **Figure** in online course

11.3.3 Select the CPU and heat sink/fan assembly

Replace the CPU when it fails or is no longer adequate for the current applications. For example, you may have a customer who has purchased an advanced graphics application, as shown in Figure 1. The application may run poorly because it requires a faster processor than the current CPU.

Before you buy a CPU, make sure that it is compatible with the existing motherboard:

- The new CPU must use the same socket type and chip set.
- The BIOS must support the new CPU.
- The new CPU may require a different heat sink/fan assembly.

Manufacturers' websites are a good resource to investigate the compatibility between CPUs and other devices. When upgrading the CPU, make sure the correct voltage is maintained. A voltage regulator module (VRM) is integrated into the motherboard. The voltage setting for the CPU can be configured with jumpers or switches located on the motherboard. Figure 2 shows two similar CPUs that use different sockets.

Refer to **Figure** in online course

11.3.4 Select RAM

New RAM may be needed when an application locks up or the computer displays frequent error messages. To determine if the problem is the RAM, replace the old RAM module as shown in Figure 1. Restart the computer to see if the application runs properly.

Note

To close a stalled application, press Ctrl-Alt-Delete to open the Task Manager. In the window, select the application. Click End Task to close it, as shown in Figure 2.

When selecting new RAM, you must ensure that it is compatible with the current motherboard. It must also be the same type of RAM as installed in the computer. The speed of the new RAM must be the same or faster than the existing RAM. It may help to take the original memory module with you when you shop for the replacement RAM.

Refer to **Figure** in online course

11.3.5 Select adapter cards

Adapter cards, also called expansion cards, add extra functionality to a computer. Figure 1 shows some of the adapter cards available. Before you purchase an adapter card, do some research:

- Is there an open expansion slot?
- Is the adapter card compatible with the open slot?

If the motherboard does not have compatible expansion slots, external devices may be an option:

- Are USB or FireWire versions of the external device available?
- Does the computer have an open USB or FireWire port?

Consider the following situation for an adapter card upgrade. A customer requires a wireless card to connect to the network. The new wireless adapter card must be compatible with the existing wireless network and with the computer.

Investigate wireless NICs before you purchase one. You should ensure that the new wireless NIC is compatible with the 802.11 wireless standard being used on the wireless network.

Examine the computer for an available expansion slot or an open USB port. Purchase either an adapter card that will fit an available expansion slot or a USB wireless NIC. Cost, warranty, brand name, and availability are the last factors for you to consider.

Refer to **Figure** in online course

11.3.6 Select storage devices and hard drives

You may need to replace a hard drive when it no longer meets your customer's needs for data storage or fails. The signs that a hard drive is failing include:

- Unusual noises
- Error messages
- Corrupt data or applications

If your hard drive exhibits any of these symptoms, you should replace it as soon as possible. Figure 1 shows PATA, SATA, and SCSI connectors.

ATA was renamed Parallel ATA, or PATA, with the introduction of Serial ATA (SATA). PATA hard drives can use a 40-pin / 80-conductor cable or a 40-pin / 40-conductor cable.

SATA

SATA hard drives connect to the motherboard using a serial interface. SATA hard drives have a higher data-transfer rate than PATA drives. The smaller data cable allows for improved airflow through the computer case. Early versions of SATA offered a speed of 1.5 Gbps. Current versions offer a speed of 3.0 Gbps.

SCSI

The small computer systems interface (SCSI) standard is usually used for hard drives and for tape storage. However, printers, scanners, CD-ROM drives, and DVD drives can also use SCSI. Today, SCSI devices are used mostly on servers or computers that require high transfer speeds and reliability.

SCSI is a more advanced interface controller than PATA or SATA. It is ideal for high-end computers, including network servers. Devices may include hard drives, CD-ROM drives, tape drives, scanners, and removable drives. SCSI devices are typically connected in a series, forming a chain that is commonly called a daisy chain, as shown in Figure 2. Each end of the daisy chain must be terminated to prevent signals from bouncing off the ends of cables and causing interference. Generally, the SCSI controller on one end of the SCSI bus has onboard termination. The other end of the SCSI cable is either terminated by a resistor on the last drive on the chain or a physical terminator on the end of the SCSI bus.

Most SCSI buses can handle a total of seven devices and a SCSI controller. The channels are numbered from 0 through 7. Some versions of SCSI support a total of 15 devices plus the SCSI controller. These channels are numbered 0 through 15. Each device on a SCSI channel must have a unique SCSI ID. For example, the primary drive would be 0, and the controller card is usually 7. The SCSI ID is generally set by jumpers on a SCSI drive.

The SCSI bus was originally 8-bits wide and operated at a transfer rate of 5 MBps. Later SCSI technologies used a 16-bit bus and operated at 320 – 640 MBps. Figure 3 shows the different types of SCSIs. Current and future SCSI technologies use a serial interface for increased speed.

Refer to **Figure** in online course

11.3.7 Select input and output devices

An input device can be any piece of equipment that transfers information into a computer:

- Mouse
- Keyboard
- Scanner
- Camera
- Process control sensor
- MIDI interface
- Microphone

An output device transfers information to the outside of the computer:

- Display monitor
- Projector
- Printer
- Process-control equipment
- Speaker

To select input and output devices, you should first find out what the customer wants. Next, you should select the hardware and software by researching the Internet for possible solutions. After you determine which input or output device the customer needs, you must determine how to connect it to the computer. Figures 1 shows common input and output port symbols.

Technicians should have a good understanding of several types of interfaces:

- USB 1.1 – Transfers data at a maximum speed of 12 Mbps

- USB 2.0 – Transfers data at a maximum speed of 480 Mbps
- FireWire – (IEEE 1394) – Transfers data at 100, 200, or 400 Mbps and IEEE 1394b at 800 Mbps
- Parallel (IEEE 1284) – Transfers data at a maximum speed of 3 MBps
- Serial (RS-232) – Early versions were limited to 20 Kbps, but newer versions can reach transfer rates of 1.5 Mbps
- SCSI (Ultra-320 SCSI) – Connects as many as 15 devices with a transfer rate of 320 MBps

Refer to **Worksheet** for this chapter

Selecting Replacement Components
Research computer components

Refer to **Figure** in online course

11.4 Upgrade and configure personal computer components and peripherals

Computer systems need periodic upgrades for various reasons:

- User requirements change
- Upgraded software packages require new hardware
- New hardware offers enhanced performance

Changes to the computer may cause you to upgrade or replace components and peripherals. You should research the effectiveness and cost for both options - upgrading and replacing.

After completing this section, you will meet these objectives:

- Upgrade and configure a motherboard.
- Upgrade and configure a CPU and a heat sink/fan assembly.
- Upgrade and configure RAM.
- Upgrade and configure BIOS.
- Upgrade and configure storage devices and hard drives.
- Upgrade and configure input and output devices.

Refer to **Figure** in online course

11.4.1 Upgrade and configure a motherboard

To upgrade or replace a motherboard, you may have to replace several other components, such as the CPU, heat sink/fan assembly, and RAM.

A new motherboard must fit into the old computer case. The power supply must also be compatible for the new motherboard and be able to support all new computer components.

You should begin the upgrade by moving the CPU and heat sink/fan assembly to the new motherboard. These are much easier to work with when they are outside of the case. You should work on an antistatic mat and wear a wrist strap to avoid damaging the CPU. Remember to use thermal compound between the CPU and the heat sink. If the new motherboard requires different RAM, install it at this time.

When it is time to remove and replace the old motherboard, remove the cables from the motherboard that attach to the case LEDs and buttons. They may have the same labels, but there may be minor differences. Make the appropriate notes in your journal to know where and how everything is connected before you start the upgrade.

Note how the motherboard secures to the case. Some mounting screws provide support, and some may provide an important grounding connection between the motherboard and chassis. In particular, you should pay attention to screws and standoffs that are non-metallic. These may be insulators. Replacing insulating screws and supports with metal hardware that conducts electricity may have disastrous results.

Make sure that you use the correct screws. Do not swap threaded screws with self-tapping metal screws; they will damage the threaded screw holes and may not be secure. Make sure that threaded screws are the correct length and have the same number of threads per inch. If the thread is correct, they will fit easily. You may make a screw fit by using force, but you will damage the threaded hole and it will not hold the motherboard securely. Using the wrong screw can also produce metal shavings that can cause short circuits.

Note

It does not matter if you replace a screw made for a slotted screwdriver with one made for a Phillips-head screwdriver, as long as the threaded part of the screw is the same length and has the same number of threads.

Next you should connect the power supply cables. If the ATX power connectors are not the same size (some have more pins), you may need to use an adapter. Connect the cables for the case LEDs and buttons.

After the new motherboard is in place and cabled, you should install and secure all expansion cards. Check your work. Make sure there are no loose parts or leftover wires. Connect a keyboard, mouse, monitor, and power. If there is any sign of trouble, you should shut the power supply off immediately.

Do not forget that an expansion card can have the same functionality that is integrated into the motherboard. In this case, you may need to disable the onboard functions in the system BIOS. Use the documentation that came with the motherboard to learn what BIOS adjustments may be required.

NIC

Refer to **Lab Activity** for this chapter

Install a NIC and disable an integrated motherboard network adapter

11.4.2 Upgrade and configure a CPU and a heat sink/fan assembly

Refer to **Figure** in online course

One way to increase the apparent power of a computer is to increase the processing speed. You can often do this by upgrading the CPU. However, there are some requirements that you must meet:

- The new CPU must fit into the existing CPU socket.
- The new CPU must be compatible with the motherboard chip set.
- The new CPU must operate with the existing motherboard and power supply.
- The new CPU must operate with the existing RAM. The RAM may need to be upgraded or expanded to take advantage of the faster CPU.

If the motherboard is older, you may not be able to find a compatible CPU. In that case, you would replace the motherboard.

Caution

Always work on an antistatic mat and wear a wrist strap when installing and removing CPUs. Place a CPU on the antistatic mat until you are ready to use it. Store CPUs in antistatic packaging.

To change the CPU, you should remove the existing CPU by releasing it from the socket using the zero insertion force lever. Different sockets have slightly different mechanisms, but all serve to lock the CPU in place after it is correctly oriented in the socket.

Insert the new CPU into place. Do not force the CPU into its socket, or use excessive force to close the locking bars. Excessive force may damage the CPU or its socket. If you encounter resistance, make sure that you have aligned the CPU properly. Most have a pattern of pins that will fit only one way. If there is a question, examine the new CPU to insure it is physically similar to the old one.

The new CPU may require a different heat sink/fan assembly. The heat sink/fan assembly must physically fit the CPU and be compatible with the CPU socket. The heat sink/fan assembly must also be adequate to remove the heat of the faster CPU.

Caution

You must apply thermal compound between the new CPU and the heat sink/fan assembly.

With some types of BIOS, you can view thermal settings to determine if there are any problems with the CPU and the heat sink/fan assembly. Third-party software applications can report CPU temperature information in an easy to read format. Refer to the motherboard or CPU user documentation to determine if the chip is operating in the correct temperature range. Some CPU and case fans turn on and off automatically depending on the CPU temperature and the internal case temperature. The temperatures are measured through thermal probes built into the fan assembly, or internal circuitry in the CPU.

Refer to **Figure** in online course

11.4.3 Upgrade and configure RAM

Increasing the amount of system RAM almost always improves overall system performance. Prior to upgrading or replacing the RAM, there are some questions you must answer:

- What type of RAM does the motherboard currently use?
- Can the RAM be installed one module at a time, or should it be grouped into matching banks?
- Are there any available RAM slots?
- Does the new RAM chip match the speed, latency, type, and voltage of the existing RAM?

Caution

When working with system RAM, work on an antistatic mat and wear a wrist strap. Place the RAM on the mat until you are ready to install it. Store RAM in antistatic packaging.

Remove the existing RAM by freeing retaining clips that secure it. Pull it from the socket. Current DIMMS pull straight out and insert straight down. Earlier SIMMS were inserted at an angle to lock into place.

When inserting the new RAM make sure the notches in the RAM and RAM slot on the motherboard align properly. Press down firmly and lock the RAM into place with the retaining clips.

Caution

Make sure to insert the memory module completely into the socket. RAM can cause serious damage to the motherboard if it is incorrectly aligned and shorts the main system bus.

The system discovers the newly installed RAM if it is compatible and installed correctly. If the BIOS does not indicate the presence of the correct amount of RAM, check to make sure that the RAM is compatible with the motherboard and is correctly installed.

Refer to **Lab Activity** for this chapter

Install RAM

Install additional RAM into the computer

Refer to **Figure** in online course

11.4.4 Upgrade and configure BIOS

Motherboard manufacturers periodically release updates for their BIOS. The release notes, such as those shown in Figure 1, describe the upgrade to the product, compatibility improvements, and the known bugs that have been addressed. Some newer devices only operate properly with an updated BIOS.

Early computer BIOS information was contained in ROM chips. To upgrade the BIOS information, the ROM chip had to be replaced, which was not always possible. Modern BIOS chips are EEPROM, or flash memory, which can be upgraded by the user without opening the computer case. This process is called "flashing the BIOS".

To view the current BIOS settings on your computer, you must enter the BIOS setup program as shown in Figure 2. Press the setup sequence keys while the computer is performing the power-on self test (POST). Depending on the computer, the setup key may be the F1, F2, or Del key. Watch the text on the screen or consult the motherboard manual to find the setup key or combination of keys.

The first part of the boot process displays a message that tells you which key to press to enter the setup, or BIOS mode. There are a variety of settings in the BIOS that should not be altered by anyone unfamiliar with this procedure. If you are unsure, it is best not to change any BIOS setting unless you research the problem in depth.

To download a new BIOS, consult the manufacturer's website and follow the recommended installation procedures as shown in Figure 3. Installing BIOS software online may involve downloading a new BIOS file, copying or extracting files to a floppy, and then booting from the floppy. An installation program prompts the user for information to complete the process.

Although it is still common to flash the BIOS through a command prompt, several motherboard manufacturers provide software on their websites that allow a user to flash the BIOS from within Windows. The procedure varies from manufacturer to manufacturer.

Refer to **Lab Activity** for this chapter

BIOS

Search for newer BIOS versions

Caution

An improperly installed or aborted BIOS update can cause the computer to become unusable.

Refer to **Figure** in online course

11.4.5 Upgrade and configure storage devices and hard drives

Instead of purchasing a new computer to get increased access speed and storage space, you may consider adding another hard drive. There are several reasons for installing an additional drive:

- To install a second operating system
- To provide additional storage space
- To provide a faster hard drive
- To hold the system swap file
- To provide a backup for the original hard drive
- To increase fault tolerance

There are several things to consider before adding a new hard drive.

If the new drive is PATA and is on the same data cable, one of the drives must be set as the master drive and the other must be set as the slave drive. Figure 1 shows jumper settings on the back of a PATA hard drive. Also, any new partitions or drive letter assignments should be well-planned. The boot order in BIOS may need to be adjusted.

Arrays, such as a redundant array of independent disks (RAID), improve fault tolerance when connecting multiple hard drives, as shown in Figure 2. Some types of RAID require two or more hard drives. You can install RAID using hardware or software. Hardware installations are usually more dependable, but are more expensive. Software installations are created and managed by an operating system, such as Windows Server 2003.

Refer to **Lab Activity** for this chapter

Up-grade and Configure Hard Drive

Install and configure a second hard drive

Refer to **Figure** in online course

11.4.6 Upgrade and configure input and output devices

If an input or output device stops operating, you may have to replace the device. Some customers may wish to upgrade their input or output devices to increase performance and productivity.

An ergonomic keyboard, shown in Figure 1, may be more comfortable to use. Sometimes a reconfiguration is necessary to enable a user to perform special tasks, such as typing in a second language with additional characters. Finally, replacing or reconfiguring an input or output device may make it easier to accommodate users with disabilities.

Sometimes it is not possible to perform an upgrade using the existing expansion slots or sockets. In this case, you may be able to accomplish the upgrade using a USB connection. If the computer does not have an extra USB connection, you must install a USB adapter card or purchase a USB hub, as shown in Figure 2.

After obtaining new hardware, you may have to install new drivers. You can usually do this by using the installation CD. If you do not have the CD, you can obtain updated drivers from the website of the manufacturer.

Note

A signed driver is a driver that has passed the Windows hardware quality lab test and has been given a driver signature by Microsoft. Installing an unsigned driver can cause system instability, error messages, and boot problems. During hardware installation, if an unsigned driver is detected you will be asked to stop or continue installation of this driver.

11.5 Identify and apply common preventive maintenance techniques for personal computer components

To keep computers working properly, you must maintain them by performing preventive maintenance. Preventive maintenance can extend the life of the components, protect data, and improve computer performance.

After completing this section, you will meet these objectives:

- Clean internal components.
- Clean the case.
- Inspect computer components.

Refer to **Figure** in online course

11.5.1 Clean internal components

One important part of computer preventive maintenance is to keep the system clean. The amount of dust in the environment and the habits of the user determines how often to clean the computer components. Most of your cleaning is to prevent the accumulation of dust.

To remove dust, do not use a vacuum cleaner. Vacuum cleaners can generate static and can damage or loosen components and jumpers. Instead, you should use compressed air to blow the dust away. If you use compressed air from a can, keep the can upright to prevent the fluid from leaking onto computer components. Always follow the instructions and warnings on the compressed air can.

Regular cleaning also gives you a chance to inspect components for loose screws and connectors. There are several parts inside the computer case that you should keep as clean as possible:

- Heat sink/fan assembly
- RAM
- Adapter cards
- Motherboard
- Case fan
- Power supply
- Internal drives

Refer to **Figure** in online course

Caution

When you clean a fan with compressed air, hold the fan blades in place. This prevents overspinning the rotor, or moving the fan in the wrong direction.

11.5.2 Clean the case

Dust or dirt on the outside of a computer can travel through cooling fans and loose computer case covers. Dirt can also enter a computer through missing expansion slot covers, as shown in Figure 1. If dust accumulates inside the computer, it can prevent the flow of air and affect cooling.

Use a cloth or duster to clean the outside of the computer case. If you use a cleaning product, do not spray it directly on the case. Instead, put a small amount onto a cleaning cloth or duster and wipe the outside of the case.

While cleaning the case, you should look for and correct things that might cause a problem later:

- Missing expansion slot covers that let dust, dirt, or living pests into the computer
- Loose or missing screws that secure adapter cards
- Missing or tangled cables that can pull free from the case

Refer to **Figure** in online course

11.5.3 Inspect computer components

The best method of keeping a computer in good condition is to examine the computer on a regular schedule. Cleaning provides a good opportunity to make this inspection. You should have a checklist of components to inspect:

- ***CPU and cooling system –*** Examine the CPU and cooling system for dust buildup. Make sure that the fan can spin freely. Check that the fan power cable is secure, as shown in Figure

1. Check the fan while the power is on to see the fan turn. Inspect the CPU to be sure that it is seated securely in the socket. Make sure that the heat sink is well attached. To avoid damage, do not remove the CPU for cleaning.

- *RAM connections –* The RAM chips should be seated securely in the RAM slots. Figure 2 shows that sometimes the retaining clips can loosen. Reseat them, if necessary. Use compressed air to remove any dust.
- *Storage devices –* Inspect all storage devices including the hard drives, floppy drive, optical drives, and tape drive. All cables should be firmly connected. Check for loose, missing, or incorrectly set jumpers, as shown in Figure 3. A drive should not produce rattling, knocking, or grinding sounds. Read the manufacturer's manual to learn how to clean optical drive and tape heads by using cotton swabs and compressed air. Clean floppy drives with a drive cleaning kit.
- *Adapter cards –* Adapter cards should be seated properly in their expansion slots. Loose cards, as shown in Figure 4, can cause short circuits. Secure adapter cards with the retaining screw to avoid the cards coming loose in their expansion slots. Use compressed air to remove any dirt or dust on the adapter cards or the expansion slots.

Note

The video adapter can sometimes become unseated because the large monitor cable can put pressure on it, or it is mishandled when someone is tightening the retainer screws.

Note

If a video adapter is used in an expansion slot, the integrated video adapter from the motherboard is likely to be disabled. If you connect a monitor to it in error, the computer appears not to work.

These are some common computer items to inspect:

- *Power devices –* Inspect power strips, surge suppressors (surge protectors), and UPS devices. Make sure that there is proper and unobstructed ventilation. Replace the power strip if there have been electrical problems or excessive thunderstorms in the area.
- *Loose screws –* Loose screws can cause problems if they are not immediately fixed or removed. A loose screw in the case may later cause a short circuit or roll into a position where the screw is hard to remove.
- *Keyboard and mouse –* Use compressed air or a small vacuum cleaner to clean the keyboard and mouse. If the mouse is the mechanical type, remove the ball and clean off any dirt.
- *Cables –* Examine all cable connections. Look for broken and bent pins. Ensure that all connector retaining screws are finger tight. Make sure cables are not crimped, pinched, or severely bent.

Refer to **Figure** in online course

11.6 Troubleshoot computer components and peripherals

The troubleshooting process helps resolve problems with the computer or peripherals. These problems range from simple, such as updating a drive, to more complex problems, such as installing a CPU. Use the troubleshooting steps as a guideline to help you diagnose and repair problems.

After completing this section, you will meet these objectives:

- Review the troubleshooting process.
- Identify common problems and solutions.
- Apply troubleshooting skills.

Refer to **Figure** in online course

11.6.1 Review the troubleshooting process

Computer technicians must be able to analyze the problem and determine the cause of the error to repair the computer. This process is called troubleshooting.

The first step in the troubleshooting process is to gather data from the customer. Figures 1 and 2 list open-ended and closed-ended questions to ask the customer.

Once you have talked to the customer, you should verify the obvious issues. Figure 3 lists issues that apply to computer hardware.

After the obvious issues have been verified, try some quick solutions. Figure 4 lists some quick solutions to computer hardware problems.

If quick solutions did not correct the problem, it is time to gather data from the computer. Figure 5 shows different ways to gather information about the problem from the computer.

At this point, you have enough information to evaluate the problem, research, and implement possible solutions. Figure 6 shows resources for possible solutions.

After you have solved the problem, close with the customer. Figure 7 is a list of the tasks required to complete this step.

Refer to **Figure** in online course

11.6.2 Identify common problems and solutions

Computer problems can be attributed to hardware, software, networks, or some combination of the three. You will resolve some types of computer problems more often than others. Figure 1 is a chart of common hardware problems and solutions.

Refer to **Figure** in online course

11.6.3 Apply troubleshooting skills

Now that you understand the troubleshooting process, it is time to apply your listening and diagnostic skills.

The first lab is designed to reinforce your skills with PC hardware problems. You will troubleshoot and repair a computer that does not boot.

The second lab is designed to reinforce your communication and troubleshooting skills with PC hardware problems. In this lab, you will perform the following steps:

- Receive the work order
- Take the customer through various steps to try and resolve the problem
- Document the problem and the resolution

Summary

In this chapter, you learned about advanced computer diagnosis and repair, and how to consider upgrades and select components. This chapter also presented some detailed troubleshooting techniques to help you locate and resolve problems, and present your findings to the customer.

- You learned about the roles of the field, remote, and bench technicians and the job possibilities that are available to those who enter the workforce with some knowledge of advanced troubleshooting skills.
- You are able to explain and perform safe lab procedures and tool use. You can describe basic electrical safety, especially as it applies to monitors and laser printers. You understand the purpose and enforcement of worker safety standards.
- You know the safe disposal procedures for various types of computer batteries and types of hardware, such as monitors.
- You have the ability to advise customers of ways to protect their computers by using good preventive maintenance practices.
- You can describe ways to clean the external components of a computer, including the monitor, case, printer, and peripherals. You can describe how to clean internal components of a computer, such as the motherboard, CPU and cooling system, RAM, and adapter cards.
- You know how to advise customers when it is best to upgrade a computer and components and when it is best to buy new products.
- You can explain the steps involved in adding and configuring a second hard drive. You can describe the steps involved in updating various computer components, such as cases, power supplies, the CPU and cooling system, RAM, hard drives, and adapter cards.
- You are able to demonstrate the use of open- and closed-ended questions that are appropriate for a level-two technician to determine the problem.
- You can describe the troubleshooting steps, including gathering data from the customer, verifying obvious issues, trying quick solutions first, evaluating problems, and implementing solutions until the problem is fixed.
- You have an understanding of the role of the level-two technician, and how to build on the troubleshooting efforts of a level-one technician.

Chapter 11 Quiz

Take the chapter quiz to test your knowledge.

Go to
the online course
to take the quiz.

Your Chapter Notes

CHAPTER 12

Advanced Operating Systems

Introduction

The installation, configuration, and optimization of operating systems are examined in greater detail in this chapter.

There are various brands of operating systems available on the market today, including Microsoft Windows, Apple Mac OS, UNIX, and Linux. A technician must consider the current computer system when selecting an operating system. Additionally, there are several versions or distributions of an operating system. Some versions of Microsoft Windows include Windows 2000 Professional, Windows XP Home Edition,Windows XP Professional, Windows Media Center, Windows Vista Home Basic, Windows Vista Business, and Windows Vista Premium.

Each of these operating systems offers many of the same features with a similar interface. However, some functions necessary for specific customer needs may not be available in all of them. You must be able to compare and contrast operating systems to find the best one based on your customer's needs.

After completing this chapter, you will meet these objectives:

- Select the appropriate operating system based on customer needs.
- Install, configure, and optimize an operating system.
- Describe how to upgrade operating systems.
- Describe preventive maintenance procedures for operating systems.
- Troubleshoot operating systems.

Refer to **Figure** in online course

12.1 Select the appropriate operating system based on customer needs

There are many operating systems to choose from, each with features that should be considered when consulting with a customer. When selecting an operating system for a customer, you should select hardware that meets or exceeds the minimum requirements for equipment called for by the operating system.

In this chapter, Windows XP Professional is used to describe the functions of an operating system. At some point during your career, you most likely will upgrade or repair a computer with a Windows operating system.

Figure 1 shows a comparison of Windows operating systems.

After completing this section, you will meet these objectives:

- Describe operating systems.
- Describe network operating systems.

Refer to **Figure** in online course

12.1.1 Describe operating systems

An operating system is the interface between the user and the computer. Without an operating system, the user would not be able to interact with the hardware or software on the computer. An operating system provides the following operational and organizational capabilities:

- Provides a bridge between the hardware and applications
- Creates a file system to store data
- Manages applications
- Interprets user commands

Operating systems have minimum requirements for hardware. Figure 1 shows the minimum hardware requirements for several operating systems.

Refer to **Figure** in online course

12.1.2 Describe network operating systems

A network operating system (NOS) is an operating system that contains additional features to increase functionality and manageability in a networked environment. The following are examples of network operating systems:

- Windows 2000 Server
- Windows 2003 Server
- UNIX
- Linux
- Novell NetWare
- Mac OS X

The NOS is designed to provide network resources to clients:

- Server applications, such as shared databases
- Centralized data storage
- Directory services that provide a centralized repository of user accounts and resources on the network, such as LDAP or Active Directory
- Network print queue
- Network access and security
- Redundant storage systems, such as RAID and backups

Network operating systems provide several protocols designed to perform network functions. These protocols are controlled by code on the network servers. Protocols used by network operating systems provide services such as web browsing, file transfer, e-mail, name resolution, and automatic IP addressing. Figure 1 shows more information.

Refer to **Interactive Graphic** in online course.

Refer to **Figure** in online course

12.2 Install, configure, and optimize an operating system

Most operating systems are easy to install. After the computer starts, the Windows XP Professional installation CD displays a wizard to guide you through the installation process with a series of questions. Once the answers to the questions are provided, the installation wizard completes the installation automatically. In this section, you will perform a custom installation of Windows XP Professional.

After completing this section, you will meet these objectives:

- Compare and contrast a default installation and a custom installation.
- Install Windows XP Professional using a custom installation.
- Create, view, and manage disks, directories, and files.
- Identify procedures and utilities used to optimize the performance of operating systems.
- Identify procedures and utilities used to optimize the performance of browsers.
- Describe installation, use, and configuration of e-mail software.
- Set screen resolution and update video driver.
- Describe installation of a second operating system.

Refer to **Figure** in online course

12.2.1 Compare and contrast a default installation and a custom installation

The default installation of Windows XP Professional is sufficient for most computers used in a home or small office network. A custom installation of Windows XP Professional is typically used in a larger network.

Default Installation

Default installation requires minimal user interaction. You are prompted to provide information for the specific computer and the owner/user.

Custom Installation

In Windows XP, the custom installation is very similar to the default installation. There are only two screens that offer a custom selection during setup. The first screen is to customize the regional settings, and the second screen is to customize the network settings as shown in Figure 1. A technician or a user with technical experience often performs the custom installation. In a custom installation, the wizard prompts the user for detailed performance information to ensure that the operating system is customized to meet the preferences or requirements of the individual user or the network administrator of a company. You can perform a custom Windows XP Professional installation on more than one computer on a network by using an answer file that contains predefined settings and answers to the questions that are asked by the wizard during setup.

The technician can automate and customize a Windows XP Professional installation to include the following features:

- Productivity applications, such as Microsoft Office

- Custom applications
- Support for multiple languages
- OS Deployment Feature Pack using Microsoft Systems Management Server (SMS)
- Hardware device drivers

Refer to **Figure** in online course

12.2.2 Install Windows XP Professional using a custom installation

The default installation of Windows XP Professional is sufficient for most computers used in a home or small-office environment. A custom installation of Windows XP Professional can save time and provide a consistent configuration of the operating system across computers on a large network.

- Unattended installation from a network distribution point using an answer file.
- Image-based installation using Sysprep and a disk-imaging program, which copies an image of the operating system directly to the hard drive with no user intervention.
- Remote installation using Remote Installation Services (RIS), which can download the installation across the network. This install can be requested by the user or forced onto the computer by the administrator.
- OS Deployment Feature Pack using Microsoft Systems Management Server (SMS), which can dramatically simplify deployment of an operating system across the organization.

Unattended Installation

The unattended installation using an unattend.txt answer file is the easiest custom installation method to perform on a network. An answer file can be created using an application called setupmgr.exe located within the deploy.cab file on the Windows XP Professional CD.

Figure 1 shows an example of an answer file. Once you have answered all of the questions, the unattend.txt file is copied to the distribution shared folder on a server. At this point, you can do one of two things:

- Run the unattended.bat file on the client machine. This prepares the hard drive and automatically installs the operating system from the server over the network.
- Create a boot disk that boots up the computer and connects to the distribution share on the server. Run the batch file to install the operating system over the network.

Image-Based Installation

When performing image-based installations, you should begin by completely configuring one computer to an operational state. Next, run Sysprep to prepare the system for imaging. A third-party drive imaging application prepares an image of the completed computer, which can be burned onto a CD or DVD. This image can then be copied onto computers with compatible HALs to complete the installation of multiple computers. Once the image has been copied, you can boot up the computer, but you may have to configure some settings, such as computer name and domain membership.

Remote Installation

With RIS, the process is very much like an image-based installation, except you would not use a drive imaging utility. You can use RIS to remotely set up new Microsoft Windows computers by using an RIS network shared folder as the source of the Windows operating system files. You can install operating systems on remote boot-enabled client computers. User computers that are connected to the network can be started by using a Pre-Boot eXecution Environment (PXE)-capable network adapter or remote boot disk. The client then logs on with valid user account credentials.

RIS is designed to be used in a relatively small network and should not be used over low-speed links of a wide area network (WAN). Microsoft System Management Server (SMS) allows a network administrator to manage large numbers of computers on a network. SMS can be used to manage updates, provide remote control, and perform inventory management. An optional feature is operating system deployment, which requires the installation of the SMS OS Deployment Feature Pack on the Windows 2003 server. SMS allows the installation of a large number of client computers across the entire network, such as a LAN or WAN.

Refer to **Lab Activity** for this chapter

Advanced Installation of Windows XP

Perform custom install of Windows XP

Refer to **Figure** in online course

12.2.3 Create, view, and manage disks, directories, and files

Within the operating system, disks and directories are locations where data is stored and organized. The file system used by the operating system determines additional factors that affect storage such as partition size, cluster size, and security features.

Disk Structure

The Disk Management utility displays information and performs services such as partitioning and formatting disks in Windows. Figure 1 shows the Disk Management utility used in Windows XP Professional.

There are several types of partitions on a hard drive:

- Primary partitions
- Extended partitions
- Logical drives

Note

At any given time, you can only designate one partition as the active partition. The operating system uses the active partition to boot up the system. The active partition must be a primary partition.

In most cases, the C: drive is the active partition and contains the boot and system files. Some users create additional partitions to organize files or to be able to dual-boot the computer.

You can access the Disk Management utility in the following ways:

- From the **Start** menu, right-click **My Computer** and then choose **Manage > Disk Management**.
- From the **Start** menu, choose **Settings > Control Panel > Administrative Tools > Computer Management**. Double-click **Storage**, then click **Disk Management**.

File System

Partitions are formatted with a file system. The two file systems available in Windows XP are FAT32 and NTFS. NTFS has greater stability and security features.

For example, Windows does not display the file extension, but this practice can cause security problems. Virus writers are able to distribute executable files disguised as a non-executable file. To avoid this security breach, you should always show file extensions by doing the following:

From the **Start** menu, choose **Control Panel > Folder Options > View**, and uncheck the "Hide extensions for known file types" check box, as shown in Figure 2.

Refer to **Lab Activity** for this chapter

Additional Partitions

Create an additional partition in Windows XP Professional

Note

Saving files to the root directory of the C: drive can cause organizational problems with data. It is a best practice to store data in folders created on the C: drive.

Refer to **Figure** in online course

12.2.4 Identify procedures and utilities used to optimize the performance of operating systems

There are several procedures and tools available to optimize the performance of an operating system. The concepts may be the same across operating systems, but the optimization methods and procedures are different. For example, while virtual memory performs the same function on a Windows 98 and Windows XP operating system, the path to find and set virtual memory settings is different.

System Tools

To maintain and optimize an operating system, you can access various tools within Windows. Some of these tools include disk error checking, which can scan the hard drive for file structure errors, and hard drive defragmentation, which can consolidate files for faster access. Figure 1 shows the hard drive management tools.

Virtual Memory

Virtual memory allows the CPU to address more memory than is installed in the computer. This is done so that every application can address the same amount of memory. Virtual memory is a swap or page file that is contantly read in and out of RAM. Typically, you should let Windows manage the size of the swap file. The only setting that you should change is the location of the swap file. You must be a member of the administrator group to make this change. Figure 2 shows virtual memory settings.

To access virtual memory settings in Windows XP, use one of the following paths:

- **Start > Settings > Control Panel >System > Advanced tab > Performance, click Settings button > Advanced tab**

  or

- **Start > Control Panel > System > Advanced tab > Performance, click Settings button > Advanced tab**

Disk Defragmenter

To help optimize the files on the hard drive, Windows operating systems provide a defragmentation utility. As files are accessed and stored on a hard drive, the files change from being contiguous on the disk to being scattered across the disk. This can cause the operating system to slow down. The hard drive has to search several areas on the hard drive platter to find the entire file. For one file, the effect of the process is minimal. When this occurs for thousands of files, however, the process will physically slow down the reading and writing of a file to a hard drive. To defragment a drive, double-click **My Computer** on the desktop. Right-click the drive that you want to optimize. Choose **Properties**. On the **Tools** tab, click **Defragment Now**.

Temporary Files

Almost every program uses temporary files, which are usually automatically deleted when the application or the operating system is finished using them. However, some of the temporary files must be deleted manually. Since temporary files take up hard drive space that could be used for other files, it is a good idea to check and delete as necessary every two or three months. Temporary files are usually located in the following locations:

- C:\temp
- C:\tmp
- C:\windows\temp
- C:\windows\tmp
- C:\documents and settings\%USERPROFILE%\local settings\temp

Services

Services are a type of application that runs in the background to achieve a specific goal or wait for a request. Only necessary services should be started to reduce unnecessary security risks. See Figure 3 for some of the services available on a computer. There are four settings, or states, that can be used to control the services:

- Automatic
- Manual
- Disabled
- Stopped

If a service, such as DHCP or Automatic Updates, is set to automatic, it will start up when the PC starts. Manual services, such as the support of an uninterruptible power supply (UPS), need to be manually configured to work. Some services may be stopped or disabled for troubleshooting purposes, such as turning off the print spooler when there are printer problems.

Refer to **Lab Activity** for this chapter

Virtual Memory

Customize the virtual memory settings

Refer to **Figure** in online course

12.2.5 Identify procedures and utilities used to optimize the performance of browsers

Web browsers and e-mail applications are typically the applications used the most on a computer. Optimizing the Web browsers and the e-mail application should increase the performance of the computer.

The Microsoft browser, Internet Explorer (IE), has general settings for changing the homepage and browser appearance settings. Additional settings allow you to view or delete the information saved by the browser:

- History
- Temporary files
- Cookies
- Passwords

- Web-form information

Note

Cookies are information transmitted between a web browser and a web server with the purpose of tracking user information to customize the page delivered to the user.

To access the settings in IE, open an IE browser window and **choose Tools > Internet Options**.

Caching, or storing, Internet files is a feature of the Web browser that is used to speed up the process of accessing previously visited websites. The file-storing tool in IE downloads copies of the images or the HTML files of sites you have visited to the hard disk. When you revisit the website, the site opens more quickly because the files are in the local disk cache and do not need to be downloaded again.

Cached files in the web browser can become outdated or may be very large. These IE settings allow you to control the size of the cache and when the cache should be refreshed:

- Every visit to the page
- Every time you start IE
- Automatically
- Never

To access the cache settings, open an IE browser window and choose **Tools > Internet Options**. In the **Temporary Internet Files** area, click **Settings**. Click the tabs in Figure 1 to explore other IE configuration options.

Refer to **Lab Activity** for this chapter

Alternate Browser (Optional)

Install an alternate browser

Refer to **Figure** in online course

12.2.6 Describe installation, use, and configuration of e-mail software

E-mail software may be installed as part of a web browser or as a standalone application. Outlook Express is an e-mail tool that is a component of the Microsoft Windows operating system. To configure Outlook Express, you must provide information about your e-mail account, as shown in Figure 1.

You should have the following information available when installing e-mail accounts into the e-mail client software:

- Display name
- E-mail address
- Type of incoming mail server, such as POP3 or IMAP
- Incoming mail server name
- Outgoing mail server name
- Username
- Account password

The protocols used in e-mail include the following:

- ***Post Office Protocol version 3 (POP3)*** – Retrieves e-mails from a remote server over TCP/IP. It does not leave a copy of the e-mail on the server; however, some implementations allow users to specify that mail be saved for some period of time.

- ***Internet Message Access Protocol (IMAP)*** – Allows local e-mail clients to retrieve e-mail from a server. Typically leaves a copy of the e-mail on the server until you move the e-mail to a personal folder in your e-mail application. IMAP synchronizes e-mail folders between the server and client.
- ***Simple Mail Transfer Protocol (SMTP)*** – Transmits e-mails across a TCP/IP network. It is the e-mail format for text that only uses ASCII encoding.
- ***Multipurpose Internet Mail Extensions (MIME)*** – Extends the e-mail format to include text in ASCII standard, as well as other formats such as pictures and word processor documents. Normally used in conjunction with SMTP.

Additional features are available with e-mail software:

- Automatic handling rules for e-mails
- Different e-mail coding, such as HTML, plain text, or rich text
- Newsgroups

Refer to **Interactive Graphic** in online course.

12.2.7 Set screen resolution and update video driver

Refer to **Figure** in online course

Once the operating system is installed, you can set the screen resolution to meet the requirements of your customer. If the screen resolution is not set properly, you may get unexpected display results from different video cards and monitors. The unexpected results could include a Windows desktop that does not take up the full area of the screen, or a blank screen if the resolution is set too high.

When using an LCD screen, the resolution should be set to native mode, or native resolution. Native mode is the screen resolution that is the same as the number of pixels that the monitor has. If you move from the native mode, the monitor does not produce the best picture. See Figure 1 for the screen resolution settings on a Windows XP Professional computer.

You can change the screen settings in the Settings tab of the Display Properties control panel applet:

- ***Screen resolution*** – Determines the number of pixels. A higher number of pixels displays a better resolution and picture.
- ***Refresh rate*** – Determines how often the image in the screen is redrawn. Refresh rate is expressed in Hertz (Hz). The higher the refresh rate, the more steady the screen image.
- ***Display colors*** – Determines the number of colors visible on the screen at once. Colors are created by varying the intensity of the three basic colors (red, green, blue). The more bits, the greater the number of colors. The following is a list of color depths:
  - 256 colors - 8-bit color
  - 65,536 colors - 16-bit color (High Color)
  - 16 million colors - 24-bit color (True Color)
  - 16 million colors - 24-bit (True Color with 8-bit padding to allow for 32-bit processing)

When troubleshooting a display problem, check that the driver is fully compatible with the graphics card. Windows may install a default driver that works, but may not provide all of the available options for best viewing and performance. See Figure 2 for the video driver update utility in Windows XP Professional. Perform the following for best graphical performance:

Step 1. Download the most recent driver from the manufacturer website.

Step 2. Remove the current driver.

Step 3. Disable anti-virus software.

Step 4. Install the new driver.

Step 5. Restart the computer.

Note

Disabling the antivirus software leaves your computer vulnerable to viruses and should not be done if you are connected to the Internet.

You may encounter problems when you install or reinstall a video driver. For example, after performing the graphical performance steps, you are unable to view the screen when you restart the computer. To investigate the problem and restore the settings, reboot the computer. During the boot phase, press the **F8** key. Enter the boot options when prompted and select **Enable VGA Mode** to use a 640 × 480 resolution. Once the operating system is loaded, you can then select **Roll Back Driver** from the **Properties** of the graphics card. You should then do some research to determine the possible issues with the driver that you tried to install.

Refer to **Figure** in online course

12.2.8 Describe installation of a second operating system

You can have multiple operating systems on a single computer. Some software applications may require the most recent version of an operating system, while other software applications require an older version. There is a dual-boot process for multiple operating systems on a computer. When the boot.ini file determines that more than one operating system is present during the boot process, you are prompted to choose the operating system that you want to load. See Figure 1 for a sample boot.ini file.

Dual-Boot Setup

To create a dual-boot system in Microsoft Windows, you typically must have more than one hard drive or the hard drive must contain more than one partition.

You should install the oldest operating system on the primary partition or the hard drive marked as the active partition first. You should then install the second operating system on the second partition or hard drive. The boot files are automatically installed in the active partition.

During the installation, the boot.ini file is created on the active partition to allow the selection of the operating system to boot on startup. The boot.ini file can be edited to change the order of the operating systems. You can also edit the file for the length of time an operating system selection can be made during the boot phase. Typically, the default time to select an operating system is 30 seconds. This always delay the boot time of the computer by 30 seconds, unless the user intervenes to select a particular operating system. In the boot.ini file, the boot time should be changed to 5 or 10 seconds to boot up the computer faster.

To edit the boot.ini file, right-click **My Computer** > **Properties** > **Advanced Tab**. In the **Startup and Recovery** area, select **Settings**. Click **Edit**.

Refer to **Figure** in online course

12.3 Describe how to upgrade operating systems

An operating system must be upgraded periodically to remain compatible with the latest hardware and software. When newer versions of an operating system are released, support for older operating systems is eventually withdrawn.

Hardware products are continually coming on the market. The new design of the products often requires that the latest operating system be installed to operate correctly. While this may be expensive, you gain advanced functionality through new features and support for newer hardware.

A Windows XP upgrade can be performed from a CD or over a network. You should ensure that the new operating system is compatible with the computer. Microsoft provides a utility called the Upgrade Advisor to scan the system for incompatibility issues before upgrading to newer Windows operating systems. You can download the Upgrade Advisor from the Microsoft Windows website free of charge. After the Upgrade Advisor is finished, a report is produced to inform you of any problems. Incompatibility in hardware is the most common reason for failure in the upgrade process.

Not all older Windows operating systems are upgradeable to the newer versions, as described in the following list:

- Windows 98, Windows 98 SE, and Windows Me can be upgraded to Windows XP Home or Windows XP Professional.
- Windows NT workstation 4.0 with Service Pack 6 and Windows 2000 Professional can be upgraded only to Windows XP Professional.
- Windows 3.1 and Windows 95 cannot be upgraded to Windows XP.

Refer to **Figure** in online course

Note

Remember to back up all data prior to beginning the upgrade.

12.4 Describe preventive maintenance procedures for operating systems

Preventive maintenance for an operating system includes automating tasks to perform scheduled updates. It also includes installing service packs that help keep the system up to date and compatible with new software and hardware.

If a driver or system becomes corrupted, you can use restore points to restore the system to a previous state. However, restore points cannot recover lost data.

After completing this section, you will meet these objectives:

- Schedule automatic tasks and updates.
- Set restore points.

Refer to **Figure** in online course

12.4.1 Schedule automatic tasks and updates

You can automate tasks in Windows XP using the Scheduled Tasks utility. The Scheduled Tasks utility monitors selected, user-defined criteria and then executes the tasks when the criteria have been met.

GUI Scheduled Tasks

Some of the common tasks that are automated using the Scheduled Tasks utility include the following:

- Disk cleanup

- Backup
- Disk defragmenter
- Starting other applications

To open the Scheduled Tasks wizard, select **Start > All Programs >Accessories > System Tools > Scheduled Tasks**. Double-click **Add Scheduled Task** as shown in Figure 1.

CLI Scheduled Tasks

The Scheduled Tasks utility is a Windows-based GUI utility. You can also use the **at** command in the command line utility to automatically schedule a command, a script file, or an application to run at a specific date and time. To use the **at** command, you must be logged in as a member of the Administrators group.

To learn more about the at command, choose **Start > Run**. At the CLI prompt, type **cmd**, and then press **Return**. At the command prompt, type **at/?**.

Windows Automatic Updates

You should use one of the following methods to configure updates for the Windows XP operating system:

- Automatic (need to specify a date and time)
- Download updates for me, but let me choose when to install them
- Notify me but don't automatically download or install them
- Turn off Automatic Updates

The Automatic Updates screen, shown in Figure 2, is found in the Control Panel.

Refer to **Lab Activity** for this chapter

Task Scheduling

Schedule and cancel a simple task

12.4.2 Set restore points

Refer to **Figure** in online course

Restore points return the operating system to a predefined point in time. In some cases, the installation of an application or a hardware driver can cause instability or create unexpected changes to the computer. Uninstalling the application or hardware driver normally corrects the problem. If uninstalling does not solve the problem, you should try to restore the computer to an earlier time when the system worked properly.

To open the System Restore utility, select **Start > All Programs > Accessories > System Tools > System Restore**.

Windows XP can create restore points in the following scenarios:

- When an install or upgrade takes place
- Every 24 hours, if the computer is running
- Manually, at any time

The restore points contain information about the system and registry settings that are used by Windows operating systems. System restore does not back up personal data files nor recover personal files that have been corrupted or deleted. To back up data, you should use a dedicated backup system, such as a tape drive, CDs, or even a USB storage device.

Refer to **Figure** in online course

12.5 Troubleshoot operating systems

The troubleshooting process helps resolve problems with the operating system. These problems range from simple, such as a driver that does not operate properly, to complex, such as a system that locks up. Use the troubleshooting steps as a guideline to help you diagnose and repair problems.

After completing this section, you will meet these objectives:

- Review the troubleshooting process.
- Identify common problems and solutions.
- Apply troubleshooting skills.

Refer to **Figure** in online course

12.5.1 Review the troubleshooting process

Computer technicians must be able to analyze the problem and determine the cause of the error to repair the computer. This process is called troubleshooting.

The first step in the troubleshooting process is to gather data from the customer. Figures 1 and 2 list open-ended and closed-ended questions to ask the customer.

Once you have talked to the customer, you should verify the obvious issues. Figure 3 lists issues that apply to the operating system.

After the obvious issues have been verified, try some quick solutions. Figure 4 lists some quick solutions to operating system problems.

If quick solutions did not correct the problem, it is time to gather data from the computer. Figure 5 shows different ways to gather information about the problem from the computer.

At this point, you will have enough information to evaluate the problem, research, and implement possible solutions. Figure 6 shows resources for possible solutions.

After you have solved the problem, you will close with the customer. Figure 7 is a list of the tasks required to complete this step.

Refer to **Figure** in online course

12.5.2 Identify common problems and solutions

Computer problems can be attributed to hardware, software, networks, or some combination of the three. You will resolve some types of computer problems more often than others. A stop error is a hardware or software malfunction that causes the system to lock up. This type of error is known as the blue screen of death (BSoD) and appears when the system is unable to recover from an error. The BSoD is usually caused by device driver errors. The Event Log and other diagnostic utilities are available to research a stop error or BSoD error. To prevent these types of errors, verify that the hardware and software drivers are compatible. In addition, install the latest patches and updates for Windows. When the system locks up during startup, the computer can automatically reboot. The reboot is caused by the auto restart function in Windows and makes it difficult to see the error message. The auto restart function can be disabled in the Advanced Startup Options menu. Figure 1 is a chart of common hardware problems and solutions.

Refer to **Figure** in online course

12.5.3 Apply troubleshooting skills

Now that you understand the troubleshooting process, it is time to apply your listening and diagnostic skills.

The first lab is designed to reinforce your skills with the operating system. You will check restore points before and after using Windows Update.

Refer to **Lab Activity** for this chapter

Remote Technician Operating System Problem

Instruct a customer on how to correct an operating system problem

The second lab is designed to reinforce your communication and troubleshooting skills. In this lab, you will perform the following steps:

- Receive the work order
- Take the customer through various steps to try and resolve the problem
- Document the problem and the resolution

Summary

This chapter discussed how to select an operating system based on the needs of the customer. You have learned the differences between operating systems and network operating systems. The labs have helped you become familiar with Windows XP, creating partitions, customizing virtual memory, and scheduling tasks. You have also learned some optimization tips for operating systems, as well as how to troubleshoot a computer problem from the perspective of a level-two technician. The following concepts discussed in this chapter will be useful to you when selecting and installing an operating system:

- Ensuring that you fully understand the technology needs of the customer.
- Knowing the differences between common operating systems.
- Carefully matching the customer needs to the proper technologies.
- Knowing the different methods to install an operating system.
- Knowing how to upgrade different operating systems.
- Understanding how preventive maintenance can stop problems before they start.
- Knowing which preventive maintenance procedures are appropriate for the customer.
- Knowing how to troubleshoot operating system problems.

Chapter 12 Quiz

Take the chapter quiz to test your knowledge.

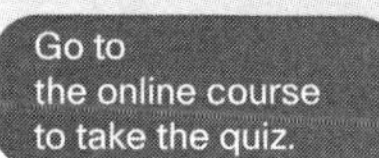

Your Chapter Notes

CHAPTER 13

Advanced Laptops and Portable Devices

Introduction

With the increase in demand for mobility, the popularity of laptops and portable devices will continue to grow. During the course of your career, you will be expected to know how to configure, repair, and maintain these devices. The knowledge you acquire about desktop computers will help you service laptops and portable devices. However, there are important differences between the two technologies.

To facilitate mobility, laptops and portable devices use wireless technologies more than desktops. All laptops use batteries when they are disconnected from a power source. Docking stations are commonly used to connect a laptop to peripheral devices. As a computer technician, you will be required to configure, optimize, and troubleshoot these docking stations and accessories, as well as the laptop or portable device that they accompany. Many laptop components are proprietary, so some manufacturers require that you complete specialized certification training to perform laptop repairs.

Servicing laptops can be very challenging. Mastering the skills necessary to work on laptops is important to your career advancement.

After completing this chapter, you will meet these objectives:

- Describe wireless communication methods for laptops and portable devices.
- Describe repairs for laptops and portable devices.
- Select laptop components.
- Describe preventive maintenance procedures for laptops.
- Describe how to troubleshoot a laptop.

Refer to **Figure** in online course

13.1 Describe wireless communication methods for laptops and portable devices

Wireless devices give people the freedom to work, learn, play, and communicate wherever they want. People using wireless-capable devices do not need to be tied to a physical location to send and receive voice, video, and data communications. As a result, wireless facilities, such as Internet cafes, are opening in many countries. College campuses use wireless networks to allow students to sign up for classes, watch lectures, and submit assignments in areas where physical connections to the network are unavailable. This trend toward wireless communications will continue to grow as more people use wireless devices.

After completing this section, you will meet these objectives:

- Describe Bluetooth Technology.
- Describe Infrared Technology.

- Describe Cellular WAN Technology.
- Describe Wi-Fi Technology.
- Describe Satellite Technology.

Refer to **Figure** in online course

13.1.1 Describe Bluetooth Technology

Bluetooth is a wireless technology that enables devices to communicate over short distances. A Bluetooth device can connect up to seven other Bluetooth devices to create a wireless personal area network (WPAN). This technical specification is described by the Institute of Electrical and Electronics Engineers (IEEE) 802.15.1 standard. Bluetooth devices are capable of handling voice and data and are ideally suited for connecting the following devices:

- Laptops
- Printers
- Cameras
- PDAs
- Cell phones
- Hands-free headsets

Refer to Figure 1 for common Bluetooth characteristics.

The distance of a Bluetooth personal area network (PAN) is limited by the amount of power used by the devices in the PAN. Bluetooth devices are broken into three classifications as shown in Figure 2. The most common Bluetooth network is Class 2, which has a range of approximately 33 feet (10 m).

Bluetooth devices operate in the 2.4 to 2.485 GHz radio frequency range, which is in the Industrial, Scientific, and Medical (ISM) band. This band often does not require a license if approved equipment is used. The Bluetooth standard incorporates adaptive frequency hopping (AFH). AFH allows signals to "hop" around using different frequencies within the Bluetooth range, thereby reducing the chance of interference when multiple Bluetooth devices are present. AFH also allows the device to learn frequencies that are already in use and to choose a different subset of frequencies hopping.

Security measures are included in the Bluetooth standard. The first time that a Bluetooth device connects, the device is authenticated using a personal identification number (PIN). Bluetooth supports both 128-bit encryption and PIN authentication.

Refer to **Figure** in online course

13.1.2 Describe Infrared Technology

Infrared (IR) wireless technology is a low-power, short-range wireless technology. IR transmits data using Light Emitting Diodes (LEDs) and receives data using photodiodes.

IR wireless networks are globally unregulated. However, the Infrared Data Association (IrDA) defines the specifications for IR wireless communication. Refer to Figure 1 for common IR characteristics.

There are four types of IR networks:

- ***Line of sight*** – Signal is transmitted only if there is a clear, unobstructed view between devices.
- ***Scatter*** – Signal is bounced off ceilings and walls.

- ***Reflective –*** Signal is sent to an optical transceiver and is redirected to the receiving device.
- ***Broadband optical telepoint –*** Transmission can handle high-quality multimedia requirements.

Infrared networks are ideal for connecting laptops to the following types of devices that are in close proximity:

- Multimedia projector
- PDA
- Printer
- Remote control
- Wireless mouse
- Wireless keyboard

The setup and configuration of IR devices is quite simple. Many IR devices connect to the USB port on a laptop or desktop computer. Once the computer detects the new device, Windows XP install the appropriate drivers as shown in Figure 2. The installation is similar to setting up a local area network connection.

IR is a practical, short-range connection solution, but it has some limitations:

- IR light cannot penetrate ceilings or walls.
- IR signals are susceptible to interference and dilution by strong light sources, such as florescent lighting.
- Scatter IR devices are able to connect without the line of sight, but data transfer rates are lower and distances are shorter.
- IR distances should be 3 feet (1 m) or less when used for computer communications.

Refer to **Figure** in online course

13.1.3 Describe Cellular WAN Technology

Originally, cellular networks were designed for voice communication only. Cellular technology has been evolving and now enables the transfer of voice, video, and data simultaneously. It also enables the use of laptops and portable devices remotely. With a cellular WAN adapter installed, a laptop user is able to travel and access the Internet. Refer to Figure 1 for common cellular WAN characteristics.

Although slower than DSL and cable connections, cellular WANs are still fast enough to be classified as a high-speed connection. To connect a laptop to a cellular WAN, you should install an adapter that is designed to work with cellular networks. A cellular adapter needs to support some or all of the following:

- ***Global System for Mobile Communications (GSM) –*** Worldwide cellular network
- ***General Packet Radio Service (GPRS) –*** Data service for users of GSM
- ***Quad-band –*** Allows a cellular phone to operate on all four GSM frequencies: 850 MHz, 900 MHz, 1800 MHz, and 1900 MHz
- ***Short Message Service (SMS) –*** Text messages
- ***Multimedia Messaging Service (MMS) –*** Multimedia messages

- ***Enhanced Data Rates for GSM Evolution (EDGE)*** **–** Provides increased data rates and improved data reliability
- ***Evolution-Data Optimized (EV-DO)*** **–** Faster download rates

Connecting to a cellular WAN is a simple process. Cellular WAN cards, as shown in Figure 2, are Plug and Play (PnP). These cards plug in to the PC Card slot or are built in to the laptop.

Refer to **Figure** in online course

13.1.4 Describe Wi-Fi Technology

The wireless technology Wi-Fi is based on IEEE 802.11 networking standards and specifications. The number 802.11 denotes a set of standards that are specified in the IEEE 802.11 documentation. Hence, the terms 802.11 and Wi-Fi are interchangeable. Figure 1 shows some characteristics of Wi-Fi.

There are currently four major Wi-Fi, 802.11 standards:

- 802.11a
- 802.11b
- 802.11g
- 802.11n (draft standard)

Technicians often refer to Wi-Fi standards by just the final letters. For example, a technician may refer to an 802.11b wireless router as simply a "b" router.

The 802.11g standard was released in 2003 and is currently the most common Wi-Fi standard. The 802.11n standard was released in draft form in 2006 and may be modified slightly before becoming an official IEEE standard.

The 802.11b, 802.11g, and 802.11n standards use the 2.4 GHz frequency band. The 2.4 GHz frequency band is unregulated and heavily used. The large amount of traffic can cause wireless signals in the 2.4 GHz range to be interfered with by other 2.4 GHz wireless devices. For this reason, the 802.11a standard was designed to use the 5.0 GHz frequency band. As a result, 802.11a is only compatible with only the 802.11n standard as it also supports 5.0 GHz frequency. See Figure 2 for data rate and range information.

Security is a major concern for wireless networks. Anyone within the coverage area of a wireless router can potentially gain access to the network. These precautions should be taken for security purposes:

- Never send login or password information using clear, unencrypted text.
- Use a VPN connection when possible.
- Enable security on home networks.
- Use Wi-Fi Protected Access (WPA) security.

Wi-Fi Protected Access standards (WPA, WPA2) are used to secure Wi-Fi networks. WPA uses a sophisticated encryption and authentication technology to protect data flow between Wi-Fi devices. WPA uses a 128-bit encryption key and should be enabled on all wireless devices. WPA was introduced to replace wired equivalent privacy (WEP), which had known security issues.

Refer to **Figure** in online course

13.1.5 Describe Satellite Technology

Satellite service is ideal for rural or remote users who require high-speed, broadband access in areas where no other high-speed services are available. However, because of the higher initial cost and relatively slower speeds, high-speed satellite network connections are recommended only if a cable or Digital Subscriber Line (DSL) connection is unavailable. Refer to Figure 1 for common satellite characteristics.

Satellite Internet connections use two-way data channels. One channel is used for uploading and another for downloading. Both download and upload can be accomplished using a satellite connection. In some cases, a telephone line and modem are used for the upload. Download speeds are typically in the 500 Kbps range, while uploads are around 50 Kbps, making this an asymmetrical connection similar to DSL. Satellite connections are slower than cable or DSL connections but faster than telephone modem connections. Connecting by satellite has some advantages:

- Two-way, high-speed Internet access, available in rural and remote areas
- Quick file downloads
- Satellite dish may be also be used for TV access

Proper placement, installation, and configuration of a satellite system are important for the system to work effectively. Even if you point the satellite dish toward the equator where most satellites orbit the Earth, obstructions and adverse weather can still interfere with signal reception.

Specific equipment is needed to set up a satellite connection:

- 24-inch (610 mm) satellite dish
- Modem for uplink and downlink
- Coaxial cable and connectors

Refer to **Interactive Graphic** in online course.

13.2 Describe repairs for laptops and portable devices

Refer to **Figure** in online course

When a laptop or portable device begins to malfunction, what should you do? There are some parts of a laptop – typically called Customer Replaceable Units (CRUs) – that can be replaced by the customer. CRUs include such components as the laptop battery and additional RAM. Parts that should not be replaced by the customer are called Field Replaceable Units (FRUs). FRUs include such components as the laptop motherboard, LCD display, and keyboard. In many cases, the device may need to be returned to the place of purchase, a certified service center, or even to the manufacturer.

A repair center can provide service on laptops made by different manufacturers, or a repair center may specialize in a specific brand and be considered an authorized dealer for warranty work and repair. The following are common repairs performed at local repair centers:

- Hardware and software diagnostics
- Data transfer and recovery
- Hard drive installation and upgrades
- RAM installation and upgrades
- Keyboard and fan replacement
- Internal laptop cleaning
- LCD screen repair
- LCD inverter and backlight repair

Most repairs to LCD displays must be performed in a repair center. The repairs include replacing the LCD screen, the backlight that shines through the screen to illuminate the display, and the inverter that produces the high voltage required by the backlight. If the backlight has failed, the screen is only visible when looking at it from an angle.

If no local services are available, you may be required to send the laptop to a regional repair center or to the manufacturer. If the laptop damage is severe or requires specialized software and tools, the manufacturer can decide to replace the laptop instead of attempting a repair.

Refer to **Worksheet** for this chapter

Investigating Repair Centers

Research repair center services

Caution

Before attempting to repair a laptop or portable device, check the warranty to see if repairs during the warranty period must be done at an authorized service center to avoid invalidating the warranty. If you repair a laptop yourself, you should always back up the data and disconnect the device from the power source.

Refer to **Figure** in online course

13.3 Select laptop components

Laptop components need to be replaced for a variety of reasons. The original part may be worn, damaged, or faulty. You may want additional functionality, such as a wireless PC card that supports new standards. You may want to improve performance by adding memory. When implementing any of these changes, make sure that all new components are physically and electrically compatible with the existing components and operating system.

It is always a good idea to purchase components from a reputable source and research the warranty information. Components generally fall into two categories: retail packaged or original equipment manufacturer (OEM). Retail packaged, or retail box, components usually come with documentation, a full warranty, cables, mounting hardware, drivers, and software.

OEM components are usually sold without packaging. OEM components require the user to locate documentation, software, drivers, and any additional hardware that may be needed. OEM components are usually less expensive and offer a shorter warranty period than similar retail packaged components. Using OEM components can result in substantial savings when upgrades are performed in bulk on many laptops and additional support is not needed.

After completing this section, you will meet these objectives:

- Select batteries.
- Select a docking station or port replicator.
- Select storage devices.
- Select additional RAM.

Refer to **Figure** in online course

13.3.1 Select batteries

How do you know when you need a new laptop battery? The signs may not always be apparent, but some are obvious:

- Laptop shuts off immediately when AC power is removed
- Battery is leaking
- Battery overheats

- Battery does not hold a charge

If you experience problems that you suspect are battery related, exchange the battery with a known, good battery that is compatible with the laptop. If a replacement battery cannot be located, take the battery to an authorized repair center for testing.

A replacement battery must meet or exceed the specifications of the laptop manufacturer. New batteries must use the same form factor as the original battery. Voltages, power ratings, and AC adapters must also meet manufacturer specifications.

Note

Always follow the instructions provided by the manufacturer when charging a new battery. The laptop can be used during an initial charge, but do not unplug the AC adapter. Ni-Cad and NiMH rechargeable batteries should occasionally be discharged completely to remove the charge memory. When the battery is completely discharged, it should then be charged to maximum capacity.

Refer to **Worksheet** for this chapter

Laptop Batteries

Research laptop batteries

Caution

Care should always be taken when handling batteries. Batteries can explode if improperly charged, shorted, or mishandled. Be sure that the battery charger is designed for the chemistry, size, and voltage of your battery. Batteries are considered toxic waste, and must be disposed of according to local laws.

13.3.2 Select a docking station or port replicator

Refer to **Figure** in online course

Docking stations and port replicators increase the number of ports available to a laptop. A port replicator may contain a SCSI port, a networking port, PS/2 ports, USB ports, and a game port. A docking station has the same ports as a port replicator, but adds the ability to connect to PCI cards, additional hard drives, optical drives, and floppy drives. Docking stations make it convenient to connect a laptop to an office network and peripherals. A laptop connected to a docking station has the same capabilities as a desktop computer. Figure 1 shows several docking stations and port replicators that support the same laptop.

Docking stations and port replicators offer several connection options:

- Ethernet (RJ-45)
- Modem (RJ-11)
- S-Video, TV out
- USB 2.0 port
- External monitor
- Parallel port
- High-speed serial port
- IEEE 1394 port
- Stereo headphone output
- Stereo microphone input
- Docking port

Some docking stations connect to a laptop using a docking station port that is located on the bottom of the laptop as shown in Figure 2. Other docking stations are designed to plug directly into a USB port of the laptop. Most laptops can be docked when in use or while shut off. The addition of new devices when docking can be handled by using PnP technology that recognizes and configures the newly added components, or by having a separate hardware profile for the docked and undocked state.

Many docking stations and port replicators are proprietary and only work with particular laptops. Before buying a docking station or port replicator, check the laptop documentation, or the website of the manufacturer to determine the appropriate make and model for the laptop.

Refer to **Worksheet** for this chapter

Docking Station

Research laptop docking stations

Refer to **Figure** in online course

13.3.3 Select storage devices

Storage devices are CRUs, unless a warranty requires technical assistance. There are several options when adding, replacing, or upgrading a storage device for a laptop:

- External USB hard drive
- Firewire hard drive
- DVD/CD burner

The form factor of an internal hard drive storage device is smaller for a laptop than for a desktop computer.

An external USB hard drive connects to a laptop using the USB port. Another type of external drive is the IEEE 1394 external hard drive that connects to the Firewire port. A laptop automatically detects when an external hard drive is plugged into a USB or Firewire port.

A DVD/CD RW drive is an optical drive that reads and writes data to and from a CD, and reads data from a DVD. This is a convenient method of creating backups and archiving data. The two most common types of writable CDs and DVDs are writable (R) and rewritable (RW).

Before purchasing a new internal or external hard drive, check the laptop documentation or the website of the manufacturer for compatibility requirements. Documentation often contains Frequently Asked Questions (FAQs) that may be helpful. It is also important to research known laptop component issues on the Internet.

Refer to **Worksheet** for this chapter

DVD Drive Research

Research DVD drives

Refer to **Figure** in online course

13.3.4 Select additional RAM

Adding RAM can make a laptop perform better. Additional RAM speeds up the process by decreasing the number of times the operating system reads and writes data to the hard drive swap file. Reading and writing data directly from RAM is faster than using swap files. Also, RAM helps the operating system run multiple applications more efficiently.

Graphic processing in laptops is usually performed by the CPU and often requires extra RAM to store the video while the CPU decodes it for viewing. New applications, such as video sharing and video editing, demand increased performance from laptops. Installing expansion RAM can help increase laptop performance.

The make and model of the laptop determines the type of RAM chip needed. It is important to select the correct memory type that is physically compatible with the laptop. Most desktop computers use memory that fits into a Dual Inline Memory Module (DIMM) slot. Most laptops use a smaller profile memory chip that is called Small Outline DIMM (SODIMM). SODIMMs are smaller than DIMMs, so they are ideal for use in laptops, printers, and other devices where conserving space is desirable. When replacing or adding memory, determine if the laptop has available slots to add memory, and that the laptop supports the quantity and type of memory to be added, as shown in Figure 1.

Before purchasing and installing additional RAM, consult the laptop documentation or the website of the manufacturer for form-factor specifications. Use the documentation to find where to install RAM on the laptop. On most laptops, RAM is inserted into slots behind a cover on the underside of the case, as shown in Figure 2. However, on some laptops, the keyboard must be removed to access the RAM slots.

Caution

Before installing RAM, remove the battery and unplug the computer from the electrical outlet to avoid damage related to ESD when you are installing memory modules.

To confirm the currently installed amount of RAM, check the POST screen, BIOS, or System Properties window. Figure 3 shows where the amount of RAM can be found in the System Properties window:

Start > Control Panel > System > General Tab

13.4 Describe preventive maintenance procedures for laptops

Preventive maintenance should be scheduled at regular intervals to keep laptops running properly. Because laptops are portable, they are more likely than desktop computers to be exposed to these harmful materials and situations:

- Dirt and contamination
- Spills
- Wear and tear
- Drops
- Excessive heat or cold
- Excessive moisture

Properly managing data files and folders can ensure data integrity.

After completing this section, you will meet these objectives:

- Describe how to schedule and perform maintenance for laptops.
- Explain how to manage data version control between desktops and laptops.

Refer to **Figure** in online course

13.4.1 Describe how to schedule and perform maintenance for laptops

Proper care and maintenance can help laptop components run more efficiently and extend the life of the equipment.

An effective preventive maintenance program must include a routine schedule for maintenance. Most organizations will have a preventive maintenance schedule in place. If a schedule does not exist, work with the manager to create one. The most effective preventive maintenance programs require a set of routines to be conducted monthly, but still allow for maintenance to be performed when usage demands it.

The preventive maintenance schedule for a laptop may include practices that are unique to a particular organization, but should also include these standard procedures:

- Cleaning
- Hard drive maintenance
- Software updates

To keep a laptop clean, be proactive, not reactive. Keep fluids away from the laptop. Do not eat when you are working on your laptop, and close the laptop when it is not in use. When cleaning a laptop, never use harsh cleaners or solutions that contain ammonia. Nonabrasive materials, as shown in Figure 1, are recommended for cleaning a laptop:

- Compressed air
- Mild cleaning solution
- Cotton swabs
- Soft, lint-free cleaning cloth

Caution

Before you clean a laptop, disconnect it from all power sources.

Routine maintenance includes the monthly cleaning of these laptop components:

- Exterior case
- Cooling vents
- I/O ports
- Display
- Keyboard

Note

At any time, if it is obvious that the laptop needs to be cleaned, clean it. Do not wait for the next scheduled maintenance.

The operating system should also be maintained. The hard drive can become disorganized as files are opened, saved, and deleted. The computer can slow down if the operating system is searching through fragmented files. Fortunately, Windows XP has two programs that help clean up the hard drive:

- Disk Cleanup
- Disk Defragmenter

To Run Disk Cleanup [Figure 2]:

. Select the hard drive that you want to clean.

. Right-click and choose **Properties**.

- On the General tab, click **Disk Cleanup**.
- A series of check boxes displays the files that are available for deletion. Check the boxes of the file that you want to delete, and click **OK**.

To Run Disk Defragmenter [Figure 3]:

- Select the hard drive that you want to clean.
- Right-click and choose **Properties**.
- On the Tools tab, click **Defragment Now**. The length of time to complete the defragmentation varies according to how fragmented the hard drive is.

Refer to **Figure** in online course

Note

It may be necessary to close all programs running in the background before running Disk Defragmenter.

13.4.2 Explain how to manage data version control between desktops and laptops

It is important to manage your data files and folders properly. Restore and recover procedures, as well as backups, are more successful if the data is organized.

Windows XP has a default location, sometimes available as an icon on the desktop called My Documents. You can use My Documents to create a folder structure and store files.

When moving files from a laptop to a desktop computer, start by creating a similar folder structure in both locations. Files can be transferred over a network, with an optical disc, or with a portable drive.

You should be careful that data copied from one computer does not inadvertently overwrite data on the other computer. When you are copying a file to a destination folder, you might encounter a "Confirm File Replacement" message as shown in Figure 1. This message indicates that Windows XP has stopped the copying process until you choose whether to replace or not to replace the original file with the file that is being transferred. If you are unsure, select "No". To determine which file to keep, compare the dates and file size. You may also open the files to view their content.

Note

No operating system allows files with the same name to exist in the same folder.

Refer to **Figure** in online course

Caution

Be careful not to unintentionally "cut" a file from its original location when you only meant to "copy" it.

13.5 Describe how to troubleshoot a laptop

The troubleshooting process helps resolve problems with the laptop or peripherals. These problems range from simple, such as updating a drive, to more complex problems, such as installing RAM. Use the troubleshooting steps as a guideline to help you diagnose and repair problems.

After completing this section, you will meet these objectives:

- Review the troubleshooting process.
- Identify common problems and solutions.
- Apply troubleshooting skills.

Refer to **Figure** in online course

13.5.1 Review the troubleshooting process

Computer technicians must be able to analyze the problem and determine the cause of the error to repair a laptop. This process is called troubleshooting.

The first step in the troubleshooting process is to gather data from the customer. Figures 1 and 2 list open-ended and closed-ended questions to ask the customer.

Once you have talked to the customer, you should verify the obvious issues. Figure 3 lists issues that apply to laptops.

After the obvious issues have been verified, try some quick solutions. Figure 4 lists some quick solutions to laptop problems.

If quick solutions did not correct the problem, it is time to gather data from the computer. Figure 5 shows different ways to gather information about the problem from the laptop.

At this point, you have enough information to evaluate the problem, research, and implement possible solutions. Figure 6 shows resources for possible solutions.

After you have solved the problem, you close with the customer. Figure 7 is a list of the tasks required to complete this step.

Refer to **Figure** in online course

13.5.2 Identify common problems and solutions

Laptop problems can be attributed to hardware, software, networks, or some combination of the three. You will resolve some types of laptop problems more often than others. Figure 1 is a chart of common laptop problems and solutions.

Refer to **Figure** in online course

13.5.3 Apply troubleshooting skills

Now that you understand the troubleshooting process, it is time to apply your listening and diagnostic skills.

The worksheet is designed to reinforce your communication skills to verify information from the customer.

Summary

This chapter has described components of laptops and portable devices. Here are some important concepts contained in this chapter:

- Bluetooth creates a small wireless PAN for connected cell phones, printers, and laptops.
- An IR network uses infrared light to create short-range networks that are primarily used to control input devices and mobile devices.
- A cellular WAN allows you to use your cell phone and laptop for voice and data communications.
- The most popular wireless technology is Wi-Fi. There are four major Wi-Fi releases, each with different speed and bandwidth ratings: IEEE 802.11 a, b, g, and n.
- Satellite networks are faster than modems, but slower than DSL and cable networks. Satellite networks are primarily used in remote locations.
- A CRU is a component that a user can easily install without technical training.
- A FRU is a component that a trained service technician may install at a remote location.
- Most repairs can be done at customers' sites or at any local repair center. However, there are occasions when a laptop must be sent directly to the manufacturer for repairs.
- Professional technicians follow preventive maintenance schedules to keep their equipment at optimal performance levels.
- Laptops are more susceptible to contamination and damage. A well-maintained laptop will reduce repair costs.
- A docking station allows a laptop to easily connect to peripheral devices similar to those found on desktop computers. A port replicator can be added to a laptop if the user needs more I/O ports.
- Mastering the steps in troubleshooting laptop problems is considered a career milestone by many technicians.
- A well-trained technician must possess good customer communications skills.

Chapter 13 Quiz

Take the chapter quiz to test your knowledge.

Go to
the online course
to take the quiz.

Your Chapter Notes

CHAPTER 14

Advanced Printers and Scanners

Introduction

This chapter explores the functionality of printers and scanners. You will learn how to maintain, install, and repair these devices in both local and network configurations. The chapter discusses safety hazards, configuration procedures, preventive maintenance, and printer and scanner sharing.

After completing this chapter, you will meet these objectives:

- Describe potential safety hazards and safety procedures associated with printers and scanners.
- Install and configure a local printer and scanner.
- Describe how to share a printer and a scanner on a network.
- Upgrade and configure printers and scanners.
- Describe printer and scanner preventive maintenance techniques.
- Troubleshoot printers and scanners.

Refer to **Figure** in online course

14.1 Describe potential safety hazards and safety procedures associated with printers and scanners

You must always follow safety procedures when working on any computer. There are also rules that you must follow as you work with printers and scanners. These rules keep you and the equipment safe.

The first rule of safety concerns moving large pieces of equipment. Always lift equipment by using the strength in your legs and knees, not your back. Wear appropriate work clothes and shoes. Do not wear loose jewelry or baggy clothes when servicing computer equipment.

Printers, scanners, and all-in-one devices that connect to AC outlets can become hot while in use. If you plan to perform any services on equipment, you should turn it off and allow it to cool before beginning any repairs on internal components. Print heads on dot matrix printers may become very hot when in use. The fuser assembly on a laser printer can also become hot.

Some printers retain a large amount of voltage even after you disconnect them from a power source. Only qualified technicians should perform advanced repairs on laser printers, particularly if the repair involves the corona wire or transfer roller assembly. These areas can retain high voltage, even after the printer has been turned off. Check the service manuals or contact the manufacturer to be sure that you know where these areas are inside the devices.

Printers and scanners can be expensive. If you do not service printers correctly, or install the wrong part, you can damage them beyond repair.

Refer to **Figure** in online course

14.2 Install and configure a local printer and scanner

A local device is one that connects directly to the computer. Before you install a local device, such as a printer or scanner, be sure that you remove all packing material. Take out anything that prevents moving parts from shifting around during shipping. Keep the original packing material in case you need to return the equipment to the manufacturer for warranty repairs.

After completing this section, you will meet these objectives:

- Connect the device to a local port.
- Install and configure the driver and software.
- Configure options and default settings.
- Verify functionality.

Refer to **Figure** in online course

14.2.1 Connect the device to a local port

Depending on the manufacturer, local printers may communicate with computers using serial, parallel, USB, FireWire, or SCSI ports and cables. Click the buttons in Figure 1 to review the characteristics of these ports. Wireless technologies, such as Bluetooth and infrared, are also used to connect these devices.

To connect a printer, attach the appropriate cable to the communication port on the back of the printer. Connect the other end of the cable to the corresponding port on the back of the computer.

After the data cable has been properly connected, attach the power cable to the printer. Connect the other end of the power cable to an available electrical outlet. When you turn on the power to the device, the computer tries to determine the correct device driver to install.

Refer to **Figure** in online course

Tip

Always check the packaging for cables when you buy a printer or scanner. Many manufacturers keep production costs down by not including a cable with the printer. If you have to buy a cable, be sure that you buy the correct type.

14.2.2 Install and configure the driver and software

Printer drivers are software programs that make it possible for computers and printers to communicate with each other. Configuration software provides an interface that enables users to set and change printer options. Every printer model has its own type of driver and software configuration software.

When you connect a new printer device to a computer, Windows XP tries to locate and install a default driver by using the Plug and Play (PnP) utility. If Windows cannot find the necessary driver on the computer, it tries to connect to the Internet to find one. Printer manufacturers frequently update drivers to increase the performance of the printer, to add new and improved printer options, and to address general compatibility issues.

Printer Driver Installation

The process of installing and updating a printer driver usually involves the following five steps:

. Determine the current version of the installed printer driver. Remember to select a newer version to increase functionality.

- Search the Internet to locate the most recent version of the driver.
- Download the driver. Follow the instructions on the website.
- Install the driver. When activated, most driver installation programs automatically install the new driver.
- Test the driver. To test the driver, choose **Start > Settings > Printers and Faxes** in Windows 2000 or **Start > Control Panel > Printers and Faxes** in Windows XP. Right-click the printer and choose **Properties**. Then choose **Print Test Page**. If the printer does not work, restart the computer and then try again.

The printed test page should contain text that you can read. If the text is unreadable, the problem could be a bad driver program or that the wrong page description language has been used.

Page Description Language (PDL)

A page description language (PDL) is a type of code that describes the appearance of a document in a language that a printer can understand. The PDL for a page includes the text, graphics, and formatting information. Software applications use PDLs to send What You See Is What You Get (WYSIWYG) images to the printer. The printer translates the PDL file so that whatever is on the computer screen is what is printed. PDLs speed up the printing process by sending large amounts of data at one time. They also manage the computer fonts.

There are three common PDLs:

- ***Printer Command Language (PCL)*** – Hewlett-Packard developed PCL for communication with early inkjet printers. PCL is now an industry standard for nearly all printer types.
- ***PostScript (PS)*** – Adobe Systems developed PS to allow fonts or text types to share the same characteristics on the screen as on paper.
- ***Graphics Device Interface (GDI)*** – GDI is a Windows component to manage how graphical images are transmitted to output devices. GDI works by converting images to a bitmap that uses the computer instead of the printer to transfer the images.

Refer to **Figure** in online course

14.2.3 Configure options and default settings

Common printer options that can be configured by the user include media control and printer output.

The following media control options set the way a printer manages media:

- Input paper tray selection
- Output path selection
- Media size and orientation
- Paper weight selection

The following printer output options manage how the ink or toner goes on the media:

- Color management
- Print speed

Some printers have control switches on the printer for users to select options. Other printers use the printer driver options. Two methods of selecting options are the global and per-document methods.

Global Method

The global method refers to printer options that are set to affect all documents. Each time a document is printed, the global options are used, unless overridden by per-document selections.

To change the configuration of a global printer, choose **Start > Control Panel > Printers and Faxes** and right-click the printer. The following examples show how you can manage printer options.

To designate a default printer, choose **Start > Control Panel > Printers and Faxes**. Right-click the printer, and then choose **Set as Default Printer**, as shown in Figure 1.

Note

Depending on the driver installed, Set as Default Printer may not appear on the menu. If this happens, double-click the printer to open the Document Status window, and then choose **Printer > Set as Default Printer.**

To limit printing to only black and white, choose **Start > Control Panel > Printer and Faxes**. Right-click the printer, and then choose **Printing Preferences**. Choose the **Color** tab. Check **Print In Grayscale** and choose the **Black Print Cartridge Only** radio button, as shown in Figure 2. Click **OK**.

Per-Document Method

Letters, spreadsheets, and digital images are some of the document types that may require special printer settings. You can change the settings for each document sent to the printer by changing the document print settings.

To change the printer settings, keep the document open and select **File > Page Setup**. The default settings are displayed, as shown in Figure 3. You can alter the colors, print quality, paper direction, and margin size for the document that you are printing without changing the default settings.

Scanner Calibrations

Calibrating a device is one of the first tasks after installing a driver. Use the bundled software that came with the device to perform this procedure. The default settings can be altered later to meet customer requirements.

Scanner calibrations can include positioning the sensor and using an IT8 target to adjust the color. An IT8 target is a color calibration chart that you use to create profiles for specific devices. A scanner analyzes the target for comparison, while a printer reproduces the target for comparison.

To ensure calibration, compare the printed output of the device to the IT8 target. Adjust the printer color settings to match. The next time you print or scan an image, the color will be as accurate as the target.

Printer Calibrations

The calibration of the printer is performed using the print driver software. This process makes sure that the print heads are aligned and can print on special paper. Inkjet print heads are usually fitted to the ink cartridge, which means that you may have to recalibrate the printer each time you change a cartridge.

Refer to **Figure** in online course

14.2.4 Verify functionality

The installation of any device is not complete until you have successfully tested all of the device functions. This includes special tasks such as the following :

- Print double-sided documents to save paper
- Use different types of paper trays for special paper sizes
- Change the settings of a color printer so that it prints in black and white or grayscale to print draft copies of documents
- Print in draft mode to save ink
- Change a scanner's scan resolution to make an image easier to view
- Edit scanned images of saved documents
- Use an optical character recognition (OCR) application

Note

Electronic manuals and support websites explain how to clear paper jams, install ink cartridges, and load all types of paper trays.

Printer Test

There are several ways to print a test page:

- Use the Print Test Page option from the printer
- Use the Print Test Page option from Windows
- Use the print function of an application
- Send a file directly to a parallel port printer using the command line

To test a printer, first print a test page from the printer, and then print from the computer properties function or from an application. This ensures that the printer is working properly, the driver software is installed and working, and the printer and computer are communicating.

Scanner Test

Test the scanner by scanning a document. Use the buttons on the device for automatic scanning. Next, initiate scans from the scanner software and make sure that the software opens automatic scan. If the scanned images appear to be the same as the image on the screen, you have successfully completed the installation.

For an all-in-one device, you should test all of the functions:

- ***Fax –*** Fax to another known working fax
- ***Copy –*** Create a copy of a document
- ***Scan –*** Scan a document
- ***Print –*** Print a document

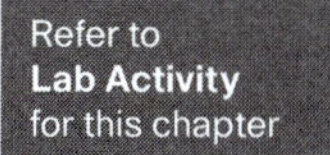

All-in-One Device Installation

Install an all-in-one device

Refer to **Figure** in online course

14.3 Describe how to share a printer and a scanner on a network

One of the primary reasons that networks were developed was to allow groups of computer users to share peripheral devices. The most common shared device is the printer. Sharing a single printer among a group of users costs much less than buying a printer for each computer.

Low-cost printers usually require a separate print server to allow network connectivity because these printers do not have built-in network interfaces. The computer that is connected to the printer can serve as the print server. Most personal computer operating systems have built-in printer sharing capability.

After you confirm that the printer sharing software is installed, the server must know which printer it is going to share. In the Printers folder, right-click the printer to share, select **Properties**, and click the **Sharing** tab. Select **Share this printer** option and assign the printer a name.

After completing this section, you will meet these objectives:

- Describe types of print servers.
- Describe how to install network printer software and drivers on a computer.

Refer to **Figure** in online course

14.3.1 Describe types of print servers

Print servers enable multiple computer users to access a single printer. A print server has three functions. The first is to provide client access to print resources. The second is to administrate print jobs, storing them in a queue until the print device is ready for them, and then feeding or spooling the print information to the printer. The third is to provide feedback to the users. This includes providing notification that a print job is finished, or error messages that something has gone wrong.

As a technician, you must choose the type of print server that best suits the customer's needs. There are three kinds:

- Network print server devices
- Dedicated PC print servers
- Computer-shared printers

Network Print Server Devices

Network print server devices allow many users on a network to access a single printer. A network print server device can manage network printing through either wired or wireless connections. Figure 1 shows a wired print server. You should consider the advantages and disadvantages of a dedicated PC print server before you install one:

- An advantage of using a network print server is that the server accepts incoming print jobs from computers, and then frees the computers for other tasks. The print server is always available to the users, unlike a printer shared from a user's computer.
- A disadvantage of a network print server is that it may not be able to use all of the functions of an all-in-one device.

Dedicated PC Print Servers

A dedicated PC print server is a computer dedicated to handling client print jobs in the most efficient manner. Since it handles requests from multiple clients, a print server is usually one of the most powerful computers on the network. Dedicated PC print servers can manage more than one printer at a time. A print server needs to have resources available to meet the requests of print clients:

- *Powerful processor* – Because the PC print server uses its processor to manage and route printing information, it needs to be fast enough to handle all incoming requests.
- *Adequate hard disk space* – A PC print server captures print jobs from clients, places them in a print queue, and sends them to the printer in a timely way. This requires the computer to have enough storage space to hold these jobs until completed.
- *Adequate memory* – The server processor and RAM handle sending print jobs to a printer. If server memory is not large enough to handle an entire print job, the hard drive must send the job, which is much slower.

Computer-shared Printers

A user's computer that has a printer attached can share that printer with other users on the network. Windows XP makes the process fast and easy. In a home network, it means users can print documents from wherever they are in the house by using a wireless laptop. In a small office network, sharing a printer means one printer can serve many users.

Sharing a printer from a computer also has disadvantages. The computer sharing the printer uses its own resources to manage the print jobs coming to the printer. If a user on the desktop is working at the same time that a user on the network is printing, the desktop user may notice a performance slowdown. In addition, the printer is not available if the user reboots or powers down the computer with a shared printer.

Refer to **Figure** in online course

14.3.2 Describe how to install network printer software and drivers on a computer

Windows XP allows computer users to share their printers with other users on the network. There are two steps:

- Configure the computer attached to the printer to share the printer with other network users.
- Configure a user's computer to recognize the shared printer and print to it.

To configure the computer with the printer attached to accept print jobs from other network users, follow these steps:

- Choose **Start > Control Panel > Printers and Other Hardware > Printers and Faxes**.
- Select the printer you want to share.
- The **Printer Tasks** box will appear on the left. Select **Share this printer**.
- The **Printer Properties** dialog box for that printer will display. Select the **Sharing** tab. Select **Share this printer** and enter the desired share name. This is the name that the printer will appear as to other users.
- Verify that sharing has been successful. Return to the **Printers and Faxes** folder and notice that the printer icon now has a hand under it, as shown in Figure 1. This shows that the printer is now a shared resource.

Other users who can now connect to the shared printer may not have the required drivers installed. These other users may also be using different operating systems than the computer that is hosting the shared printer. Windows XP can automatically download the correct drivers to these other users. Click the **Additional Drivers** button to select operating systems that the other users may be using. When you close that dialog box by clicking OK, Windows XP will ask to obtain those additional drivers. If all of the other users are also operating Windows XP, you do not need to click the **Additional Drivers** button.

Connecting Other Users

Other users on the network can now connect to this printer by following these steps:

- Choose **Start > Control Panel > Printers and other Hardware > Add a Printer**.
- The Add Printer wizard appears. Click **Next**.
- Select **A network printer, or a printer attached to another computer**, as shown in Figure 2. Click **Next**.
- Type in the name of the printer, or browse for it on the network using the **Next** button. A list of shared printers will appear.
- After you select the printer, a virtual printer port is created and displayed in the **Add a Printer** window. The required print drivers are downloaded from the print server and installed on the computer. The wizard then finishes the installation.

Refer to **Lab Activity** for this chapter

Printer Sharing

Share a printer over a network

Refer to **Figure** in online course

14.4 Upgrade and configure printers and scanners

Some printers can be expanded to print faster and to accommodate more print jobs by adding hardware. The hardware may include additional paper trays, sheet feeders, network cards, and expansion memory.

Scanners can also be configured to do more to meet customer needs. Examples for scanner optimization include color correction and resizing. These tasks cannot be completed with the default settings.

After completing this section, you will meet these objectives:

- Describe printer upgrades.
- Describe scanner optimization.

Refer to **Figure** in online course

14.4.1 Describe printer upgrades

Upgrading the printer memory improves the printing speed and enhances the ability to perform complex print jobs. All printers today have at least a small amount of RAM. The more memory a printer has, the more efficiently it works. The added memory helps with tasks such as job buffering, page creation, improved photo printing, and graphics.

Print job buffering is when a print job is captured into the internal printer memory. Buffering allows the computer to continue with other work instead of waiting for the printer to finish. Buffering is a common feature in laser printers and plotters, as well as in advanced inkjet and dot matrix printers.

Printers usually arrive from the factory with enough memory to handle jobs that involve text. However, print jobs involving graphics, and especially photographs, run more efficiently if the printer memory is adequate to store the entire job before it starts. If you receive errors that indicate the printer is "out of memory" or that there has been a "memory overload", you may need more memory.

Installing Printer Memory

The first step in installing additional printer memory is to read the printer manual to determine the following:

- ***Memory type –*** Physical type of memory, speed, and capacity; some are standard types of memory, whereas others require special or proprietary memory
- ***Memory population and availability –*** Number of memory upgrade slots in use, and how many available; this may require opening a compartment to check RAM

Printer manufacturers have set procedures for upgrading memory, including the following tasks:

- Removing covers to access the memory area
- Installing or removing memory
- Initializing the printer to recognize the new memory
- Installing updated drivers if needed

Additional Printer Upgrades

These are some of the additional printer upgrades:

- Duplex printing to enable dual-sided printing
- Extra trays to hold more paper
- Specialized tray types for different media
- Network cards to access a wired or wireless network
- Firmware upgrades to add functionality or to fix bugs

Follow the instructions included with the printer when you install or upgrade components. Contact the manufacturer or an authorized service technician for additional information if you have any problems when installing upgrades. Follow all safety procedures outlined by the manufacturer.

Refer to **Figure** in online course

14.4.2 Describe scanner optimization

Scanners work well for most users without any changes to the default settings. There are, however, features that can improve document or image scans depending on user requirements. These are the most common types of scanner options:

- Resizing
- Sharpening
- Brightening or darkening
- Color correction
- Resolution changes

- Output file format
- Color inversion

Scanning resolution affects the size of the output file. The end use of the image determines the required resolution. If the image is for use on a web publication, you only need low resolution and a small file size. This makes it possible for browsers to load the image quickly. Medium resolution images are normally used for laser prints. In commercial printing, where the quality of the image is very important, a higher resolution is the best setting. Low resolution means small file size; high resolution means large file size. Figure 1 shows the settings for resolution and output type.

Scanners may allow you to choose different file formats for the scanned output, as shown in Figure 2.

If a scanner does not produce output in a file format required by the customer, the format can be converted later using software tools. After changing device settings, you should test the changes by making some sample printouts.

Refer to **Lab Activity** for this chapter

Scanner Optimization

Change the resolution on a scanner

Refer to **Figure** in online course

14.5 Describe printer and scanner preventive maintenance techniques

Preventive maintenance decreases downtime and increases the service life of the components. You should maintain printers and scanners to keep them working properly. A good maintenance program guarantees good quality prints and scans. The printer or scanner manual contains information on how to maintain and clean the equipment.

After completing this section, you will meet these objectives:

- Determine scheduled maintenance according to vendor guidelines.
- Describe a suitable environment for printers and scanners.
- Describe cleaning methods.
- Describe how to check the capacity of ink cartridges and toners.

Refer to **Figure** in online course

14.5.1 Determine scheduled maintenance according to vendor guidelines

Read the information manuals that come with every new piece of equipment. Follow the recommended maintenance instructions. Also, use the supplies listed by the manufacturer. Less expensive supplies can save money, but may produce poor results, damage the equipment, or void the warranty.

When maintenance is completed, reset the counters to allow the next maintenance to be completed at the correct time. On many types of printers, the page count is viewed through the LCD display or a counter located inside the main cover.

Most manufacturers sell maintenance kits for their printers. Figure 1 shows a sample maintenance kit. The kit has instructions that any technician can follow. For laser printers, the kit may contain replacement parts that often break or wear out:

- Fuser assembly
- Transfer rollers

- Separation pads
- Pickup rollers

Each time you install new parts or replace toners and cartridges, do a visual inspection of all the internal components:

- Remove bits of paper and dust
- Clean spilled ink
- Look for any worn gears, cracked plastic, or broken parts

Users that do not know how to maintain printing equipment should call a manufacturer-certified technician.

Refer to **Worksheet** for this chapter

Certified Printer Technician

Research printer service technician requirements

Refer to **Figure** in online course

14.5.2 Describe a suitable environment for printers and scanners

Printers and scanners, like all other electrical devices, are affected by temperature, humidity, and electrical interference. For example, laser printers produce heat. Operate them in well-ventilated areas to prevent overheating. If possible, store all printers, scanners, and supplies in a cool and dry place, away from dust. This will help to ensure that they will work properly and for a long time.

Keep paper and toner cartridges in their original wrappers and in a cool, dry environment. High humidity causes paper to absorb moisture from the air. This makes it difficult for the toner to attach to the paper correctly. If the paper and printer are dusty, you may use compressed air to blow away the dust.

Refer to **Figure** in online course

14.5.3 Describe cleaning methods

Always follow the manufacturer's guidelines when cleaning printers and scanners. Information on the manufacturer's website or in the user manual explains the proper cleaning methods.

Caution

Remember to unplug scanners and printers before cleaning to prevent danger from high voltage.

Printer Maintenance

Make sure that you turn off and unplug any printer before performing maintenance. Use a damp cloth to wipe off any dirt, paper dust, and spilled ink on the exterior of the device.

Print heads in an inkjet printer are replaced when the cartridges are replaced. However, sometimes print heads become clogged and require cleaning. Use the utility supplied by the manufacturer to clean the print heads. After you clean them, you should test them. Repeat this process until the test shows a clean and uniform print.

Printers have many moving parts. Over time, the parts collect dust, dirt, and other debris. If not cleaned regularly, the printer may not work well, or could stop working completely. When working with dot matrix printers, clean the roller surfaces with a damp cloth. On inkjet printers, clean the paper-handling machinery with a damp cloth.

Caution

Do not touch the drum of a laser printer while cleaning. You may damage the surface of the drum.

Laser printers do not usually require much maintenance unless they are in a dusty area or they are very old. When cleaning a laser printer, use a specially designed vacuum cleaner to pick up toner particles. Figure 1 shows a vacuum designed for electronic equipment. A standard vacuum cleaner cannot hold the tiny particles of toner and may scatter them about. Use only a vacuum cleaner with HEPA filtration. HEPA filtration catches microscopic particles within the filters.

Choosing the correct paper type for a printer helps the printer last longer and print more efficiently. Several types of paper are available. Each type of paper is clearly labeled with the type of printer for which it is intended. The manufacturer of the printer may also recommend the best type of paper. Check the printer manual.

Information about the brands and types of ink recommended by the manufacturer is also found in the manual. Using the wrong type of ink may cause the printer not to work or may reduce the print quality. To prevent ink leaks, do not refill ink cartridges.

Scanner Maintenance

You should clean scanners regularly to prevent dirt, fingerprints, and other smudges from showing in scanned images. On flatbed scanners, keep the lid closed when the scanner is not in use. This will help to prevent dust build-up and accidental fingertip smudges. If the glass becomes dirty, consult the user guide for the manufacturer's cleaning recommendations. If the manual does not list any recommendations, use a glass cleaner and a soft cloth to protect the glass from scratching. Even very small scratches can be visible on high-resolution scans. If dirt becomes lodged in the scratches, the scratches will become more visible.

If the inside of the glass becomes dirty, check the manual for instructions on how to open the unit or remove the glass from the scanner. If possible, thoroughly clean both sides and replace the glass as it was originally installed in the scanner.

Refer to **Figure** in online course

14.5.4 Describe checking capacity of ink cartridges and toners

When an inkjet printer produces blank pages, the ink cartridges may be empty. Laser printers, however, do not produce blank pages, but do begin to print very poor-quality printouts. Most inkjet printers provide a utility that shows ink levels in each cartridge, as shown in Figure 1. Some printers have LCD message screens or LED lights that warn users when ink supplies are low.

A method for checking ink levels is to look at the page counter inside the printer or the printer software to determine how many pages have been printed. Then look at the cartridge label information. The label should show how many pages the cartridge can print. You can then easily estimate how many more pages you can print. For this method to be accurate, each time you replace the cartridge, you must remember to reset the counter. In addition, some printouts use more ink than others do. For example, a letter uses less ink than a photograph.

You can set the printer software to reduce the amount of ink or toner that the printer uses. This setting may be called "toner save" or "draft quality". This setting reduces the print quality of laser and inkjet products, and reduces the time it takes to print a document on an inkjet printer.

Refer to **Figure** in online course

14.6 Troubleshoot printers and scanners

With printer and scanner problems, a technician must be able to determine if the problem exists with the device, cable connection, or the computer that it is attached to. Follow the steps outlined in this section to accurately identify, repair, and document the problem.

After completing this section, you will meet these objectives:

- Review the troubleshooting process.
- Identify common problems and solutions.
- Apply troubleshooting skills.

Refer to **Figure** in online course

14.6.1 Review the troubleshooting process

Printer and scanner problems can result from a combination of hardware, software, and connectivity issues. Computer technicians must be able to analyze the problem and determine the cause of the error to repair the printer and scanner issues.

The first step in the troubleshooting process is to gather data from the customer. Figures 1 and 2 list open-ended and closed-ended questions to ask the customer.

Once you have talked to the customer, you should verify the obvious issues. Figure 3 lists issues that apply to printers and scanners.

After the obvious issues have been verified, try some quick solutions. Figure 4 lists some quick solutions to printer and scanner problems.

If quick solutions did not correct the problem, it is time to gather data from the computer. Figure 5 shows different ways to gather information about the printer and scanner problem.

At this point, you will have enough information to evaluate the problem, research, and implement possible solutions. Figure 6 shows resources for possible solutions.

After you have solved the problem, you will close with the customer. Figure 7 is a list of the tasks required to complete this step.

Refer to **Figure** in online course

14.6.2 Identify common problems and solutions

Printer and scanner problems can be attributed to hardware, software, networks, or some combination of the three. You will resolve some types of problems more often than others. Figure 1 is a chart of common problems and solutions.

Refer to **Figure** in online course

14.6.3 Apply troubleshooting skills

Now that you understand the troubleshooting process, it is time to apply your listening and diagnostic skills.

The first lab is designed to reinforce your skill with printers. You will troubleshoot and fix a printer problem.

The second lab is designed to reinforce your communication and troubleshooting skills with printers. In this lab, you will perform the following steps:

- Receive the work order

- Take the customer through various steps to try and resolve the problem
- Document the problem and the resolution

Refer to **Lab Activity** for this chapter

Fix a Printer

Fix a printer problem

Remote Technician

Instruct a customer on how to correct a printer problem

Summary

This chapter reviewed and discussed information about printers and scanners. The chapter explored hazards and safety procedures associated with printers and scanners. You have learned preventive maintenance methods, and have installed, configured, and upgraded a printer or scanner, both locally and on a network. Here are some other important facts covered in this chapter:

- Always follow safety procedures when working with printers and scanners. There are many parts inside printers that contain high voltage or become very hot with use.
- Use the device manual and software to install a printer or scanner. After the installation, update the drivers and firmware to fix problems and increase functionality.
- Use the Windows interface to share printers and scanners across the network.
- Consult the customers to determine how best to upgrade and configure printers and scanners to meet their needs.
- Keep printers, scanners, and supplies clean and dry. Keep supplies in their original packaging to prevent breakdowns and downtime. Develop a maintenance schedule to clean and check devices on a regular basis.
- Use a sequence of steps to fix a problem. Start with simple tasks before you decide on a course of action. Call a qualified or certified printer technician when a problem is too difficult for you to fix.

Chapter 14 Quiz

Take the chapter quiz to test your knowledge.

Go to
the online course
to take the quiz.

Your Chapter Notes

CHAPTER 15

Advanced Networks

Introduction

This chapter focuses on advanced networking topics, including network design, network component upgrades, and e-mail server installations. Basic networking topics such as safety, network components, and preventive maintenance are also discussed.

To meet the expectations and needs of your customers and network users, you must be familiar with networking technologies. You must understand the basics of how a network is designed and why some components affect the flow of data on a network. Troubleshooting advanced network situations is also described in this chapter.

After completing this chapter, you will meet these objectives:

- Identify potential safety hazards and implement proper safety procedures related to networks.
- Design a network based on the customer's needs.
- Determine the components for your customer's network.
- Implement the customer's network.
- Upgrade the customer's network.
- Describe installation, configuration, and management of a simple mail server.
- Describe preventive maintenance procedures for networks.
- Troubleshoot the network.

Refer to **Figure** in online course

15.1 Identify potential safety hazards and implement proper safety procedures related to networks

Installing network cables, whether copper or fiber optic, can be dangerous. Often, cables must be pulled through ceilings and walls where there are obstacles and unexpected or toxic materials. You should wear clothing that protects you from these materials. For example, wear long pants, long-sleeved shirts, sturdy shoes that cover your feet, and gloves. Most importantly, wear safety glasses. If possible, ask building management, or someone responsible for the building, if there are any dangerous materials or obstacles that you need to be aware of before entering the ceiling area.

Be aware of the safety issues when using a ladder:

- Read the labels on the ladder and follow any safety instructions written on it.
- Never stand on the top rung of the ladder. You could easily lose your balance and fall.
- Make sure that people in the area know you will be working there.
- Cordon off the area with caution tape or safety cones.

- When you are using a ladder that leans up against a wall, follow the instructions written on the ladder, and have someone hold the ladder for you to help keep the ladder steady.

The tools required to install copper and fiber-optic cable may be dangerous to use. Rules should always be followed when working with cables:

- Make sure that the tools you are using are in good working order.
- Watch what you are doing and take your time. Make sure that you do not cut yourself or place anyone in danger.
- Always wear safety glasses when cutting, stripping, or splicing cables of any kind. Tiny fragments can injure your eyes.
- Wear gloves whenever possible and make sure to dispose of any waste properly.

Use common sense when you take care of any problems. Call another person to help you if you need help.

After completing this section, you will meet these objectives:

- Explain fiber-optic safety.
- Explain cable, cable cutters, and cable cutting safety hazards.

Refer to **Figure** in online course

15.1.1 Explain fiber-optic safety

Fiber optics are useful for communications, but they have certain hazards:

- Dangerous chemicals
- Light that you cannot see that can burn your eyes
- Tools with sharp edges that produce glass splinters

Specific types of tools and chemicals are used when working with fiber-optic cable. These materials must be handled safely.

Chemicals

The solvents and glues used with fiber optics are dangerous. You should handle them with extreme care. Read any instructions and follow them carefully. Also, read the MSDS that accompanies the chemicals to know how to treat someone in an emergency.

Tools

When working with any tool, safety should always be your first priority. Any compromise in safety could result in serious injury or even death. The tools used for working with fiber optics have sharp cutting surfaces that are used to scribe glass. Other tools pinch cables with high pressure to fasten connectors to them. These tools can produce shards of glass that can splinter and fly into the air. You must avoid getting them in your skin, mouth, or eyes.

Harmful Light

Protect your eyes from the harmful light that may be in the fiber-optic strands. The light is a color that humans cannot see. It can damage your eyes before you can feel it. When you use a magnifier to inspect fiber-optic cable and connectors, the light emitted from the fiber could be directed into your eye. When working with fiber, be sure to disconnect the light source. Special detectors can tell you if a fiber is energized.

Glass Shards

The process of cutting and trimming the strands of fiber-optic cables can produce tiny fragments of glass or plastic that can penetrate your eyes or skin and cause severe irritation. The fibers can be extremely difficult to see on your skin because they are clear and small. When working with fiber-optic cabling, the working surface should be a dark mat so that tiny glass or plastic fragments can be seen. The mat should also be resistant to chemical spills.

You should keep the work area clean and neat. Never pick up fiber-optic fragments with your fingers. Use tape to pick up small fragments and dispose of them properly. Use a disposable container, such as a plastic bottle with a screw-on lid, to store fiber fragments. Close the lid tightly before disposing of the container.

Refer to **Figure** in online course

Caution

Obtain proper training before you attempt to cut, strip, or splice fiber-optic cable. An experienced technician should supervise you until you become adequately skilled.

15.1.2 Explain cable, cable cutters, and cable cutting safety hazards

All levels of technicians should know the hazards before working with network cable and equipment.

Caution

When handling cable, always wear eye protection. Never touch the ends of any type of cable with bare skin.

Copper Cable Hazards

Copper cables can also be dangerous to handle. When you cut copper cable, the small copper strands can puncture your skin or cut you. The small pieces that come off after cutting cables often fly into the air. Remember to always wear safety glasses when cutting any type of cable.

The cutting and crimping tools used to repair or terminate copper cables can be dangerous if not used properly. Read the documentation that comes with the tool. Practice using the tool on scrap cable, and ask an experienced installer for help if you need it.

Remember that copper cable conducts electricity. An equipment fault, static electricity, or lightning can energize even a disconnected cable. If in doubt, test the cable you are working on with a simple voltage detector before touching it.

Refer to **Figure** in online course

15.2 Design a network based on the customer's needs

A network works best if it is designed to meet the needs of the customer. Building a network requires analysis of the environment and an understanding of networking options. You should interview the customer, as well as any other people involved in the project. It is important to have a general idea about the hardware and software that will be used on the network. You should inquire about future growth of the company and the network.

After completing this section, you will meet these objectives:

- Determine a topology.
- Determine protocols and network applications.

Refer to **Figure** in online course

15.2.1 Determine a topology

Understanding the needs of the customer and determining the general layout of the new network are required to properly determine the network topology. These important issues need to be discussed with the customer:

- Cable and wireless types
- Expandability
- Number and location of users

The number of users and the estimated amount of future growth determines the initial physical and logical topology of the network. You should create a checklist to record the needs of your customer.

An inspection, called a site survey, should be done early in the project. A site survey is a physical inspection of the building that helps determine a basic logical topology, which is the flow of data and protocols. The number of users and the estimated amount of future growth determines the initial physical and logical topology of the network. You should consider the following factors:

- Where the users' end-station computers will be.
- Where to position network equipment such as switches and routers.
- Where the servers will be positioned. This may be in the same room as the network equipment, or it could be elsewhere. The decision is often based on available space, power, security, and air conditioning.

A floor plan or blueprint is helpful to determine the physical layout of equipment and cables. Figure 1 shows a comparison of network topologies. If a floor plan or blueprint is not available, you should make a drawing of where the network devices will be located, including the location of the server room, the printers, the end stations, and cable runs. This drawing can be used for discussions when the customer makes the final layout decisions.

Refer to **Figure** in online course

15.2.2 Determine protocols and network applications

In the design of a network, you must determine the protocols that are going to be used. Some protocols are proprietary and only work on specific equipment, while other protocols are open standards and work on a variety of equipment. Figure 1 shows details of the various network protocols.

Consider the following when selecting protocols:

- The TCP/IP suite of protocols is required for every device to connect to the Internet. This makes it a preferred protocol for networking.
- NetBEUI is a small, fast protocol that is useful in low security networks. NetBEUI performs well in a small network that is not connected to the Internet. It is easy to install and requires no configuration. However, NetBEUI can cause unnecessary traffic on a large network, so it is not a good choice if there will be network growth.

- IPX/SPX is a protocol that belongs to older versions of Novell Netware. Because of the growth of the Internet, newer versions of Novell Netware use TCP/IP instead of IPX/SPX.
- Apple Macintosh networks have abandoned the AppleTalk protocol for the TCP/IP suite of protocols to ensure connectivity with other TCP/IP networks, most notably the Internet.

When the TCP/IP protocol stack is enabled, other protocols become available on specific ports, as shown in Figure 2.

Refer to **Worksheet** for this chapter

Protocols

Identify the proper protocol to use in different network configurations

Refer to **Figure** in online course

15.3 Determine the components for your customer's network

The choice of network topology determines the type of devices, cables, and network interfaces that will be required to construct the network. In addition, an outside connection to an Internet service provider must be set up. One of the steps in building a network is to determine suitable network components that work with user devices and the cabling of the network.

After completing this section, you will meet these objectives:

- Select cable types.
- Select ISP connection types.
- Select network cards.
- Select the network device.

Refer to **Figure** in online course

15.3.1 Select cable types

Select the cable type that is the most beneficial and cost effective for the users and services that will connect to the network.

Cable Types

The size of the network determines the type of network cable that will be used. Most networks today are wired using one or more kinds of types of twisted-pair copper cable:

- Cat5
- Cat5e
- Cat6
- Cat6A

Cat5 and Cat5e cables look the same, but Cat 5e cable is manufactured with a higher standard to allow for higher data transfer rates. Cat6 cable is constructed with even higher standards than Cat5e. Cat6 cable may have a center divider to separate the pairs inside the cable.

The most common type of cable used in a network is Cat5e. Cat5e is suitable for Fast Ethernet up to 330 feet (100 m). Some businesses and homes have installed Cat6 cable so that they are prepared for additional bandwidth requirements in the future. Applications such as video, videoconferencing, and gaming use a large amount of bandwidth.

The most recent type of twisted-pair cable available is Cat6A. Cat6A cable carries Ethernet signals at a rate of 10 Gbps. The abbreviation for 10 Gb Ethernet over twisted-pair cable is 10GBase-T, as defined in the IEEE 802.3an-2006 standard. Customers who need high bandwidth networks can benefit from installing cable that can support Gigabit Ethernet or 10 Gb Ethernet.

New or renovated office buildings often have some type of UTP cabling that connects every office to a central point called the Main Distribution Facility (MDF). The distance limitation of UTP cabling used for data is 330 feet (100 m). Network devices that are farther than this distance limitation need a repeater or hub to extend the connection to the MDF.

Cost

When designing a network, cost is a consideration. Installing cables is expensive, but after a one-time expense, a wired network is normally inexpensive to maintain. Most of the devices on a wired network cost much less than the devices on a wireless network.

Security

A wired network is usually more secure than a wireless network. The cables in a wired network are usually installed in walls and ceilings, and therefore not easily accessible. Wireless is easier to eavesdrop. The signals are available to anyone who has a receiver. To make a wireless network as secure as a wired network requires the use of encryption.

Design for the Future

Many organizations install the highest grade cable available to ensure that their networks can handle the network speeds that will be available in the future. The organizations want to avoid having to do expensive reinstalling of cable later. You and your customer must decide if the cost of installing a higher grade cable is necessary.

Wireless

A wireless solution may be possible in places where cables cannot be installed. Consider an older, historic building where local building codes do not permit structural modifications. In this case, installing cable is not possible and therefore a wireless connection is the only solution.

15.3.2 Select ISP connection type

Refer to **Figure** in online course

The ISP (Internet service provider) that you choose can have a noticeable effect on network service. Some private resellers that connect to a phone company may sell more connections than allowed, which slows the overall speed of the service to customers.

There are three main considerations for an Internet connection:

- Speed
- Reliability
- Availability

POTS

A plain old telephone system (POTS) connection is extremely slow but it is available wherever there is a telephone. The modem uses the telephone line to transmit and receive data.

ISDN

The Integrated Services Digital Network (ISDN) offers faster connection times and has faster speeds than dial-up, and allows multiple devices to share a single telephone line. ISDN is very reliable because it uses POTS lines. ISDN is available in most places where the telephone company supports digital signaling.

DSL

Digital Subscriber Line (DSL), like ISDN, allows multiple devices to share a single telephone line. DSL speeds are generally higher than ISDN. DSL allows the use of high-bandwidth applications or multiple users to share the same connection to the Internet. In most cases, the copper wires already in your home or business are capable of carrying the signals needed for DSL communication.

There are limitations to DSL technology. DSL service is not available everywhere, and it works better and faster the closer the installation is to the telephone provider's central office (CO). Also, DSL is much faster when receiving data over the Internet than it is when sending it. In some cases, the lines that are in place to carry telephone signals do not technically qualify to carry DSL signals.

Cable

Cable Internet connection does not use telephone lines. Cable uses coaxial cable lines originally designed to carry cable television. Like DSL, cable offers high speeds and an "always-on" connection, which means that even when the connection is not in use, the connection to the Internet is still available. Many cable companies offer telephone service as well.

Because cable television reaches many homes, it is an alternative for people unable to receive DSL service. Theoretically, the bandwidth of cable is higher than DSL, but can be affected by limitations of the cable provider. Most homes that have cable television have the option to install high-speed Internet service.

Satellite

For people that live in rural areas, broadband satellite Internet connections provide a high-speed connection that is always on. A satellite dish is used to transmit and receive signals to and from a satellite that relays these signals back to a service provider.

The cost of installation and the monthly service fees are much higher than those for DSL and cable subscribers. Heavy storm conditions can degrade the quality of the connection between the user and the satellite, or the satellite to the provider, slowing down or even disconnecting the connection. In most cases, the service provider provides a dial-up connection as a backup.

Wireless

Many types of wireless Internet services are available. The same companies that offer cellular service may offer Internet service. PCMCIA and PCI cards are used to connect a computer to the Internet. The service is not available in all areas.

Service providers may offer wireless Internet service using microwave technology in limited areas. Signals are transmitted directly to an antenna on the roof of the house or building.

Research the connection types that the ISPs offer before selecting an ISP. Check the services available in your area. Compare connection speeds, reliability, and cost before committing to a service agreement.

Refer to **Worksheet** for this chapter

ISP Connections

Identify the best ISP based on a given scenario

15.3.3 Select network cards

Refer to **Figure** in online course

Every device on a network requires a network interface. There are many types of network interfaces:

- Most network interfaces for desktop computers are either integrated into the motherboard or are an expansion card that fits into an expansion slot.
- Most laptop network interfaces are either integrated into the motherboard or fit into a PC Card or ExpressBus expansion slot.

- USB network adapters plug into any available USB port and can be used with both desktops and laptops.

Before purchasing a NIC, you should research the speed, form factor, and capabilities the card offers. Check the speed and capabilities of the hub or switch that will be connected to the computer.

Ethernet NICs may be backward-compatible:

- If you have a 10/100 Mbps NIC and a hub that is only 10 Mbps, the NIC will operate at 10 Mbps.
- If you have a 10/100/1000 Mbps NIC and a switch that is only operating at 100 Mbps, the NIC will operate at 100 Mbps.

However, if you have a gigabit switch, you will most likely need to purchase a gigabit NIC to match speeds. If there are any plans to upgrade the network in the future to Gigabit Ethernet, make sure to purchase NICs that are able to support the speed. Costs can vary greatly, so select NICs that match the needs of your customer.

Wireless NICs are available in many formats with many capabilities. You should select wireless NICs based on the type of wireless network that is installed, as described in these examples:

- 802.11b NICs can be used on 802.11g networks.
- 802.11a can be used only on a network that supports 802.11a.
- 802.11a, 802.11b and 802.11g NICs can be used on 802.11n networks.

Choose wireless cards that match the needs of your customers. You should know what wireless equipment is in use and what will be installed on the network to ensure compatibility and usability.

Refer to **Figure** in online course

15.3.4 Select the network device

Several types of devices are available to connect components on a network. Select network devices to meet the needs of your customer.

Hubs

A hub is used to share data between multiple devices on a section of the network. The hub may connect to another networking device like a switch or router that connects to other sections of the network. The maximum speed of the network is determined by the speed of the hub.

Hubs are used less often today because of the effectiveness and low cost of switches. Hubs do not segment network traffic, so they decrease the amount of available bandwidth to any device. In addition, because hubs cannot filter data, a lot of unnecessary traffic constantly moves between all the devices connected to it.

One advantage of a hub is that it regenerates the data that passes through it. This means that a hub can also function as a repeater. A hub can extend the reach of a network because rebuilding the signal pulses overcomes the effects of distance.

Switches

In modern networks, switches have replaced hubs as the central point of connectivity. Like a hub, the speed of the switch determines the maximum speed of the network. However, switches filter and segment network traffic by sending data only to the device to which it is sent. This provides higher dedicated bandwidth to each device on the network.

Switches maintain a switching table. The switching table contains a list of all MAC addresses on the network, and a list of which switch port can be used to reach a device with a given MAC address. The switching table records MAC addresses by inspecting the source MAC address of every incoming frame, as well as the port on which the frame arrives. The switch then creates a switching table that maps MAC addresses to outgoing ports. When a frame arrives that is destined for a particular MAC address, the switch uses the switching table to determine which port to use to reach the MAC address. The frame is forwarded from the port to the destination. By sending frames out of only one port to the destination, other ports are not affected, and bandwidth on the entire network is not affected.

Routers

Routers connect networks together. On a corporate network, one router port connects to the WAN connection and the other ports connect to the corporate LANs. The router becomes the gateway, or path to the outside, for the LAN. In a home network, the router connects the computers and network devices in the home to the Internet. In this case, the router is a home gateway. The wireless router, shown in Figure 1, serves as a firewall and provides wireless connectivity. When the home router provides multiple services, it may be called a multifunction device.

ISP Equipment

When subscribing to an ISP, you should find out what type of equipment is available so that you can select the most appropriate device. Many ISPs offer a discount on equipment that is purchased at the time of installation.

Some ISPs may rent equipment on a month-to-month basis. This may be more attractive because the ISP supports the equipment if there is a failure, change, or upgrade to the technology. Home users may select to purchase equipment from the ISP because, after a period of time, the initial cost of the equipment will be lower than the cost of renting the equipment.

Refer to **Interactive Graphic** in online course.

15.4 Implement the customer's network

Refer to **Figure** in online course

Installing and implementing a network can be a complicated task. Even a small home network installation can become difficult and time consuming. However, careful planning helps ensure an easier and faster installation.

During the installation, there may be some downtime for the existing network. For example, disruptions can be caused by building modifications and network cable installation. The project is not complete until all devices have been installed, configured, and tested.

After completing this section, you will meet these objectives:

- Install and test the customer's network.
- Configure the customer's Internet and network resources.

15.4.1 Install and test the customer's network

Once you have determined the location of all network devices, you are ready to install the network cables. In some new or newly renovated buildings, network cables may be installed to avoid the problem of installing cables in finished walls later. If there is no preinstalled cable, you have to install it or have it installed.

Network Installation Steps

If you are going to install the cable yourself, you need time to prepare. All of the necessary materials should be available at the site at the time of installation, as well as the layout plan of the cable.

These steps outline the process for physically creating a network:

Step 1. To install the cable in ceilings and behind walls, you perform a cable pull. One person pulls the cable, and the other feeds the cable through the walls. Make sure to label the ends of every cable. Follow a labeling scheme that is already in place, or follow the guidelines outlined in TIA/EIA 606-A.

Step 2. After the cables have been terminated on both ends, you should test them to make sure there are no shorts or interference.

Step 3. Make sure that network interfaces are properly installed in the desktops, laptops, and network printers. After the network interfaces have been installed, configure the client software and the IP address information on all of the devices.

Step 4. Install switches and routers in a secured, centralized location. All of the LAN connections terminate in this area. In a home network, you may need to install these devices in separate locations, or you may have only one device.

Step 5. Install an Ethernet patch cable from the wall connection to each network device. Check to see if you have a link light on all network interfaces. In a home network, make sure that each network device port that connects to a device is lit.

Step 6. When all devices are connected and all link lights are functioning, you should test the network for connectivity. Use the **ipconfig /all** command to view the IP configuration on each workstation. Use the **ping** command to test basic connectivity. You should be able to ping other computers on the network, including the default gateway and remote computers. Once you have confirmed basic connectivity, you must configure and test network applications such as e-mail and an Internet browser.

Refer to **Figure** in online course

15.4.2 Configure the customer's Internet and network resources

After the network has been set up and tested, you should configure a web browser, such as Microsoft Internet Explorer (IE). You can configure browser settings and perform maintenance tasks in the Internet Properties dialog box, as shown in Figure 1.

Temporary Internet Files

When an operating system such as Windows XP has been installed, IE is also installed by default. With IE, every time that you visit a website, many files are downloaded to your computer in the Temporary Internet Files folder. Most of these files are image files that represent banners and other components of the website.

Temporary Internet files are stored on your computer so that the browser can load content faster the next time you visit a website that you have been to before. Depending on the number of websites you visit, the Temporary Internet Files folder can fill up quickly. While this may not be an urgent problem, you should delete, or flush out, the files occasionally. This is especially important after you have done online banking or have entered other personal information into the Web browser.

Default Browser

You can confirm which browser Windows uses by default. Choose **Start > Run**, enter a website address, and click **OK**. The website opens in the browser that is currently set as the default.

If you want IE to be your default browser, start by opening IE. On the toolbar, select **Tools > Internet Options...** On the **Programs** tab, you can check to see if IE is your default browser, and select it if desired.

File Sharing

Users can share resources over the network. You can share a single file, specific folders, or an entire drive, as shown in Figure 2.

To share a file, you should first copy it to a folder. Right-click the folder and select **Sharing and Security**. Next select **Share this folder**. You can identify who has access to the folder and what permissions they have on the objects in the folder. Figure 3 shows the permissions window of a shared folder.

Permissions define the type of access a user has to a file or folder:

- ***Read –*** Allows the user to view the file and subfolder names, navigate to subfolders, view data in files, and run program files.
- ***Change –*** Allows all of the permissions of the Read permission but allows the user to add files and subfolders, change the data in files, and delete subfolders and files.
- ***Full Control –*** Allows all of the permissions of Change and Read. If the file or folder is in an NTFS partition, Full Control allows you to change permissions on the file or folder, and take ownership of the file or folder.

Windows XP Professional is limited to a maximum of 10 simultaneous file-sharing connections.

Printer Sharing

To share a printer, select **Start > Control Panel > Printers and Faxes**. Right-click the printer icon and select **Sharing**. Click **Share this Printer** and then click **OK**. The printer is now available for other computers to access.

To access a printer shared by another computer, select **Start > Control Panel > Printers and Faxes**. Click **File > Add Printer**. Use the Add Printers wizard to find and install the shared network printer.

Refer to **Lab Activity** for this chapter

Browser Configuration

Configure an Internet browser

Network resource Sharing

Share and configure a network folder and printer

Refer to **Figure** in online course

15.5 Upgrade the customer's network

You must be able to upgrade, install, and configure components when a customer asks for increased speed or new functionality to be added to a network. Devices such as wireless access points, wireless network cards, and faster network equipment and cable can be integrated into a network to allow the customer to communicate wirelessly or more quickly.

If your customer is adding additional computers or wireless functionality, you should be able to recommend equipment based on their needs. The equipment that you suggest must work with the existing equipment and cabling, or the existing infrastructure must be upgraded.

After completing this section, you will meet these objectives:

- Install and configure wireless NIC.
- Install and configure wireless routers.
- Test connection.

15.5.1 Install and configure wireless NIC

Refer to **Figure** in online course

To connect to a wireless network, your computer must have a wireless network interface. A wireless network interface is used to communicate with other wireless devices, such as computer, printer, or wireless access points.

Before purchasing a wireless adapter, you should make sure that it is compatible with other wireless equipment that is already installed on the network. Also, verify that the wireless adapter is the correct form factor to fit in a desktop or laptop. A wireless USB adapter can be used with any desktop or laptop computer that has an open USB port.

To install a wireless NIC on a desktop computer, you must remove the case cover. Install the wireless NIC into an available PCI slot or PCI express slot. Some wireless NICs have an antenna connected to the back of the card. Some antennas are attached with a cable so that they can be moved around or away from objects that may cause a poor connection.

Once the wireless adapter is installed, there are additional configuration steps. These include configuring device drivers and entering network address information. When this is complete, the computer should be able to detect and connect to the wireless LAN.

Wireless network adapters may use a wizard to connect to the wireless network. In this case, you would insert the CD that comes with the adapter and follow the directions to get connected.

Refer to **Lab Activity** for this chapter

Wireless NIC Installation

Install a wireless NIC

15.5.2 Install and configure wireless routers

Refer to **Figure** in online course

When installing a wireless network, you have to decide where you want to put access points, and then configure them. The following steps describe the installation of an access point:

- Use a floor plan to find the locations for access points that allow maximum coverage. The best place for a wireless access point is at the center of the area you are covering, with a line of sight between the wireless devices and the access point.
- Connect the access point to the existing network. On the back of the Linksys WRT300N router, there are five ports. Connect a DSL or cable modem to the port labeled "Internet". The switching logic of the device forwards all of the packets through this port when there is communication to and from the Internet and other connected computers. Connect one computer to any of the remaining ports to access the configuration web pages.
- Turn on the broadband modem and plug in the power cord to the router. When the modem finishes establishing connection to the ISP, the router automatically communicates with the modem to receive network information from the ISP that is necessary to gain access to the Internet: IP address, subnet mask, and DNS server addresses.
- When the router has established communication with the modem, you must configure the router to communicate with the devices on the network. Turn on the computer that is connected to the router. Open a web browser. In the Address field, enter **192.168.1.1**. This is the default address for router configuration and management.

- A security window prompts you for authentication to access the router configuration screens. The user name field should be left empty. Enter **admin** as the default password. When logged in, the first setup screen opens.
- Continue with the setup. There are tabs that have sub-tabs on the setup screen. You must click **Save Settings** at the bottom of each screen after making any changes.

When you use the configuration screens of the 300N router, you can click the help tab to see additional information about a tab. For information beyond what is shown on the help screen, consult the user manual.

Refer to **Lab Activity** for this chapter

Wireless Router Installation

Install a wireless router

Refer to **Figure** in online course

15.5.3 Test connection

It may be difficult to know if your wireless connection is working properly, even when Windows indicates that you are connected. You may be connected to a wireless access point or home gateway, but you may not be connected to the Internet. The easiest way to test for an Internet connection is to open a web browser and see if the Internet is available. To troubleshoot a wireless connection, you can use the Windows GUI or CLI.

Network Connections

To verify a wireless connection using the Windows XP GUI, select **Start > Control Panel > Network Connections**, as shown in Figure 1. Double-click on the wireless network connection to display the status.

The **Connection Status** screen shown in Figure 2 displays the number of packets that have been sent and received. The packets are the communication between the computer and the network device. The window shows whether or not the computer is connected, along with the speed and duration of the connection.

To display the **Address Type**, as shown in Figure 3, choose the **Support** tab on the **Connection Status** screen. The Connection Status information includes either a static address, which is assigned manually, or a dynamic address which is assigned by a DHCP server. The subnet mask and default gateway are also listed. To access the MAC address and other information about the IP address, click **Details...**. If the connection is not functioning correctly, click **Repair** to reset the connection information and attempt to establish a new connection.

Ipconfig

The **ipconfig** command is a command line tool that is used to verify that the connection has a valid IP address. The window displays basic IP address information for network connections. To perform specific tasks, add switches to the **ipconfig** command, as shown in Figure 4.

Ping

Ping is a CLI tool used to test connectivity between devices. You can test your own connection by pinging your computer. To test your computer, ping your NIC. Select **Start > Run > cmd**. At the command prompt, enter **ping localhost**. This command lets you know if your adapter is working properly.

Ping your default gateway to check if your WAN connection is working properly. You can find the address for the default gateway by using the **ipconfig** command.

To test the Internet connection and DNS, ping a popular website. Select **Start > Run > cmd**. At the command prompt, enter **ping destination name**.

The response of the **ping** command displays the IP address resolution of the domain. The response shows replies from the ping or that the request timed out because there is a problem.

Tracert

Tracert is a CLI tool that traces the route that packets take from your computer to a destination address. Select **Start > Run > cmd**. At the command prompt, enter **tracert**.

The first listing in the window for the tracert result is your default gateway. Each listing after that is the router that packets are traveling through to reach the destination. Tracert shows you where packets are stopping, indicating where the problem is occurring. If there are listings that show problems after the default gateway, it may mean that the problems are with the ISP, the Internet, or the destination server.

Refer to **Lab Activity** for this chapter

Wireless NIC Connection Test

Test the connection of the wireless NIC

Refer to **Figure** in online course

15.6 Describe installation, configuration and management of a simple mail server

An e-mail system uses e-mail client software on the users' devices, and e-mail server software on one or more e-mail servers. Clients read e-mail from the e-mail server using one of two protocols:

- Post Office Protocol (POP)
- Internet Message Access Protocol (IMAP)

Clients send e-mail to an e-mail server, and e-mail servers forward e-mail to each other, using Simple Mail Transfer Protocol (SMTP).

You need to know how to configure a client computer to accept the correct incoming mail format, and also understand the process for setting up a mail server. Configuring the e-mail client software can be done using connection wizards such as shown in Figure 1. The advantages and disadvantages of each e-mail protocol are shown in Figure 2.

SMTP

SMTP sends e-mail from a e-mail client to an e-mail server, or from one e-mail server to another. SMTP has these characteristics:

- Simple, text-based protocol
- Sent over TCP using port 25
- Must be implemented to send e-mail
- Message is sent after receipients are identified and verified

POP

Post Office Protocol (POP) is used by an e-mail client to download e-mail from an e-mail server. The most recent version of POP is POP3. POP3 usually uses port 110.

POP3 supports end users that have intermittent connections, such as dial-up. A POP3 user can connect, download e-mail from the server, delete the e-mail, and then disconnect.

IMAP

Internet Message Access Protocol (IMAP) is similar to POP3, but has additional features. Like POP3, IMAP allows you to download e-mail from an e-mail server using an e-mail client. The difference is that IMAP allows the user to organize e-mail on the network e-mail server. IMAP is faster than POP3 and requires more disk space on the server and more CPU resources. The most recent version of IMAP is IMAP4. IMAP4 is often used in large networks such as a university campus. IMAP usually uses port 143.

E-mail Server

An e-mail server is a computer that can send and receive e-mail on behalf of e-mail clients. These are some common e-mail servers:

- Microsoft Exchange
- Sendmail
- Eudora Internet Mail Server (EIMS)

As shown in Figure 3, there are often wizards and tools available to guide you in setting up an e-mail server. To install and set up an e-mail server, such as Microsoft Exchange, you must first make sure that the network has all of the proper qualifications in place and that it is properly configured. Active directory servers, global catalog servers, and domain name servers (DNS) must all be in place and functioning before Exchange can be installed and work properly. An active directory server is a computer that hosts a database that allows centralized administration over an enterprise network. A global catalog server is a centralized repository that contains information about every domain in an enterprise network.

Exchange must be installed on a domain where every computer runs at least Windows 2000. This is known as native mode. Windows NT domain controllers cannot function in a native environment.

The Active Directory database is organized in a pattern called a schema. One server running Windows 2003 is designated as the Schema Master. This is the only server that can change the way the Active Directory user database is organized. When the network administrator needs to modify the Active Directory structure, the change is made on the Schema Master. Active Directory then automatically copies the update to all the rest of the authentication servers.

E-mail Server Installation

You should test the environment before you install Exchange. To prevent the installation from affecting the daily operation of your network, set up the services required and install Exchange on a dedicated set of servers away from the main network. Keep the installation of Exchange separated from your production network until you are sure that it is functioning properly.

Before you install Exchange, be prepared with the proper equipment and information:

- Fully functional and reliable DNS deployment
- Active Directory domain
- At least one Global Catalog
- Windows 2000 or higher native domain functionality
- Exchange server software

- Windows server support tools
- Schema master server
- High-speed Internet connection

You are ready to install the mail server when all of the qualifications of your network are in place. You will have to add Internet Information Services (IIS) using the Add/Remove Windows Components wizard before initiating the installation of the Exchange server. IIS is a server that has programs used for building and administering website services. After IIS has been installed, Exchange can be installed. Insert the installation CD and begin the New Exchange installation wizard.

The installation wizard will take you through a series of steps to verify that Exchange is ready to be installed. The wizard will check to make sure that IIS is installed, the domain servers are running properly, and the Windows support tools are installed. The setup program will notify you of any problems with the installation environment. Restart the setup program from the beginning after fixing any issues.

Once Exchange is installed, the Microsoft Management Console plug in for Exchange, shown in Figure 4, will provide access to many settings at one convenient location. Make sure to install all updates so that the server will run properly. The Exchange System Manager, which is a console that controls the Exchange deployment, can be used to manage the options of the server.

Use the Active Directory Users and Computer (ADUC) console to configure a user's mailbox. This is also known as making the user "mailbox-enabled".

Open the ADUC to create a new user. Fill out the username and password information according to the domain security policy, as shown in Figure 5. The user's mailbox will be created by the exchange server when the user receives the first e-mail.

Setting up Exchange takes careful planning, including ensuring that the servers, services, and technologies are in place and working correctly on the network. In some cases, during an installation, if there is a failure, you may need to reinstall the operating system and start the Exchange installation from the beginning.

Refer to **Figure** in online course

Note

Before planning an e-mail server installation, consult with network professionals, experienced Windows networking experts, or experienced e-mail technicians.

15.7 Describe preventive maintenance procedures for networks

Preventive maintenance is just as important for the network as it is for the computers on a network. You must check the condition of cables, network devices, servers, and computers to make sure that they are kept clean and are in good working order. You should develop a plan to perform scheduled maintenance and cleaning at regular intervals. This will help you to prevent network down-time and equipment failures.

As part of a regularly scheduled maintenance program, inspect all cabling for breaks. Make sure that cables are labeled correctly and labels are not coming off. Replace any worn or unreadable labels. Check that cable supports are properly installed and no attachment points are coming loose. Cabling can become damaged and worn. You should keep the cabling in good repair to maintain good network performance.

As a technician, you may notice if equipment is failing, damaged, or making unusual sounds. Inform the network administrator to prevent unnecessary network downtime.

Cables at workstations and printers should be checked carefully. Cables are often moved or kicked when they are underneath desks, and can be bent. These conditions can result in loss of bandwidth or connectivity. You should also be proactive in the education of network users. Demonstrate to network users how to properly connect and disconnect cables, as well as how to move them if necessary.

Refer to **Figure** in online course

15.8 Troubleshoot the network

To begin troubleshooting a network problem, you should first try to locate the source of the problem. Check to see if a group of users or only one user has the problem. If the problem is with one user, begin troubleshooting the problem starting with their computer.

After completing this section, you will meet these objectives:

- Review the troubleshooting process.
- Identify common problems and solutions.
- Apply troubleshooting skills.

Refer to **Figure** in online course

15.8.1 Review the troubleshooting process

Network problems can result from a combination of hardware, software, and connectivity issues. Computer technicians must be able to analyze the problem and determine the cause of the error in order to repair the network issue. This process is called troubleshooting.

The first step in the troubleshooting process is to gather data from the customer. Figures 1 and 2 list open-ended and closed-ended questions to ask the customer.

Once you have talked to the customer, you should verify the obvious issues. Figure 3 lists issues that apply to networks.

After the obvious issues have been verified, try some quick solutions. Figure 4 lists some quick solutions to network problems.

If quick solutions did not correct the problem, it is time to gather data from the computer. Figure 5 shows different ways to gather information about the network problem.

At this point, you will have enough information to evaluate the problem, research, and implement possible solutions. Figure 6 shows resources for possible solutions.

After you have solved the problem, you will close with the customer. Figure 7 is a list of the tasks required to complete this step.

Refer to **Figure** in online course

15.8.2 Identify common problems and solutions

Network problems can be attributed to hardware, software, networks, or some combination of the three. You will resolve some types of problems more often than others. Figure 1 is a chart of common network problems and solutions.

Refer to **Figure** in online course

15.8.3 Apply troubleshooting skills

Now that you understand the troubleshooting process, it is time to apply your listening and diagnostic skills.

The first lab is designed to reinforce your skills with networks. You will will troubleshoot and fix a computer that does not connect to the network.

The second lab is designed to reinforce your communication and troubleshooting skills. In this lab, you will perform the following steps:

- Receive the work order
- Take the customer through various steps to try and resolve the problem
- Document the problem and the resolution

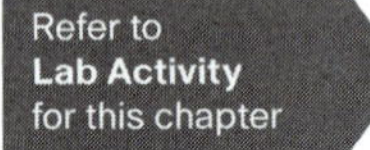

Remote Tech Network Problem

Instruct a customer on how to correct a network problem

Summary

The advanced networks chapter discussed the planning, implementation, and upgrading of networks and network components. The following are some of the important concepts to remember from this chapter:

- There are many safety hazards associated with network environments, devices, and media. You should follow proper safety procedures at all times.
- Networks must be designed around the needs of your customer. Make design decisions that will meet the needs and the goals of your customers.
- Select network components that offer the services and capabilities necessary to implement a network based on the needs of the customer.
- Plan network installations based on the services and equipment necessary to provide the network that is needed.
- Upgrading a network may involve additional equipment, advanced equipment, or cabling. Discuss how upgrading can help to enhance the usability of the network in the future.
- Plan for an e-mail installation before deployment. Consult a specialist to make sure the installation and configuration of an e-mail server goes smoothly.
- Prevent network problems by developing and implementing a solid preventive maintenance policy.
- Follow a logical methodology to troubleshoot advanced network problems.

Chapter 15 Quiz

Take the chapter quiz to test your knowledge.

Go to
the online course
to take the quiz.

Your Chapter Notes

CHAPTER 16

Advanced Security

Introduction

This chapter reviews the types of attacks that threaten the security of computers and the data contained on them. A technician is responsible for the security of data and computer equipment in an organization. The chapter describes how you can work with customers to ensure that the best possible protection is in place.

Risks to computers and network equipment come from both internal and external sources. Risks include physical threats, such as theft or damage to equipment, and data threats, such as the loss or corruption of data.

After completing this chapter, you will meet these objectives:

- Outline security requirements based on customer needs.
- Select security components based on customer needs.
- Implement customer's security plan.
- Perform preventive maintenance on security.
- Troubleshoot security.

Refer to **Figure** in online course

16.1 Outline security requirements based on customer needs

An organization should strive to achieve the best and most affordable security protection against data loss or damage to software and equipment. Network technicians and the organization's management should work together to develop a security policy to ensure that data and equipment have been protected against all security threats. A security policy includes a comprehensive statement about the level of security required and how this security will be achieved.

You may be involved in developing a security policy for a customer or organization. When creating a security policy, you should ask the following questions to determine security factors:

- Is the computer located at a home or a business?

Home computers generally are more vulnerable to wireless intrusion than business computers. Business computers have a higher threat of network intrusion, due to users abusing their access privileges.

- Is there full-time Internet access?

The more a computer is exposed to the Internet, the greater the chance of attacks from other infected computers. A computer accessing the Internet should include firewall and anti-virus solutions.

- Is the computer a laptop?

Physical security is an issue with laptop computers. There are measures to secure laptops, such as cable locks.

After completing this section, you will meet these objectives:

- Outline a local security policy.
- Explain when and how to use security hardware.
- Explain when and how to use security application software.

Refer to **Figure** in online course

16.1.1 Outline a local security policy

A security policy is a collection of rules, guidelines, and checklists. Network technicians and managers of an organization work together to develop the rules and guidelines for the security needs of computer equipment. A security policy includes the following elements:

- Defines an acceptable computer usage statement for an organization.
- Identifies the people permitted to use the computer equipment in an organization.
- Identifies devices that are permitted to be installed on a network, as well as the conditions of the installation. Modems and wireless access points are examples of hardware that could expose the network to attacks.
- Defines the requirements necessary for data to remain confidential on a network.
- Determines a process for employees to acquire access to equipment and data. This process may require the employee to sign an agreement regarding the company rules. It also lists the consequences for failure to comply.

The security policy should also provide detailed information about the following issues in case of an emergency:

- Steps to take after a breach in security
- Who to contact in an emergency
- Information to share with customers, vendors, and the media
- Secondary locations to use in an evacuation
- Steps to take after an emergency is over, including the priority of services to be restored

Refer to **Worksheet** for this chapter

Security Policy

Contribute to a security policy

Caution

A security policy must be enforced and followed by all employees to be effective.

Refer to **Figure** in online course

16.1.2 Explain when and how to use security hardware

The security policy should identify hardware and equipment that can be used to prevent theft, vandalism, and data loss. There are four interrelated aspects to physical security, which are access, data, infrastructure and the computer, as illustrated in Figure 1.

Restrict access to premises with the following:

- Fences
- Security Hardware

Protect the network infrastructure, such as cabling, telecommunication equipment, and network devices:

- Secured telecommunications rooms
- Wireless detection for unauthorized access points
- Hardware firewalls
- Network management system that detects changes in wiring and patch panels

Protect individual computers:

- Cable locks
- Laptop docking station locks
- Lockable cases
- Secured cages surrounding desktop cases

Protect data with hardware that prevents unauthorized access or theft of media:

- Lockable HD carriers
- Secure storage and transport of backup media
- USB security dongles

The Right Security Mix

Factors that determine the most effective security equipment to use to secure equipment and data include the following:

- How will the equipment be used?
- Where is the computer equipment located?
- What user access to data is required?

For instance, a computer in a busy public place, such as a library, requires additional protection from theft and vandalism. In a busy call center, a server may need to be secured in a locked equipment room.

Where it is necessary to use a laptop computer in a public place, a security dongle, shown in Figure 2, ensures that the system locks if the user and laptop are separated.

Refer to **Figure** in online course

16.1.3 Explain when and how to use security application software

Security applications protect the operating system and software application data.

The following products and software applications can be used to protect network devices:

- ***Software Firewall*** – Filters incoming data and is built into Windows XP
- ***Intrusion Detection Systems (IDS)*** – Monitors and reports on changes in program code and unusual network activity
- ***Application and OS Patches*** – Updates applications and the operating system to repair security weaknesses that are discovered

There are several software applications available to protect computers from unauthorized access by malicious computer code:

- Virus protection
- Spyware protection
- Adware protection
- Grayware protection

In small offices and homes, computers generally connect directly to the Internet rather than through a protected LAN that organizations use. This puts computers outside of a LAN at high risk for viruses and other attacks. At a minimum, these computers should use anti-virus and anti-malware protection programs. Application software and the operating system should be updated with the latest patches. A software firewall may also be part of the solution.

The security policy should determine the level of security applications put in place. Each step that increases protection costs money. In developing a policy, management should calculate the cost of data loss versus the expense of security protection and determine what tradeoffs are acceptable.

Refer to **Figure** in online course

16.2 Select security components based on customer needs

The security policy helps customers to select the security components necessary to keep equipment and data safe. If there is no security policy, you should discuss security issues with the customer.

Use your past experience as a technician and research the current security products on the market when selecting security components for the customer. The goal is to provide the security system that best matches the customer's needs.

After completing this section, you will meet these objectives:

- Describe and compare security techniques.
- Describe and compare access control devices.
- Describe and compare firewall types.

Refer to **Figure** in online course

16.2.1 Describe and compare security techniques

A technician should determine the appropriate techniques to secure equipment and data for the customer. Depending on the situation, more than one technique may be required.

Passwords

Using secure, encrypted login information for computers with network access should be a minimum requirement in any organization. Malicious software monitors the network and may record plain-text passwords. If passwords are encrypted, attackers would have to decode the encryption to learn the passwords.

Logging and Auditing

Event logging and auditing should be enabled to monitor activity on the network. The network administrator audits the log file of events to investigate network access by unauthorized users.

Wireless Configurations

Wireless connections are especially vulnerable to access by attackers. Wireless clients should be configured to encrypt data.

Encryption

Encryption technologies are used to encode data being transmitted on a network. Each technology is used for a specific purpose:

- ***Hash encoding –*** Hash encoding, or hashing, ensures that messages are not corrupted or tampered with during transmission. Hashing uses a mathematical function to create a numeric value that is unique to the data. If even one character is changed, the function output, called the message digest, will not be the same. However, the function is one way. Knowing the message digest does not allow an attacker to re-create the message. This makes it difficult for someone to intercept and change messages. Hash encoding is illustrated in Figure 1. The names of the most popular hashing algorithms are SHA and MD5.
- ***Symmetric encryption –*** Symmetric encryption requires both sides of an encrypted conversation to use an encryption key to be able to encode and decode the data. The sender and receiver must use identical keys. Symmetric encryption is illustrated in Figure 2.
- ***Asymmetric encryption –*** Asymmetric encryption requires two keys, a private key and a public key. The public key can be widely distributed including emailing in clear text or posting on the web. The private key is kept by an individual and must not be disclosed to any other party. There are two ways these keys can be used. Public key encryption is used when a single organization needs to receive encrypted text from a number of sources. The public key can be widely distributed and used to encrypt the messages. The intended recipient is the only party to have the private key which is used to decrypt the messages. In the case of Digital Signatures, a private key is required for encrypting a message and a public key is needed to decode the message. This approach allows the receiver to be confident about the source of the message as only a message encrypted using the originator's private key could be decrypted by the public key. Asymmetric encryption using digital signatures is illustrated in Figure 3.
- ***Virtual private network (VPN) –*** A virtual private network uses encryption to secure data as if it was traveling in a private, corporate LAN, even though the data actually travels over any network, for example, the Internet. The secured data pipelines between points in the VPN are called "secure tunnels". The process is illustrated in Figure 4.

Refer to **Figure** in online course

16.2.2 Describe and compare access control devices

Computer equipment and data can be secured using overlapping protection techniques to prevent unauthorized access to sensitive data. An example of overlapping protection is using two different techniques to protect an asset. This is known as two-factor security, as shown in Figure 1. When considering a security program, the cost of the implementation has to be balanced against the value of the data or equipment to be protected.

Physical Security

Use security hardware to help prevent security breaches and loss of data or equipment. Physical security access control measures include the following:

- ***Lock –*** The most common device for securing physical areas. If a key is lost, all identically keyed locks must be changed.

- ***Conduit –*** A casing that protects the infrastructure media from damage and unauthorized access.
- ***Card key –*** A tool used to secure physical areas. If a card key is lost or stolen, only the missing card must be deactivated. The card key system is more expensive than security locks.
- ***Video equipment –*** Records images and sound for monitoring activity. The recorded data must be monitored for problems.
- ***Security Guard –*** Controls access to the entrance of a facility and monitors the activity inside the facility.

Network equipment should be mounted in secured areas. All cabling should be enclosed in conduits or routed inside walls to prevent unauthorized access or tampering. Network outlets that are not in use should be disabled. If network equipment is damaged or stolen, some network users may be denied service.

The security policy should specify the level of security required for the organization. Biometric devices, which measure physical information about a user, are ideal for use in highly secure areas. However, for most small organizations, this type of solution would be too expensive.

Data Security

You can protect data by using data security devices to authenticate employee access. Two-factor identification is a method to increase security. Employees must use both a password and a data security device similar to those listed here to access data:

- ***Smart card –*** A device that has the ability to store data safely. The internal memory is an embedded integrated circuit chip (ICC) that connects to a reader either directly or through a wireless connection. Smart cards are used in many applications worldwide, like secure ID badges, online authentication devices, and secure credit card payments.
- ***Security key fob –*** A small device that resembles the ornament on a key ring. It has a small radio system that communicates with the computer over a short range. The fob is small enough so that many people attach them to their key rings. The computer must sense the signal from the key fob before it will accept a username and password.
- ***Biometric device –*** Measures a physical characteristic of the user, such as their fingerprints or the patterns of the iris in the eye. The user is granted access if these characteristics match its database and the correct login information is supplied.

The level of security that the customer needs determines which devices to select to keep data and equipment secure.

Refer to **Interactive Graphic** in online course.

Refer to **Figure** in online course

16.2.3 Describe and compare firewall types

Hardware and software firewalls protect data and equipment on a network from unauthorized access. A firewall should be used in addition to security software.

Hardware and software firewalls have several modes for filtering network data traffic:

- ***Packet filter –*** A set of rules that allow or deny traffic based on criteria such as IP addresses, protocols, or ports used.
- ***Proxy firewall –*** A firewall that inspects all traffic and allows or denies packets based on configured rules. A proxy acts as a gateway that protects computers inside the network.
- ***Stateful packet inspection –*** A firewall that keeps track of the state of network connections traveling through the firewall. Packets that are not part of a known connection are not allowed back through the firewall.

Hardware Firewall

A hardware firewall is a physical filtering component that inspects data packets from the network before they reach computers and other devices on a network. Hardware firewalls are often installed on routers. A hardware firewall is a free-standing unit that does not use the resources of the computers it is protecting, so there is no impact on processing performance.

Software Firewall

A software firewall is an application on a computer that inspects and filters data packets. Windows Firewall is an example of a software firewall that is included in the Windows operating system. A software firewall uses the resources of the computer, resulting in reduced performance for the user.

Consider the items listed in Figure 1 when selecting a firewall.

Refer to **Worksheet** for this chapter

Firewalls

Research hardware and software firewalls

Note

On a secure network, if computer performance is not an issue, you should enable the internal operating system firewall for additional security. Some applications may not operate properly unless the firewall is configured correctly for them.

Refer to **Figure** in online course

16.3 Implement customer's security policy

Adding layers of security on a network can make the network more secure, but additional layers of security protection can be expensive. You must weigh the value of the data and equipment to be protected with the cost of protection when implementing the customer's security policy.

After completing this section, you will meet these objectives:

- Configure security settings.
- Describe configuring firewall types.
- Describe protection against malicious software.

Refer to **Figure** in online course

16.3.1 Configure security settings

Two common security errors are incorrect permissions on folders and files and incorrect configuration of wireless security.

Levels of Permission for Folders and Files

Permission levels are configured to limit individual or group user access to specific data. Both FAT and NTFS allow folder sharing and folder-level permissions for users with network access. Folder permissions are shown in Figure 1. The additional security of file-level permissions is provided with NTFS. File-level permissions are shown in Figure 2.

Wireless Security Configuration

The following tools, which are shown in Figure 3, are used to configure wireless security:

- ***Wired Equivalent Privacy (WEP)*** – Encrypts the broadcast data between the wireless access point and the client using a 64-bit or 128-bit encryption key. Figure 4 shows WEP configuration.

- *Wi-Fi Protected Access (WPA) –* Provides better encryption and authentication than WEP.
- *MAC address filtering –* Restricts computer access to a wireless access point to prevent the casual user from accessing the network. MAC address filtering, as shown in Figure 5, is vulnerable when used alone and should be combined with other security filtering.
- *Service Set Identifier (SSID) –* The wireless access point broadcasts the SSID, WLAN name of the network. Turning off the SSID makes the network seem to disappear, but this is an unreliable form of wireless network security.
- *Wireless antennae –* The gain and signal pattern of the antenna connected to a wireless access point can influence where the signal can be received. Avoid transmitting signals outside of the network area by installing an antenna with a pattern that serves your network users.

Refer to **Figure** in online course

16.3.2 Describe configuring firewall types

A firewall selectively denies outside users from establishing connections to a computer or network segment. Firewalls generally work by opening and closing the ports that various applications use. By opening only the required ports on a firewall, you are implementing a restrictive security policy. Any packet not explicitly permitted is denied. In contrast, a permissive security policy permits access through all ports except those explicitly denied. At one time, software and hardware was shipped with all settings being permissive. As many users neglected to configure their equipment, the default permissive settings left many devices exposed to attackers. Most devices now ship with settings as restrictive as possible, while still allowing easy setup.

Software Firewall

Software firewalls usually exist as a software application running on the computer being protected, or as part of the operating system. There are several third-party software firewalls. There is also a software firewall built into Windows XP, as shown in Figure 1.

The configuration of the Windows XP firewall can be completed in two ways:

- *Automatically –* The user is prompted to "Keep Blocking", "Unblock", or "Ask Me Later" for any unsolicited requests. These requests may be from legitimate applications that have not been configured previously or may be from a virus or worm that has infected the system.
- *Manage Security Settings –* The user manually adds the program or ports that are required for the applications in use on the network.

To add a program, select:

Start > Control Panel > Security Center > Windows Firewall > Exceptions > Add Program.

To disable the firewall, select:

Start > Control Panel > Security Center > Windows Firewall.

16.3.3 Describe protection against malicious software

Malware is malicious software that is installed on a computer without the knowledge or permission of the user. Certain types of malware, such as spyware and phishing attacks, collect data about the user that can be used by an attacker to gain confidential information.

You should run virus and spyware scanning programs to detect and clean unwanted software. Many browsers now come equipped with special tools and settings that prevent the operation of several forms of malicious software. It may take several different programs and multiple scans to completely remove all malicious software:

- *Virus protection –* Anti-virus programs typically run automatically in the background and monitor for problems. When a virus is detected, the user is warned and the program attempts to quarantine or delete the virus.
- *Spyware protection –* Anti-spyware programs that scan for keyloggers and other malware so it can be removed from the computer.
- *Adware protection –* Anti-adware programs look for programs that display advertising on your computer.
- *Phishing protection –* Anti-phishing programs block the IP addresses of known phishing websites and warn the user about suspicious websites.

A dangerous form of malicious software that incorporates elements of social engineering is the phishing attack.

Refer to **Figure** in online course

Note

Malicious software may become embedded in the operating system. Special removal tools are available from the operating system manufacturer to clean the operating system.

16.4 Perform preventive maintenance on security

Several maintenance tasks are necessary to ensure that security is effective. This section covers how to maximize protection by performing updates, backups, and reconfiguration of the operating systems, user accounts, and data.

After completing this section, you will meet these objectives:

- Describe the configuration of operation system updates.
- Maintain accounts.
- Explain data backup procedures, access to backups, and secure physical backup media.

Refer to **Figure** in online course

16.4.1 Describe the configuration of operating system updates

An operating system is a likely target of attack because obtaining control of it can provide control of the computer. Then the compromised computer can be seized and put to work by the criminals. One popular use is to turn targeted computers into spam generators that launch attacking e-mails without the user being able to stop them. A computer compromised in this way is called a "zombie".

Windows XP automatically downloads and installs updates to operating systems by default. However, this may not be the best way to update systems. The updates may conflict with the security policy of an organization or may conflict with other settings on a computer. Furthermore, a network administrator may wish to test the updates before the updates are distributed to all of the network computers. The following options available in Windows XP give users the ability to control when software is updated:

- *Automatic –* Downloads and installs updates automatically without user intervention

- *Only download updates* – Downloads the updates automatically, but the user is required to install them
- *Notify me* – Notifies the user that updates are available and gives the option to download and install
- *Turn off automatic updates* – Prevents any checking for updates

If the user is on a dial-up network, the Windows Update setting should be configured to notify the user of available updates, or it should be turned off. The dial-up user may want to control the update by selecting a time when the update does not interrupt other network activity or use the limited resources available.

Refer to **Figure** in online course

16.4.2 Maintain accounts

Employees in an organization may require different levels of access to data. For example, a manager and an accountant may be the only employees in an organization with access to the payroll files.

Employees can be grouped by job requirements and given access to files according to group permissions. This process helps manage employee access to the network. Temporary accounts can be set up for employees that need short-term access. Close management of network access can help to limit areas of vulnerability that allow a virus or malicious software to enter the network.

Terminating Employee Access

When an employee leaves an organization, access to data and hardware on the network should be terminated immediately. If the former employee has stored files in a personal space on a server, eliminate access by disabling the account. If at a later time the employee's replacement requires access to the applications and storage space, re-enable the account and change the name to the name of the new employee.

Guest Accounts

Temporary employees and guests may need access to the network. For example, many visitors may require access to e-mail, the Internet, and a printer on the network. These resources can all be made available to a special account called Guest. When guests are present, they can be assigned to the Guest account. When no guests are present, the account can be suspended until the next guest arrives.

Some guest accounts may require extensive access to resources, as in the case of a consultant or a financial auditor. This type of access should be granted only for the period of time required to complete the work.

Refer to **Figure** in online course

16.4.3 Explain data backup procedures, access to backups, and secure physical backup media

A data backup stores a copy of the information on a computer to removable backup media that can be kept in a safe place. If the computer hardware fails, the data backup can be restored so that processing can continue.

Data backups should be performed on a regular basis. The most current data backup is usually stored offsite to protect the backup media if anything happens to the main facility. Backup media is often reused to save on media costs. Always follow your organization's media rotation guidelines.

Backup operations can be performed at the command line or from a batch file using the NTBACKUP command. The default parameters for NTBACKUP will be the ones set in the Windows backup utility. Any options you want to override must be included in the command line. The NT-BACKUP command cannot be used to restore files.

A combination of backup types, as shown in Figure 1, allow the data to be backed up efficiently. A full backup is a copy of all files on the drive. An incremental backup backs up only those files created or changed since the last normal or incremental backup. It marks files as having been backed up. A differential backup copies files created or changed since the last normal or incremental backup, but it does not mark files as having been backed up. Backing up data can take time, so it is preferable to do backups when the network traffic is low. Other types of backups include daily backup and copy backup, which do not mark the files as having been backed up.

The data backup media is just as important as the data on the computer. You should store the backup media in a climate-controlled offsite storage facility with adequate physical security. The backups should be readily available for access in case of an emergency.

Refer to **Figure** in online course

16.5 Troubleshoot security

The troubleshooting process is used to help resolve security issues. These problems range from simple, such as creating a backup, to more complex, such as firewall configuration. Use the troubleshooting steps as a guideline to help you diagnose and repair problems.

After completing this section, you will meet these objectives:

- Review the troubleshooting process.
- Identify common problems and solutions.
- Apply troubleshooting skills.

16.5.1 Review the troubleshooting process

Computer technicians must be able to analyze a security threat and determine the appropriate method to protect assets and repair damage. This process is called troubleshooting.

The first step in the troubleshooting process is to gather data from the customer. Figures 1 and 2 list open-ended and closed-ended questions to ask the customer.

Once you have talked to the customer, you should verify the obvious issues. Figure 3 lists issues that apply to security.

After the obvious issues have been verified, try some quick solutions. Figure 4 lists some quick solutions to security problems.

If quick solutions did not correct the problem, it is time to gather data from the computer. Figure 5 shows different ways to gather information about the security problem.

At this point, you will have enough information to evaluate the problem, research, and implement possible solutions. Figure 6 shows resources for possible solutions.

After you have solved the problem, you will close with the customer. Figure 7 is a list of the tasks required to complete this step.

Refer to **Figure** in online course

16.5.2 Identify common problems and solutions

Security problems can be attributed to hardware, software, networks, or some combination of the three. You will resolve some types of security problems more often than others. Figure 1 is a chart of common problems and solutions.

Refer to **Figure** in online course

16.5.3 Apply troubleshooting skills

Now that you understand the troubleshooting process, it is time to apply your listening and diagnostic skills.

The first lab is designed to reinforce your skills with security issues. You will instruct the customer on how to correct a security problem that is preventing connection to the wireless network.

The second lab is designed to reinforce your communication and troubleshooting skills. In this lab, you will perform the following steps:

- Receive the work order
- Take the customer through various steps to try and resolve the problem
- Document the problem and the resolution

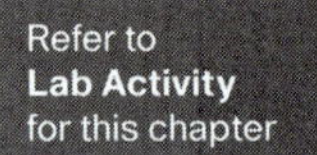

Windows XP Firewall

Configure a Windows XP firewall

Summary

This chapter discussed computer security and why it is important to protect computer equipment, networks, and data. Threats, procedures, and preventive maintenance relating to data and physical security were described to help you keep computer equipment and data safe. Security protects computers, network equipment, and data from lose and physical danger. The following are some of the important concepts to remember from this chapter:

- Security threats can come from inside or outside of an organization.
- Viruses and worms are common threats that attack data.
- Develop and maintain a security plan to protect both data and physical equipment from loss.
- Keep operating systems and applications up to date and secure with patches and service packs.

Chapter 16 Quiz

Take the chapter quiz to test your knowledge.

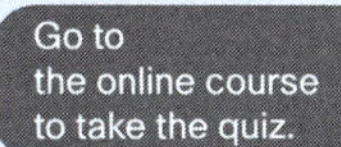

Your Chapter Notes

Glossary

1000BASE-T
Gigabit Ethernet specification that uses UTP Cat5, 5e, or 6. Each network segment can have a maximum distance of 328 feet (100 m) without a repeater. Also known as 801.3ab.

100BASE-TX
100-Mbps baseband Fast Ethernet specification that uses two pair of UTP or STP wiring. Based on the IEEE 802.3 standard.

100BASE-X
100-Mbps baseband Fast Ethernet specification that refers to the 100BASE-FX and 100BASE-TX standards for Fast Ethernet over fiber-optic and copper cabling. Based on the IEEE 802.3 standard.

10BASE-T
10-Mbps baseband Ethernet specification that uses two pairs of Category 3, 4, or 5 twisted-pair cabling. One pair of wires is used to receive data and the other pair is used to transmit data. 10BASE-T, which is part of the IEEE 802.3 specification, has a distance limit of approximately 328 feet (100 m) per segment.

AC power connector
Socket that is used to connect the AC power adapter to a computer or docking station.

AC power cord
Cable that transfers electricity from the AC power supply to the computer power supply.

Accelerated Graphics Port (AGP)
High-speed, 32-bit bus technology designed to support the acceleration of 3D computer graphics.

Access Control List (ACL)
List managed by a network administrator that itemizes what a user is permitted to access and the type of access granted.

access point
Device that connects wireless devices to form a wireless network. An access point usually connects to a wired network, and can relay data between wired and wireless devices. Connectivity distances can range from several feet or meters, to several miles or kilometers.

active partition
Partition on a hard disk drive that is set as the bootable partition and usually contains the operating system to be used on the computer. Only one partition on a computer can be set as an active or bootable partition on a hard disk drive.

ActiveX
Applet or small program created by Microsoft to control interactivity on web pages that has to be downloaded to gain access to the full functionality.

adapter card
Expansion card that increases the number of controllers and ports available on a computer.

Address Resolution Protocol (ARP)
Discovers the local address (MAC address) of a station on the network when the IP address is known. End stations as well as routers use ARP to discover local addresses:

-a Switch used with the ARP command that displays the cache.
-d Switch used with the ARP command that deletes an entry from the ARP cache.
-s Switch used with the ARP command that adds a permanent IP-to-MAC address mapping.

administrator
Person who queries the User Registrar to analyze individual subscriber status and to gather data.

Advanced Configuration and Power Interface (ACPI)
Interface that allows the operating system to control power management. Replaces Advanced Power Management (APM).

Advanced Power Management (APM)
Interface that allows the BIOS to control the settings for power management. This has been replaced by the Advanced Configuration and Power Interface (ACPI).

Advanced Technology Extended (ATX) power connector
20-pin or 24-pin internal power supply connector.

Advanced Technology Extended (ATX)
Standard computer case form factor for modern computers.

adware
Software program that displays advertising on a computer, usually distributed with downloaded software.

all-in-one type printer
Multi-functional device designed to provide services such as printing, fax, and copier functions.

alternating-current (AC)
Current that changes direction at a uniformly repetitious rate. This type of electricity is typically provided by a utility company and is accessed by wall sockets.

American National Standards Institute (ANSI)
Private, nonprofit organization that administers and coordinates the US voluntary standardization and conformity assessment system. ANSI identifies industrial and public requirements for national consensus standards and coordinates and manages their development, resolves national standards problems, and ensures effective participation in international standardization.

American Standard Code for Information Interchange (ASCII)
8-bit code for character representation (7 bits plus parity).

analog transmission
Signal transmission over wires or through the air in which information is conveyed through the variation of some combination of signal amplitude, frequency, and phase.

answer file
File that contains predefined settings and answers to the questions that are required by the operating system setup wizard.

antistatic bag
Packaging material that protects components from ESD.

antistatic mat
Surface that provides a safe environment for computer components by dissipating ESD.

antistatic wrist strap
Device worn on the wrist to dissipate ESD between a person and electronic equipment.

anti-virus application
Program that is installed on a system to prevent computer viruses from infecting the computer.

AppleTalk
Protocol suite to network Macintosh computers. It is comprised of a comprehensive set of protocols that span the seven layers of the OSI reference model.

application layer
Layer 7 of the OSI reference model. This layer provides services to application processes such as electronic mail, file transfer, and terminal emulation that are outside of the OSI model. The application layer identifies and establishes the availability of intended communication partners and the resources required to connect with them, synchronizes cooperating applications, and establishes agreement on procedures for error recovery and control of data integrity. Corresponds roughly with the transaction services layer in the Systems Network Architecture (SNA) model. The OSI reference model includes application layer, presentation layer, session layer, transport layer, network layer, data link layer, and physical layer.

application software
Program that performs a specific function by accepting input from the user and then manipulating it to achieve a result, known as the output.

arm (Acorn RISC Machine) architecture
Low-power RISC CPU.

Asymmetric DSL (ADSL)
Currently the most common DSL implementation. Speeds vary from 384 kbps to more than 6 Mbps downstream. The upstream speed is typically lower.

asymmetric encryption
Method for encrypting data on a network. Uses a private key for writing messages and a public key to decode the messages. Only the private key needs to be kept secret. Public keys can be distributed openly.

attention (AT) command set
Issues dial, hang up, reset, and other instructions to the modem. It is based on the Hayes command set.

Automatic Private IP Addressing (APIPA)
Operating system feature that enables a computer to assign itself an address if it is unable to contact a DHCP server. The Internet Assigned Numbers Authority (IANA) has reserved private IP addresses in the range of 169.254.0.0 -169.254.255.255 for APIPA.

Automatic Update
Utility to schedule the Windows Update feature to check for critical updates.

auxiliary (AUX) power connector
4-, 6-, or 8-pin connector that supplies extra voltage to the motherboard from the power supply.

backplane
Physical connection between an interface processor or card, the data buses, and the power distribution buses inside a chassis.

backup
Copy of data saved onto alternate media, and should be physically removed from the source data.

backward compatible
Hardware or software systems that can use interfaces and data from earlier versions of the system or with other systems. Also known as backward-compatible or backwards compatible.

bandwidth
Amount of data that can be transmitted within a fixed time period.

base station
Device that attaches a laptop to AC power and to desktop peripherals.

Basic Input/Output System (BIOS)
Program stored in a ROM chip in the computer that provides the basic code to control the computer's hardware and to perform diagnostics on it. The BIOS prepares the computer to load the operating system.

Basic Rate Interface (BRI)
ISDN interface composed of two B channels and one D channel for circuit-switched communication of voice, video, and data. Compare with PRI.

battery latch
Tool used to insert, remove, and secure the laptop battery.

battery status indicator LED
Light that indicates the condition of the laptop battery.

battery
Electrical device that converts chemical energy into electrical energy.

beep code
Audible reporting system for errors that are found by the BIOS during the POST, represented by a series of beeps.

Berg power connector
Keyed connector that supplies power to a floppy drive.

biometric device
Tool that uses sensors, such as a fingerprint or retinal scanner, that identify physical characteristics of the user to allow access to a device or a network.

bit rate
Speed at which bits are transmitted, usually expressed in bits per second (bps).

bit
Smallest unit of data in a computer. A bit can take the value of either 1 or 0. A bit is the binary format in which data is processed by computers.

blackout
Complete loss of AC power.

Bluetooth
Wireless industry standard that uses an unlicensed radio frequency for short-range communication enabling portable devices to communicate over short distances.

boot
To start a computer.

boot record
512-byte file containing a table that describes the partition, the number of bytes per sector, and the number of sectors per cluster.

bootable disk
Troubleshooting tool that allows the computer to boot from a disk when the hard drive will not boot.

broadband
Multiple signals using multiple frequencies over one cable.

broadband optical telepoint
Infrared broadband transmission capable of handling high-quality multimedia requirements.

broadband satellite
Network connection using a satellite dish.

brownout
Temporary drop in AC power.

buffer
Storage area used for handling data in transit. Buffers are used in internetworking to compensate for differences in processing speed between network devices. Bursts of data can be stored in buffers until they can be handled by slower processing devices. Sometimes referred to as a packet buffer.

bus topology
Network with each computer connecting on a common cable.

bus
Media through which data is transferred from one part of a computer to another. The bus can be compared to a highway on which data travels within a computer.

byte
A unit of measure that describes the size of a data file, the amount of space on a disk or other storage medium, or the amount of data being sent over a network. One byte consists of 8 bits of data.

C: drive
Generally the label for the first hard drive in a computer system. Drive A and Drive B are reserved for floppy drives. Drive B is rarely used on current computers.

cable modem
Acts like a LAN interface by connecting a computer to the Internet. The cable modem connects a computer to the cable company network through the same coaxial cabling that feeds cable TV (CATV) signals to a television set.

cable tie
Fastener used to bundle cables inside and outside of a computer.

cable
Set of conductors, bundled and sheathed together, made of insulated copper or optical fiber that transport signals and power between electrical devices.

cache
Data storage area that provides high-speed access for the system.

Caps lock indicator LED
Light that shows the on/off status of the caps lock.

card key
Identity card with a chip that stores user data, including the level of access.

Category 3
Cable that is primarily used in telephone connections.

Category 5
Cable that contains four pairs of wires, with a maximum data rate of 1 Gbps.

Category 5e
Cable that provides more twists per foot than Category 5 at the same data rate of 1 Gbps.

Category 6
Cable that is enhanced with more twists than Category 5e cable. It contains a plastic divider that separates the pairs of wires to prevent crosstalk.

cellular WAN
Wide area network that has the technology for the use of a cell phone or a laptop for voice and data communications.

central processing unit (CPU)
Interprets and processes software instructions and data. Located on the motherboard, the CPU is a chip contained on a single integrated circuit called the microprocessor. The CPU contains two basic components, a control unit and an Arithmetic/Logic Unit (ALU).

chip
Small slice of silicon or germanium processed to have electrical characteristics so that it can be developed into an electronic component. Also called semiconductor.

chip set
Chips on a motherboard that enable the CPU to communicate and interact with the other components of the computer.

CHKDSK
Command used to check the integrity of files and folders on a hard drive by scanning the disk surface for physical errors.

client/server network
Network in which services are located in a dedicated computer that responds to client, or user, requests.

cluster
Smallest unit of space used for storing data on a disk. Also called file allocation unit.

CMOS battery
Battery that supplies power to maintain basic configuration information, including the real time clock, when the computer is turned off.

CMYK
Display colors: cyan, magenta, yellow, and black.

coaxial cable
Copper-cored cable surrounded by a heavy shielding used to connect computers in a network.

cold boot
To power up a computer from the off position.

color ink jet printer
Type of printer that uses liquid-ink–filled cartridges that spray ink to form an image on the paper.

Comité Consultatif International Téléphonique et Télégraphique (CCITT)
Committee that defines international communications standards. The CCITT defines the standards for sending fax documents and the standards for data transmission over telephone lines.

command line interface (CLI)
Interface, such as a DOS prompt, that requires commands to be entered manually on the command line.

compact disc - read only memory (CD-ROM)
Optical storage media for audio and data.

compact disc (CD) drive
Optical device that reads compact discs.

compact disc-recordable (CD-R)
Optical media that allows data to be recorded but not modified.

compact disc-rewritable (CD-RW)
Optical storage media that allows data to be recorded and modified.

Complementary Metal Oxide Semiconductor (CMOS)
Type of semiconductor, or low-power memory firmware, that stores basic configuration information.

Complex Instruction Set Computer (CISC)
Architecture that uses a broad set of instructions, with several choices for almost every operation. The result is that a programmer can execute precisely the command needed, resulting in fewer instructions steps per operation.

compressed air
Air under pressure in a can that blows dust off of computer components without creating static. Also called canned air.

computer
Electrical machine that can execute a list of instructions and perform calculations based on those instructions.

computer network
Two or more computers connected together by some medium to share data and resources.

computer system
Combination of hardware and software components. Hardware is the physical equipment such as the case, floppy disk drives, keyboards, monitors, cables, speakers, and printers. Software describes the programs that operate the computer system.

computer-aided design (CAD)
Application used for creating architectural, electrical, and mechanical design. More complex forms of CAD include solid modeling and parametric modeling, which allow objects to be created with real-world characteristics.

conduit
Casing that protects the infrastructure media from damage and unauthorized access.

configuration tool
Service management tool or a Element management service tool with a GUI.

connector
Device used to terminate cable.

conventional memory
All memory addresses from 0 to 640 KB.

cookie
Small text file that is stored on the hard disk that allows a website to track the user's association to that site.

copy backup
Backs up user-selected files to tape. This backup does not reset the archive bit.

crosstalk
Interfering energy, such as Electro Magnetic Interference (EMI) that is transferred from one circuit to another.

current (I)
Flow of electrons in a conductor that is measured in amperes.

customer replaceable unit (CRU)
Component that customers may install at their location.

cylinder
All the tracks on a hard disk with the same number. Collectively, the same track on all platters of a multi-platter hard drive.

daily backup
Backs up only the files that are modified on the day of the backup. This backup does not reset the archive bit.

data backup
Information on a computer stored on removable backup media that can be kept in a safe place. If the computer hardware fails, the data backup can be restored so that processing can continue.

data transfer rate
Refers to how fast the computer can transfer information into memory.

database
Organized collection of data that can be easily accessed, managed, indexed, searched, and updated.

data-link layer
Layer 2 of the OSI reference model. This layer provides reliable transit of data across a physical link. The data-link layer is concerned with physical addressing, network topology, line discipline, error notification, ordered delivery of frames, and flow control. The IEEE has divided this layer into two sub layers, the MAC sub layer and the LLC sub layer. Sometimes simply called link layer. Roughly corresponds to the data link control layer of the SNA model. The OSI reference model includes application layer, presentation layer, session layer, transport layer, network layer, data link layer, and physical layer.

default gateway
Route taken so that a computer on one segment can communicate with a computer on another segment.

default installation
Installation that requires minimal user interaction. Also called a typical installation.

default printer
First option that an application uses when the user clicks the printer icon. The default printer can be changed by the user.

DEFRAG
Command that rearranges the data and rewrites all the files on the hard drive to the beginning of the drive, making it easier and faster for the hard drive to retrieve data.

denial of service (DoS)
Form of attack that prevents users from accessing normal services, such as e-mail or a web server, because the system is busy responding to abnormally large amounts of requests. DoS works by sending an abundance of requests for a resource to cause the system to overload and cease to operate.

desktop
Metaphor used to portray file systems. A desktop consists of pictures, called icons, which show files, folders, and any resource available to a user in a GUI operating system.

desktop computer
Type of computer designed to fit on top of a desk, usually with the monitor on top of the computer to conserve space. Desktop computers are not mobile like laptop computers.

Device Manager
Application that displays a list of all the hardware that is installed on the system.

diagnostic software
Programs that assist in the troubleshooting process.

diagnostic tools
Utilities that monitor the network server.

dial-up networking (DUN)
Using the public telephone system or network to communicate.

differential backup
Backs up all the files that have been created or modified since the last full backup. It does not reset the archive bit.

digital audio tape (DAT)
Tape standard that uses 4 mm digital audiotapes to store data in the Digital Data Storage (DSS) format.

digital linear tape (DLT)
Technology offers high capacity and relatively high-speed tape backup capabilities.

digital multimeter (DMM)
Tool that combines the functionality of a voltmeter, ohmmeter, and ammeter into one easy measuring device.

digital subscriber line (DSL)
Public network technology that delivers high bandwidth over conventional copper wiring at limited distances. Always-on technology that allows users to connect to the Internet.

digital versatile disc (DVD)
Removable media that is used primarily for movie and data storage.

Digital Visual Interface (DVI)
Interface that supplies uncompressed digital video to a digital monitor.

direct memory access (DMA)
Method for bypassing the CPU when transferring data from the main memory directly to a device.

direct-current (DC)
Current flowing in one direction, as used in a battery.

directory
1) Type of file that organizes other files in a hierarchical structure. 2) Related program and data files organized and grouped together in the DOS file system.3) Place to store data in the Windows file-management system.

disk cleanup
Disk management software that is used to clear space on a hard drive by searching for files that can be safely deleted, such as temporary Internet files.

disk management
System utility used to manage hard drives and partitions, such as initializing disks, creating partitions, and formatting partitions.

disk operating system (DOS)
Collection of programs and commands that control overall computer operations in a disk-based system.

display
Computer output surface and projecting mechanism that shows text and graphic images.

DNS poisoning
Changing the DNS records on a system to point to false servers where the data is recorded

docking connector
Socket used to attach a docking station to the laptop.

docking station
Device that attaches a laptop to AC power and desktop peripherals.

domain
Logical group of computers and electronic devices with a common set of rules and procedures administered as a unit.

Domain Name System (DNS)
System that provides a way to map friendly host names, or URLs, to IP addresses.

dot matrix printer
Printer that operates by impacting the ribbon to place an image on the paper.

dots per inch (dpi)
Measurement of print quality. How the quality of print is measured on a dot matrix printer, and the higher the dpi, the higher the quality of print.

drive bay
Standard-sized area for adding hardware to a computer case. The two most common drive bays are used to house a CD\DVD drive and a floppy drive.

drive letter
Designation that distinguishes the physical or logical drives in Windows.

drive mapping
Process of assigning a letter to a physical or logical drive.

dual core CPU
Two cores inside a single CPU chip. Both cores can be used together to increase speed, or they can be used in two locations at the same time.

dual in-line memory module (DIMM)
Circuit board with a 64-bit data bus that holds memory chips. Memory module with 168 pins. Supports 64-bit data transfers.

dual ring
All the devices on the network connect to two cables and the data travels in both directions. Only one cable is used at a time. In the event of a failure of one ring, data is transmitted on the other ring.

DVD drive
Optical device that reads DVDs. A DVD-ReWritable (DVD-RW) drive can write to DVD-RWs.

DVD-ROM
DVD format that is designed for storing computer files.

DVD-RW
Technology that allows the media to be recorded multiple times.

DVD-Video
DVD format that is used by standalone DVD players for movies and extras.

dye-sublimation printer
Printer that uses solid sheets of ink that change from solid to gas, in a process called sublimating. The gas then passes through the paper, where it turns back to a solid. The print head passes over a sheet of cyan, magenta, yellow, and a clear overcoat (CMYO). Also called thermal dye printer.

Dynamic Host Configuration Protocol (DHCP)
Software utility that automatically assigns IP addresses to client devices in a large network.

dynamic RAM (DRAM)
RAM that stores information in capacitors that must be periodically refreshed. Delays can occur because DRAMs are inaccessible to the processor when refreshing their contents. However, DRAMs are less complex and have greater capacity than SRAMs.

dynamic routing
Routing that adjusts automatically to network topology or traffic changes. Also called adaptive routing.

eject button
Lever that releases an object, such as the button on a floppy drive.

Electronic Industries Association (EIA)
Group that specifies electrical transmission standards. The EIA and TIA have developed numerous well-known communications standards, including EIA/TIA-232 and EIA/TIA-449.

electronic mail (e-mail)
Ability for users to communicate over a computer network. The exchange of computer-stored messages by network communication.

electrophotographic drum
Central part of the laser printer that acquires the toner to be printed on paper.

electrostatic discharge (ESD)
Discharge of static electricity from one conductor to another conductor of a different potential.

encryption
Security feature that applies a coding to a file so that only authorized users can view the file.

Encryption File System (EFS)
Microsoft specific file system for encryption.

Enhanced Integrated Drive Electronics (EIDE)
Enhanced version of the standard IDE interface that connects hard disks, CD-ROM drives, and tape drives to a PC.

Ethernet
Baseband LAN specification invented by Xerox Corporation and developed jointly by Xerox, Intel, and Digital Equipment Corporation. Ethernet networks use CSMA/CD and run over a variety of cable types at 10 Mbps or more. Ethernet is similar to the IEEE 802.3 series of standards.

Ethernet port
RJ-45 socket that is used to connect a computer to a cabled local area network.

event
Network message indicating operational irregularities in physical elements of a network or a response to the occurrence of a significant task, typically the completion of a request for information.

Event Viewer
Application that monitors system events, application events, and security events.

exhaust vent
Outlet that expels hot air from the interior of a device or room.

expansion card modem
Modem that is inserted into a motherboard expansion slot (ISA or PCI). Also called an internal modem.

expansion slot
Opening in a computer where a PC card can be inserted to add capabilities to the computer.

ExpressCard
High-throughput, laptop expansion card standard that was developed by the PCMCIA. The ExpressCard expansion slot uses the built-in PCI Express (x1) and/or USB bus of a laptop. ExpressCards have a 26-pin connector and are hot-swappable.

extended memory
Memory above 1 MB.

extended partition
Second partition on the hard drive.

extended-star topology
Star topology that is expanded to include additional networking devices.

external hard drive
Device that connects to the computer to provide additional data storage.

external modem
Modem that connects to the serial port (COM1 or COM2) of most computers. An external modem, such as a cable modem, is typically used for high-speed connections.

Fast Ethernet
Any of a number of 100-Mbps Ethernet specifications. Fast Ethernet offers a speed increase ten times that of the 10BASE-T Ethernet specification, while preserving such qualities as frame format, MAC mechanisms, and MTU. Such similarities allow the use of existing 10BASE-T applications and network management tools on Fast Ethernet networks. Based on an extension to the IEEE 802.3 specification. Compare with Ethernet.

FDISK
Command used to delete and create partitions on the hard drive:\STATUS Switch that displays partition information when used with the FDISK - command.

Fiber Distributed Data Interface (FDDI)
Type of Token Ring network that is used in larger LANs.

fiber-optic cable
Physical medium capable of conducting modulated light transmission. Compared with other transmission media, fiber-optic cable is more expensive, but is not susceptible to electromagnetic interference, and is capable of higher data rates. Sometimes called optical fiber.

fiber-optic cable
Uses glass or plastic wire, also called fiber, to carry information as light pulses. Conducts modulated light to transmit data.

field-replaceable unit (FRU)
Component that a trained service technician may install at a remote location.

file
A block of logically related data that is given a single name and is treated as a single unit.

file allocation table (FAT)
Table that the operating system uses to store information about the location of the files stored on a disk. This file is stored in track 0 on the disk.

file extension
Designation that describes the file format or the type of application that created a file.

file management
Hierarchical structure of files, folders, and drives in Windows.

file system
The two file systems available in Windows XP are FAT32 and NTFS. NTFS has greater stability and security features.

File Transfer Protocol (FTP)
Set of rules governing how files are transferred. FTP allows multiple simultaneous connections to remote file systems.

fingerprint reader
Input device that scans fingerprints to authenticate login using biometric identification.

firewall
Router or access server, or several routers or access servers, designated as a buffer between any connected public networks and a private network. A firewall router uses access lists and other methods to ensure the security of the private network.

FireWire
High-speed, platform-independent communication bus. FireWire interconnects digital devices such as digital video cameras, printers, scanners, digital cameras, and hard drives. FireWire is also known as IEEE 1394, i.Link (Sony proprietary), and linear heat detecting cable (LHDC) in the U.K.

firmware
Program that is embedded in a silicon chip rather than stored on a floppy disk.

Flash memory
Rewritable memory chip that retains data after the power is turned off.

flat-head screwdriver
Tool used to loosen or tighten slotted screws.

floppy data cable
External cable that transfers data between the computer and the floppy drive.

floppy disk drive (FDD)
Device that spins a magnetically coated floppy disk to read data from and write data to it.

floppy drive cable
External cable that connects the computer and the floppy drive.

form factor
Physical size and shape of computer components. Components that share the same form factor are physically interchangeable.

format
To prepare a file system in a partition to store files.

full backup
Backs up all files on a disk. Also called a normal backup.

full-duplex transmission
Data transmission that can go two ways at the same time. An Internet connection using DSL service is an example.

function key (Fn key)
Modifier key usually found on laptop computers. It is used in combination with other keys to perform specific functions.

gamepad
External controller used as an input device, primarily for gaming.

gigahertz (GHz)
Common measurement of a processor equal to one billion cycles per second.

Global System for Mobile Communications (GSM)
World-wide cellular network.

graphical user interface (GUI)
Interface that allows the user to navigate through the operating system using icons and menus.

graphics application
Creates or modifies graphical images. The two types of graphical images include object- or vector-based images, and bitmaps or raster images.

Graphics Device Interface (GDI)
Windows component to manage how graphical images are transmitted to output devices. GDI works by converting images to a bitmap that uses the computer instead of the printer to transfer the images.

grayware
Spyware that installs on a computer without being prompted and downloads additional applications without permission from the user.

half-duplex transmission
Data transmission that can go two ways, but not at the same time. A telephone and two-way radio are examples.

handshaking sequence
Series of short communications that occur between the two modems. This establishes the readiness of the two modems and computers to engage in data exchange.

handwriting recognition
Ability of computer, especially mobile devices, to recognize letters and numbers written by hand and convert them to ASCII text.

hard disk drive (HDD)
Device that stores and retrieves data from magnetic-coated platters that rotate at high speeds. The hard drive, or HDD, is the primary storage medium on a computer.

Hardware Abstraction Layer (HAL)
Library of hardware drivers that communicate between the operating system and the hardware that is installed.

Hardware Compatibility List (HCL)
Utility that verifies existing hardware is compatible with an operating system.

hardware firewall
Hardware device that filters data packets from the network before reaching computers and other devices on a network.

hardware
Physical electronic components that make up a computer system.

Hayes-compatible command set
Set of AT commands that most modem software uses. This command set is named after the Hayes Microcomputer Products Company, which first defined them.

headphone jack
Socket that is used to attach an audio output device.

heat sink and fan assembly
Device that dissipates heat from electronic components into the surrounding air.

hex driver
Driver used to tighten nuts. Sometimes called a nut driver,

Hibernate/Standby indicator LED
Light that shows if the computer is in standby or hibernate mode.

hierarchical star topology
Extended star topology where a central hub is connected by vertical cabling to other hubs that are dependent on it.

High Data Rate DSL (HDSL)
Provides a bandwidth of 768 kbps in both directions.

High Definition Multimedia Interface (HDMI)
Video, plasma, LCD, or DLP projector.

HKEY_
Designation at the beginning of Windows Registry boot file names.

host
Computer system on a network. Similar to the term node except that host usually implies a computer system, whereas node generally applies to any networked system, including access servers and routers.

hot-swappable interface
Allows peripherals to be changed while the system is running. USB is an example.

hub
1) Generally, a term used to describe a Layer 1 device that serves as the center of a star-topology network.

2) Hardware or software device that contains multiple independent but connected modules of network and internetwork equipment. Hubs can be active (where they repeat signals sent through them) or passive

(where they do not repeat, but merely split, signals sent through them).

3) In Ethernet and IEEE 802.3, an Ethernet multiport repeater, sometimes referred to as a concentrator.

Hypertext Markup Language (HTML)
Page-description language used by browser applications such as Windows Internet Explorer or Mozilla Firefox.

Hypertext Transfer Protocol (HTTP)
Governs how files are exchanged on the Internet.

I/O shield
Grounded metal plate installed in the rear of the case that enables the motherboard connectors to be accessed from the outside of the case.

icon
Image that represents an application or a capability.

IEEE 802.1
IEEE specification that describes an algorithm that prevents bridging loops by creating a spanning tree. The algorithm was invented by Digital Equipment Corporation. The Digital algorithm and the IEEE 802.1 algorithm are not exactly the same, nor are they compatible.

IEEE 802.12
IEEE LAN standard that specifies the physical layer and the MAC sub layer of the data-link layer. IEEE 802.12 uses the demand priority media-access scheme at 100 Mbps over a variety of physical media.

IEEE 802.2
IEEE LAN protocol that specifies an implementation of the LLC sub layer of the data-link layer. IEEE 802.2 handles errors, framing, flow control, and the network layer, Layer 3, service interface. Used in IEEE 802.3 and IEEE 802.5 LANs.

IEEE 802.3
IEEE LAN protocol that specifies an implementation of the physical layer and the MAC sub layer of the data-link layer. IEEE 802.3 uses CSMA/CD access at a variety of speeds over a variety of physical media. Extensions to the IEEE 802.3 standard specify implementations for Fast Ethernet. Physical variations of the original IEEE 802.3 specification include 10BASE2, 10BASE5, 10BASE-F, 10BASE-T, and 10Broad36. Physical variations for Fast Ethernet include 100BASE-T, 100BASE-T4, and 100BASE-X.

IEEE 802.3i
Physical variation of the original IEEE 802.3 specification that calls for using Ethernet type signaling over twisted pair networking media. The standard sets the signaling speed at 10 megabits per second using a baseband signaling scheme transmitted over twisted pair cable employing a star or extended star topology.

IEEE 802.4
IEEE LAN protocol that specifies an implementation of the physical layer and the MAC sub layer of the data-link layer. IEEE 802.4 uses token-passing access over a bus topology and is based on the token bus LAN architecture.

IEEE 802.5
IEEE LAN protocol that specifies an implementation of the physical layer and MAC sub layer of the data link-layer. IEEE 802.5 uses token passing access at 4 or 16 Mbps over shielded twisted-pair (STP) cabling and is similar to IBM Token Ring.

IEEE 802.6
IEEE MAN specification based on DQDB technology. IEEE 802.6 supports data rates of 1.5 to 155 Mbps.

impact printer
Class of printer that includes dot matrix and daisy wheel.

incremental backup
Procedure to back up all the files and folders that have been created or modified since the last full or normal backup.

infrared (IR)
Electromagnetic waves whose frequency range is above that of microwaves, but below that of the visible spectrum. LAN systems based on this technology represent an emerging technology.

infrared port
Line-of-sight wireless transceiver that is used for data transmission.

infrared scatter
Infrared signal that is bounced off ceilings and walls. Devices are able to connect without the line of sight, but data transfer rates are lower and distances are shorter.

inkjet printer
Type of printer that uses liquid-ink–filled cartridges that spray ink to form an image on the paper.

input/output (I/O)
Any operation, program, or device that transfers data to or from a computer.

input/output (I/O) address
Unique hexadecimal memory address that is associated with a specific device on a computer.

installation CD
Compact disc that includes new software with drivers and manuals. Additionally, may include diagnostic tools and trial software.

instant messaging (IM)
Real-time text-based method of communication conducted over a network between two or more users.

Institute of Electrical and Electronics Engineers (IEEE)
Organization that oversees the development of communication and network standards.

insulation
High resistance material that inhibits the flow of current between conductors in a cable.

Integrated Services Digital Network (ISDN)
Communication protocol, offered by telephone companies, that permits telephone networks to carry data, voice, and other source traffic.

interface
1) Connection between two systems or devices.

2) In routing terminology, a network connection.

3) In telephony, a shared boundary defined by common physical interconnection characteristics, signal characteristics, and meanings of interchanged signals.

4) The boundary between adjacent layers of the OSI model.

Interior Gateway Protocol (IGP)
Internet protocol that is used to exchange routing information within an autonomous system. Examples of common Internet IGPs include EIGRP, OSPF, and RIP.

International Electrotechnical Commission (IEC)
Industry group that writes and distributes standards for electrical products and components.

International Organization for Standardization (ISO)
International organization that sets standards for networking. ISO developed the OSI reference model, a popular networking reference model.

Internet
Largest global internetwork that connects tens of thousands of networks worldwide.

Internet Architecture Board (IAB)
Board of internetwork researchers who discuss issues pertinent to Internet architecture. Responsible for appointing a variety of Internet-related groups such as the IANA, IESG, and IRSG. The IAB is appointed by the trustees of the ISOC.

Internet Control Message Protocol (ICMP)
Used for network testing and troubleshooting, it enables diagnostic and error messages. ICMP echo messages are used by the ping utility to determine whether a remote device is reachable.

Internet Message Access Protocol (IMAP)
Used by local e-mail clients to synchronize and retrieve e-mail from a server.

Internet Protocol (IP)
Network layer protocol in the TCP/IP stack that offers a connectionless internetwork service. IP provides features for addressing, type-of-service specification, fragmentation and reassembly, and security. Documented in RFC 791.

Internet service provider (ISP)
Company that provides Internet service to home users, such as the local phone or cable company.

Internetwork Packet Exchange/Sequenced Packet Exchange (IPX/SPX)
Used by Novell Netware; IPX is a connectionless communication and SPX is the transport layer (Layer 7 of the OSI model).

interrupt request (IRQ)
A request from a device for communication with the CPU.

Java
Programming language for applets to run within a web browser. Examples of applets include a calculator or a counter.

JavaScript
Programming language developed to interact with HTML source code for interactive websites. Examples include a rotating banner or a popup window.

jumper
Electrical contact points used to set a hard drive as master or slave.

keyboard port
PS/2 socket used to attach an external keyboard.

keyboard
Input device with multi-functional keys.

kilobytes per second (KBps)
Measurement of the amount of data that is transferred over a connection such as a network connection. A data transfer rate of 1 KBps is a rate of approximately 1,000 bytes per second.

laptop battery
Rechargeable battery that powers the laptop.

laptop connector
Socket that is used to attach the laptop to a docking station.

laptop keyboard
Input device that includes alphanumeric, punctuation, and special function keys.

laptop latch
Lever used to open the laptop lid.

laptop
Small form factor computer designed to be mobile, but operates much the same as a desktop computer. Laptop hardware is proprietary and usually more expensive than desktop hardware.

laser printer
Type of printer that uses static electricity and a laser to form the image on the paper.

latent image
In laser printers, the undeveloped image.

LCD monitor
Output device that passes polarized light through liquid crystals to produce images on the screen.

light-emitting diode (LED)
Type of semiconductor that emits light when current is passed through it. The LED indicates whether components inside the computer are on.

line of sight
Characteristic of certain transmission systems such as laser, microwave, and infrared systems in which no obstructions in a direct path between transmitter and receiver can exist.

line-in connector
Socket that is used to attach an audio source.

liquid crystal display (LCD)
Type of light-weight, high-resolution display that works by blocking light rather than creating it.

local area network (LAN)
Communication network that covers a small geographical area and is under the control of a single administrator.

local security policy
Combination of security settings that define the security of the computer on which the settings reside.

logical drive
Section that a partition is divided into.

logical topology
Actual method (ring or bus) by which different computers and other equipment in a network communicate with one another. Contrast with physical topology.

loopback plug
Diagnostic tool that redirects signals back to the transmitting port to troubleshoot connectivity.

MAC address
Standardized data link layer address that is required for every port or device that connects to a LAN. Other devices in the network use these addresses to locate specific ports in the network and to create and update routing tables and data structures. MAC addresses are 6 bytes long and are controlled by the Institute of Electrical and Electronics Engineers (IEEE). Also known as a hardware address, a MAC-layer address, burnt-in address, or a physical address.

main distribution facility (MDF)
Primary communications room for a building. Also, the central point of a star networking topology where patch panels, hubs, and routers are located.

malware
Term taken from the words malicious and software. Malware is software designed to infiltrate or damage a computer system without the consent of the user.

Master Boot Record (MBR)
Program on the first sector of a hard disk that starts the boot process. The MBR determines which partition is used for booting the system and then transfers control to the boot sector of that partition, which continues the boot process. MBR allows programs such as DOS to load into RAM.

Material Safety and Data Sheet (MSDS)
A fact sheet that identifies hazardous materials.

mean time between failures (MTBF)
Average length of time that the device will work without failing. Information is found in the manual or on the manufacturer website.

media
The plural form of medium. The various physical environments through which transmission signals pass. Common network media include twisted-pair, coaxial and fiber-optic cable, and the atmosphere (through which microwave, laser, and infrared transmission occurs).

Media Access Control (MAC)
Lower of the two sub layers of the data link layer defined by the Institute of Electrical and Electronics Engineers (IEEE). The MAC sub layer handles access to shared media, such as whether token passing or contention will be used. Also the rules for coordinating the use of the medium on a LAN.

media-handling options
Options by which a printer handles media, including the orientation, size, and weight of the paper.

megabit
1,048,576 bits (approximately 1 million bits).

megabits per second (Mbps)
Common measurement of the amount of data that is transferred over a connection in one second. A data transfer rate of 1 Mbps is a rate of approximately 1 million bits or 1,000 kilobits per second.

megabyte (MB)
1,048,576 bytes (or approximately 1 million bytes).

mesh grip
Tool attached to the end of a cable to help pull cable.

mesh topology
Method of connecting users that provides alternate paths for data. If one path is severed or unusable, the data can take an alternate path to its destination.

microphone
Audio input device.

microphone jack
Socket used to connect a microphone used for audio input.

microwave
Electromagnetic waves that range from 1 to 30 GHz. Microwave-based networks are an evolving technology gaining popularity due to high bandwidth and relatively low cost.

mobile processor
CPU that is optimized to use less power allowing laptop batteries to last longer.

modem port
RJ-11 jack that connects a computer to a standard telephone line. The modem port can be used to connect the computer to the Internet, to send and receive fax documents, and to answer incoming calls.

modulator/demodulator (modem)
Device that converts digital computer signals into a format that is sent and received over an analog telephone line.

Molex power connector
Four-wire computer power connector used to connect many devices such as optical drives and hard drives.

monitor
Display device that works with the installed video card to present output from a computer. The clarity of a CRT monitor is based on video bandwidth, dot pitch, refresh rate, and convergence.

motherboard
Main printed circuit board that connects all the components of the computer such as the CPU, BIOS, memory, mass storage interfaces, serial and parallel ports, expansion slots, and controllers required for standard peripheral devices.

mouse port
PS/2 socket that is used to attach an external mouse.

MSCONFIG
Windows utility designed to aid in the troubleshooting of the operating system. Allows the user to edit start-up applications and access the BOOT.INI, SYSTEM.INI, and WIN.INI files.

multimeter
Troubleshooting tool that measures electrical voltage, resistance, and current.

multimode
Optical fiber that has a thicker core than single-mode. It is easier to make, can use simpler light sources, such as LEDs, and works well over short distances. This type of fiber allows light waves to be dispersed into many paths as they travel through the fiber.

multiprocessing
To enable programs to share two or more CPUs.

Multipurpose Internet Mail Extensions (MIME)
Standard that extends the e-mail format to include text in ASCII standard, as well as other formats such as pictures and word processor documents. Normally used in conjunction with SMTP.

multitask
To run two or more applications at the same time.

multithread
To divide a program into smaller parts that can be loaded as needed by the operating system. Multithreading allows individual programs to be multitasked.

multi-user
Two or more users running programs and sharing peripheral devices, such as a printer, at the same time.

My Computer icon
Desktop icon that provides access to the installed drives and other computer properties.

near letter quality (NLQ)
Quality of print that is better than draft quality, but not as good as letter quality.

needle-nose pliers
Tool with long and slender jaws that can be used to grasp small objects.

NetView
IBM network management architecture and related applications. NetView is a virtual telecommunications access method (VTAM) application used for managing mainframes in Systems Network Architecture (SNA) networks.

network
Group of two or more electronic devices, such as computers, PDAs, and smartphones which communicate with each other to share data and resources.

Network Access Point (NAP)
Point at which access providers are interconnected.

network administration
Task of maintaining and upgrading a private network that is done by network administrators.

Network Basic Input/Output System (NetBIOS)
Application programming interface (API) used by applications on an IBM LAN to request services from lower-level network processes. These services might include session establishment and termination, and information transfer.

network cable
Physical media used to connect devices together for communication.

network file services
Allow documents to be shared over a network to facilitate the development of a project.

network indicator LED
Light that shows the status of the network connection. The green link light indicates network connectivity. The other LED light indicates traffic.

network interface card (NIC)
Computer interface with the LAN. This card typically is inserted into an expansion slot in a computer and connects to the network medium.

network layer
Layer 3 of the Open System Interconnection (OSI) reference model. This layer provides connectivity and path selection between two end systems. The network layer is the layer at which routing occurs. Corresponds roughly with the path control layer of the Systems Network Architecture (SNA) model. The OSI reference model includes application layer, presentation layer, session layer, transport layer, network layer, data link layer, and physical layer.

network operating system (NOS)
Operating system designed specifically to provide additional network features.

network printer
Printer connected to the computer network that is set up to be shared by multiple users.

network server
Computer that provides some network service, such as file sharing, and is capable of handling multiple users and multiple jobs.

network topology
Way that computers, printers, and other devices are connected.

networking media
Material (either cable or air) by which signals are sent from one network device to another.

New Technology File System (NTFS)
Type of file system that provides improved fault tolerance over traditional file systems, and also provides file-level security.

nibble
Half a byte, or four bits.

node
1) The endpoint of a network connection or a junction common to two or more lines in a network. Nodes can be processors, controllers, or workstations. Nodes, which vary in routing and other functional capabilities, can be interconnected by links, and serve as control points in the network. Node is sometimes used generically to refer to any entity that can access a network, and is frequently used interchangeably with device.

2) In Systems Network Architecture (SNA), the basic component of a network, and the point at which one or more functional units connect channels or data circuits.

noise
Interference, such as EMI or RFI, that causes unclean power and may cause errors in a computer system.

non-bootable disk
Damaged or missing disk, or a disk that does not contain one or more system boot files.

northbridge
One of the two chips in the core logic chipset of a PC motherboard. It typically handles communications between the CPU, RAM, AGP, PCIe, and the southbridge core chip. Also called a Memory Controller Hub (MCH).

NSLOOKUP
Command that returns the IP address for a given host name. This command can also do the reverse and find the host name for a specified IP address.

NTDETECT
Program used by Intel-based systems to detect installed hardware.

Num lock indicator LED
Light that shows the on/off status of the 10-key number pad.

Ohm's Law
The mathematical relationship between current, resistance, and voltage where voltage is equal to the current multiplied by the resistance.

operating system
Software program that performs general system tasks, such as controlling RAM, prioritizing the processing, controlling input and output devices, and managing files.

optical drive activity indicator LED
Light that shows drive activity.

optical drive
Disk drive that uses a laser to read and/or write CDs and DVDs.

packet
Logical grouping of information which includes a header that contains control information and usually user data. Packets are most often used to refer to network layer units of data. The terms datagram, frame, message, and segment are also used to describe logical information groupings at various layers of the Open System Interconnection (OSI) reference model and in various technology circles.

Packet Internet Gopher (ping)
Simple but highly useful command-line utility that is included in most implementations of TCP/IP. Ping can be used with either the host name or the IP address to test IP connectivity. Determines whether a specific IP address is accessible by sending an ICMP echo request to a destination computer or other network device. The receiving device then sends back an ICMP echo reply message.

Page Description Language (PDL)
Code that describes the contents of a document in a language that the printer can understand.

pages per minute (ppm)
Designation for measuring the speed of a printer.

Parallel Advanced Technology Attachment (PATA)
Standard for connecting hard drives and optical drives into computer systems and uses a parallel signaling technology.

parallel ATA (PATA) data cable
Internal cable that transfers data between the motherboard and an ATA drive.

parallel cable
External cable that connects the parallel port of the computer to a printer or another parallel communications device. Also known as a printer cable.

parallel port
Socket used to connect a device such as a printer or scanner.

partition
To divide memory or mass storage into isolated or logical sections. Once a disk is partitioned, each partition will behave like a separate disk drive.

PC Card
Expansion card used in laptops to conform to PCMCIA standards.

peer-to-peer computing
Each network device runs both client and server portions of an application. Also describes communication between implementations of the same Open System Interconnection (OSI) reference model layer in two different network devices.

Personal Computer Memory Card International Association (PCMCIA)
Industry trade association that defines laptop expansion card standards.

personal digital assistant (PDA)
Stand-alone, hand-held device with computing and communicating abilities.

Phillips-head screwdriver
Tool used to tighten or loosen cross-head screws

phishing
Type of spam intended to persuade the recipient to provide the sender with information that will enable the sender to access personal information of the recipeint.

physical layer
Layer 1 of the Open System Interconnection (OSI) reference model. The physical layer defines the electrical, mechanical, procedural and functional specifications to activate, maintain, and deactivate the physical link between end systems. Corresponds with the physical control layer in the Systems Network Architecture (SNA) model. The OSI reference model includes application layer, presentation layer, session layer, transport layer, network layer, data link layer, and physical layer.

physical topology
Physical layout of the components on the network.

piezoelectric
For printers, an electrically charged plate changes the size and shape of the nozzle. This change in size causes the nozzle to act like a pump. The pumping action forces ink out through the nozzle and onto the paper.

plain old telephone service (POTS)
The regular phone system which typically uses analog signals to transmit voice and data. Sometimes called Public Switched Telephone Network (PSTN).

platen
Large roller in a dot matrix printer that applies pressure to keep the paper from slipping. If a multiple-copy paper is used, the platen gap can be adjusted to the thickness of the paper.

plug-and-play (PnP)
Technology that allows a computer to automatically configure the devices that connect to it.

point of presence (POP)
Point of interconnection between the communication facilities provided by the telephone company and the main distribution facility of the building.

port replicator
Fixed base unit where a laptop is inserted and able to connect to peripheral devices.

power adaptor
Device that transforms AC to DC to provide electricity to the computer and charge the battery.

power button
Control that turns a device on and off.

power cable
External cable consisting of color-coded conductors that transfer electricity to a computer and attached electrical devices.

power line communication (PLC)
Communication method that uses power distribution wires (local electric grid) to send and receive data.

power on indicator LED
Light that shows the on/off status of the laptop.

power supply
Converts AC (alternating current) into the lower voltages of DC (direct current) which powers all components of the computer. Power supplies are rated in watts.

power-on self-test (POST)
Diagnostic test of memory and hardware when the system is powered up.

presentation layer
Layer 6 of the Open System Interconnection (OSI) reference model. This layer ensures that information sent by the application layer of one system will be readable by the application layer of another. The presentation layer is also concerned with the data structures used by programs and therefore negotiates data transfer syntax for the application layer. Corresponds roughly with the presentation services layer of the Systems Network Architecture (SNA) model. The OSI reference model includes application layer, presentation layer, session layer, transport layer, network layer, data link layer, and physical layer.

preventive maintenance policy
Detailed program that determines maintenance timing, the type of maintenance performed, and the specifics of how the maintenance plan is carried out.

preventive maintenance
Regular and systematic inspection, cleaning, and replacement of worn parts, materials, and systems.

primary corona wire
Voltage device that erases the charge on the printing drum. Also called the grid or conditioning roller.

primary partition
First partition on a hard drive. A primary partition cannot be subdivided into smaller sections.

Primary Rate Interface (PRI)
Integrated Services Digital Network (ISDN) interface to primary rate access. Primary rate access consists of a single 64-Kbps D channel plus 23 (T1) or 30 (E1) B channels for voice or data. Compare to BRI.

print resolution
Number of tiny dots that the print head is capable of placing per inch on the paper when forming an image.

Printer Control Language (PCL)
Developed by Hewlett-Packard to allow software applications to communicate with HP and HP-compatible laser printers. PCL is now an industry standard for most printer types.

printer driver
Software that must be installed on a PC so that the printer can communicate and coordinate the printing process.

printer network interface card (NIC)
Adapter that the printer uses to access the network media.

printer queue
Temporary holding area for print jobs. The jobs in the queue are fed to the printer when it is ready for the next job.

printer-output options
Determine how the ink or toner is transferred to the paper and include color management, print quality, and speed.

protected mode
Allows programs to access more than 1 MB of physical memory, and protects against misuse of memory, such as programs that can not execute a data segment, or write into a code segment.

protocol
1) Formal description of a set of rules and conventions that govern how devices on a network exchange information.

2) Field within an IP datagram that indicates the upper layer (Layer 4) protocol that sent the datagram.

protocol data unit (PDU)
A unit of data that is specified in a protocol of a layer of the Open System Interconnection (OSI) Model. For example, the PDU for Layer 1 is bits or the data stream, Layer 2 is framing, Layer 3 is the packet, and Layer 4 is the segment.

proxy
Entity that, in the interest of efficiency, acts on behalf of another entity.

Public Switched Telephone Network (PSTN)
General term that refers to the variety of telephone networks and services in place worldwide. Sometimes called plain old telephone service (POTS).

radio frequency (RF)
Generic term that refers to frequencies that correspond to radio transmissions. Cable TV and broadband networks use RF technology.

radio frequency interference (RFI)
Radio frequencies that create noise that interferes with information being transmitted across unshielded copper cabling.

random access memory (RAM)
Memory that temporarily stores data for processing by the CPU. Also called physical memory.

read only memory (ROM)
Memory that permanently stores prerecorded configuration settings and data on a chip, that can only be read. This type of memory retains its contents when power is not being supplied to the chip.

Reduced Instruction Set Computer (RISC)
Architecture that uses a relatively small set of instructions. RISC chips are designed to execute these instructions very rapidly.

Redundant Array of Independent Disks (RAID)
Provides fault tolerance to prevent loss of data in the event of a disk drive failure on a network server. Also known as Redundant Array of Inexpensive Disks.

Regedit
Windows application that allows users to edit the registry.

registry
System-wide database used by the Windows operating system to store information and settings for hardware, software, users, and preferences on a system.

remote access server (RAS)
Server that is dedicated to users that need to gain access to files and print services on the LAN from a remote location.

remote installation services (RIS)
Ability to download a Windows operating system installation across the network. This install can be requested by the user or forced onto the computer by the administrator.

removable drive
Drive that can be removed from a computer to transport data.

resistance (r)
Measurement, expressed in ohms, of the opposition of a material to the flow of current.

resolution
Number of distinct pixels in each dimension that can be displayed on a computer screen. The higher the resolution, the better quality the screen display is. Also referred to as display resolution.

restore point
Utility in Microsoft's Windows Me, XP, and Vista operating systems. It allows the rolling back of system files, registry keys, and installed programs to a previous state in the event of a system failure. User data is not affected by performing a restore point.

ring topology
Network topology that consists of a series of repeaters connected to one another by unidirectional transmission links to form a single closed loop. Each station on the network connects to the network at a repeater. While logically a ring, ring topologies are most often organized in a closed-loop star.

router
A network layer device that uses one or more metrics to determine the optimal path along which network traffic should be forwarded. Routers forward packets from one network to another based on network layer information. Occasionally called a gateway, although this definition of gateway is becoming increasingly outdated.

Routing Information Protocol (RIP)
Interior Gateway Protocol (IGP) supplied with UNIX Berkeley Standard Distribution (BSD) systems. The most common IGP on the Internet. RIP uses hop count as a routing metric.

safe mode
Option when booting the system that loads only the basic devices that Windows needs to run. It is used for troubleshooting.

satellite communication
The use of orbiting satellites to relay data between multiple earth-based stations. Satellite communications offer high bandwidth and broadcast capability at a cost that is not related to distance between earth stations. Because of the altitude of the satellite, satellite communications can be subject to long propagation delays.

SCANDISK
Windows utility used to examine all files on a drive.

security key fob
Small radio system that communicates with the computer over a short range. The computer must sense the signal from the key fob before it will accept the user login name and password.

security keyhole
Hard point in the case that is used to attach a security cable.

segment
Portion of a computer network in which every device communicates using the physical layer of the OSI Model. Hubs and repeaters extend and become part of a network segment, while switches and routers define and separate network segments.

semiconductor
Material used to make computer chips that can be either a conductor or an insulator, depending on the control signals applied to it. The most common semiconductor materials are silicon and germanium. These materials then have other materials added to them to increase conductivity.

serial cable
External cable that connects the serial port on the computer to a peripheral device.

serial data transfer
Movement of single bits of information in a single cycle.

serial port
Socket that is used to connect a device such as a mouse or trackball.

serial transmission
Method of data transmission in which the bits of a data character are transmitted sequentially over a single channel.

server
Repository for files, or other resources, that can be accessed and shared across a network by many users.

service level agreement (SLA)
Contract that defines expectations between an organization and the service vendor to provide an agreed upon level of support.

session layer
Layer 5 of the Open System Interconnection (OSI) reference model. This layer establishes, manages, and terminates sessions between applications and manages data exchange between presentation layer entities. The OSI reference model includes application layer, presentation layer, session layer, transport layer, network layer, data link layer, and physical layer.

shielded twisted pair (STP)
Two-pair wiring medium used primarily for token ring networks. STP cabling has a layer of shielded insulation to reduce electromagnetic interference (EMI). Compare with UTP.

shortcut
Keyboard combination that activates a command.

Simple Mail Transfer Protocol (SMTP)
E-mail protocol used by servers to send ASCII text messages. When augmented by the MIME protocol, SMTP can carry e-mail with pictures and documents. SMTP is sometimes used by e-mail clients to retrieve messages from an e-mail server. However, due to the limited ability to queue messages at the receiving end, other protocols such as POP or IMAP are typically used to receive e-mail.

simplex
Capability for data transmission in only one direction between a sending station and a receiving station.

single-mode
Fiber cable that has a very thin core. Uses a high-energy laser as a light source and can transmit signals over longer distances than multi-mode fiber optic cable.

site survey
Physical inspection of the building that will help determine a basic network topology.

Small Computer System Interface (SCSI)
Parallel interface standard that supports multiple devices on the same cable and achieves faster data transmission rates than standard buses.

Small Computer System Interface (SCSI) cable
External or internal cable that connects the SCSI controller to SCSI ports of multiple internal and external devices.

smart card
Credit card sized device that includes a processor and memory, used to store information and authenticate network users. Smart cards provide two-factor identification because the user must have both the card and a password to access the network.

software firewall
Application on a computer that inspects and filters data packets.

solenoid
Coil of wires that form electromagnets that fire the pins in the dot matrix printer.

solid-ink printers
Printer that uses solid sticks of ink rather than toner or ink cartridges. Solid-ink printers produce high-quality images. The ink sticks are nontoxic and can be handled safely.

sound card
Integrated circuit board that enhances the audio capabilities of the computer.

southbridge
Chip that implements the slower capabilities of the motherboard. It is connected to the CPU through the northbridge chip. Also known as the Input/Output (I/O) Controlling Station (ICH).

spam
Unsolicited e-mail.

speaker
Audio output device.

spike
Sudden increase in voltage that is usually caused by lightning strikes.

spoof
To gain access to resources on devices by pretending to be a trusted computer.

spooling
Process of loading documents into a buffer (usually an area on a hard drive) until the printer is ready to print the documents.

spyware
Malware that monitors activity on the computer. The spyware then sends this information to the organization responsible for launching the spyware.

standby power supply (SPS)
Battery backup that is enabled when voltage levels fall below normal.

standoff
Barrier used to physically separate parts.

star topology
LAN topology in which end points on a network are connected to a common central switch by point-to-point links. A ring topology that is organized as a star, and implements a unidirectional closed-loop star, instead of point-to-point links.

static RAM (SRAM)
Type of RAM that retains its contents for as long as power is supplied. SRAM does not require constant refreshing, like dynamic RAM (DRAM).

static random access memory (SRAM)
Memory that holds data as long as there is voltage applied. Used mainly as cache memory for the CPU.

stylus
Writing utensil. Typically used as an input method for the touch-sensitive screens of PDAs and graphics tablets.

subnet mask
Second group of numbers used when configuring an IP address on a device. The subnet mask is used by end devices to determine the network portion of an IP address.

subnetting
Logical division of a network. It provides the means to divide a network, and the subnet mask specifies how it is subdivided.

surge
Any voltage increase above 110 percent of the normal voltage carried by a power line.

surge protector
Suppressor that regulates the voltage going to a device.

surge suppressor
Device that makes sure that the voltage going to another device stays below a certain level.

S-video port
Four-pin mini-DIN connector that is used to output video signals to a compatible device. S-video separates the brightness and color portions of a video signal.

switch
1) Operation that is added to a DOS command to modify the output of that command. 2) A Layer 2 network device also known as a multiport bridge.

Symmetric DSL (SDSL)
Version of a Digital Subscriber Line (DSL) service that provides the same speed for uploads and downloads.

Symmetric encryption
Encryption that requires both sides of an encrypted conversation to use an encryption key to be able to encode and decode the data. The sender and receiver must use the same key at the same time.

SYN flood
Randomly opens TCP ports, tying up the network equipment or computer resources with a large amount of false requests, causing sessions to be denied to others. Also see Denial of Service (DoS).

System Restore
Windows XP service that runs in the background and allows the user to restore the OS to a predefined point in time.

tape drive
Device used for data backup on a network server drive.

Task Manager
Displays active applications and identifies those applications that are not responding so that they can be shut down.

Taskbar
Utility within Microsoft Windows that graphically represents open applications, computer contents, and other information. Also provides a way to quickly access these resources.

Telecommunications Industry Association (TIA)
Organization that develops standards that relate to telecommunications technologies. Together, the TIA and the Electronic Industries Alliance (EIA) have formalized standards, such as EIA/TIA-232, for the electrical characteristics of data transmission.

telnet
Remote access application used to provide remote terminal access between hosts on a network. As a troubleshooting tool, telnet can verify the application layer software between source and destination stations. This is the most complete test mechanism available for the OSI Model.

thermal paper
Chemically treated paper with a waxy quality. It becomes black when heated. Most thermal printer print heads are the width of the paper. The paper is supplied in the form of a roll.

thermal printer
A printer that marks special thermal paper by applying heat to areas of the paper that are to be darkened to represent characters.

Thicknet
Coaxial cable that was used in older networks and operated at 10 megabits per second with a maximum length of 500 meters. Also called 10BASE5 .

Thinnet
Coaxial cable that was used in older networks and operated at 10 megabits per second with a maximum length of 185 meters. Also called 10BASE2.

three claw part retriever
Tool used to retrieve and manipulate small parts.

Token Ring network
Uses a ring topology and a token-passing methodology to create collision-free data transmission.

toner
Powder-type ink used in laser printers and photocopiers to form text and images on printer paper.

topology
Actual physical layout of a network or in the case of a logical topology, the signal or data flows in a network.

torx screwdriver
Tool used to tighten or loosen screws that have a star-shaped depression on the top, a feature that is mainly found on laptop screws.

touch screen
Interactive LCD or CRT monitor that detects when something is pressed on it.

touchpad
Pressure-sensitive input pad that controls the cursor.

tracert
Windows utility that traces the route that a packet takes from source computer to destination host.

track
Complete circle around a hard drive platter made up of groups of 512-byte sectors.

trackball
Ball that is rotated to control the cursor.

trackpoint
Input stick that controls the cursor.

Transmission Control Protocol (TCP)
Primary Internet protocol for the delivery of data. TCP includes facilities for end-to-end connection establishment, error detection and recovery, and metering the rate of data flow into the network. Many standard applications, such as e-mail, web browser, file transfer, and Telnet, depend on the services of TCP.

Transmission Control Protocol/Internet Protocol (TCP/IP)
Common name for the suite of protocols developed by the U.S. Department of Defense (DoD) in the 1970s to support the construction of worldwide internetworks. TCP and IP are the two best-known protocols in the suite.

transport layer
This is Layer 4 of the Open System Interconnection (OSI) reference model. This layer is responsible for reliable network communication between end nodes. The transport layer provides mechanisms for the establishment, maintenance, and termination of virtual circuits, transport fault detection and recovery, and information flow control. Corresponds to the transmission control layer of the SNA model. The OSI reference model includes application layer, presentation layer, session layer, transport layer, network layer, data link layer, and physical layer.

troubleshooting
Systematic approach to locating the cause of a fault in a computer system.

tweezers
Tool used to retrieve and manipulate small parts.

twisted pair
A pair of insulated wires wrapped together in a regular spiral pattern to control the effects of electrical noise. The pairs can be shielded or unshielded. Twisted pair is common in telephony applications and in data networks. Category 3, Category 5, Category 5e, and Category 6 twisted pair cables all contain 4 twisted pairs in a common jacket.

unattended installation
Custom installation of an operating system with minimal user intervention. Windows performs unattended installations by using an answer file called unattend.txt.

universal bay status indicator LED
Light that shows that a device is installed in the laptop bay.

Universal Serial Bus (USB) cable
External cable that connects the USB port on the computer to a peripheral device.

Universal Serial Bus (USB) port
External, hot-swappable, bi-directional connection for USB cables connecting to peripheral devices.

Universal Serial Bus (USB)
External serial bus interface standard for the connection of multiple peripheral devices. USB can connect up to 127 USB devices at transfer rates of up to 480 Mbps, and can provide DC power to connected devices.

UNIX
Operating system that is used primarily to run and maintain computer networks.

unshielded twisted pair (UTP)
Four-pair wire medium used in a variety of networks. UTP is rated in categories, with higher categories providing the best performance and highest bandwidth. The most popular categories are Category 3, Category 5, Category 5e, Category 6, and Category 6A.

User Datagram Protocol (UDP)
Connectionless service for delivery of data with less overhead than TCP and designed for speed. Network management applications, network file system, and simple file transport use UDP.

user interface
Part of the operating system that allows the user to communicate with the computer. User interfaces can provide a Command Line Interface (text) or Graphical User Interface (GUI).

user profile
Specific setting for the user who is logged on to the computer.

ventilation
Series of vents that allow hot air to be expelled from the interior of the device.

very high data rate DSL (VDSL)
Broadband data transfer capable of bandwidths of 13 Mbps to 52 Mbps.

video accelerator card
Integrated circuit board that contains a processor and memory to increase the speed of video graphics. Video accelerator cards are primarily used for 3D and gaming applications.

video adapter
Integrated circuit board that stores digital data in VRAM and converts it to analog data.

video graphics array (VGA)
Supplies analog video to an analog monitor. The connector is a 15-pin D-sub type connector.

video memory
Dedicated random access memory on a video graphics adapter (video RAM or VRAM).

video surveillance equipment
Used to record images and sound for monitoring activity.

virtual memory
Memory created and controlled by the operating system by manipulating free hard disk space to mimic more RAM than is actually installed in the system.

virtual private network (VPN)
Encryption system that protects data as it travels, or tunnels, over the Internet or other unsecured public network.

virtual
Something that is conceptual rather than something that is physical.

Virus Scan
Utility that checks all hard drives and memory for viruses.

virus
In computer terms, a malicious piece of software or code that can copy itself and infect a computer without the knowledge or permission of the user. Some viruses are benign and do not adversely affect a computer, while other viruses can damage or delete operating system and data files.

Voice over IP (VoIP)
Method to transmit telephone calls over the Internet using packet-switched technology.

voltage (V)
Force that creates a current by moving electrons. Electromotive force or potential difference expressed in volts.

volume control
Button that adjusts audio output.

warm boot
Restarting a computer that is already turned on without first turning it off.

What You See Is What You Get (WYSIWYG)
Printer output that matches what the user sees on-screen.

wide-area network (WAN)
Data communications network that serves users across a broad geographic area and often uses transmission devices provided by common carriers. Frame Relay, SMDS, and X.25 are examples of WANs.

Wi-Fi Protected Access (WPA)
Security standard for Wi-Fi wireless technology. Provides better encryption and authentication than earlier WEP system.

Wi-Fi
Brand originally licensed by the Wi-Fi Alliance to define the embedded technology of a wireless network, and is based on the IEEE 802.11 specifications.

Windows Explorer
Windows utility that graphically represents the file-management structure.

wire cutters
Tool used to strip and cut wires.

Wired Equivalent Privacy (WEP)
First-generation security standard for wireless technology.

wireless connection
Connection to a network using radio signals, infrared technology (laser), or satellite transmissions.

wireless indicator LED
Light that shows activity of the wireless network connection.

wireless network
Extension of a wired network using radio frequency (RF) signals to connect to access points. Wireless signals can be repeated to additional access points, extending the distance of the network.

wireless NIC
Expansion card that enables a computer to connect to a wireless modem using RF signals.

Wireless Transport Layer Security (WTLS)
Layer that provides security for mobile devices that use Wireless Applications Protocol (WAP).

workgroup
Collection of workstations and servers on a LAN that are designed to communicate and exchange data with one another.

zero insertion force (ZIF) socket
Chip socket that permits the insertion and removal of a chip without using tools or force. This is common for delicate chips like a CPU.